11|5|13
# 39.95

# ALFRED ADLER
# REVISITED

# ALFRED ADLER REVISITED

EDITED BY Jon Carlson AND Michael P. Maniacci

Routledge
Taylor & Francis Group
New York London

Routledge
Taylor & Francis Group
711 Third Avenue
New York, NY 10017

Routledge
Taylor & Francis Group
27 Church Road
Hove, East Sussex BN3 2FA

International Standard Book Number: 978-0-415-88446-4 (Hardback) 978-0-415-88447-1 (Paperback)

### Library of Congress Cataloging-in-Publication Data

Alfred Adler revisited / Jon Carlson & Michael Maniacci. -- 1st ed.
      p. cm.
   Includes bibliographical references and index.
   ISBN 978-0-415-88446-4 (hardback : alk. paper) -- ISBN 978-0-415-88447-1 (pbk. : alk. paper)
   1. Adlerian psychology. 2. Adler, Alfred, 1870-1937. I. Carlson, Jon. II. Maniacci, Michael.

   BF175.5.A33A44 2011
   150.19'53092--dc22                                                        2011011250

**Visit the Taylor & Francis Web site at**
**http://www.taylorandfrancis.com**

**and the Routledge Web site at**
**http://www.routledgementalhealth.com**

# Contents

# Acknowledgments

We wish to thank the Provost's Office at Governors State University (GSU) for providing state-of-the-art digital scanning equipment for use in reproducing the original manuscripts in a digital format. We also wish to thank the Division of Psychology and Counseling at GSU for help in preparing the manuscripts for republication and obtaining permission for their use. Specifically we want to acknowledge Dr. Shannon Dermer, Raquel Rios-Aguirre, Mona Douglas, Nanette Nelson, Lindsey Raske, Robert Rauworth, and Nicole Roy.

We thank Margot Adler for her support of this project through her permission to use her grandfather's writings.

We are indebted to the work of Heinz L. and Rowena R. Ansbacher for their comprehensive translation and interpretation of Adler's writing from 1907 to 1937. It is only through their personal relationship with Alfred Adler and their scholarship that these ideas are available today.

We are also indebted to the ongoing support of our editor George Zimmar for making this project a reality.

# Contributors

**James Robert Bitter**, EdD, is professor of counseling at East Tennessee State University in Johnson City, Tennessee. He is a Diplomate in Adlerian Psychology and a former editor of the *Journal of Individual Psychology*. He is also on the faculty of the Adlerian Training Institute in Port St. Lucie, Florida.

**Donald L. Bubenzer**, PhD, is an emeritus professor in the Counseling and Human Development Services Program at Kent State University.

**Arthur J. Clark**, EdD, is a professor and coordinator of the Counseling and Human Development Program at St. Lawrence University in Canton, New York. His professional background includes positions in the schools and agencies as a counselor and psychologist. He is the author of *Early Recollections: Theory and Practice in Counseling and Psychotherapy* (2002), published by Routledge.

**Jill D. Duba**, PhD, is an associate professor and the coordinator of the Clinical Mental Health Counseling Program in the Department of Counseling and Student Affairs at Western Kentucky University; she also has a small private practice. She has been a long-standing board member of the International Association of Marriage and Family Counselors. She is engaged in research projects related to long-term marital satisfaction and religious training in counselor education.

**Daniel Eckstein**, PhD, is a professor of medical psychology, Saba University School of Medicine, Saba, National Caribbean Netherlands. He has a Diplomate in Adlerian Studies and is a past president of the North American Society of Adlerian Psychology (http://www.leadershipbyencouragment.com).

**Timothy S. Hartshorne**, PhD, is a professor of psychology at Central Michigan University. A longtime Adlerian, he frequently addresses applications of Adlerian psychology to the issues of children and young adults with disability (http://www.chsbs.cmich.edu/timothy_hartshorne).

**Melissa Heston**, PhD, is an associate professor in the Department of Curriculum and Instruction at the University of Northern Iowa. She currently teaches introductory courses in teacher education and upper-level courses in child development. Dr. Heston's scholarship centers on the self-study of teacher education practices and leadership, and she has drawn upon the work of Adler and his disciples in her research and writing.

**Terry Kottman**, PhD, is the director of The Encouragement Zone, a training center for play therapists, in Cedar Falls, Iowa (http://www.encouragementzone.com).

**Frank Main**, EdD, is professor emeritus at the University of South Dakota. He recently served a guest editor of a special issue of the *Journal of Individual Psychology* and continues to deliver training workshops in marriage and family therapy and family therapy supervision.

**Guy J. Manaster**, PhD, is the Spence Professor Emeritus in Education, Department of Educational Psychology, University of Texas at Austin. He is a former chair of the department and director of the Counseling Psychology and the Social-Developmental-Personality Area. He was an editor of the *Journal of Individual Psychology* for 19 years and was president of the North American Society of Adlerian Psychology. He is presently president of the International Association of Individual Psychology.

**Robert McBrien**, PhD, is a licensed clinical professional counselor consulting in child and adolescent development, early childhood mental health, and family leadership training. As a consultant he introduces the optimistic psychology of Adler to professionals and parents on the eastern shore of Maryland and southern Delaware. A Diplomate in Adlerian Psychology, he has presented encouragement-focused programs at regional, national, and international Adlerian conferences for more than 30 years.

**Gary D. McKay**, PhD, is the coauthor of 14 books and programs, including *Systematic Training for Effective Parenting* (STEP), the world's leading parent-education program used by over 4 million parents in the United States alone (published by STEP Publishers). He is a retired psychologist and a Diplomate in Adlerian Psychology from the North American Society of Adlerian Psychology.

**Bret A. Moore**, PsyD, is a board-certified clinical psychologist, prescribing psychologist, and former active-duty Army psychologist. He is a graduate of the Adler School of Professional Psychology, Chicago, Illinois, and Fairleigh Dickinson University.

**Kevin P. Moore** attends the undergraduate psychology program at Furman University. He plans to pursue a degree in clinical psychology upon completing his undergraduate studies.

**Gerald J. Mozdzierz**, PhD, is a clinical and consulting psychologist in private practice and a professor of psychiatry and behavioral neuroscience at Loyola University Stritch School of Medicine in Maywood, Illinois. His private practice is located in Lombard, Illinois. Dr. Mozdzierz is a Diplomate of the American Board of Professional Psychology and a Fellow of the American Academy of Clinical Psychologists.

**Paul R. Peluso**, PhD, is an associate professor at Florida Atlantic University. He is the coauthor of *Couples Therapy: Integrating Theory, Research, & Practice*; *Principles of Counseling and Psychotherapy: Learning the Essential Domains and Nonlinear Thinking of Master Practitioners*; and *Infidelity: A Practitioner's Guide to Working With Couples in Crisis*. Dr. Peluso is the author of over 25 articles and chapters related to family therapy, couples counseling, and Adlerian theory. He writes a blog at http://drpaulpeluso.com.

**Dorothy E. Peven**, MSW, is a licensed clinical social worker in private practice in the Chicago metropolitan area and has served as professor at the Adler School of Professional Psychology, Chicago, Illinois. She has published 25 articles on Adlerian theory and practice as well as a book with Bernard Shulman, *Who Is Sylvia? Case Studies in Psychotherapy* (http://www.dorothyepevenmsw.com).

**Paul R. Rasmussen**, PhD, is a core faculty member in clinical psychology at the Adler School of Professional Psychology in Chicago, Illinois. He is the author of numerous professional articles and four books, most recently, *The Quest to Feel Good*.

**Mary Frances Schneider**, PhD, directs the doctoral program in school and educational psychology at National Louis University in Chicago, Illinois. Her current research and writing focus on school-wide practices in social and emotional learning with an emphasis on evidence-based interventions for internalizing disorders and family–school partnerships.

**Len Sperry**, MD, PhD, is a professor at Florida Atlantic University and a clinical professor at the Medical College of Wisconsin. He is board certified in clinical psychology, psychiatry, and preventive medicine, has 600 publications, and is a member of 12 editorial boards.

**Alan E. Stewart**, PhD, works as an associate professor in the University of Georgia's Department of Counseling. His research interests include psychological birth order, Adlerian psychology, and the psychology of weather and climate.

**Sharyl M. Trail**, PsyD, is a lieutenant in the U.S. Public Health Service Commissioned Corps (PHS). She currently works as a clinical psychologist and PHS officer at the Indian Health Service in Zuni, New Mexico. Her clinical focus includes addressing PTSD, historical trauma, and suicide prevention in the Native American community. Dr. Trail is an Adlerian parent educator. Her research interests include the lesbian, gay, bisexual, and transgendered community as well as understanding social justice and social exclusion from an Adlerian perspective. Dr. Trail is a member of NASAP and in the past has participated in ICCASI and the International Congress of Adlerian Psychology.

**Francis X. Walton** has been a psychologist in private practice in Columbia, South Carolina, for over 40 years. He is a frequent consultant and lecturer in North America and Europe. Dr. Walton is the founder of Adlerian Child Care Center, Inc., is a former president of the North American Society of Adlerian Psychology, and has been a member of the faculty of the International Adlerian Summer Institute (ICASSI) for 31 years. His most popular publications, *Winning Teenagers Over in Home and School* and *Winning Children Over* (with R. L. Powers), have been published in 13 languages. Dr. Walton's DVDs include *Use of the Most Memorable Observation in Counseling* and *Parent Consultation and Teen Suicide: An Approach to Prevention*. Contact him at his website, http://www.drfrankwalton.com.

**Richard E. Watts**, PhD, is professor and director of the Center for Research and Doctoral Studies in Counselor Education at Sam Houston State University. He is the author of over 100 professional publications, a Diplomate in Adlerian Psychology, and a Fellow of the American Counseling Association (http://sites.google.com/site/richardwattswebsite/Home).

**John D. West**, EdD, is a professor in the Counseling and Human Development Services Program at Kent State University.

**JoAnna White**, EdD, is chair of the Department of Counseling and Psychological Services at Georgia State University. Her research interests are in individual psychology and play therapy. She is the coauthor of the White–Campbell Psychological Birth Order Inventory.

# 1

# An Introduction to Alfred Adler

Michael P. Maniacci

Alfred Adler (1870–1937) was a physician, psychiatrist, author, professor, and husband and father who lived at a significant time in our era. We were about to experience two world wars, the dawning of the nuclear age, social and political upheaval, and revolution. Medicine in specific, and science in general, was ascending, as people began to move more toward scientific and away from traditional folk and religious explanations for the assorted troubles that were emerging. People were feeling lost, if not scared and anxious, about themselves, their children, and their worlds. The physician was becoming the source of hope, if not faith and salvation, for what disturbed us. It was into this context that three men stepped up to declare they had *the* answers to what was wrong: Sigmund Freud, Carl Jung, and Alfred Adler.

This book is intended to explore one of those men's answers, Alfred Adler. Those were heady times. People listened, and read, and studied, and practiced. Perhaps, just perhaps, if we learned from these men and others like them, we could feel better, do better, and act better. Maybe, just maybe, we could change things—and be better.

Like Plato and Aristotle, Freud, Jung, and Adler have become common knowledge to today's world. Most of Western civilization knows their names, something about their theories, terms, and ideas. Even though the average person may not know any particulars, words and concepts like drives, unconscious, inferiority complex, lifestyle, psyche, ego, introvert, extrovert, and the significance of dreams and the early childhood years have become commonplace. In particular, Adler wrote 13 books, authored dozens and dozens of articles, gave hundreds of lectures, and taught classes for both professionals and interested laypersons. He was interviewed all over the world and treated like a celebrity, with his life and work discussed, processed, debated, and challenged. Like his onetime associates, Adler thought he had answers, and he felt almost compelled to share them with the world, for the world's sake. Twice in his lifetime, he saw his country devastated by war, political upheaval, and social unrest. He and his family had to flee their country for their lives, and he lost one of his children to the political revolution the world was experiencing because she was on the front line, trying to intervene. This last pain was almost more than he could bear and shortly after he found out about it, he was struck with a near fatal illness that most likely took his life several brief months later.

This book is intended to bring some of his original writings back to life. To these original writings, contemporary experts have been asked to comment and introduce Adler's work through the prism of the 21st century. Repeatedly, they note how contemporary his ideas seem, and how prescient he seemed to be. A possible reason for this will be explored below. Perhaps readers of this work will agree, and the debating, discussing, and challenging can continue.

## ALFRED ADLER: A BRIEF BIOGRAPHICAL SKETCH

Ansbacher (1978), Ellenberger (1970), Furtmuller (1964), Hoffman (1994), Manaster, Painter, Deutsch, and Overholt (1977), Mosak and Maniacci (1999), and Orgler (1939/1963) provide the details highlighted in this and the previous section. Adler was the second of six children. He woke one morning to find one of his brothers dead in the bed next to him. Twice in his life, he was run over in the street outside his home. Once, he contracted a pneumonia that almost killed him. In fact, he heard the physician tell his father, "Your boy is lost" (Orgler, 1939/1963, p. 16). He suffered from poor eyesight, and his family was told he should be apprenticed to a shoemaker because his studies were so bad. With glasses, his academics improved so much he became one of the best students.

Adler learned the importance of health, how crucial the support of family was, and the necessity of constructively compensating for illness or weakness. He went to medical school, studied to be a clinician (as opposed to a researcher, like Freud), and specialized in ophthalmology. He quickly expanded to general practice, and eventually, psychiatry. He met and married a brilliant woman, Riassa Timofeyewna Epstein, a scholar who was multilingual and politically active. He set up practice in the lower- to middle-class part of town and treated the circus sideshow performers on a regular basis. He was struck by their ability to compensate, and overcompensate, for their deformities and still meet the tasks of life: work, friendship, and love.

Partially under the influence of his wife, Adler was very politically active, attending meetings, writing pamphlets, and marching in various rallies, including for women's liberation. It was around this time, when he was beginning his practice, starting his family, and establishing himself in the community, that he met Freud.

## ADLER AND FREUD: COWORKERS AND RIVALS

Adler was 14 years Freud's junior. Freud was much better established in the community. He had been practicing longer, had published more and lectured to professionals longer, and had done extensive research in neurology, particularly aphasia. He was a professor at the country's prestigious medical school. They were both working professionals and colleagues, and while Adler deferred to Freud in many ways, as would have been expected given the differences in their ages and professional experience, Adler was not a disciple. Within a short time, Adler and Freud (and three others) started the Wednesday Night Meetings, soon to become the first psychoanalytic society, and invited others to join. Adler, not Freud, was the first president of the society, and coeditor (with Freud) of the journal they started. Over the years, they began to differ on several points, and soon, it came to a head over two issues: repression and the masculine protest.

Freud felt that repression was a product of living in a society, a community, and a consequence of having to adapt to communal life. If people did not repress their drives, they would kill each other, assault each other, and tear society apart. Only by repressing these drives could people live together. Adler disagreed. He felt that only *poorly adjusted* individuals had to repress their drives. If they were well integrated into the society, at peace with themselves and others, individuals could live in harmony and satisfy their drives with others, in cooperative ways. Freud felt this was naïve, even foolish, and stated that Adler was grossly underestimating the true depth of pathology that rested inside people. He called Adler superficial, a label that would haunt him his entire professional life, and well after his death. Adler stated that Freud was not describing normal individuals but childlike people who were poorly socialized and overindulged, and that people who were raised well and with love and compassion could achieve what Adler was advocating, and they did it every day, in many communities. Adler called Freud's views the psychology of pampered children who would not accept no for an answer, who were self-serving and self-centered. They did not take into consideration the welfare of others. They may have had good reasons for developing such attitudes, including poor social conditions and possibly inferior organs, but no such reasons were acceptable for maintaining such a stance.

Similarly, Freud felt that women were constitutionally and biologically inferior. Because they were born without a penis, they could not experience the Oedipal conflict the way men did, they would not fear castration, and therefore, they would not develop a superego, a sense of morality and conscience. Adler forcefully disagreed, but he attempted to remain diplomatic. Yes, women may have difficulties in greater numbers than men (and therefore be utilizing more psychoanalytic services), but this was because of the *social situation* in which they found themselves. Women were treated as second-class citizens and told from an early age that men were more powerful, and they were not given the same choices and freedoms men had. They therefore exhibited what Adler termed the masculine protest: They were attesting to the fact that they were as powerful as men, but in many instances, in socially useless ways, such as through psychological symptoms. It was only through their symptoms that they could gain power, recognition, and some sense of control in their lives and families. If women were given the rights and privileges of men, not only would they be better, so would society. Freud was unmovable.

A vote was taken, and Freud and his growing followers felt that Adler and those who thought as he did were wrong. They were no longer welcome in the new psychoanalytic movement. Adler and his followers tried to negotiate, but to no avail. Adler left and started his own group, originally called the Society for Free Psychoanalytic Research. Apparently, the *free* meant free from Freud. Many early members tried to keep membership in both groups, but Freud would have none of it. He declared that membership in one precluded membership in the other. Members would have to choose. Eleven members resigned from Freud's group and joined Adler. A bright, young Swiss psychiatrist was recruited to replace Adler. His name was Carl Jung. He became the new head of the society and within just a few years, he too was voted out, by Freud and his loyal followers who felt that he too, as Adler before him, had deviated too far from psychoanalytic doctrine and that his new concepts were not compatible with Freud's.

## ADLER: THE MOVEMENT TOWARD INDIVIDUAL PSYCHOLOGY

As stated above, Adler wanted to originally call his group the Society for Free Psychoanalytic Research, but Freud objected to Adler using the term *psychoanalytic*, so Adler began exploring for new titles. He considered Personality Psychology, but that was already being used. He then wanted Holistic Psychology, but that too was being used by a new and up-and-coming group that would become known as the Gestalt Psychologists (*Gestalt*, in German, meaning *whole*). He chose *Individual Psychology*, meaning *individuum*, a Latin term for *indivisible*. The proper English translation should have been *Indivisible Psychology*, but as will be noted below, poor translation would become a curse to Adler and his writings to the present day.

Adler and his followers began meeting. Adler (1907/1917) had written one book as a member of the Freudian group, *Study of Organ Inferiority and Its Psychical Compensation: A Contribution to Clinical Medicine*. It was well received and even praised by Freud. Now, on his own, he needed a declaration of independence, and he had been preparing one for months even while still in the Freudian circle. He would rush its completion and submit it to the medical school where Freud taught so he could gain an appointment and train other physicians and thus grow his movement. It was his most important work, and Adler (1912/2002) called it, *The Neurotic Character: Fundamentals of Individual Psychology and Psychotherapy*.

He was still rather polite to Freud, giving his senior colleague credit and playing down any bad feelings toward him. Nonetheless, he outlined in exquisite detail his differences from mainstream psychoanalysis and pointed toward a new direction not just for psychiatry but for medical practice as well. It was two and a half years before Adler would receive a response. He was unanimously rejected by 25 professors. Freud had been teaching there for 15 years already. The rejection was unequivocal, yet unclear. In part, it may have been Adler's radical political leanings that damned him. His once close association with Freud did not help either—Freud was not popular among the academics at the medical school because of his "speculations." In fact, Freud had not submitted any psychoanalytic works as a basis for his appointment: He submitted his research on aphasia. After he was appointed, he began teaching psychoanalysis. This did not please the faculty, but it was tolerated well enough to keep Freud on a limited basis. Adler was reportedly devastated. He would never teach in his home country, nor did he ever apply again. As will become detailed below, he would never write a book again.

## ADLER AND SOCIAL PSYCHOLOGY

For the rest of his life, Adler would continue to write articles, but his books would be "assembled" for him from two sources. Either his articles would be gathered together and anthologized, or his lectures to lay audiences would be hastily put together from his notes and transcriptions and published as "books." He came to America and received academic appointments to universities, but almost always in departments of education, social work, or medical psychology. The Freudians had a stranglehold in the medical schools in America, and the psychology departments were dominated by a young psychologist named John Watson, with his new system he labeled *behaviorism*. The behaviorists had no tolerance for the Freudian speculators, and the Freudians had little patience for the naïve behaviorists; hence, the (almost) tragic split began in the 1920s between the medical schools and psychology departments of the major universities. Adler found himself welcomed in neither; he was not psychoanalytic enough for the Freudians, and the behaviorists considered him just another Freudian. He came up with an idea. He would turn to the people themselves, and he began teaching and writing for them, directly.

Adler opened clinics for the poor. He taught teachers and set up offices in the public schools, training teachers, counselors, and social workers in his methods. He lectured to whoever would listen, at churches, public meeting halls, community organizations, and the community mental health clinics he was instrumental in establishing. He provided consultations to prisons, sanitariums, mental institutions for the "insane," and magazines and newspapers. His popular self-help "books" became global best-sellers, much to the annoyance of Freud, whose books did not sell well, especially in America. He became a media sensation and one of the most famous people in the world.

## ADLER AS WRITER

Adler wrote in German. Later in life, he wrote in English, but how much he actually "wrote," versus was written for him, remains speculation. He did lecture in English, but while he was reportedly a dynamic and captivating speaker, his English retained much of the Germanic structure from his native tongue. Adler turned over the editing of his works to translators, editors, and colleagues as he became increasingly popular. His global reach was unprecedented, and as he grew increasingly busy, he did not closely attend to their work. Frankly, some of his early translations were simply wrong. As noted earlier, Adler did not intend (primarily) the word *individual* to mean "unique person"; he meant "indivisible." When he used words like *lacking courage*, he was not sympathetically translated—the more accurate translation is "discouraged." Similarly, though the term *pampered* became synonymous with Adler, the more accurate translation is "tenderized." In many of his early works, he appeared to have used the word *soul*; the more accurate translation of the same term from German is "mind." When he apparently used the term *failure*, an alternate translation is "to breakdown" or "refuse." The list could continue, but the point is clear. Adler should have checked more closely, but he was both too busy and too avoidant to address writing in great detail ever again, using a safeguarding operation he would later identify as "distance." His lack of attentiveness hurt his reputation with scholars and unsympathetic students. (For the record, Freud fared little better in certain crucial instances. Freud was poorly translated as well, with words like *id* being an inaccurate translation of "it" and *ego* being a poor choice for "self.")

To read Adler with such modified translations in mind helps. He was brilliant, but not scholarly. He was busy in private practice, not teaching. He did not have the time or structure of an academician. That was not his goal, and his behavior fell in line with that. He wanted to help as many people as directly as possible, and he did. He was considered a master clinician by those who knew him, but the effect upon his academic reputation was devastating. He is difficult to follow at times, unclear in his points, and apparently lacking in references and citations to other authors or experts (though not in his one scholarly book, *The Neurotic Character*). The articles presented in this text are an attempt to clarify some of this. In most of the articles in this book, Adler was direct, clear, and to the point. Some of the translations are still stilted but, in the interest of historical accuracy, are left in their original form. In the article format, Adler was sharp and often as penetrating as any physician or psychiatrist, and in many instances far more astute than scholars of his or our day. He was attentive!

## ADLER AND THE NATURE OF HIS THEORETICAL MODEL

When Freud, Adler, and Jung met, wrote, discussed, and analyzed, they were not modest. They wanted to create a new discipline, even a new science. They were global (at best) and grandiose (at worst) in their aspirations. They wanted to explain everything. They did. How successfully they attained that goal is open to question, but they did try. It is fascinating to compare their writings with contemporaries from our era. The articles written by today's scholars and professionals are typically much more scientific, far more scholarly, and more tightly focused. Yet, they lack something. Experts in the social sciences today, especially psychiatry and psychology, are generally aiming much lower. They achieve their aims with precision and pedantry, but their global reach is limited, partially due to information overload among the general public, but also because many of them lack the vision—or hubris—to try.

The founding three (Freud, Adler, Jung) wanted to be taken seriously, and respect for a new discipline can be hard won. Freud's answer was to model his system after the prevailing dominant science of his day: physics. It was, and is, considered to be the grandparent of all science. He began a tradition that continues to this day, that is, of using models from physics to explain the functioning of the mind and brain, thereby giving an apparent sophistication—and prestige—to his theories.

The machine of the day in Freud's time was the steam engine. Newtonian physics could explain the workings of the world, and any science that was worth its salt had to at least implicitly acknowledge Newton. Freud's terminology was consistent with this: *energy, force, resistance, pressure, blocking*. As the technology of the day changed, so too did the metaphor. When the telephone and telegraph arose, psychology and psychiatry began using images of wiring, circuits, and communication theory. The model then became computers, and neural networks, nodes, and complex systems grounded in information processing emerged. Freud's system, like much in brain science, constantly undergoes revision as the models in physics change. With the new models of chaos theory and fractal mathematics emerging, psychiatry and psychology will scramble yet again to revise their languages, metaphors, and terminologies.

Interestingly, Adler tried this language of Newtonian physics in his first book on organ inferiority in 1907. It did not work for him. Perhaps he too was fascinated by trying to emulate traditional scientific methodology, or he was still swayed by Freud's views. He never returned to that language or its metaphors again after 1907. Slowly, his language, and thinking, began to change. By 1912, he found three new sources, and a major conceptual shift happened. He found Nietzsche, Vaihinger, and Shakespeare. Their influence upon the way Adler not only phrased his system but conceptualized his theory was enormous. He began a conceptual shift that was more than terminological. Adler began *thinking* differently. A brief examination of each thinker will clarify.

With Nietzsche (1901/1967), he found a gadfly, a rebel who provoked, challenged, and disrupted practically everything he touched. Adler was drawn to this for many reasons, but one key was that Adler was a second-born who also enjoyed challenging others. Adler's (favored) older brother was named Sigmund, and Adler saw in Sigmund Freud someone who was an oldest-born authority figure. Nietzsche delighted in questioning, and overthrowing, traditional values, assumptions, and pretenses. Nietzsche developed ideas such as the prime motivating force behind all human functioning as the will to power. He believed that people attempted to distance themselves from responsibilities and that most problems people developed were due to the fact that they were competitive and their unwillingness to acknowledge such competitive striving fostered all sorts of dysfunctions. Unconscious processes led people to make choices for which they were responsible, but unaware. There was an ideal type for which all people strove, and challenging that ideal produced panic, hostility, and dissimulation from people.

Vaihinger (1911/1965) elaborated upon concepts from Immanuel Kant. People formed cognitive assumptions, what he called fictions, and those fictions served as a map of the world. Some of those maps were just that, maps. They were useful expedients to navigate through the world. Some people, however, took those maps too seriously. They confused the map with the terrain and became too rigid.

With Shakespeare, Adler discovered a unique thinker. Though writing in the late 16th and early 17th centuries, Shakespeare's influence seemed unbounded. Especially during his prime writing period (from about 1595 till his retirement in 1611), Shakespeare changed the way people thought about human motivation and the world. He seems to have created the notion of the human as we know it today (Bloom, 1998; Nuttall, 2007). In Shakespeare, people were often victims of life and other people, but something new was added. People also brought their own downfall upon themselves. They had a unique, distinguishable character that was the source of both their strengths and their weakness. The same characteristics that made Hamlet, Othello, or Cleopatra great also brought them down. Their "destinies" were largely self-created, through flaws that could be directly correlated to a mismatch between what they brought to situations and the requirements of the situations themselves. To truly understand human nature, one had to know both the character and the life situation (with its trials and challenges). It was the mismatch between those two forces that led to tragedy, not one or the other.

In *The Neurotic Character*, Adler often cites Nietzsche, Vaihinger, and Shakespeare. The consequence is more than superficial; yes, other authors and physicians are cited, as is research, but there is a clear difference in his thinking from other things he had written thus far. Adler was not thinking like an aspiring physicist. He was thinking like a philosopher or writer, and he had excellent taste. The insights these three individuals had were profound and not tied to any fashion of the time. Since he was not tying himself to any particular system in science, as the science changed, Adler did not seem out of step. The insights of Nietzsche and Shakespeare, in particular, have stood the test of time. Both those men are often cited as among the towering geniuses of all time (e.g., Bloom, 2003). By building his thinking, and his system, upon their styles of thinking, Adler seemed to become "timeless" himself.

Adler's theory has been relatively unchanged since he first articulated it. His assumptions are as valid today as they were back then. Some of the postulates derived from his assumptions have come under criticism, and in cases such as his stance toward "homosexuality" appropriately so, but he was a man of his times. His assumptions, though, are still amazingly relevant. Because his focus was clinically oriented, not academically driven, he developed numerous tactics for achieving change in characters and the situations they find themselves in. While his theory is consistent, his tactics are diverse. Today's Adlerian practitioners are diverse in their styles of counseling and therapy. Their theory is homogeneous. It appears to have stood the test of time. Freud, however, has not had the same fate. He was much more research and academically oriented. He only would work with patients that fit his system. If they did not, he would refer them out (often to Adler, at least early on it appears). That was not the case with Adler: He would modify his style to suit the needs of the patient.

Freud, till his death, advocated psychoanalysis as a research method. He wanted to be a researcher, but his desire to marry and start a family "got in the way," so to speak. He found he could not support his growing family on a researcher's salary, so reluctantly he began a private practice. He wanted to understand human nature, and the best way to do that (he thought) was to study cases in depth. He adopted a researcher's stance: He would sit away from the subject, not interfere with the process, and take copious notes. He saw patients four to six times per week. Too much interference from the researcher might contaminate the data, so professional distance was required. His original research was on aphasia— the loss of speech. He was fascinated about how and why people lost the ability to speak, to articulate their issues. Psychoanalysis was a method of transferring his academic research on aphasia into clinical practice. He found, as most of us do, only what he was looking for, and his theory closely resembles his biases and personality dynamics (Mosak & Kopp, 1973).

Adler was different. He wanted to overcome death. He wanted individuals to compensate for their weaknesses and unfortunate circumstances of life. He wanted to make life fair and better for all. He was clinically driven. He took any number of individuals, and types of individuals, into his practice. He worked with psychotics, criminals, children, families, couples, teachers, and school systems, as well as traditionally defined neurotics. He even advocated group psychotherapy. He found what he looked for as well, but he had a different outlook on life and himself than Freud (Mosak & Kopp, 1973).

It is within this context that *Alfred Adler Revisited* is presented. Following are some of his most important articles. Their selection was not exhaustive, nor was it comprehensive. They were picked because of their seeming relevance to today's issues and their importance in Adlerian theory and practice. They are relatively self-explanatory. Their selection will detail the core elements of his theory and some of the tactics he used and advocated for changing both individuals and the systems (e.g., families, schools, communities) in which they found themselves. We hope you enjoy them and look forward to the debate continuing.

## REFERENCES

Adler, A. (1917). *Study of organ inferiority and its psychical compensation: A contribution to clinical medicine* (S. E. Jelliffe, Trans.). New York: Nervous and Mental Diseases Company. (Original work published 1907)

Adler, A. (2002). *The neurotic character: Fundamentals of Individual Psychology and psychotherapy* (C. Koen, Trans., & H. T. Stein, Ed.). San Francisco: Classical Adlerian Translation Project. (Original work published 1912)

Ansbacher, A. (1978). Essay: Adler's sex theories. In A. Adler, *Cooperation between the sexes: Writings on women, love, and marriage, sexuality and its disorders* (H. I., Ansbacher & R. R. Ansbachers, Eds., & Trans.; pp. 248–412). New York: Jason Aronson.

Bloom, H. (1998). *Shakespeare: The invention of the human.* New York: Riverhead Books.

Bloom, H. (2003). *Genius: A mosaic of one hundred exemplary creative minds.* New York: Grand Central Publishing.

Ellenberger, H. F. (1970). *The discovery of the unconscious: The history and evolution of dynamic psychiatry.* New York: Basic Books.

Furtmuller, C. (1964). Alfred Adler: A biographical essay. In A. Adler, *Superiority and social interest: A collection of later writings* (H. L. Ansbacher & R. R. Ansbacher, Eds., & Trans.; pp. 309–393). Evanston, IL: Northwestern University Press.

Hoffman, E. (1994). *The drive for self: Alfred Adler and the founding of Individual Psychology.* New York: Addison-Wesley.

Manaster, G. J., Painter, G., Deutsch, J., & Overholt, B. (Eds.). (1977). *Alfred Adler: As we remember him.* Chicago: North American Society of Adlerian Psychology.

Mosak, H. H., & Kopp, R. R. (1973). The early recollections of Adler, Freud and Jung. *Journal of Individual Psychology, 29,* 157–166.

Mosak, H., & Maniacci, M. (1999). *A primer of Adlerian psychology: The analytic-behavioral-cognitive psychology of Alfred Adler.* Philadelphia: Brunner/Mazel.

Nietzsche, F. (1967). *The will to power* (W. Kaufman & R. J. Hollingdale, Trans.; W. Kaufman, Ed.). New York: Vintage. (Original work published 1901)

Nuttall, A. D. (2007). *Shakespeare the thinker.* New Haven, CT: Yale University Press.

Orgler, H. (1963). *Alfred Adler: The man and his works: Triumph over the inferiority complex.* New York: Mentor Books. (Original work published 1939)

Vaihinger, H. (1965). *The philosophy of "as if"* (C. K. Ogden, Trans.). London: Routledge, Kegan, Paul. (Original work published 1911)

# 2

# The Fundamental Views of Individual Psychology

## Francis X. Walton

It is a pleasure to offer this commentary as to how the fundamental principles of Individual Psychology, as set forth by Adler in the following article, help provide direction for solving problems that face society in 2011.

As a practitioner, I am continually faced with the remarkably encouraging moment adult clients experience when they begin to understand the powerful hand they have had in creating their personal set of beliefs and the manner in which their idiosyncratic interpretation of themselves and their problems brought them to the troubles they have presented in therapy. Adler's contributions to the clinician's ability to help the client understand "the bricks which he uses in his own 'creative' way" and his "individual way of using these bricks" has become more systematized and elaborated upon especially by psychiatrists Rudolf Dreikurs, Kurt Adler, and Bernard Shulman, as well as psychologist Harold Mosak in the period following Alfred Adler's death, and subsequently by many others. Lifestyle formulation has become the precursor to counseling and therapy for a great many Adlerian clinicians.

When working with children I am often reminded how parents, educators, physicians, and mental health clinicians could be of so much more help to young people if they would use Adler's understanding of the development of lifestyle when dealing with the most commonly diagnosed childhood disorder of our time: attention deficit hyperactivity disorder. Sadly, one of the psychologists who has been particularly prolific and influential in his publications about ADHD, Russell Barkley, explains the etiology of ADHD as follows: "For most children, ADHD is a biologically based inborn temperamental style that predisposes them to be inattentive, impulsive, and psychically restless as well as deficient in their capacity for role governed behavior" (Barkley, 1990). This understanding of ADHD is prevalent in the medical community despite the fact it does not fit with the facts. Peter Freer in connection with the esteemed Drug Effectiveness

Review Project at Oregon State University writes, "Dr. Russell Barkley just spoke at a national conference citing that medication is by far the best and most trusted method. Unfortunately, dinosaurs like Barkley do exist, are respected, and yet completely propagate information that has no substance in current research" (Freer, 2010). Despite this fact, more than 2.5 million children in the United States alone take ADHD drugs.

My point is that the conclusions Adler offers in the following article direct practitioners where we need to go when attempting to understand and help children who manifest behavior that meets the criteria for the ADHD diagnosis. Adler shows us a two-pronged approach, namely, help parents, children and teachers understand the particular way the child has learned to approach life, and help parents and teachers understand how children manifesting these characteristics very commonly are influenced by a substantially underdeveloped sense of the social interest or social feeling and spirit of cooperation to which Adler refers in this article (Walton, 1996). I offer you the observation that so many clinicians, educators, and parents are accustomed to looking for the causes of behavior that they ignore the belief system and the style of behavior the child uses to create the difficulties he is experiencing. Adler emphasizes the need to understand the individual in the light of his own "peculiar" development and avoid the "unfruitful roads of classification," and yet we continue to see mental health workers adopt the language and labeling of the *Diagnostic and Statistical Manual* as if placing clients in diagnostic categories is in any way similar to understanding the unique belief system that takes the client to his successes and to his difficulties.

Speaking further about the capacity to develop the social interest that Adler cites, it is probably not possible to overemphasize how important the "degree of social feeling and cooperation" is to individual and community mental health. Adler has helped us understand how important it is for the child to learn to approach life's problems with concern for himself or herself, but also to develop concern for how the solution to problems will influence him and his mother, or him and other members of the family, and as the child grows older, him and his classmates, or him and other members of the football team, or him and other members of the community, or him and other inhabitants of his country, and, finally, him and others in the world. The closest to a guarantee that we may live in a world with peace and harmony is that we capitalize upon the capacity we possess to learn to care about the welfare of fellow human beings.

Probably the influence that most undermines the development of social interest in young people today is pampering. Since Adler regards the development of social interest as having such importance for successful interaction with fellow human beings, it behooves us to emphasize how the pampered child learns to see himself as the center of the universe. His belief system includes the thinking that he is entitled to special treatment, and consequently he frequently can picture himself as being mistreated when the special treatment he thinks should be awarded to him does not materialize. The common reaction of such a person is to attempt to force others to treat him as special, and if that is not successful, he frequently attempts to punish others. Adler attempts to help us understand that life calls for cooperation, for a give-and-take, but the understanding of the pampered human being is that you give and I take. Carried on without modification, the absence or low state of social interest in the pampered child dooms him to a life of poor relationships in work and social situations and in love. The blame and hate that such individuals are capable of calling upon can be seen in many sorts of antagonistic and harmful behaviors including suicide, which so very often has in it the motive of revenge.

It is noteworthy at this time in the history of society that we are faced with an increase in bullying, substantial violence, and other sorts of abuse of human beings by fellow human beings. Adler proposes that "the treatment and cure of the numerous failures and mal-adjustments of our time are wholly dependent upon increasing the degree of social feeling and cooperation." Support for his position is abundant, but some very recent empirical support of his position is found in research conducted in areas as diverse as penology and parenting. It is noteworthy that the cutting edge to improving penal systems is found in the country of Norway, where penologists have instituted a system designed to bring about much greater respect and caring between guards and inmates as well as between fellow inmates. The guiding principles are that repressive systems do not work, and that treating prisoners humanely boosts their chance of reintegration into society. Within 2 years of their release 20% of Norway's prisoners end up in jail. In the United Kingdom and the United States the figure is between 50% and 60% (Adams, 2010). A study reported by Tulane University researchers found that 5-year-old children who had been spanked frequently as 3-year-olds were more likely to demonstrate aggressive behavior including defiance, cruelty, screaming, bullying or meanness to others, frequent threatening of others, temper tantrums, destruction of things, and lashing out physically against people or animals (Taylor, Manganello, Lee, & Rice, 2010). Thus, whether our mistaken approaches to leadership consist of pampering or overcontrol, we steal away opportunities for others to develop social interest. In summary, Adler helps us understand how we behave in ways consistent with our belief system. It is very difficult to mistreat fellow human beings when we have made concern for fellow human beings part of our belief system. He writes that a great improvement in "the next generation" can be assured by preventive work. Of course, that work can be carried out in the family, but absolutely not only in the family. In this day when a great many young children commonly spend as much time in the early childhood education center as they do with parents, we have begun to recognize the tremendous opportunity that exists to teach preschool children to care about fellow human beings. There probably is no better opportunity to systematically work at "increasing the degree of social feeling and cooperation" for which Adler has called than in early childhood education centers. Finally, while the education of parents in groups in preschool centers, elementary schools, and churches is an important resource to continue the work Adler pioneered in his child guidance centers in Vienna, let us not ignore a huge opportunity that has been largely wasted—that is, the opportunity for students from kindergarten through secondary school to acquire and practice socially interested behavior, so that schools ultimately operate much more in the manner of a caring extended family.

## REFERENCES

Adams, W. L. (2010). A look inside the world's most humane prison. *TIME, 175*(21), 14.

Barkley, R. A. (1990). *Attention deficit hyperactivity disorder*. New York: The Guilford Press.

Freer, P. (2010). ADHD medications and neurofeedback. *Drug Effectiveness Review Project—Attention deficit*. Retrieved April 28, 2010, from http://playattention.com/attention-deficit/articles/category/drug-effectiveness-review-project/

Taylor, C. A., Manganello, J. A., Lee, S. J., & Rice, J. C. (2010, May). Mother's spanking of 3-year old children and subsequent risk of children's aggressive behavior. *Pediatrics, 125*, e1057–e1065.

Walton, F. X. (1996). Understanding and helping children who manifest symptoms that meet the criteria for the attention-deficit hyperactivity disorder diagnosis. *Journal of Individual Psychology, 63*(2), 235–280.

## The Fundamental Views of Individual Psychology

*Alfred Adler*

In introducing the *International Journal* of *Individual Psychology* in the United States and Great Britain, it seems fitting to describe the basic structure of Individual Psychology, in order to show the contributions of this science to modern psychology and psychiatry. I do not want to go into details here. Those details will be found in the articles of the contributors to this Journal. It is only the scientific framework that I want to explain very briefly.

The raw material with which the Individual Psychologist works is: The *relationship* of the individual to the problems of the outside world. The Individual Psychologist has to observe how a particular individual relates himself to the outside world. This outside world includes the individual's own body, his bodily functions, and the functions of his mind. He does not relate himself to the outside world in a pre-determined manner as is often assumed. He relates himself always according to his own interpretation of himself and of his present problem. His limits are not only the common human limits, but also the limits which he has set himself. It is neither heredity nor environment which determines his relationship to the outside world. Heredity only endows him with certain abilities. Environment only gives him certain impressions. These abilities and impressions, and the manner in which he "experiences" them—that is to say, the interpretation he makes of these experiences—are the bricks which he uses in his own "creative" way in building up his attitude toward life. It is his individual way of using these bricks—or in other words, it is his attitude toward life which determines his relationship to the outside world.

He meets problems which are entirely different from those of his forebears. He sees all his problems from a perspective which is his own creation. He sees the environment which trains him, with his own self-created perspective, and accordingly changes its effect upon him for better or worse. There is a task in life which no individual can escape. It is to solve a great number of problems. These problems are in no way accidental. I have divided them for clarity into three parts: problems of behavior toward others; problems of occupation; and problems of love. The manner in which an individual behaves toward these three problems and their subdivisions—that is his answer to the problems of life.

Life (and all psychic expressions as part of life) moves ever toward "overcoming," toward perfection, toward superiority, toward success. You cannot train or condition a living being for defeat. But what an individual thinks or feels as success (i.e., as a goal acceptable to him), that is his own matter. In my experience I have found that each individual has a different meaning of, and attitude toward, what constitutes success. Therefore a human being cannot be typified or classified. I believe it is because of the parsimony of language that many scientists have come to mistaken conclusions—believing in types, entities, racial qualities, etc. Individual Psychology recognizes, with other psychologies, that each individual must be studied in the light of his own peculiar development. To present the individual understandably, in words, requires an extensive reviewing of all his facets, the elaborate demands of which are apparent in the articles which follow. Yet, too often, psychologists are tempted away from this recognition, and take the easier but unfruitful roads of classification. That is a temptation to which, in practical work, we must never yield. It is for teaching purposes only—to illuminate the broad field—that I designate here four different types, in order, temporarily, to classify the attitude and behavior of individuals toward outside problems.

Thus, we find individuals whose approach to reality shows, from early childhood through their entire lives, a more or less dominant or "ruling" attitude. This attitude appears in all their relationships. A second type—surely the most frequent one—expects everything from others and leans on others. I might call it the "getting" type. A third type is inclined to feel successful by avoiding the solution of problems. Instead of struggling with a problem, a person of this type merely tries to "sidestep" it, in an effort thereby to avoid defeat. The fourth type struggles, to a greater or lesser degree, for a solution of these problems in a way which is useful to others.

It is necessary to say here that each special type retains his style from childhood to the end of his life, unless he is convinced of the mistake in his creation of his attitude toward reality. As I have said before, this style is the creation of the child himself, who uses inheritance and impressions of the environment as bricks in building his particular avenue for success—success according to his own interpretation.

Individual Psychology goes beyond the views of philosophers like Kant and newer psychologists and psychiatrists who have accepted the idea of the *totality* of the human being. Very early in my work, I found him to be a *unity!* The foremost task of Individual Psychology is to prove this unity in each individual—in his thinking, feeling, acting; in his so-called conscious and unconscious—in every expression of his personality. This unity we call the "Life-Style" of the individual. What is frequently labeled "the ego" is nothing more than the style of the individual.

Individual Psychology has shown that the first three types mentioned above—the "ruling" type, the "getting" type, and the "avoiding" type—are not apt, and are not prepared, to solve the problems of life. These problems are always social problems. Individuals of these three types are lacking in the ability for co-operation and contribution. The clash between such a life-style (lacking in social interest) and the outside problems (demanding social interest) results in shock. This shock leads up to the individual's failures—which we know as neurosis, psychosis, etc. Significantly, the failure shows the same style as the individual. As I mentioned before, the life-style persists.

In the fourth type (the socially useful type), prepared for co-operation and contribution, we can always find a certain amount of *activity* which is used for the benefit of others. This activity is in agreement with the needs of others; it is useful, normal, rightly imbedded in the stream of evolution of mankind.

The first type also has activity, but not enough social interest. Therefore, if confronted strongly by a situation which he feels to be in the nature of an examination, a test of his social value, a judgment upon his social usefulness, a person of this type acts in an unsocial way. The more active of this type attack others directly: they become delinquents, tyrants, sadists. It is as if they said, with Richard III, "And therefore, since I cannot be a lover, I am determined to prove a villain." To this type also belong suicidals, drug-addicts, drunkards—whose lesser degree of activity causes them to attack others indirectly: They make attacks upon themselves for the purpose of hurting others. The second and third types show even less activity, and not much social interest. This lack appears also in the expression of their shock results, which are neuroses and psychoses.

The principles which guide me when grouping individuals into these four types are (1) the degree of their approach to social integration and (2) the form of movement which they develop (with greater or lesser activity) to maintain that degree of approach in a manner which they regard as most likely to achieve success (in their own interpretation).

But it is the individual shade of interpretation that matters in the end. And when reconstructing the unity of a personality in his relationships to the outer world, Individual Psychology fundamentally undertakes to delineate the individual form of creative activity—which is the life-style.

I should not like to close this short introduction to Individual Psychology without saying that a great improvement in the next generation can be assured by preventive work; while the treatment and cure of the numerous failures and mal-adjustments of our time are wholly dependent upon increasing the degree of social feeling and co-operation. For difficult times like ours, the inherited potentiality for human co-operation does not suffice. It must be further developed. The necessity and importance of this development are inherent in the discoveries of Individual Psychology—and the scientific method by which it may be accomplished is its contribution to the advancement of mankind.

People are always blaming their circumstances for what they are. I don't believe in circumstances. The people who get on in this world are the people who get up and look for the circumstances they want, and, if they can't find them, make them.

—G. B. Shaw, *Mrs. Warren's Profession*

# 3

# A Basic Difference Between Individual Psychology and Psychoanalysis

JOHN D. WEST AND DONALD L. BUBENZER

Although Sigmund Freud (1856–1939) was 14 years older than Alfred Adler (1870–1937), from some perspectives they lived in a similar context. Both were part of what today would be considered fairly large families. Both were born into Jewish households and spent most of their lives in Vienna, Austria. Both became physicians and were educated at the University of Vienna. And, both seemed to be highly influenced by personal experiences in developing their theories of personality and therapy. Adler wrote of overcoming the influence of a sickly childhood and Freud developed many of his ideas while dealing with his own obsessions and fears. Yet their theories of personality and related therapies diverged greatly. Freud was much more influenced by science and the "objective," particularly the principles of physics. He saw humans from a more pessimistic perspective where they could at best manage negative energy and influences through an array of maneuvers that might prevent them from manifesting destructive primal instincts. Adler, on the other hand, was more drawn by goals and the ability to contribute to life through social involvements. He was captured by the subjectivity of life and his work may have portended the social constructionist ideas of the current day (Hall, 1954; Heer, 1972; Orgler, 1963).

   In the chapter titled "The Differences Between Individual Psychology and Psychoanalysis" (Ansbacher & Ansbacher, 1973), Adler wrote of distinctions between Individual Psychology and Psychoanalysis; for example, he commented on how Individual Psychology would view censorship, the Oedipus complex, the construct of narcissism, the notion of a death wish, the castration complex, and the ego ideal and superego. While commenting on these constructions he also commented on the idea of moving from a feeling of inferiority to a sense of excellence. He wrote concerning the basic difference between Individual Psychology and Psychoanalysis and stated "that Freud starts with the assumption that by nature man only wants to satisfy his drives—the pleasure principle—and must, therefore, from the viewpoint of culture be regarded as completely bad" (Ansbacher & Ansbacher, 1973, p. 210). Individual Psychology, however, indicates "development of man . . . is subject to the redeeming influence of social interest, so that all his drives can be guided in the direction of the generally useful. . . . We find neurotics, psychotics, suicides, etc., only when social interest is throttled" (Ansbacher & Ansbacher, 1973, p. 211). As opposed to social interest, on the other hand, he wrote that there are also those who are seeking their personal interest rather than focusing on the well-being of others (Ansbacher & Ansbacher, 1956, p. 253).

Regarding the striving for significance, Adler noted, "It is the striving for superiority which is behind every human creation and it is the source of all contributions which are made to our culture. The whole of human life proceeds along this great line of action—from below to above, from minus to plus, from defeat to victory" (Ansbacher & Ansbacher, 1956, p. 255). Of social interest he acknowledged that it "is innate, just as the striving for overcoming is innate, with the important difference, however, that social interest must be developed, and that it can be developed only when the child is already in the midst of life" (Ansbacher & Ansbacher, 1956, p. 134). He also explained, "The only individuals who can really meet and master the problems of life, however, are those who show in their striving a tendency to enrich all others. . . . All human judgements of value and success are founded, in the end, upon cooperation; this is the great shared commonplace of the human race" (Ansbacher & Ansbacher, 1956, p. 255). It was Adler's thought concerning the striving for significance and social interest that we believe holds great value today, and it is the idea of social interest that we would like to comment on as it pertains to our current life and to the foreseeable future.

## SOCIAL INTEREST IN TODAY'S CLIMATE

It is in moving from a sense of inferiority to superiority that people can become frightened about life and the unknown or potential outcomes of their encounters with life. At these times it appears that some human beings, suffering from a desire for protection and wanting guarantees and assurances about their futures, focus on assumed personal interests rather than social interest—for example, when preemptive strikes as in war seem to be based in limited evidence but a lot of fear, when concerns around personal interests appear to replace interests in national health care, when it appears that personal interests have allowed greed to direct behavior, when desires for profit shares seem to have supported abuse of natural resources, when anxieties about performance appear to lead to compulsive behaviors, or when unfamiliarity and discomfort with cultural pluralism seems to spark an evangelical commitment toward a monoculture. Indeed, as Adler noted, "the lines along which the development both of the individual and the community . . . proceed are prescribed by the degree of social feeling" (Adler, 1964, p. 104).

In juxtaposition to seemingly self-interested positions noted above, and on a more optimistic and helpful note, we have seen educators sending faculty and students out of the country—and welcoming international students into the country—in an effort to stimulate familiarity and cooperation and hopefully reduce suspicions and fears that may lead to conflict. We have heard reports of legislators voting for universal health care, we have heard of government officials advocating for citizens by trying to regulate how large financial institutions use the resources of constituencies, and companies of volunteers assign themselves to work details after a natural disaster. Consequently, it can be said that even in a time when our world is far from the ideal there are illustrations of social interest.

Those who work to help create better families, communities, and countries, as well as a better world, are certainly emblematic of a courageous people. The courage in the stories they live reflects a "confidence in oneself and one's ability to cope either with the particular situation at hand or, even more importantly, with whatever situation may arise" (Dinkmeyer & Dreikurs, 1963, p. 33). Here there is no need to explain away one's performance and no need to locate guarantees or assurances for the future. Instead, when writing of "the courage to be imperfect," Dreikurs and Soltz (1964) mentioned that the issue becomes one of what to do once a mistake occurs and this, rather than focusing on the mistake, promotes courage (p. 108). Indeed, "the courage to be imperfect" would seem to be an essential ingredient for social interest, for it becomes difficult to hold a genuine interest in the welfare of others while also working to elevate or protect one's personal status. If we want to increase concern for others and social interest, a question becomes, "How do we shine a light on stories of caring such that others see this commitment as a worthy investment?"

At times it would appear that we have grown quite adept at highlighting stories in which abuse and neglect occur and much less proficient at highlighting moments where a caring commitment for the well-being of others has occurred. The latter stories may be present in a couple's commitment to act as foster parents, a grandparent's decision to once more assume parenting responsibilities, a daughter's commitment to return home to care for an ailing parent, a couple's investment in a long-term relationship, a country's decision to send aid to a foreign land, or one community's decision to help another when a river is at risk of flooding its banks. Historically, research has been interested in understanding conditions from which problems arise. We may, however, be better served by investing in the study of the spirit of commitment that supports the advancement and well-being of others. For, as human beings, we are not independent of one another but, rather, we are interdependent creatures who benefit from an ecological perspective indicating that we will only survive and flourish in light of a demonstrated concern for each other.

Indeed, meaning and pleasure in life are not derived from inwardly focusing on one's own security or advancement but in transcending the focus on oneself through concern and commitment to others. We have both been fortunate to experience this in our lives and are aware that it can also play out on a larger stage. On a personal note, one of the authors has a story about moving with his family to accept a new position. This event occurred some time ago and as with the narratives in each of our lives, the event is remembered in a way that brings meaning to the storyteller. In applying for his counselor license he understood that clarification for one of the courses he had taken in graduate school was needed. A letter was drafted to the professor who had taught the course explaining the nature of the request. John then followed up with a telephone call and discovered that his teacher had retired and was given the home telephone number. When the telephone call was placed the wife answered and mentioned that her husband had been resting but she was sure he would not mind coming to the phone. It was good to talk with the gentleman, for John had remembered him as kindly and helpful. He remembered the course and agreed to write a description of the course for the licensure application. Eventually John received his license and wanted to call his teacher back and thank him for his assistance, but he had lost the telephone number and so called the counselor education department again and talked with a member of the staff. She mentioned remembering the day that the retired faculty member's wife brought him back to the department office so that he could dictate the letter. She mentioned that at some point after that visit the wonderful gentleman died. It was clear to John that this individual had inconvenienced himself with what was probably a noticeable level of discomfort to be helpful to someone else. John has tried to never forget that event or the realization that the real mission in life, and that of a university faculty member, is to try to be of service to others.

It seems that narratives around social interest are easily identifiable by others and, consequently, have the strength to move people to concern and caring. Another illustration of social interest that touched both of us concerns the village of Rothenburg ob der Tauber, Germany. The village arose around 950 AD. The medieval town with its surrounding 30-foot wall remained intact until near the end of World War II, the 31st of March, 1945 (Kootz, 2007), when the allies bombed the city, destroying about 40% of it. In the final months of the war Lieutenant General Max Simon and his German forces sought refuge in Rothenburg after fleeing from the bombing of Nurnberg. He had orders to fight until the last man. Knowing that Simon and his troops were ensconced in Rothenburg, the allies had orders to bomb the rest of the city (Darheim & Baumgartner, 2004).

John McCloy, a US undersecretary of state, learned of these orders. McCloy remembered a picture of Rothenburg that hung on his mother's wall in Los Angeles and his mother's fondness for the village. As an expression of humanity he contacted the American general, Devers, to see if a meeting might be arranged with the Germans for purposes of securing a surrender of the city. The Germans agreed, and the meeting took place outside the city wall. The German negotiator, Major Friedrich Thommes, at risk of his own life for disobeying orders, agreed to surrender the city. The German troops vacated the city by the following morning and the bombing was averted (Darheim & Baumgartner, 2004).

The action took special courage on the part of a few men, supposed enemies, who resisted authority for the well-being of a community and a way of life. This story of valor and social interest related to Rothenburg was followed by another. After the war the village was faced with a need to rebuild with dire financial coffers, but the community had a good idea. Citizens pooled their resources and took out advertisements in leading newspapers around the world stating their plight and soliciting funds to rebuild the village (Darheim & Baumgartner, 2004). For example, by providing a stated contribution people could rebuild 1 meter of the wall. The plea was heard by folks who had memories of the idyllic Rothenburg and by empathic others. The funds poured in and the city was rebuilt.

Both instances, the surrender and the rebuilding of the city, are examples of risk and courage and of working together for a cause much larger than any single player. The actions required tremendous presence to the posed contexts and to opportunities for the well-being of humanity.

## OUR FUTURES WITH SOCIAL INTEREST AND CONCLUDING THOUGHTS

The metaphor of the "rugged individualist" that appears to have captured parts of the Western world may have outlived its usefulness or at least may be in need of major alteration. This type of thinking may at times become associated with limited consideration of others, self-promotion, and competition among people—for example, competition in schools where some excel and some others may become discouraged, competition between employees for merit pay or bonuses where some succeed and some others may feel underappreciated, and competition between departments and companies where the goal may become one of gaining the advantage rather than finding ways to cooperate. This focus on the individual and supporting personal interests rather than social interest may also be joined with a limited understanding and appreciation of others and marginalization of some citizens.

It seems essential for our future that we help people to understand that as human beings we often have similar needs, hopes, and concerns, and that "human kind is our kind," that "you are me and I am you," and that we can no longer live in "gated communities." Whether we are considering our place in a family, our lives at work, or our connectedness with various communities, we need to become mindful and accountable for the welfare of others, in order that those we leave behind might inherit a more sustainable world. This we see as the essence of Alfred Adler's social interest, for as he said, "The only thing that can save us from being crucified on a harmful fiction . . . is the guiding star of universal welfare" (Adler, 1964, p. 278).

## REFERENCES

Adler, A. (1964). *Social interest: A challenge to mankind* (J. Linton & R. Vaughan, Trans.). New York: Capricorn Books.

Ansbacher, H. L., & Ansbacher, R. R. (Eds.). (1956). *The individual psychology of Alfred Adler: A systematic presentation in selections from his writings.* New York: Basic Books.

Ansbacher, H. L., & Ansbacher, R. R. (Eds.). (1973). *Superiority and social interest: A collection of later writings* (3rd rev. ed.). New York: Viking Press.

Darheim, J., & Baumgartner, H. G. (Producers). (2004). *The history of Rothenburg ob der Tauber* [DVD]. Available from http://www.EuroFocus.com

Dinkmeyer, D., & Dreikurs, R. (1963). *Encouraging children to learn: The encouragement process.* Englewood Cliffs, NJ: Prentice-Hall.

Dreikurs, R., & Soltz, V. (1964). *Children: The challenge.* New York: Hawthorn Books.

Hall, C. S. (1954). *A primer of Freudian psychology.* London: The World Publishing Company.

Heer, F. (1972). Freud the Viennese Jew (W. A. Littlewood, Trans.). In J. Miller (Ed.), *Freud: The man, his world, his influence* (pp. 1–21), Prescott, Great Britain: George Weidenfeld and Nicholson Ltd.

Kootz, W. (2007). *Rothenburg ob der Tauber.* Rothenburg, Germany: Simon Sauer.

Orgler, H. (1963). *Alfred Adler: The man and his work.* New York: Mentor Book.

## The Differences Between Individual Psychology and Psychoanalysis (1931)[1,2]

*Alfred Adler*

## INTERPRETATION OF PSYCHOANALYTIC TERMS

### CENSORSHIP

Who creates and guides the censorship? According to which viewpoints does the censorship work? Is it not a striving for significance and superiority, to get away from a feeling of inferiority and to hold on to a feeling of totality, of equality?

I should like to say that we cannot possibly be satisfied by assuming that the censorship plays a role biologically. If such a thing exists, it could have meaning only if it veiled and changed some unconscious impulses for some purpose. For what purpose? We shall hardly be able to find any other purpose than one which serves to hold and enhance the feeling of one's own value. This would mean that the deeper basis for such a concept would again be found in the observations of Individual Psychology, in the striving to get away from a feeling of inferiority to some kind of superiority.

But this would also mean that in the work of a man who has explained the concept of a censorship, the idea is active which has been stated by Individual Psychology, namely, the upward striving. This would mean that in the unconscious of Freud the Individual Psychology conception is confirmed. If this conception does not become conscious, one would have to assume in Freud, according to his own view, the existence of a censorship which veils this deeper foundation. This censorship also would be guided by the striving from below to above.

### OEDIPUS COMPLEX

Since one often comes across the claim that psychoanalysis goes deeper, we may indicate that the Individual Psychology conception also points the way for the thinking of the psychoanalyst in the instance of the Oedipus complex, i.e., the idea that the child would like to possess the opposite-sexed parent libidinally.

---

[1] Original translation of A19310, with some rearrangements.

[2] The further footnotes here are supplementations from an unpublished English manuscript by Adler, titled "Individual Psychology and Psychoanalysis" (A1930m), which despite the same title differs from the present paper. Footnotes 6 and 11 are exceptions in that they are citations from a later paper (A1935i).

The view has changed of late—girls do not have an Oedipus complex—because with growing experience the Oedipus complex could not be retained as the fixed pole.

One thing is certain, that this thesis also could not be conceived without at the same time thinking that the son strives for the laurels, the possibilities, the strength of his father. Whether one conceives this as sexual libido or sees it in broader terms, it is certain that this view could not be held if the thinker were not unconsciously influenced by the idea that the boy wants to grow beyond himself, wants to attain a superiority over his father.

We see how strongly the fact of the striving for significance influences all our thoughts, as well as the thoughts of other schools. I do not think one could ask for more from a theory. In this conception also the deeper dynamics of Individual Psychology can be seen.

## NARCISSISM

Freud announced his concept of narcissism during a period in which Individual Psychology sharply pointed out the egocentric aspect of the neurotic. It is a question of terminology. If I understand by narcissism only sexual self-love, then narcissism is no more than one of a thousand variations of self-love. When sexual self-love appears, it is merely one of the many manifestations of a person thinking only of himself. This, however, takes place not only within his developing sexuality, but in all relationships of his live. We then find the picture of a child or adult turned in upon himself, a life style which can come about only when one was previously able to exclude all other persons from one's experience.

Since the natural progression of development is not like this, we cannot regard a phenomenon such as narcissism an innate component or phase of development. We regard it as a secondary phase which occurs when a person has excluded social relationships that are self-understood and naturally given, or when he has never found them. In this event, nothing is left.

If one expands the concept of the narcissist enormously, as in psychoanalysis, it shows nothing but the type of egocentric person whom we have described extensively. We shall have to observe that this exclusion of others signifies a lack of social interest. This lack must have arisen because the person does not have the self-confidence and has not learned how to do justice to the tasks with which he is confronted within the frame in which he is placed, the human context.

Thereby we say that in the conception of the narcissist the most important part has been overlooked: the permanent exclusion of others, the narrowing of the sphere of action. From this we justly conclude that such a person is one who does not consider himself strong, that narcissism signifies a feeling of weakness which originated from a feeling of inferiority. At the same time this feeling seeks compensation through seemingly making the situation easier.

That this attitude comes into conflict with the social questions of life is obvious. Thus we find here a lack of social interest corresponding to a stronger feeling of inferiority, when a child sees himself as if in enemy country and believes he cannot accomplish anything any more, or only if he refers all events almost compulsively to himself and excludes every obligation.

## DEATH WISH

The death wish, which later played a great role in psychoanalysis, is similar to narcissism in every way. It is nothing by the further exclusion of all relationships to life. It also is the expression of a feeling of weakness.

This death wish runs parallel to the idea of pessimism. Psychoanalysis is pessimistic. The death wish is perhaps an unrecognized confession of weakness in the face of reality, as well as a lack of interest in others, of cooperation. We find in it a lack of social feeling; it is a last resource for the weak in heart. An author who arrives at the view that the death wish is the general condition thereby confesses to being weak in heart. He experiences the world full of unrest and difficulties and capitulates before it. Here too it is the expression of an inferiority feeling presented in scientific form.

## CASTRATION COMPLEX

Some psychoanalysts have themselves pointed out that the castration complex has developed from the "masculine protest." In our culture the error is inherent to regard feminine form and behavior as inferior, as a diminished form of life. In *The Neurotic Constitution* cases are described of patients who express their feeling of being diminished by talking of loss of penis.

## EGO IDEAL AND SUPEREGO

The ego ideal is a late conception of psychoanalysis. It is mighty similar to social interest. The ego ideal means nothing other than the ideal represented by social interest: the striving towards a goal of fellowmanship. Thus we find hidden in the ego ideal the finalistic view of Individual Psychology.

Regarding the superego, we would say that it is a later conception of what we have come to know as the fictive goal of superiority. It is only a new and unattractive work, modeled after "superman." If it were named thus, everybody could recognize the imprint of the striving for godlikeness. It is not called so because [superman is Nietzsche's term and] Individual Psychology has erroneously been placed near Nietzsche. In the superego we find nothing other than the Individual Psychology goal of superiority.

## BASIC DIFFERENCE

With these discussions I have not yet touched on much of what is important. I could talk about the different significance which we attribute to childhood recollections. We do not distinguish a type of child who has the Oedipus complex, but a child who is pampered. We also know other types, children with inferior organs, and those who never have had the experience of fellowmanship. Here the frame is much wider than in the psychoanalytic view. Also the views on the dream are fundamentally different.

Now I should like to show the decisive basic difference between psychoanalysis and Individual Psychology. It is not that Freud has taken up drive psychology, which was first created by Individual Psychology and was then left behind as incorrect when I brought the striving for significance to the foreground. This is not the basic difference. The difference is that Freud starts with the assumption that by nature man only wants to satisfy his drives—the pleasure principle—and must, therefore, from the viewpoint of culture be regarded as completely bad.

## Concept of Human Nature

The Freudian view is that man, by nature bad, covers this unconscious badness through censorship merely to get along better in life. Individual Psychology, on the other hand, states that the development of man, by virtue of his inadequate physique, is subject to the redeeming influence of social interest, so that all his drives can be guided in the direction of the generally useful. The indestructible destiny of the human species is social interest. In Individual Psychology that is the truth; in psychoanalysis it is a trick.

Individual Psychology, accordingly, maintains that, due to his physique, i.e., physical condition, a biological factor, man is inclined toward social interest, toward the good. We find neurotics, psychotics, suicides, etc., only when social interest is throttled. In this case the child becomes egotistic, loses interest in others, and presses his biologically founded striving for significance toward the useless side reach his goal of personal superiority.

If one has clearly comprehended this difference, one will not be able to think that these two theories have anything more in common than a few words. That much any theory has in common with any dictionary. It is not admissible to rely on such things.

## Basic Drives and Heredity

It seems to me that in the entire problem of basic drives and heredity there prevails great confusion. Let us assume that in the life of a person nothing develops for which the possibility has not been present from the start. Then we see how this undeniable fact can be abused. Anything which shows later in life is already present in the embryo as a possibility. But this does not imply that what we see in later life before us was already present in the embryo in this very form. Each possibility can materialize in different ways.

If we want to illuminate a conception of the striving for significance in this light, we must say: Of course, it can come about only if it is founded in the original disposition. But what we see, such as the character, cannot be thought of outside society, because the striving for significance, seen as character, must be regarded as a social function which can show itself only within a social frame.

We shall not forget that the child experiences in his first days his physical weakness in the face of the cultural demands, and that this acts as a sting to the child, especially when he begins to make comparisons. Whatever the opportunities may be to develop a striving for power, the sting always leads to wanting to be more. Since the factor of evolution is incessantly effective—and the striving for significance is its psychological expression—the striving can degenerate into a striving for personal power.

Here social interest steps in as a regulator. The striving for power is only the distorted aspect of the striving for perfection. The child is urged daily to get beyond his difficulties to a point where he finds security, where he can expect satisfaction of his needs. *But goal setting must precede this.* Thus we must understand the striving for significance as a function rooted in biology, although not in the form in which we see it later on as striving for superiority. If this were the case, then of course one would arrive at the conclusion that man, so often greedy for egotistical power, is evil by nature. What we do find is always that the personal striving for power comes about through an error from earliest childhood when the mind of the child is not sufficiently mature to draw correct conclusions.

We see that after the fourth or fifth year of life a *prototype* forms itself, an original form of life, *a psychological constitution*, which will act independently, draw independent conclusions, develop in a thousand variations according to the individual's original peculiarity. From our viewpoint we can trace to what extent and why this original development of the child deviates from our comprehension of a social being. One cannot talk of an original drive of egotistical power striving, because power striving is a realization in the face of a social context, a phenomenon of social relations.

## Pleasure Principle and Social Interest

I have never yet heard of an attempt to establish a relationship between the pleasure principle and social interest. The pleasure principle, according to Freud, is connected with the drive life. Social interest is the compensatory factor for the physical inferiority feeling of man. One cannot conceive of man in his weakness in any other way than being supported through society. One could say that this creature cannot live in isolation, that he is viable only through the aid of society. We can regard society as the most important compensatory factor for human weakness.

The experience of social interest has nothing to do with pleasure [in the sense of lust]. It is pleasurable for the social person only because he is embedded in society; it is unpleasurable for one who experiences society as a chain to which he is tied, and who desires only personal satisfaction. E.g., for the murderer it is pleasurable to act against social interest; for the neurotic it is pleasurable to lean on others.

It is the goal, the style of life, which will force pleasure or displeasure. In this connection I must comment that the fellow man strives in his goal not for pleasure but for happiness.

Since we Individual Psychologists emphasize so very much *the unity of psychological life* ("as in a kind of elephantiasis," Pfaundler), it is beyond any question that the feeling of pleasure must run parallel to the goal. Nietzsche said approximately: "Pleasure sets in when it is in accord with a person's gait [in the sense of his characteristic way of walking through life]." Therefore the pleasure principle cannot be used as a regulative concept. Only the striving for the ideal end form can be used in this way.

For some time I have tried to discover a biological analogy here. I do not know if it is more than a smile, but there is in the organic realm a similar process. The possibility, e.g., that a chicken's egg always develops into a chicken, rests in the germ cell. Here is an organic process which has a finalistic tendency, which, in turn, is latent in the original germ cell. Obviously a finalistic tendency is also admixed to the original psychological process and will seek to penetrate somehow. Thus I arrived at the concept of the *striving for totality* which can only mean the seeking of a situation in which all forces, drives, feelings, conscious and unconscious impulses, etc., strive in a self-consistent fashion toward overcoming the difficulties of life. This search, this movement takes on a form. Thus I may speak of an ideal end form.

## DREAM INTERPRETATION

With Freud the dream was at first a wish fulfillment—to bring infantile sexual impulses to a release and gratification. In consequence he had to comprehend sexually everything that happens in dreams, and there arose the view of the sexual symbols.

Freud assumes the dreamer wants to look backward. I have pointed out that the dreamer looks forward; he intends the solution of a task. This is the basic difference here. I do not believe that Freud has taken over this viewpoint, that the dream attempts to bring a present problem to a solution.

In due course new aspects were added to our view—e.g., what is the purpose of the dream?—and, what occupied me most—why do people dream if they do not understand their dreams? The answer which Freud gave is quite unfounded: Man is supposed to dream in order not to wake up, to be occupied with the fulfillment of his infantile impulses and not to disturb the sleep. I often find that patients wake up when they dream.

Why does a person dream? I did not find an adequate solution until the thought came: It is the intention of the dreamer not to understand his dreams. He *wants* to withdraw the dream from understanding. This must mean that something happens in the dream which he cannot justify with reason. The intention of the dream is to deceive the dreamer. The person attempts in a certain situation to deceive himself. I have also understood why one does not understand the dream. Its purpose is only to create a *mood*. This emotion must not be clarified: it must exist and act as an emotion, created from the individuality of the dreamer. This apparently corresponds to the desire to solve a problem by an emotional episode and in accordance with his life style, since he is not confident of solving his problem in accordance with the common sense.

Examination of the dream devices shows them to represent the right arsenal for self-deception.

1. *Selection of certain pictures.* The explanation is not to be found in the pictures but in their selection; i.e., the dreamer is guided by a tendency in the selection of his thoughts. We know the force which select; it is the individuality of a person, his unity, his goal; and so we find in this one aspect already that here the individuality reigns and not the common sense. The person attempts to solve the problem by selecting a picture which produces an emotion suitable to his life style. What happens through the emotion is what he would have done anyway on account of his individuality. The dreamer wants only to strengthen himself, to justify himself. Thus I could understand that the dream represents the bridge from the present problem to the individuality.

2. *Similes and symbols.* Other dream devices for the purpose of auto-intoxication are similes and symbols. Here also the most important questions are: Why these similes in particular? Why a simile at all? In the psychological structure of the simile the inclination toward self-deception is also contained. It would be very interesting to uncover the psychological structure of the poetic simile; here also there is a deception, a deception in the broader sense of doing justice to an intention through a detour, in this case for the purpose of poetic transfiguration. All symbols have the purpose of filling the person in question with a mood through which he does what he would do on the basis of his individuality alone.

3. *Simplification.* There are a number of further devices, such as the simplification in the dream. This is the significant device of

self-deception, to narrow down a problem so much that nothing is left but a small "harmless" remainder. Then the dreamer does not experience the problem as a whole, but only as a small part; he has a better possibility of going the way he wants to go than if he were to look all around.

These devices are not unique for the dream. If a person wants to deceive himself during waking life, he uses the same devices. He works with the selection of certain memories and pictures, he uses similes and symbols, and also simplification.

Thus our result is completely different from that of psychoanalysis, which considers, "The dream is the royal road to the unconscious." This signifies a contrast to waking thought. We say this contrast does not exist. The unconscious is no contrast to the conscious. If, in analyzing it, one tears the conscious from its context, one can also discover differences within it. But he who learns to interpret the conscious appreciates that it may be as little understood as the unconscious, i.e., remain as unconscious as the latter. A contrast does not exist here. Therefore Freud's view that neurosis arises from the conflict between the conscious and the unconscious was not tenable.

## CONCLUSION

One cannot understand the psychological structure of a person through the drive life because the drive is "without direction" (see also Hermann Schwarz). The main problem of psychology is not to comprehend the causal factors as in physiology, by the direction-giving, pulling forces and goals which guide all other psychological movements. Thus Individual Psychology arrived at its finalistic conception.

The necessity for ego formation is founded in the evolutionary tendency of the original germ cell (of men and other living creatures). The cell with its evolutionary tendency represents the ego. Outside of this ego there is nothing—no "id" and no "drive" and no "libido"—that would furnish material for taking a stand towards the problems of life. Wanting to develop the ego from the drives—to crown it all, from the sadistic and masochistic drives—means to attribute these drives the figure of the ego. It means to place knowledge and cunning into the censorship and into the development of the superego and the ego ideal; likewise, to put direction into all three against persons, persons who appear only after birth; to put a striving for significance into the Oedipus complex, into the ego ideal, into the castration complex; to put a goal into the alterable sexual tendencies, etc. In short, the drive here becomes a demon in ready form.

The problem of the wholeness of the personality, which represents the essential contribution of Individual Psychology to modern medicine, appears in psychoanalysis as unessential. How this wholeness penetrates every psychological part-phenomenon and colors it individually is omitted from the considerations of psychoanalysis which, as if it were hypnotized, looks in each part for the sexual-libidinal structure.

Although it would take us too far afield to prove in this paper, Freud's psychology is *taken from the psychopathology of the pampered child, and describes it in sexual dialect.*

In all points one finds the sad results of overlooking the whole as that which gives form to, and is the basic melody of, the penetrating motive which compels all parts, forces, and drives—including sexuality—toward a self-consistent stand. Consequently, the misunderstanding of a contrast between conscious and unconscious; consequently also, the enthusiastic acceptance of ambivalence—both in contrast to the unity of the personality.

In treatment also psychoanalysis shows itself as inadequate. This is not to deny that there are patients who have been cured. We are attacking the basic principles—transference and the weak expedient of sublimation.

Transference in psychoanalysis has two faces. In the first there is nothing more than the unalterable wholeness of the personality, including its stand toward the therapist. This aspect, then, belongs to the Individual Psychology personality theory. The second face is the continuous underscoring of sexual connections whether they exist or not. As always in life, such underscoring brings about a sexual atmosphere, and this leads to approach or rejection.

To point to cured or improved cases is not sufficient proof for the goodness of a method. Uncured cases would be more suitable. For despite all formulas the physician is forced to bring to bear his ability to take the common sense into account. Also, the patient can free his own common sense in the course of discussions, perhaps often without the physician noticing it. Common sense—that means thinking which corresponds to the human community.

Despite the many scientific contrasts between Freud and myself, I have always been willing to recognize that he has clarified much through his endeavors; especially, he has severely shaken the position of positivistically (materialistisch) oriented neurology and opened a wide door to psychology as an auxiliary science to medicine. This is his chief merit, next to his detective art of guessing through common sense. That he did not get any further is due to the limits of his personality and the limits of the personalities of his disciples.

In a future history of psychology and psychopathology Freud's doctrine will figure as the admirable attempt to describe, in the strongest expressions of sexual terminology, the psychological life of the pampered child as a generally valid psychology.

# 4

# *The Progress of Mankind*

## Bret A. Moore

Alfred Adler's paper "The Progress of Mankind" was originally published in 1937. For Adlerians, this is a memorable year as it is the last year he edited the *International Journal of Individual Psychology* and the year his body was laid to rest. As I read this paper, I couldn't help but wonder if Adler somehow knew that his final minutes were fast approaching. Although the main focus of this paper is on how social interest is connected to the continued evolution of man and society, Adler touched on the philosophical question of what man leaves behind after death. Regarding the motivations and striving of previous generations with adequate social interest, he stated, "This is the inheritance from our forebears which falls to us for administration. It is their contribution in which their spirit lives on immortally after the body has fallen." For those who have not pondered or questioned the importance of social connection and decided to follow the useless trail of life, he wondered, "What happened to the earthly life of those who contributed nothing, or who interfered with the developmental process? The answer is: It has disappeared. Nothing from their lives can be found."

Although I recognize the above may be a tad melodramatic, the underlying message is very real and serious. The message is one that Adler put forth in almost all of his writings since his "split" with Freud; man can only find meaning and purpose and society can only progress within the context of social collaboration, which includes working toward similar goals.

How can this permanently fixed tenant of Adler's theory be placed into a contemporary context? Consider the current state of affairs of the United States.[3]

At the time of this writing, the United States is dealing with several crises. The economy is at its lowest point in decades, the eventual design and functionality of health care is uncertain, and a colossal oil spill in the Gulf of Mexico threatens the solvency of an entire section of the country and the survival of a delicate

---

[3] The author chose to focus on the United States as the example of how democracy can be strengthened by social interconnectedness and collaboration. This was due to space and time limitations. Without question, the leadership of other countries could have been used.

ecosystem. The question that invariably surfaces on television and radio and in coffee houses and living rooms across the nation is "What progress are we making?" The answer is usually one of disappointment, frustration, and uncertainty. To understand this tone one needs to look no further than to the leaders of the country.

If Adler was right and that progress only happens when all people work together toward common goals, then it is no wonder why average citizens of the United States feel angry and hopeless. Effective examples of unity and collaboration between political leaders within the halls of the US government are the exception and not the rule. For various reasons, so many that the limits of this paper do not allow analysis, the two dominant parties of the federal government work primarily in opposition to each other instead of in partnership and collaboration. And as Adler and common sense tells us, progress will be stymied and unnecessary suffering will continue.

One can argue that dissent and stubborn discourse are essential to the survival of a democracy. However, it must be done without any personal gain or ill will toward others. If it is done within the context of true social interest and by the selflessness of those entrusted to represent American citizens, then expedient and meaningful progress has a chance. Unfortunately, it has become apparent that disagreement within the political system of the United States is fueled by personal reward (e.g., ego, money, power) and the instinctual desire to defend one's beliefs no matter how much those beliefs are bathed in private versus common logic. And it is troubling that there is no reason to believe that this tendency will change as leaders are imperfect humans and are not versed in the psychological, social, and yes, the political principles of Individual Psychology.

As in most other areas of daily life, Adler's principles of social interconnectedness are relevant to successful leadership. It is my hope that, somehow, leaders who are chosen to represent the masses consider their own legacies. What will they leave behind? Will the knowledge of their existence, or at least the positive impact of their existence, be nonexistent within a few generations? Or, will the positive effects of their selfless sacrifices made in collaboration with others reverberate infinitely? It is my hope that the latter will be the case. One only needs to look at Adler himself to understand the lasting effects that cooperation and personal sacrifice have on a society.

# The Progress of Mankind[4]

## *Alfred Adler*

The question of whether progress of mankind is possible, probable, impossible, or certain moves everyone today more than ever. But even regarding the meaning of progress there is disagreement. The explanation for this is probably that people in general tend to overlook the larger contexts, and to regard all problems, including scientific ones, from their own, usually too narrow, personal perspective. This is also true for the problem of progress.

Everyone subordinates all experiences and problems to his own conception. This conception is usually a tacit assumption and as such unknown to the person. Yet he lives and dies for the inferences he draws from such a conception. It is amusing, and sad at the same time, to see how even scientists—especially philosophers, sociologists, and psychologists—are caught in this net. Individual Psychology is no exception, in that it also has its assumptions, its conception of life, its style of life. But it differs in that it is well aware of this fact.

## BASIC ASSUMPTIONS OF INDIVIDUAL PSYCHOLOGY

Individual Psychology was the first school of psychology to break with the assumption of inner forces, such as instincts, drives, unconsciousness, etc., as irrational material. When it comes to the understanding and appraisal of an individual or a group, this break has proved most helpful. On the positive side, Individual Psychology makes the following assumptions:

Individual Psychology has established the presupposition, against which no argument can be found, of the *unity and self-consistency of the personality.*

Individual Psychology finds its firm, rational field of activity in the manner in which the always unique individual behaves towards the changing problems of life. Decisive for his behavior is the individual's *opinion of himself and of the environment* with which he has to cope.

Individual Psychology assumes further the individual's *striving for success* in the solution of his problems, this striving being anchored in the very structure of life. But the judgment of what constitutes success is again left to the opinion of the individual.

Our criterion for appraising a specific variant, whether a given individual or a group, is always the direction towards the ascending development and welfare of mankind. In other words, it is the degree and kind of *social interest* necessary to arrive at this goal of general welfare and upward development.

---

[4] This paper appeared originally in 1937, the year of Adler's death, in German, under the title "Ist Fortschritt der Menschheit moglich? wahrscheinlich? unmoglich? sicher?" (*Int. Z. Indiv. Psychol.,* 15, 1–4). Reprinted from *The Journal of Individual Psychology*, Volume XIII, Number 1, May, 1957.

The weightiest reason for this assumption is our finding that the individual is faced exclusively with such problems as can be solved only with sufficient social interest. He may have had this from childhood, or may have acquired it later. All problems of life merge into the three social problems of neighborly love, work, and sexual love. One finds a degree of social interest, although this is usually inadequate, in all men, with the exception of idiots, and even in animals. We therefore feel justified in assuming that this social interest which is demonstrated throughout life is rooted in the germ cell. But it is rooted as a potentiality, not as an actual ability.

Social interest, like all innate human potentialities, will develop in accordance with the individual's self-consistent *style of life*.

The style of life arises in the child out of his *creative power*, i.e., from the way he perceives the world and from what appears to him as success.

Such a foundation of a psychology greatly supports the certainty of the observer. Firstly, since the assumptions are made explicit, he gains certainty in that he knows and understands them well and can check them at any time. Secondly, he is especially protected from false conclusions and mistaken appraisals regarding an individual or a group, because he is forced to seek the existing degree of social interest in all the expressive movements, personality traits, and symptoms. This latter advantage he owes to the basic view of the unity and self-consistency of the personality in thinking, feeling, willing, and acting.

## THE IDEA OF PROGRESS

From our basic assumptions there follows an important conclusion bearing on the problem of the progress of mankind.

We may define human progress as a function of a higher development of social interest. Admittedly the level of social interest is presently still low, as indicated by such phrases as "Why should I love my neighbor?" and "After me the deluge." But social interest is continually pressing and growing. For this reason, no matter how dark the times may be, in the long-range view there is the assurance of the higher development of the individual and the group. Social interest is continually growing; human progress is a function of the higher development of social interest; therefore, human progress will be inevitable as long as mankind exists.

## THREE PROSPECTIVE CONSIDERATIONS

In the following we wish to support through three brief prospects the view that evolution leads to the success of social interest. Such a view gives Individual Psychology the imprint of a gay and optimistic science.[5]

---

[5] The expression "gay science" is undoubtedly borrowed from Nietzsche's book of that title. (Original footnote by H. & R. Ansbacher.)

(1) The first prospect is in the nature of an anecdote. I once read it in an American article, the author of which I have unfortunately forgotten, and it moved me very strongly. A multimillionaire who had spent a hard youth in poverty and misery wanted to protect his descendants from similar deprivations. He consulted a lawyer and told him the size of his fortune, as well as that he wanted to protect his descendants to approximately the tenth generation. The lawyer took his pen and began to figure. When he was finished he turned to his client and said: "Your fortune is so great that it is completely sufficient to provide for your descendants adequately up to the tenth generation. But do you know that if you do this, you are protecting children, each of whom is related to over 1,000 persons of your generation as closely as he is related to you?"

It follows from this consideration, if we widen our view to include 100 and more generations, that everything that people have contributed, even if only in the apparent interest of their own families, is irrevocably for the benefit of the whole of mankind. This "equalization process" may be slowed down at times for lack of useful contributions, but it cannot be stopped.

(2) A consideration from my forthcoming book *Social Interest; a Challenge to Mankind* supplements the first. I raise the question, "What do we find when we are born into this world?" The answer is: We find all the previous useful contributions which have been supplied by our forebears. We find human beings in their bodily and mental development, social institutions, art, science, lasting traditions, social relations, values, schooling, etc. We receive all these and build upon them, advancing, improving, and changing, always in the sense of a further durability. This is the inheritance from our forebears which falls to us for administration. It is their contribution in which their spirit lives on immortally after the body has fallen.

What happened to the earthly life of those who contributed nothing, or who interfered with the developmental process? The answer is: It has disappeared. Nothing from their lives can be found. Does this not appear like an inviolable law aimed against all who supply no contributions for later generations? Their trace on earth is lost forever.

This train of thought, against which it would be difficult to find any counter-argument, is closely related to my findings that the life of the individual as well as of the group presents itself as a "compensation process." This process attempts to overcome felt or alleged "inferiorities," in a physical or psychological manner. One goal of this compensatory striving is the steadily growing culture of mankind which collects all useful and productive contributions of the various generations and passes them on.

The power of social interest which is inherent to the life of mankind, which as innate aptitude determines human nature in great part, and which is lacking only in the feeble-minded, comes to life and becomes productive through the creative power of the child, as pointed out above. Although not strong enough at present to solve human difficulties for the benefit of the entire human family, the existing social interest is nevertheless so powerful that individuals and groups must refer to it. Human judgment can do no more than consider whether the line of a proposed movement will ultimately merge into the well-being of man in general. Political movements, the utilization of the advances of science and technology, laws, and social norms are included in this evaluation. Claims of interest in the well-being of the community, however, have power in the long run only if their professed accord with the general well-being finds confirmation.

(3) A third prospect has a much more serious background but leads to the same result, namely, that progress is forced upon men. This consideration is that the finality of the individual life merges into the progress of mankind. Even though we are tragically affected by withered and rapidly withering life, we realize that its rejuvenation in the next generation, enriched by the earlier generation, forces new contributions and progress. Rejuvenation raises new problems and meets them. No heredity has matured for these problems because they have never arisen before. Again and again the creative power of the child and of the adult come under new tensions until new solutions have been brought into being and useless ones have been removed.

Each new generation struggles afresh with old and new tasks and, pitted against the environment, is forced as a whole to maintain its equilibrium (Cannon) physically and psychologically with growing senses and growing understanding. This equilibrium can be gained only if the sum of the energies of the individual, supported through the growth of a rational picture of the world, is successful in bringing the problems of the environment closer to a solution.

In the holistic relationship between man and cosmos progress will rule until the decline of the human family. "The environment molds man, but man molds the environment" (Pestalozzi). With the limitation of our senses and our understanding of the ultimate things, rational science speaks the last word. At this point, a strong word is spoken by Individual Psychology with its emphasis on the whole and on social interest.

# 5

# On the Origin of the Striving for Superiority and of Social Interest

RICHARD E. WATTS

Adler died in 1937 having created a personality theory and approach to therapy so far ahead of its time that many contemporary psychological approaches are only now "discovering" many of Adler's fundamental conclusions, but typically without reference to or acknowledgment of Adler (Watts, 1999). In reading his 1933 paper "On the Origin of Striving for Superiority and Social Interest," one can see the contemporary relevance of Adler's thinking in several streams of psychological thinking. In particular, I would like to address Adler's thoughts on striving and *gemeinschaftsgefuhl* (community feeling/social interest) as evincing Adlerian psychology's position as arguably the first *positive psychology* in the 20th century. Prochaska and Norcross (2010), echoing Ellenberger (1970), stated that many of "Adler's ideas have quietly permeated modern psychological thinking, often without notice. It would not be easy to find another author from which so much has been borrowed from all sides without acknowledgment than Alfred Adler" (p. 91). This appears particularly true in the positive psychology movement. Adlerian ideas are replete in the positive psychology literature, but there is no substantive mention of Adler or Adlerian psychology. In this brief introduction addressing the contemporary relevance of Adler's ideas, I will first address striving for perfection or superiority, next gemeinschaftsgefuhl, and finally the remarkable common ground between Adler's ideas and the contemporary positive psychology.

## STRIVING FOR PERFECTION OR SUPERIORITY

Adler's understanding of "striving" evolved over time, and he used various words like *completion*, *mastery*, *perfection*, and *superiority* to describe how humans seek to move from "the present situation, as observed and interpreted, to a better one, one that was superior to the present status" (Manaster & Corsini, 1982, p. 41). According to Adler, the central human directionality is toward competence or self-mastery, what Adler called *striving for perfection or superiority*. This is the individual's creative and compensatory answer to the normal and universal feelings of insignificance and disempowerment, and the accompanying beliefs that one is less than what one should be (i.e., *feelings of inferiority*). Thus, striving for perfection or superiority is the natural human desire to move from a perceived negative position to a perceived positive one.

This concept of striving or teleological/teleonomical movement is seen in the writings of various personality theorists including Kurt Goldstein, Karen Horney, Carl Jung, Abraham Maslow, Otto Rank, Carl Rogers, and Robert White (Jorgensen & Nafstad, 2004; Manaster & Corsini, 1982). One can find similar ideas in various contemporary theoretical perspectives, including constructivist, evolutionary, and positive psychologies (Linley & Joseph, 2004; Mahoney, 2003; Rasmussen, 2010; Snyder, Lopez, & Pedrotti, 2011). For example, in discussing happiness and human potential, Ryan and Deci (2001) described optimal functioning and development as "the striving for perfection that represents the realization of one's true potential" (p. 144).

All of the aforementioned personality theorists agree with Adler that humans are striving, seeking to actualize potential, and in the process of "becoming," and most of the theories created by these theorists are listed as early exemplars of positive psychology in that literature. Adler's theory, however, is not found in the various lists; the positive psychology literature typically lists Maslow and Rogers as the earliest exemplars, even though Adler clearly preceded both in his formulation of an optimistic, growth-oriented psychology.

## GEMEINSCHAFTSGEFUHL (COMMUNITY FEELING/SOCIAL INTEREST)

Adlerian psychology is a relational theory. It asserts that humans are socially embedded and that knowledge is relationally distributed. Adler stressed that persons cannot be properly understood apart from their social context. Consequently, the Adlerian perspective on the tasks of life—love, society, work, spirituality, and self—is a strongly relational one. These tasks of life address intimate love relationships, relationships with friends and fellow beings in society, our relationships at work, our relationship with self, and our relationship with God or the universe (Carlson, Watts, & Maniacci, 2006; Watts, 2003; Watts, Williamson, & Williamson, 2004).

According to Manaster and Corsini (1982), the most unique and valuable concept in Adlerian psychology is *Gemeinschaftsgefuhl*. The cardinal tenet of Adler's theory, it is typically translated as "social interest or community feeling" and emphasizes the relational, social-contextual nature of the theory. I believe both community feeling and social interest are needed for a holistic understanding of gemeinschafts-gefuhl; that is, *community feeling* addresses the affective and motivational aspects and *social interest* the cognitive and behavioral ones. Thus, true community feeling (e.g., sense of belonging, empathy, caring, compassion, acceptance of others) results in social interest (thoughts and behaviors that contribute to the common good, the good of the whole at both micro- and macro-systemic levels); true social interest is motivated by community feeling (Watts & Eckstein, 2009).

A significant difference between Adler and other personality theorists regarding the aforementioned "striving" is the role of community feeling/social interest. Adler emphasized that striving for perfection or superiority occurs in a relational context and this striving may occur in either a socially useful or a socially useless manner. How one strives, and the manifest behaviors, are predicated on one's community feeling/social interest. Thus, in Adler's mature theoretical formulation, as evidenced in the 1933 paper, *striving for perfection* means that one is striving toward greater competence, both for oneself and the common good of humanity. This is a horizontal striving that is useful both for self and for others, seeking to build both self- and other-esteem. *Striving for superiority* means to move in a self-centered manner, seeking to be superior over others. This is a vertical striving that primarily pursues personal gain without contribution to or consideration of others and the common good. The manner one chooses to strive constitutes the Adlerian criterion for mental health: healthy development follows the goal of community feeling and social interest; maladjustment is the consequence of pursuing narcissistic self-interest (Manaster & Corsini, 1982).

Recent research by Leak and Leak (2006) and Barlow, Tobin, and Schmidt (2009) indicated that social interest is related to numerous aspects of positive psychology (e.g., hope, other-centered values, optimism, prosocial moral reasoning, psychosocial maturity, subjective well-being). Nevertheless, positive psychology authors appear to have ignored an important early positive psychology construct: Adler's *Gemeinschaftsgefuhl.*

## ADLERIAN THEORY AND POSITIVE PSYCHOLOGY

Snyder and Lopez (2002) identified the positive psychology movement as a "new approach" because "psychology and its sister disciplines . . . focus on the weaknesses in humankind" (p. ix). In affirming the positive qualities of humankind, the editors state, "*no science, including psychology, looks seriously at this positive side of people*" [emphasis in original, p. x]. Seligman (2002) noted that the goal of positive psychology is to move from a preoccupation with pathology to a more balanced perspective that includes the idea of "a fulfilled individual and a thriving community" by emphasizing that building strengths in people "is the most potent weapon in the arsenal of therapy" (p. 3). It is remarkable that Seligman's goal is exactly the evolution of Adler's theory development. Prior to

World War I, Adler was more focused on deficits, pathology, and remediation. Adler's mature theory, however, focused on strengths, healthy human development, and prevention.

Given Adler's evolution from a deficit and pathology focus to one emphasizing strength, health, and prevention, it is not surprising to find significant common ground between Adlerian theory and the positive psychology movement. Although not an exhaustive list, Carlson, Watts, and Maniacci (2006) identified the following shared emphases: normal human growth and development; prevention/education rather than merely remediation; moving away from the medical model perspective; a focus on mental health and clients' strengths, resources, and abilities rather than psychopathology and clients' disabilities; and holism, spirituality, wellness, multiculturalism, and social justice. Adler's 1933 paper on striving and social interest alludes to several of the emphases listed above.

Cowen and Kilmer (2002) criticized the positive psychology literature for its lack of attention to prior literature regarding prevention and wellness, its lack of a cohesive undergirding theoretical framework, and its lack of a developmental perspective. Adlerian theory has a rich literature addressing prevention and healthy development, and could serve as a useful cohesive theoretical framework that Cowen and Kilmer indicated is lacking in positive psychology.

Adlerian psychology is a growth model that emphasizes the holistic, phenomenological, teleological, field-theoretically, and socially embedded aspects of human functioning. It is an optimistic perspective that views people as unique, creative, capable, and responsible. Adlerians disdain the deficit or "medical model" orientation to maladjustment, preferring a nonpathological perspective. Thus, clients are not sick (as in having a disease) and are not identified or "labeled" by their diagnoses. Because Adlerians believe the growth model of personality makes more sense than the sickness model, they see clients as discouraged rather than sick. Thus, Adlerians are not about "curing" anything; therapy is a process of *encouragement*. In fact, Adlerians consider encouragement a crucial aspect of human growth and development (Carlson, Watts, & Maniacci, 2006; Manaster & Corsini, 1982; Mosak & Maniacci, 1999).

Adlerian therapists focus on developing a respectful, egalitarian, optimistic, and growth-oriented therapeutic alliance that emphasizes clients' assets, abilities, resources, and strengths. Watts (1998) noted that Adler's descriptions of therapist-modeled social interest look very similar to Rogers's descriptions of the core facilitative conditions of client change: congruence, unconditional positive regard, and empathic understanding. The above qualities and characteristics of the therapeutic alliance are embedded in what Adlerians have historically called encouragement, or *the therapeutic modeling of social interest* (Carlson, Watts, & Maniacci, 2006; Mosak and Maniacci, 1999). Stressing the importance of encouragement in therapy, Adler (1956) stated, "Altogether, in every step of the treatment, we must not deviate from the path of encouragement" (p. 342). In addition,

Dreikurs (1967) stated that therapeutic success was largely dependent upon "(the therapist's) ability to provide encouragement" and failure generally occurred "due to the inability of the therapist to encourage" (pp. 12–13). Encouragement skills include demonstrating concern for clients through active listening and empathy, communicating respect for and confidence in clients, focusing on clients' strengths, assets, and resources, helping clients generate perceptual alternatives for discouraging fictional beliefs, focusing on efforts and progress, and helping clients see the humor in life experiences (Carlson, Watts, & Maniacci, 2006; Watts & Pietrzak, 2000).

Adler and many subsequent Adlerians have focused on prevention rather than simply remediation and, consequently, they have been extensively involved in education. Throughout his career, Adler was actively involved in public health, medical and psychological prevention, and social welfare. He wrote, lectured on, and advocated for children at risk, women's rights and the equality of the sexes, women's rights to abortion, adult education, teacher training, community mental health, family counseling and education and the establishment of family counseling clinics, experimental schools for public students, and brief psychotherapy. Adlerians have continued Adler's emphasis on prevention and education. For example, they have been perhaps the strongest proponents of child guidance and parent and family education, and have written extensively on parent and family education, couple-enrichment, and teacher education (Carlson, Watts, & Maniacci, 2006; Mosak & Maniacci, 1999).

## CONCLUSION

As noted earlier, the basic tenets of Adlerian theory and therapy permeate contemporary psychology, typically without acknowledgment of Adler's pioneering influence (Mosak & Maniacci, 1999). This appears to be evident in the positive psychology literature as well. Seligman (2002), considered the "Father of Positive Psychology," stated: "I well recognize that positive psychology is not a new idea. It has many distinguished ancestors" (p. 7). The two examples he mentions are Gordon Allport and Abraham Maslow. I can find no evidence of Seligman ever acknowledging Adler's pioneering positive psychology. As the 1933 paper on striving and social interest demonstrates, Adler clearly addressed key positive psychology tenets long before the "ancestors" (e.g., Allport, Maslow, Rogers) typically identified in the positive psychology literature (Jorgensen & Nafstad, 2004; Seligman, 2002; Seligman, Steen, Park, & Peterson, 2005; Snyder & Lopez, 2002; Snyder, Lopez, & Pedrotti, 2011). Thus, Adlerian theory is clearly relevant for today's psychological zeitgeist because it has evinced the characteristics of positive psychology long before the emergence of the positive psychology movement. As Bitter (1998) suggested, "the more the fields of psychology and psychotherapy develop, the more relevant the ideas and processes of Adlerian psychology become" (p. 412). All things considered, one can plausibly argue that Alfred Adler should be acknowledged as the "Grandfather of Positive Psychology."

## REFERENCES

Adler, A. (1956). *The individual psychology of Alfred Adler* (H. L. Ansbacher & R. R. Ansbacher, Eds.). New York: Harper Torchbooks.
Barlow, P. J., Tobin, D. J., & Schmidt, M. M. (2009). Social interest and positive psychology: Positively aligned. *Journal of Individual Psychology, 65,* 191–202.
Bitter, J. R. (1998). Thanks for the opportunity. *Journal of Individual Psychology, 54,* 411–412.
Carlson, J., Watts, R. E., & Maniacci, M. (2006). *Adlerian therapy: Theory and practice.* Washington, DC: American Psychological Association.
Cowen, E. L., & Kilmer, R. P. (2002). "Positive psychology": Some plusses and some open issues. *Journal of Community Psychology, 30,* 449–460.
Dreikurs, R. (1967). *Psychodynamics, psychotherapy, and counseling.* Chicago, IL: Alfred Adler Institute of Chicago.
Ellenberger, H. (1970). *The discovery of the unconscious: The history and evolution of dynamic psychiatry.* New York: Basic Books.
Jorgensen, I. S., & Nafstad, H. E. (2004). Positive psychology: Historical, philosophical, and epistemological perspectives. In S. Joseph & P. A. Linley (Eds.), *Positive psychology in practice* (pp. 15–34). New York: Wiley.
Leak, G. K., & Leak, K. C. (2006). Adlerian social interest and positive psychology: A conceptual and empirical investigation. *Journal of Individual Psychology, 62,* 207–223.
Linley, P. A., & Joseph, S. (Eds.). (2004). *Positive psychology in practice.* New York: Wiley.
Mahoney, M. J. (2003). *Constructive psychotherapy: A practical guide.* New York: Guilford.
Manaster, G. J., & Corsini, R. J. (1982). *Individual psychology: Theory and practice.* Itasca, IL: Peacock.
Mosak, H. H., & Maniacci, M. (1999). *A primer of Adlerian psychology: The analytic-behavioral-cognitive psychology of Alfred Adler.* Philadelphia, PA: Accelerated Development/Taylor and Francis.
Prochaska, J. O., & Norcross, J. C. (2010). *Systems of psychotherapy: A transtheoretical analysis* (7th ed.). Belmont, CA: Brooks/Cole.
Rasmussen, P. R. (2010). *The quest to feel good.* New York: Routledge/Taylor & Francis.
Ryan, R. M., & Deci, E. L. (2001). On happiness and human potentials: A review of research on hedonic and eudaimonic well-being. *Annual Review of Psychology, 52,* 141–166.
Seligman, M. E. P. (2002). Positive psychology, positive prevention, and positive therapy. In C. R. Snyder & S. J. Lopez (Eds.), *Handbook of positive psychology* (pp. 3–9). New York: Oxford.
Seligman, M. E. P., Steen, T. A., Park, N., & Peterson, C. (2005). Positive psychology progress: Empirical validation of interventions. *American Psychologist, 60,* 410–421.
Snyder, C. R., & Lopez, S. J. (2002). Preface. In C. R. Snyder & S. J. Lopez (Eds.), *Handbook of positive psychology* (pp. ix–x). New York: Oxford.
Snyder, C. R., Lopez, S. J., & Pedrotti, J. T. (2011). *Positive psychology: The scientific and practical explorations of human strengths* (2nd ed.). Los Angeles, CA: Sage.
Watts, R. E. (1998). The remarkable similarity between Rogers's core conditions and Adler's social interest. *Journal of Individual Psychology, 54,* 4–9.
Watts, R. E. (1999). The vision of Adler: An introduction. In R. E. Watts & J. Carlson (Eds.), *Interventions and strategies in counseling and psychotherapy* (pp. 1–13). Philadelphia, PA: Accelerated Development/Taylor & Francis.

Watts, R. E. (2003). Adlerian therapy as a relational constructivist approach. *The Family Journal: Counseling and Therapy for Couples and Families, 11,* 139–147.

Watts, R. E., & Eckstein, D. (2009). Individual Psychology. In American Counseling Association (Ed.), *The ACA encyclopedia of counseling* (pp. 281–283). Alexandria, VA: American Counseling Association.

Watts, R. E., & Pietrzak, D. (2000). Adlerian "encouragement" and the therapeutic process of solution-focused brief therapy. *Journal of Counseling and Development, 78,* 442–447.

Watts, R. E., Williamson, J., & Williamson, D. (2004). Adlerian psychology: A relational constructivist approach. *Adlerian Yearbook: 2004* (pp. 7–31). London: Adlerian Society (UK) and Institute for Individual Psychology.

## On the Origin of the Striving for Superiority and of Social Interest (1933)

*Alfred Adler*

It sounds almost like a timely problem to speak on the striving for perfection and the roots of social interest. For Individual Psychology, however, it is an old problem. I may well say that in these two questions and their solution rests the entire value and the entire significance of Individual Psychology.

The emphasis on these two questions has never been lacking in our work, but you, like myself, will probably have felt the need to have the questions for once treated in a fundamental form, so that we can avoid the vacillation and uncertainty which we have met occasionally among our friends, still more often among our opponents. I don't believe that outside our circle it is very well known what we understand by striving for perfection. I am obliged to add further supplements to the knowledge up to now. This knowledge cannot be comprehended immediately; it cannot be found through an analysis of the visible phenomena and facts, as, altogether, something new can never be created through analysis. Here we would have parts in our hands instead of the whole. To us Individual Psychologists, the whole tells much more than the analysis of the parts. Also, nothing new can emerge through synthesis if one simply puts the parts together.

### THE STRIVING FOR PERFECTION

Where must we begin with our considerations, if we want to get beyond the position of what has already been reached? Regarding the striving for perfection, or as it manifests itself sometimes, the striving for superiority, or the striving for power which authors of less understanding sometimes attribute to us, some few have always known about it. But their knowledge was not so thorough that they could communicate it to a larger number, or could illuminate the fundamental significance of this striving for the structure of the entire personality. It took Individual Psychology to point out that every individual is seized by this striving for perfection, that we find it in every individual. It is not at all necessary first to inoculate man with the desire to develop into superman, as the daring attempt of Nietzsche has maintained. Individual Psychology has shown that every individual is seized by the striving for perfection, by the upward striving. He who can read between the lines will have realized that we are continuously aware of the fundamental importance of the striving for perfection. In the consideration of a case of illness we have always uncovered the individual direction of this striving.

And yet one question remains which always returns whenever this problem appears, a question emphasized by friends and opponents, a question which perhaps in our circle as well has not yet been completely clarified. I shall attempt today to bring it nearer to a solution because I have always considered it necessary to create on this point clarity for all.

## PART OF EVOLUTIONARY PRINCIPLE

Thus I should first of all like to stress that the striving for perfection is innate. However, it is not innate in a concrete way, since we find it again and again in the various individuals in thousandfold variation. It is not innate in the sense of a drive which would later in life be capable of bringing everything to completion and which only needs to unfold itself. Rather, the striving for perfection is innate as something which belongs to life, a striving, an urge, a developing, a something without which one could not even conceive of life.

The scientists, especially the biological scientists, have always stressed this evolutionary principle in the body. Especially since Darwin, Lamarck, and others, it is a matter of course to take the evolutionary thought into account. If we go a step further here and emphasize more strongly what these ingenious researchers envisioned, we want to state: To live means to develop.

The human mind is accustomed to bring all flow into a form, to regard not the movement but the frozen movement, movement which has become form. However, we have always been intent to resolve into movement what we comprehend as form. Thus we must ascertain for the single individual of our time as well as for the development of living creatures in general that to live means to develop. Everyone knows that the complete man originates from an ovular cell. But one should also properly understand that in this ovular cell rest the fundaments for the development.

How life came on this earth is an uncertain matter; possibly we shall never reach a final answer. We could assume that there is life even in inanimate matter, as for example the ingenious attempt of Smuts[6] has done. Such a view becomes quite plausible through modern physics which shows that the electrons move around the proton. Whether this view will be further vindicated, we do not know. But it is certain that our concept of life as development can no longer be doubted. Thereby movement is ascertained at the same time, movement toward self-preservation, procreation, contact with the surrounding world, victorious contact in order not to perish. We must take our point of departure from this path of development, of a continuous active adaptation to the demands of the external world, if we want to understand in which direction life moves.

We must keep in mind that we are dealing here with something primary, something which adhered already to primordial life. It is always a matter of overcoming, of the existence of the individual and the human race, of establishing a favorable relationship between the individual and the surrounding

---

[6] Smuts, J. C. (1926). *Holism and evolution*. New York: Macmillan.

world. *This coercion to carry out a better adaptation can never end.* Herein lies the foundation for our view of the striving for superiority.

Probably much of what I have just discussed seems familiar, and it certainly was also known to others. Individual Psychology has only the one merit, to have established a connection and to have shown which form this force, called life, takes in each single individual and how it prevails. We are in the midst of the stream of evolution but notice it as little as the rotation of the earth. In this cosmic relation, in which the life of the single individual is a part, the striving for *victorious adaptation to the external world is a precondition.* Even if one doubted that the striving for superiority existed already at the beginning of life, the course of the billions of years puts it clearly before us that today the striving for perfection is an innate factor which is present in every man.

## Individual Conceptions of Perfection

This consideration may show us something else. None of us knows which is the only correct way to perfection. Mankind has variously made the attempt to imagine this final goal of human development. The best conception gained so far of this ideal elevation of mankind is the concept of God. There is no question but that the concept of God actually includes this movement toward perfection in the form of a goal, and that as a concrete goal of perfection it corresponds best to man's dark longing to reach perfection. Of course, it seems to me that each person imagines his God differently. Thus there are conceptions of God which from the outset are not equal to the principle of perfection. But of the purest formulation of God we can say: Here the concrete formulation of the goal of perfection has been accomplished.

There are, of course, countless attempts among men to imagine this goal of perfection differently. We physicians who deal with failures, with persons who have fallen sick from a neurosis or psychosis, who have become delinquents, alcoholics, etc., we see this goal of superiority in them also, but in another direction, one which contradicts reason in so far as we cannot acknowledge in it a correct goal of perfection. When, for example, someone attempts to concretize this goal by wanting to dominate over others, such a goal of perfection appears to us incapable to steer the individual and the group. The reason is that not every one could make this goal of perfection his task, because he would be forced to come into conflict with the coercion of evolution, to violate reality, and to defend himself full of anxiety against the truth and its confessors. When we find persons who have set themselves as a goal of perfection to lean on others, this goal of perfection also appears to us to contradict reason. When someone perhaps finds the goal of perfection in leaving the tasks of life unsolved in order not to suffer *certain defeats which would be the opposite of the goal of perfection,* this goal also appears to us altogether unsuited, although it appears to many persons as acceptable.

Let us enlarge our prospect and raise the question: What has become of those creatures who posited for themselves an incorrect goal of perfection, whose active adaptation has not succeeded because they took the incorrect path, who did not find the path toward the advancement of all (Sinn des Lebens [A1933b])? Here the extinction of species, races, tribes, families, and thousands of individual persons of whom nothing has remained, teaches us how necessary it is for the individual to find a halfway correct path to the goal of some kind of perfection. After all, it is understood in our day and by the individual among us that the goal of perfection gives the direction for the development of his entire personality, for all his expressive movements, his perceiving, his thinking, his feeling, his view of the world. It is equally clear and understandable for every Individual Psychologist that a direction which deviates in a considerable degree from the truth must turn out to the detriment of the one in question, if not to his doom. This being the case, it would be a lucky find if we knew more about the direction which we have to take since we are, after all, embedded in the stream of evolution and must follow it. Here as well, Individual Psychology has performed a great achievement, as it has with the ascertainment of the general striving for perfection. From thousandfold experience it has gained a view which is capable of understanding to some degree the direction toward ideal perfection, through its ascertainment of the norms of *social interest*.

## SOCIAL INTEREST

Regarding social interest, you will also have observed certain fluctuations in the Individual Psychology literature, and it is for this reason that I wanted to talk about it. I do not wish to say much about the usual and thoughtless case which is occasionally found within our circle among beginners, and outside our circle—the mistake of understanding what we call community as a private circle of our time, or a larger circle which one should join. Social interest means much more. Particularly it means *feeling with the whole, sub specie aeternitatis*, under the aspect of eternity. It means a striving for a form of community which must be thought of as everlasting, as it could be thought of if mankind had reached the goal of perfection. It is never a present-day community or society, nor a political or religious form. Rather the goal which is best suited for perfection would have to be a goal which signifies the ideal community of all mankind, the ultimate fulfillment of evolution.

### Normative Ideal

Of course, one will ask, how do I know this? Certainly not from immediate experience. I must admit that those who find a piece of metaphysics in Individual Psychology are right. Some praise this, other criticize it. Unfortunately, there are many who have an erroneous view of metaphysics, who would like to see everything eliminated from the life of mankind which they cannot comprehend immediately. But by doing so we would interfere with the possibilities of development, prevent every new thought. Every new idea lies beyond immediate experience; immediate experiences never yield anything new. Only a synthesizing idea can do this. Whether you call it speculation or transcendentalism, there is no science which does not have to enter the realm of metaphysics. I see no reason to be afraid of metaphysics; it has had a very great influence on human life and development. We are not blessed with the possession of the absolute truth, and on that account we are compelled to form theories for ourselves about our future, about the results of our actions, etc.

We conceive the idea of social interest, social feeling, as the ultimate form of mankind, a condition in which we imagine all questions of life, all relationship to the external world as solved. It is a normative ideal, a direction-giving goal. This goal of perfection must contain the goal of an ideal community, because everything we find valuable in life, what exists and what will remain, is forever a product of this social feeling.

I want to repeat what I have mentioned in another connection. The newborn child always finds in life only what the others have contributed to life, to welfare, to security. What we find when we enter our life is always the contribution of our forebears. This one fact alone could enlighten us as to how life will move on: We shall approach a condition of larger contributions, of greater ability to cooperate, where every individual presents himself more fully as a part of the whole—a condition for which of course all forms of our societal movement are trials, preliminary trials, and only those will endure which are situated in the direction of this ideal community.

We do not want to judge; only one thing we can say: A movement of the individual or a movement of the masses can for us pass as valuable only if it creates values for eternity, for the higher development of all mankind. Maybe you will understand this fact better if I raise once more the question: What happens to those persons who have contributed nothing? They have disappeared, have become extinct. There you see again how the force of evolution, how this urge to achieve a higher stage physically and mentally, how this urge extinguishes everything which does not go along and contributes nothing.

If one is a friend of formulations, one could say there is a basic law in development which calls to those who are negating: Away with you; you do not understand what counts! Thus duration emphasizes itself, the eternal duration of the contribution of persons who have done something for the common good. Of course we are thoughtful enough not to assume that we have the key for telling in each case exactly what is calculated for eternity and what not. We are convinced that we can err, that only a very exact, objective investigation can decide, often also only the course of events. It is perhaps already a great step that we can avoid what does not contribute to the striving for perfection.

## SOCIAL CONTEXT

I could talk more about this and show how all our functions are calculated not to disturb the community of man, to connect the individual with the community. To see means to receive, to make fertile that which falls on the retina. This is not only a physiological process; it shows the person as part of the whole, who takes and gives. In seeing, hearing, speaking we connect ourselves with the others. Thus all functions of our organs are correctly developed only if they are not detrimental to the social interest.

We speak of virtue, and mean that one participates in the game; of vice, and mean that one disturbs cooperation. I could also point out how everything which signifies a failure is a failure because it disturbs the development of the community, whether we are dealing with problem children, neurotics, criminals, or cases of suicide. In all cases you see that the contribution is lacking.

In the entire history of mankind you will find no isolated persons. The development of mankind was possible only because mankind was a community and in striving for perfection strove for an ideal community. All movements, all functions of a person express whether or not he has found this direction in the stream of evolution which is characterized by the community ideal. The reason is that man is inviolably guided by the community ideal. He becomes impeded, punished, praised, and advanced by it, so that each individual becomes not only responsible for each deviation but must also suffer for it. This is a hard law, virtually a cruel law. Those who have already developed in themselves a strong social feeling constantly endeavour to ameliorate the hardships of anyone who proceeds erroneously. They do this as if they knew that here is a man who has missed the way for reasons which only Individual Psychology is able to demonstrate. If a man understood how he erred, stepping out of the way of evolution, he would leave this course and join general humanity.

## INNATE SUBSTRATUM

Finally, I should like to submit a thought which has much in its favor and which I should like you to consider. If you agree with my arguments, you will have to raise the question: Is social interest innate or must one bring it to man? Of course it is also innate, like the striving for perfection, except that it must be developed and can be developed only when the child is already in the midst of life.

Like the character traits which depend on it, social interest can come to life only in the social context. By social context, of course, is meant the child's subjective understanding of the same. The decision [as to how he will interpret the essentially ambiguous social context] rests in the creative power of the child, which, however, is guided by the environment and educational measures, and influenced by the experience and evaluation of his body.[7] At the present stage of mankind's psychological and possibly also physical development, we must consider the innate substratum of the social interest as too small, as not strong enough, to become effective or to develop without the benefit of social understanding. This is in contrast to abilities and functions which succeed almost all on their own, such as breathing. But with social interest we are far from having reached this stage. We have not developed it to the same extent as breathing. And yet we must expect the development of social interest so strongly in the ultimate goal of perfection that mankind of the future will possess and activate it like breathing.

## CONCLUSION

What we have to do in the present critical state follows automatically. Unquestionably this consideration gives us a certain and firm foundation not only for the evaluation of a person and for the education of a child but also for the improvement and guidance of one who has gone astray. But this succeeds only through explanation and understanding. We must talk about it, because we are not certain whether every child and every adult knows where the way leads. This is why one must talk about it so long until perhaps in the course of thousands of years talking also will have become superfluous, as perhaps it has today become superfluous to talk about correct breathing.

The talking about social interest as belonging to the evolution of man, as a part of human life, and the awakening of the corresponding understanding is today being attended to by Individual Psychology. This is its fundamental significance, its claim to existence, and this is what represents its strength. Today everybody speaks about community and community feeling. We were not the very first, but we are the first to have strongly emphasized the basic nature of the social feelings.

The concept of community and community feeling can also be abused. But one who has properly understood knows that in the nature of community and community feeling rests an evolutionary factor which turns against everything which resists this direction. He will be able to avoid the abuse of the concept of the community or to let himself be abused by others in its name.

---

[7] By "experience and evaluation of his body," Adler means that the child is not directly influenced by his physique but by how he subjectively experiences and evaluates it. Thus a beautiful girl who feels that boys are attracted by her beauty rather than by her brains (for which she would like to be admired) will evaluate her beauty negatively. (Original footnote by H. & R. Ansbacher.)

This represents the practical value and the significance of Individual Psychology: It has clarified the fundamental significance of social interest for the development, the higher development, of the individual and of the whole of mankind.

## SUMMARY

Individual Psychology has shown that the striving for superiority and perfection is not limited to the characterization of *certain* individuals, nor is it *brought to them from the outside*; rather, it is given to *every* person and must be understood as *innate*, as a *necessary and general foundation of the development of every person.*

The originators of the concept of evolution in the field of general organic life, such as Darwin and Lamarck, have pointed out that life must be understood as *movement toward a goal*, and that this goal—the preservation of the individual and the species—is attained through the overcoming of resistances with which the environment confronts the organism. Thus *mastery of the environment* appears to be inseparably connected with the concept of evolution. If this striving were not innate to the organism, no form of life could preserve itself.

The goal of mastering the environment in a superior way, which one can call the striving for perfection, consequently also characterizes the development of man. It is expressed most clearly in the concept of God. In the individual case, however, the striving for superiority takes on very different concrete forms. Typical is, e.g., the striving to *master one's fellow man*, Exactly this form was shown by Individual Psychology to be erroneous, contradicting the concept of evolution. Individual Psychology has uncovered the fact that the deviations and failures of the human character—neurosis, psychosis, crime, drug addiction etc.—are nothing but forms of expression and symptoms of the striving for superiority directed against fellowmanship,[8] which presents itself in one case as striving for power, in another case as an evasion of accomplishments by which another might benefit. Such erroneous striving leads to the psychological decline and fall of the individual, as any biological erroneous striving has led to the physical decline and fall of entire species and races.

Individual Psychology has found a special formula for the correct striving for perfection of man: The goal which the individual must pursue must lie in the direction which leads to the perfection of *all of mankind sub specie aeternitatis.* "Virtue" means advancement, "vice" means disturbance of the common work which aims at perfection. Never can the individual be the goal

---

[8] The German original for fellowmanship is *Mitmenschlichkeit,* meaning "being a fellow man," as well as "co-humaneness." (Original footnote by H. & R. Ansbacher.)

of the ideal of perfection, but only mankind as a *cooperating community*. A *partial community* of any kind—perhaps groups that are associated through certain political, religious, or other ideals—is also not sufficient. Neither do we mean the *existing* society, but an *ideal* society yet to be developed, which comprises all men, all filled by the common striving for perfection.

This is how the Individual Psychology concept of social interest (*Gemeinschaftsgefuhl*) is to be understood. This is to be considered as innate— "innate" also in the categorical (metaphysical) sense, namely as the necessary and general premise for human cultural development. Every human being brings the disposition for social interest with him; but then it must be *developed* through *upbringing*, especially through correct guidance of the creative power of the individual. We can assume that the innate substratum of the ability to cooperate will become increasingly stronger through the training of the generations.

An important aid in this training is that the individual become *conscious* of the importance of social interest as the form of the striving for perfection which is appropriate for man. Exactly in this work of information rests the foremost practical task of Individual Psychology.

# 6

## *Personality as a Self-Consistent Unity*
### A Contemporary View

PAUL R. PELUSO

The article "Personality as a Self-Consistent Unity" is taken from a lecture that Adler gave in Vienna in the early 1930s (the publication date of the article is 1932, and in it Adler references his book *Problems of Neurosis,* which was originally published in 1929). It reminds me of how I first came to know Shakespeare in high school: by reading his plays. Although this was supposed to be my introduction to the legendary Bard, unfortunately nothing could be more *boring* for a teenager than reading spoken words whose origin was an English that was no longer spoken (Elizabethan)! It was only when I began to see the plays in action (especially the humor and the bawdiness), and hear the words spoken in the way they were meant to be received, that I saw how his work resonated with my experiences of love, jealousy, fear, and wonder over 500 years after he wrote them. I became enthralled with the construction of these great works and wanted to reread and memorize them as much for their wit as for their iambic pentameter and rhythms. I think that it is the same way with many of Adler's lectures that were later turned into articles. At first they may seem to be dull, dry, and lifeless. I remember struggling through Adler's words in Ansbacher and Ansbacher's (1964) famous anthology and wondering where was the "great man" that I was supposed to learn from, whose ideas were supposed to inspire me. It was only after I began to practice as an Adlerian therapist, and saw the theoretical concepts and clinical interventions come to life, that I discovered new meanings from the once arcane and incomprehensible words of Adler (not surprisingly, much of the text for that work came from a series of lectures). I reread them (and other of his works) with new interest and excitement.

So as I read and reread this article, I had three competing thoughts. First, I had to focus on the contemporary aspects of article so that I could speak to its contemporary value. Second, I was trying to read it as an Adlerian practitioner. I was looking for some new insight or shading from a great mind that I admired and whose work has been meaningful to me. Third, I was trying to read it and imagine that I was in a lecture hall and hearing these words spoken to me. I was trying to imagine the heavily accented broken English, of which I have only heard a snippet from an old Movietone newsreel, that would be pronouncing these words

It was interesting for me to discover that Adler delivered this lecture with several overlapping thoughts, or agendas of his own that he was trying to convey. First, he devoted a fair amount of time to being an apologist for Individual Psychology. His theory was still under attack from competing schools of psychotherapy (most notably the Psychoanalytic school) and he felt that he had to defend it from contemporary critics (many of whom were recycling arguments that were almost 20 years old). You can almost hear the weariness in his voice as he had to (once again) dispel many of the myths that had arisen around Individual Psychology. While this may have some interest to readers as a historical point, I will not embellish much on it here (I think Adler does a good enough job without any help from me). Second, he was acting as a philosopher and theoretician. Here he was expounding on a theory that had both complexity and simplicity at its core; it was familiar and common sense, and at the same time it was revolutionary and ahead of its time. These elements may be the most resounding to a modern audience, and I will discuss in some detail. Third, he was acting as a clinician and giving a clinical demonstration of his therapeutic insight and incisiveness. Even in his brief recall of several cases to illustrate his point, we can see some forward-thinking clinical approaches that echo many of the "cutting-edge" perspectives today. It is from the multiple perspectives of Adler as a theoretician and Adler as a clinician that I will make some commentary on this article and draw out those elements that are still noteworthy to an audience a century removed from the original delivery of this oratory.

## ADLER AS A THEORETICIAN

In the article "Personality as a Self-Consistent Unity," Adler tackles several theoretical issues that were avant-garde for his time (the 1930s) and seems on-target in today's world (2010s). One of the first issues that he tackles is the unconscious. At the time of this article, the existence and influence of the unconscious was considered to be beyond question. This was primarily due to the strong influence of psychoanalysis, which considered the unconscious to be central to shaping the personality and creating psychopathology. The unconscious was also seen as key to delivering any treatment. However, Adler refuted the idea of an unconscious that was mysterious and out of our ability to observe (directly or indirectly) or bring under any kind of conscious control. He believed that an unconscious that could not be directly influenced was not consistent with human experience:

> Animals have, of course, a consciousness without concepts; but doesn't an infant have the same things, and doesn't he behave exceptionally rationally? Aren't we all able to carry things in the consciousness which we do not grasp conceptually, but which nevertheless are there? (p. 436)

This idea is reminiscent of the current thinking in cognitive psychology about automatic (or implicit) processing, which may be outside of conscious awareness but is not *un*conscious. An example of this is adults riding a bicycle. This task is so automatic that few get on the bicycle and have to consciously recall how to balance, peddle, steer, or brake. Instead, they just *ride*. However, if required to, a person can describe the process for doing this step-by-step, even though he or she may have not thought about it for some time. Today most clinicians (from cognitive-behaviorists to constructionists) as well as cognitive scientists agree with Adler's conceptualization and reject the idea of a "dark" unconscious.

Another central tenet of the philosophy behind Individual Psychology, and the focus of his article, is the holistic nature of the person. Again, this is in direct contrast to the dominant idea of the time that human beings could be thought of as machines, or that cognitive processes could be best represented by mechanical processes that could be broken down to their constituent parts. In fact, Adler references this dominant idea by discussing one of the more sophisticated machines of his time: the Dictaphone (a vocal recording device before magnetic tape recorders). Many practitioners and scientists felt that human personality operated along the lines of a Dictaphone—that it simply recorded whatever it was exposed to and then played back whichever record was installed (sometimes jazz, sometimes opera, etc.) depending on the situation. While this was not the best metaphor for human functioning, the psychoanalytic view of unconscious forces was rooted in the metaphor of hydraulic steam engines that would exert pressure and forces that the individual had to balance to maintain order. Interestingly, this dominant mechanistic metaphor would be replaced in modern times with the "human as computer" model, or the "human information processing model" that had separate processes and subroutines that could be broken down and "reprogrammed."

Adler rejected the idea that humans were automatons "ruled" by these forces, instead suggesting that people were active decision makers and shaped both their experiences of the world and their behavior (or movement) in it: "The creative force arranges: it has the ability to look ahead and see what it must do" (p. 432). In addition, Adler believed that this creative force was goal-directed and directed by the individual. Indeed, this was a radical departure from the idea that personality was "force-driven" and able to be broken into subroutines. Instead, the personality (or "style of life"/lifestyle) is unique, and each person decides how to act to meet the particular goal. Furthermore, this personality style does not change with a person's context (work, home, etc.), but remains constant and whole. All things are arranged by it to consciously meet this goal. At times this may become automatic and out of the awareness of the individual, but it can be recalled (sometimes with some therapeutic intervention). This idea goes against a mechanistic view of the human as a machine, and from a clinical standpoint, it is consistent with many Constructivist approaches and reflected in other, postmodern approaches (e.g., NLP, ACT).

## ADLER AS A CLINICIAN

In the last section of the article (and lecture), Adler demonstrates the theoretical points that he is trying to make. It was not surprising that he borrows a character from Shakespeare to illustrate his point about the personality! And like a great Shakespeare play, this is where his mastery as a clinician shines. First, he sets the framework for how Individual Psychology works: "All we undertake to do is to be in a position to replace larger errors with smaller ones. Larger errors hinder the active adaptation to life" (p. 433). In other words, the goal of therapy is not a long-term "reconstruction" of the individual, but to help individuals to see where their persistent errors in judgment (perception) "gets in the way" of their own functioning. If clients can be made to stop making the "big mistakes" in their lives, then they will be able to find relief and sort out the rest. For many in his time[9] (and some in modern time), this is too simplistic. Adler himself even talks about how his approach is considered "simple" or too "common sense." Today, however, most clinicians would recognize this approach as "brief" or "solution-focused" or even "results-oriented."

Adler also emphasizes in his clinical examples how the therapist needs to be mindful of every behavior and statement from the client to understand the style of life and the goal that drives it. "It is not given to us directly; only from the forms of expression and their system of context can we understand it. . . . This much show itself in everything, in his bearing and in his achievements" (pp. 436–437). From this understanding of the "style of life," the clinician can then intervene. In the first clinical example, Adler demonstrates how a brief interaction with a person can reveal his or her goal. Adler discovers that the successful but depressed businessman operates under the assumption "if I am pitiful, people will take care of me" and how his goal of pitifulness makes his success intolerable to him. It puts him onto a "double bind" because he can have no joy or comfort in his success, because to do so would risk the only method that he knows to connect and get his needs met by others (by being pitiful). Adler is able to take this dominant image (the "beggar") and illuminates it for the client, saying, "We are forced to establish the connection" (p. 439). The internal constancy of this image (goal)

---

[9] See Rollo May's recollection of his time with Adler in 1933 in *The Art of Counseling.*

was then validated by the client sending Adler a newspaper article that the client had written 10 years earlier on that topic! In terms of modern approaches, this is reflective of what schema-focused therapists and emotion-focused counselors do in finding the dominant underlying themes of the clients' lives.

However, Adler cautions against being too confident or too complacent as a therapist. This admonishment is just as true today as it was almost 100 years ago:

> Making the portrait completely true to life, so that the patient is convinced of its correctness, requires further, more subtle work. Where we come across the unsolvable contradictions our interpretation is incorrect and must be altered. This is an indication of the seriousness, misunderstood by many, with which Individual Psychology bears in mind and pursues the self-contained unity of the person. (1932, p. 440)

In this way, Adler may be the most like modern practitioners. He was cautious about being too presumptuous and sure of oneself. Unlike many of his contemporaries, he was mindful of the possibility that his own interpretations could be wrong. This forced him to attend to the client and not only co-create a treatment that would address the client's concern but also tailor a treatment that relied less on the therapist being "brilliant" or masterful and more on forging a collaboration with clients and demonstrating a spirit of *Gemeinschaftsgefuhl* (social interest/community feeling) that he wished to inspire in them. Of course this is consistent with the literature on effective therapy and the importance of a strong, positive therapeutic alliance.

As one reads *Personality as a Self-Consistent Unity*, I would encourage the modern reader to consider all of the audiences that Adler was speaking to. I would also submit that Adler may have been speaking to one more audience as well: us—the audience of practitioners that would read his work nearly a century later.

## REFERENCE

Adler, A. (1964). The individual psychology of Alfred Adler. In H. L. Ansbacher & R. R. Ansbacher (Eds.), *The individual psychology of Alfred Adler*. New York: Harper & Row.

## Personality as a Self-Consistent Unity[10,11]

### Alfred Adler

### Translation by Michael Cicero

The importance of a discussion on this theme may be shown by the fact that, even more outside the circle of Individual Psychology than within it, there have piled up a great number of misunderstandings, which, for us, act as a powerful incentive. We are often forced to help along the powers of understanding of those who stand outside our circle. We don't know what it is the others are missing, but since the assault against Individual Psychology has sharpened in recent years, we have at our disposal the inexhaustible material of their errors. It is a rewarding task to throw some light on these misunderstandings.

I refer to the position of many authors who treat Individual Psychology as if it were an environmental theory *(Milieutheorie)*, as if the whole mentality of a human being could be traced back to the effect of the outside world on him. If one took a closer look at this position, he would have to ask: who seeks out, who answers, who processes the impressions? Is a human being a dictaphone? A machine? There must be something at the bottom of this! Similarly, we cannot approve of the heredity theory. There we raise the most strenuous objections. Research on twins has shown that, there too, there is less to this than at first meets the eye. One speaks of the influence of the upbringing, saying that social life is a modifying influence. Who does the modifying? Is it a mathematical calculation? In contrast, Individual Psychology takes the following position: when we begin to speak of the "psychic life" *(Seelenleben)*, we go off into transcendental areas. We know something only of the effects, of the results, of the relationships which make themselves noticeable. We must make assumptions which someone who has a fixed, preconceived notion of the "psychic life" no longer thinks about, or, like the behaviorist, denies altogether. But, even with regard to behaviorism, we have to emphasize that there must be psychic impulses which are responsible for the outpourings of our thoughts, feelings, and actions which become visible; psychic impulses of which we can say that we are much better off than the physicists when they speak of electricity. Just as it is with every science, Individual Psychology merges into metaphysics. We can smile about those objections which say that Individual Psychology dispenses with metaphysical foundations. There we are dealing with an area of our insight which we must presuppose: we cannot

[10] This article is a translation of Personlichkeit als geschlossene Einheit, *Internationale Zeitschrift fur Individualpsychologie*, 10, 81–88, 1932.

[11] From a lecture held in the Society for Individual Psychology, Vienna.

work there because we want to order the impressions which lie before us, and we want to designate them as psychic impressions. It is an a priori interpretation, one that we must make and which serves us well in ordering events and placing them under a common light.

We can say even more about our psychic life if we stay in the transcendental realm. If we want to construct the psychic life, we must be sure that it agrees with our conception of time and space, i.e., we must not only apply the conception of time to it, thus considering its movement, but we must also consider the *direction*. Where does the direction come from? It cannot be derived from hereditary forces. If one propounds a drive psychology *(Triebpsychologie)*, the movement can be determined, but not the direction. Here we come to that puzzle, upon which Individual Psychology has thrown itself, in accord with investigators dating back to times long past. There is a creative force at hand in the psychic life which is identical to the life force itself. This creative force arranges: it has the ability to look ahead and see what it must do. Indeed, such *looking ahead* seems necessary in the psychic life, since man is mobile. Psychic life is movement and direction, both placed under one goal. Since man is not isolated, the goal of a creative force must be formed from the stress of the overcoming of social difficulties which place themselves in opposition to movement. There must always be a goal of overcoming, of the carrying through of the purpose of self-preservation, of completion. Always before us there hangs also the threat of damage, of listlessness—of death.

We are pleased to stick with the general expression: *overcoming*. The misunderstanding that Individual Psychology not only interprets the psychic life as a striving for power, but also seeks to propagate that idea, inserts itself here. This striving for power is not our madness: it is the madness which we find in others. A goal of overcoming as an abstract formulation is unacceptable in the general stream of human thought. There, one finds a much more concrete formulation. According to this formulation, every individual comes to a concrete goal of overcoming through his creative force, which is identical to the ego. Our task is to ascertain the direction in which a person endeavors to overcome. His own opinion of this direction commands and directs him. All we can say of this opinion is that it is more, or that it is less, incorrect. We have never maintained that we were in possession of an absolute truth. All we undertake to do is to be in a position to replace larger errors with smaller ones. Larger errors hinder the active adaptation to life. In the very moment in which we speak of singleness of purpose, in that moment when we can better grasp the concrete concept of a goal, there crops up a huge difficulty: that we have to do it with thousands of variations, each time in a unique case, with a unique concrete objective. Here, we come upon the fairy tale, which is imputed to us, that we have presupposed the equality of human beings or that we have striven for it. The truth is that we only undertake to investigate the nuances, the uniqueness of the objective, the uniqueness of a person's opinion of himself and of the tasks of life. That is the task of Individual Psychology, to understand individual wrongheadedness *(Abwegigkeit)*. If I insert a few concepts here, as for instance that one seeks a goal of superiority in the domination of others or the evasion of duties, so that another becomes the object of exploitation, these are calm and composed positions, which, along with their variations, it is the task of Individual Psychology to clarify.

When someone doesn't know anything else to hold against Individual Psychology, he says: If we don't believe at all in heredity, then it ought to be possible for a human being to develop into a goose. One should think, of course, that among serious people we wouldn't need to speak about such things. Possibilities must be granted. Nothing can be developed which isn't present somehow or other in the human embryo. Such objections, however, could mislead us toward the belief that in odd cases such a development is possible.

Another misunderstanding exists in the notion that it should have occurred to us that we could raise children to complete maturity, children from whom, as from the feebleminded, all capability of development has been taken away. That would be as if we were to demand right-handed drawings from one who has lost his right hand. I would never have believed that I would have to deal with such nuisances in the criticism of my work. It stands to reason that, if somehow the scope of humanity is narrowed, this incapability of development will show itself in the behavior of the person, e.g., in feebleminded children, or accordingly in people with unfit organs, such as the brain or endocrine glands. In such a case we make no claim of bringing them up to a level which to us seems normal.

In recent years, the vicious attacks against Individual Psychology have increased. For those in the know, it is easy to see how all the hard work of standing up for some different point of view, which is then raised up to high heaven, or which may on occasion coyly come to light in the notes of a margin, fogs the senses of the critic. Impartial observation allows us to distinguish several points of departure. The most humorous comes from the beginners and those ignorant in the area of modern psychology. Sworn to the word of their teacher, or of some textbook, they are full of indignation at how one "could doubt heredity"; "how one could overlook sexuality"; how one could believe that the "striving for power" rules everything; whether they realize that others as well . . . that "even *Plato*, . . . especially *Guyeau*—that every school of psychology speaks of the feeling of community, of the totality of the personality. . . ."

Then there are also the snappish critics. Mostly they speak of "depth" assuming, therefore, that people will recognize the depth in them, start off wildly in the beginning, then more moderately, until they have snatched a little more of Individual Psychology for themselves. [They] write often in magazines whose publishers are either asleep or wishing they were [and] are occasionally taken seriously by these, otherwise, by no one.

Then comes the "entrance march of the plagiarists." They cannot get over the fact that they must eke out a living while they undertake, from time to time, a "reception" of Individual Psychology. Often they don't know it and are strengthened by the well-wishing silence of insiders in their projects. New words of insult don't occur to them, which speaks poorly of the fruitfulness of their imaginations. Occasionally one notices how they, as eternal recruits, snap after the approval of the leaders of their sect. Words like "banal," "superficial," and "unscientific" recur as stereotypical expressions. The conduct of their patrons, the publishers, etc., is thereby more stigmatized than that of the recruits themselves. If one lets oneself get involved in this, making use of more than one shameless expression, one shows one's ignorance to a shocking degree.

The "great expansion" of Individual Psychology permits them no rest. "There must be a mistake hidden in there somewhere or other."

Of course, there are books and writings which cannot be considered fully and completely as Individual Psychology. Such writings, for example in politics and religion, believe it necessary to make use of psychoanalytic terminology. Recently there have appeared authors who seek the way to brain pathology with treacherous fervor. But although they strive to misuse Individual Psychology for their own personal views, they only barely nose out those who have learned nothing of Individual Psychology at all. Therefore, leave them to me unmolested, even if they occasionally recommend a liqueur or swear on the corpus striatum, whether they seek to help God or politics. Sometimes, they instruct me about Individual Psychology.

Thus, according to one psychoanalyst: Since, however, isolation is not a part of the life plan of human creation, since community and social behavior are commands of nature, of whom one cannot escape without punishment. . . ."

An open-minded Freudian examines, "moreover," the holistic personality: It must be kept clearly in mind that all classifications have only abstract meaning. If one confuses intellectual differences with real separation of outlook, then one falls back into the old ability psychology *(Vermogenpsychologie)*. There is much sexuality hidden in the urge for admiration, and much striving for admiration in the sexual development; but it won't do to have the one constantly reduced to the other or to award genuine causality to only one or the other of these desires. It would be as tasteless as if we were to subordinate all human activities to the urge for food and were to produce art and science merely as a means to obtain nutrition. We should not forget that all psychic functions are elements of one organism. Since 1916, I have struggled unceasingly for the "organic approach," according to which every psychic activity is only understandable in connection with the wholeness of life. The isolating of individual drives (aside from their most elementary expression), the general subjugation of the one area of drive to the other, leads to errors and outrages. —The sexual drive seems to be one of the exceptions.

Likewise, another: "Furthermore, within the assertion of sexuality, there is always self-assertion."

Another well-informed Theban: "Self-confidence and a serious will for achievement—nothing more is necessary." Thus, an optimist without equal.

"Of course, behind it all, a world view which is not very deep, a psychotherapy for high school teachers, as Individual Psychology proudly claims himself to be."

". . . , for Adler, there is nothing but the striving for power." As we can see, this one is an illiterate, and hardly a high school teacher himself.

Herbart: "Just because a village schoolteacher has practiced his failed method for 30 years, he shouldn't expect us to believe in his results."

On the other hand: "Whoever really understands homosexuals—assuming the reader believes he can say that of himself—must be astounded by the basic points of the foreword (Alfred Adler's, *Das Problem der Homosexualitat*, Leipzig, S. Hirzel, 1930) which contradict all experience. According to these assertions, homosexuality represents a kind of training since childhood for the discouraged human being, for the purpose of switching to the path of the exclusion of possibilities of defeat—in the case of the homosexual, the path of exclusion from the other sex—and an evasion of the normal solution to the love question."

I can only assume that the author has only dealt with exceptional cases.

"The reader who is not already sworn to Adlerian theory will find in these formulations no increase in his knowledge."

And also no decrease? "He who is perfect, always feels that it is others who need to be set right."

The poor ego has been shoved far into the background, as if it were impossible for a fertilized egg cell to be already a complete entity. To speak of drives which supposedly generate the ego is far-fetched. It is the ego, which grows its way into life, which we see later as the creative force. If one believes that he can locate in the various drives what belongs to the ego, the seeking, questioning, doubting, thinking, feeling, desiring, striving for goals, etc., this is nothing more than sleight of hand. The most important question is: who moves the psychic life, and in which direction does he move it? Always, the answer is the ego.

I would like to give expression to a thought which has recently occupied my attention especially. An error has crept unnoticed into the whole psychological literature, to the effect that only a part of a mental concept which is explicitly expressed belongs properly to the consciousness. If this were correct, then there would be no consciousness in animals. Animals have, of course, a consciousness without concepts; but doesn't an infant have the same thing, and doesn't he behave exceptionally rationally? Aren't we all able to carry things in the consciousness which we do not grasp conceptually, but which nevertheless are there? Why should someone depend only upon words? Maybe this discussion doesn't seem extraordinarily important, but if I draw attention to the fact that when we think of the unconscious as that which cannot be conceptualized, it suddenly appears to be "conscious" as soon as we grasp the concept, then one comes to understand that the assertion of the unconscious does not concern the *inseparable, unified ego*. Non-conceptual thinking, with which we are filled every moment of our lives, is conscious in the sense of consciousness, because we always have it before us and because it never disappears.

In the course of this line of thought we come to information which confronts other views very sharply. The form of life *(Lebensform)* is also established through the setting of one's goal in the psychic life. If for every impulse there is a goal at hand, then the form is also at hand. If everything (thoughts, feelings, desires, achievement) strives after this goal, then a life-style *(Lebensstil)* is established, to which every part of the psychic life must adapt itself, and of which every portion is only a fragment of the whole. Therefore, out of fragments and the arrangement of the same, [and] through their relationship to one another, we are able to guess the form of life, *the individual law of movement*. It is not given to us directly; only from the forms of expression and their system of context can we understand it. We can only say: this is a person who has set himself the goal of leaving all tasks undone. This must show itself in everything, in his bearing and in his achievements. And through them we also take into account the thousand variations of such a life-style.

In order to take a step out of theory and into practice, I would like, as I usually do, to give a hypothetical case. I love to present cases in which the uniformity of the whole person is apparent *to everyone*. There is much talk about this idea of wholeness, but I have looked in vain in the literature for an example of proof that all thoughts, feelings, desires, memories, dreams, in short, every portion could be related to the same form of life. What we encounter are devout wishes. When I and others tried to represent this unity more sharply, these attempts of ours were the only attempts up to now to demonstrate the uniformity of the whole person.

That isn't totally correct, since there have been men of the past and men of the present who have done the same thing. They are to be found among the poets, painters, and musicians who create unified personalities, just as the child creates the adult out of himself, in his unique and never to be repeated individuality and unity, where every part fits into the whole. Schopenhauer expresses his admiration for Shakespeare for the way he portrays the character of Northumberland in a unified form in three of his dramas: a jovial henchmen until the king falls into danger. Then he betrays the king three times. This looks like "ambivalence": submissive and rebellious. We do not have a single concept for the millions of variations. Here is a man whose loyalty extends to a certain point and no further. What follows is no longer loyalty. This is the great merit of Individual Psychology to have shown that the best way to measure [a person] is by the capability of cooperative achievement. Thus, it stands to reason that the yardstick for the characterization of a form of life derives exactly from this one point of view; how far the feeling of community (*Gemeinschaftsgefuhl*), reaches, and where it ends. This is not a mathematical problem, but rather an artistic one. We must find out at what point one is no longer in a position to provide this feeling of community (*Gemeinschaftsgefuhl*), at what point one no longer insists on the test of social interest (*soziales Intresse*). Here, too, we are not speaking of a moral ideal, not in the sense of a religious concept, but rather in the sense of a thoroughly scientific consideration of the human psychic life (*Seelenlebens*). All capabilities can be developed only on the basis of the feeling of community. It is in this area that one person develops more, the other less. The feeling of community must be bred in the person. That doesn't mean that environmental theory can celebrate a victory here. Knowledgeable educators have the task of linking the creative force of the child to the path of the feeling of community. This means more than just weighing influences. One must look at *how the creative force* of *the child grasps* the influence, [and] whether in doing so he stays on the right path.

In order to give an example of the unity of the personality, I refer back to a case which appeared in *Problems of Neurosis*.[12] A man in his fifties came up to me after a lecture and complained about depression: he was constantly inclined to cry. In spite of this, he had been successful in his job and had amassed some wealth. I was short of time and tried to snatch a few fragments from his life history. His earliest memory was: he was the youngest of many children in a family which lived for many years in the greatest poverty. He used to sneak about, pale and hungry, so that the neighbors took care of him and gave him gifts. Even at that time he suffered from his melancholy. Individual Psychology has shown that the form of life is apparent, to the expert, after the age of three or four years. I doubt that it *exists* prior to that, but it becomes clearly visible only later. He was the darling of his mother and very spoiled. Once, when she wanted to get a job in order to earn some money, he cried so violently that she said: "I won't go away. I would rather starve here with you." He had a speech impediment and was often urged by

---

[12] Kegan Paul, London, 1929.

others, for the sake of fun, to recite poems. Finally, he took his hat and went around collecting coins. He conducted himself like a beggar. The adult had retained the form of life of a beggar. I told him, that. It made a great impression on him. He said: "I remember the great impression it made, when, as a child, I saw a beggar in the street and heard him singing as people gave him coins. And the man still deported himself as a beggar, causing people to deal much more gently with him. I did not see the man again, but he wrote me a letter in which he made clear to me how very correct I had been. And he sent me a newspaper article, which he had written 10 years before with the title, "An Organization of Beggars." Was the beggar idea supposed to be only in the man's unconscious? We see unity in all his thoughts, in the way in which he wrote the article, in the feeling, the attitude, [and] also ultimately in the nature of his achievements. He approaches all the problems of life like a beggar. This is his law of movement.

A salesman, 30-years-old, [is] the youngest in his family. The situation of the youngest as we know from our experience, is a special case. The youngest grows up in a unique situation. After every child comes a new one. Only in his case is this not true. He has no one bringing up the rear. This is very significant in the manner of our upbringing. Each of the children has his day to be dethroned by a new arrival. The youngest never experiences this. Furthermore, the earlier children are bigger, they satisfy greater standards and are able to achieve more. This becomes a significant incentive for the youngest. Every youngest child is nuanced by it. This is where the creative force of the individual enters the picture. But the strong incentive for the youngest cannot be overlooked (Joseph in the Bible, the youngest in fairy tales). This particular youngest child had outdone all his siblings: he was his parents' favorite, the best in school, a very ambitious child who trembled before every test. This man married a girl whom he believed he could totally dominate. It was characteristic of his case that he didn't really have any friends. This shows that he loved only those situations in which he was the master. All other situations he tried to shut out. It happened that he suffered from nervous symptoms whenever something should happen where he wasn't the leading figure, where he felt pressure from outside, for example as in the theater, when he sat in an isolated space. This situation, in which he was not aware of his commanding influence, seemed to be a danger to him.

I want to digress and speak about intellectual processes. It is not true that we could have intellectual processes within us without their being followed by desire and feeling. But people come in different sorts, some of whom look more to the intellectual, others more to the emotional, and still others more to the will. We are forced to establish the connection. If I think: I am not free—then, as a man who tolerates no coercion, I will develop feelings and emotions which militate against it. These are persons who, for instance, only take the end seat in a theater in order to feel free. The man in question was distinct from the other type of anxious neurotic (*Angstneurotiker*); he fought against it but it was clearly visible that he was urged on by the motor of his ambition. He always wanted to be the leader, to outshine the others, which he succeeded in doing more easily through the impression that his symptoms made. *No wonder that the incentive to ward them off was slight.* I would like to point out that we could observe the same mechanism in the theory of dreams where we find an intellectual content that is not supposed to be understood. Dreams, too, contain a fragment of the personality: feelings are awakened which the dreamer needs.

First dream: Its setting was the school. He was not properly prepared.

If we look at that in context it says: The teacher is the doctor who knows better than I. After that, a worsening must ensue. This is one danger.

Second dream: He had some calculations to perform, among which some were done by him, some by others. The calculations of the others were wrong. His own were right. This is an attempt to create for himself an incentive to rise above others. The calculations are not correct and neither are those of the doctor. We see that this "resistance" has nothing to do with love and sexuality. Rather, the patient wants to correspond to his own notion of a leader. Thus the others are not permitted any leadership activity.

Third dream: He sees himself having to wear an old jacket home. He says: "The most unpleasant thing for me was always when I was given something to wear."

Fourth dream: He has two hats, a stiff one and a soft one. The latter he treats with great care. Asked what he does with two hats, he says: It is true that, in order to preserve the soft one, I wear the stiff hat in bad weather; that means, in order to prevent damage, so as not to *have* to spend so much money on hats. He is invoking his thriftiness. He springs all mines in order to force me, who must be paid, into the background.

The four dreams say: I won't stand for it. Someone like a teacher stands before me; perhaps he gives me orders, and he believes that he understands things better than I do, while at the same time he lets me pay him money for it.

Making the portrait completely true to life, so that the patient is convinced of its correctness, requires further, more subtle work. Where we come across the unsolvable contradictions our interpretation is incorrect and must be altered. This is an indication of the seriousness, misunderstood by many, with which Individual Psychology bears in mind and pursues the self-contained unity of the person.

# 7

# Position in Family Constellation Influences Lifestyle

GARY D. McKAY

While many theorists have discussed birth order, only Adler addressed this concept as family constellation—it's not only the position into which one is born but *how* one interprets the position, or how it manifests as behavior. For example, most firstborns retain their desire to be the "good" one when the second child is born, while some feel dethroned by the second born and become the best at being "bad" while the second born becomes the good one.

Adler points out that people in the same family constellation position are more like each other than they are to their own siblings unless dethronement has taken place. For example, most firstborns demonstrate leadership and responsibility, whereas second children strive to catch up or overtake the firstborn. If this is not possible, the second born may become the "bad" child as mentioned above or develop positive traits the oldest doesn't have. For example, if the oldest is a good student, the second child may think he can't match or overtake his or her sibling in that field, and become good at sports.

Youngest children never have to face someone younger trying to take their place. They have always been babies. The youngest may subsume to the spoiling of the parents and often older siblings. Or, this child may decide that he or she wants to strive to overtake his siblings, gaining their power. A youngest with this desire and behavior can be termed a "speeder."

Adler suggests that families with only children may not feel up to raising more than one child and use birth control to avoid more children, failing to mention that some people have only children because the mother can't have any more children. I am an only child, and this was the situation with my mother.

Adler discusses the difficulties of an only child. An only child retains the center of attention without effort and is usually pampered. Thus he or she develops a lifestyle that "calls for his being supported by others and at the same time ruling them."

In the article Adler discusses eldests, second children, onlys, and youngest children. For some reason, he doesn't discuss middle children. Perhaps this is because many families had several children at the time that the article was published (1937). So the kids may have been in groups of oldests, seconds, and youngests. With large families this is often the case because if a child is 5 years older or younger than a sibling, that sibling has a limited effect on the child, for the lifestyle is formed somewhere between 4 and 6 years of age. For example, in a family with six children the oldest is going to be several years older than the youngest. Families are generally smaller today than they were then. Table 7.1 points out the possible characteristics of a child today in each family constellation position.

In today's world we find many stepfamilies. When both stepparents have their own children, kids from each family may influence the children of their stepparent. For example, there could be two oldests who both compete for the top position, which means one could be newly dethroned.

Throughout the article, Adler uses case examples to show how family constellation influences lifestyle. For example, he discusses the case of a 60-year-old man, the youngest of three, who was still in the care of his two older sisters. Needless to say, he was very worried about what would happen to him when his sisters died.

Adler discusses homosexual development in relation to family constellation. For example, being an only boy or only girl in the sibling ship also affects the development of that individual. The only boy in a family of girls may decide to become "a real man" or decide to join the feminine ship as one of the girls and strive to be the "best" girl in the crew, whereas being an only girl in the family may result in a masculine tendency for being the best guy in the pack.

He points out that only children or children reared in a family where all their siblings are from the opposite sex can be more prone to develop homosexual lifestyles. I'm not aware of any research that supports this theory even though it appears logical. Additionally, some of the language Adler uses to describe homosexuals such as *pervert* or *abnormal*, or the word *homosexual* itself—instead of *gay* or *lesbian*—is unacceptable in society today. Again, we have to realize when this article was written and the social norms at that time.

Getting back to typical characteristics of family constellation positions, Table 7.1 outlines these characteristics. Of course it can always be different depending on how the child sees his or her position in relation to the others.

As you read this article, you will see how the characteristics of each position influence one's outlook on life. But remember, as said above: "It can always be different."

## REFERENCES

Dinkmeyer, D., McKay, G. D., & Dinkmeyer, D. (1997). *STEP (Systematic Training for Effective Parenting) leader's resource guide.* Bowling Green, KY: STEP Publishers.

**Table 7.1** Some Typical Characteristics of Family Constellation Positions

| Position | Strives To | Possible Positive Traits | Possible Negative Traits |
| --- | --- | --- | --- |
| Only Child | Get own way (may play "divide and conquer") | • Is creative[a]<br>• Has positive peer relationships as an adult[b]<br>• Is selective about choosing who to please | • May be pampered or spoiled, or self-centered<br>• Feels incompetent, feels adults are more capable<br>• Relies on service from others rather than being self-reliant |
| Oldest Child | Be first | • Is leader<br>• Is helpful and responsible<br>• Is selective about choosing who to please | • Is bossy<br>• Believes *must* please others<br>• Becomes discouraged if can't be best (becomes "best at being worst") |
| Second Child | Catch up or overtake | • Is sociable<br>• Puts forth effort<br>• Develops abilities lacking in oldest | • May rebel<br>• Can become "bad" child if oldest is "good" child<br>• Is uncertain of abilities if oldest child is successful |
| Middle Child of Three[c] | Make life fair | • Is adaptable<br>• Is concerned with justice<br>• Knows how to get along with all kinds of people | • Feels "squeezed"—May push others down to elevate self<br>• May be "problem" child<br>• Feels doesn't have a place |
| Youngest child | Get service | • Knows how to influence others<br>• Is charming<br>• Is friendly | • May be manipulative<br>• Expects others to take care of his or her responsibilities<br>• Feels inferior or overtakes older siblings |

a  Only children may have to learn to operate in a world made up exclusively of adults and may have to entertain themselves. This may develop their creative side.

b  When growing up, only children may want to be adults and may have poor peer relationships as a result. When they become adults, they often believe they've "made it" and can now relate better to adults as peers.

c  Middle children in a large family don't compete as much as middle child of three, since their parents don't have as much time to reinforce the competition. Middle children from large families are usually more cooperative.

Source: This chart comes from Dinkmeyer, D., McKay, G. D., & Dinkmeyer, D., *STEP (Systematic Training for Effective Parenting) Leader's Resource Guide*, STEP Publishers, Bowling Green, KY, p. 1997, 12. It is not available for commercial purposes without permission from the publisher.

## Position in Family Constellation Influences Life Style[13]

*Alfred Adler*

It is a common fallacy to imagine that children of the same family are formed in the same environment. Of course there is much which is the same for all children in the same home, but the psychic situation of each child is individual and differs from that of others, because of the order of their succession.

There has been some misunderstanding of my custom of classification according to position in the family. It is not, of course, the child's number in the order of successive births which influences his character, but the *situation* into which he is born and the way in which he *interprets* it. Thus, if the eldest child is feeble-minded or suppressed, the second child may acquire a style of life similar to that of an eldest child; and in a large family, if two are born much later than the rest, and grow up together separated from the older children, the elder of these may develop like a first child. This also happens sometimes in the case of twins.

### POSITION OF THE FIRST CHILD

The first child has the unique position of having been the only one at the beginning of his life. Being thus the central interest he is generally spoiled. In this he resembles the only child, and spoiling is almost inevitable in both cases. The first child, however, usually suffers an important change of situation, being dethroned when the second baby is born. The child is generally quite unprepared for this change, and feels that he has lost his position as the center of love and attention. He then comes into great tension for he is far from his goal and there begins a striving to regain favor. He uses all the means by which he has hitherto attracted notice. Of course he would like to go the best way about it, to be beloved for his goodness; but good behavior is apt to pass unnoticed when everyone is busied with the new-comer. He is then likely to change his tactics and to resort to old activities which have previously attracted attention—even if it was unfavorable attention.

If intelligent, he acts intelligently, but not necessarily in harmony with the family's demands. Antagonism, disobedience, attacks on the baby, or even attempts to play the part of a baby, compel the parents to give renewed attention to his existence. A spoiled child must have the spotlight upon himself, even at the cost of expressing weakness or imitating a return to babyhood. Thus, under the influence of the past, he attains his goal in the present by unsuitable means; suddenly showing inability to function alone, needing assistance in eating and excretion and requiring constant watching, or compelling

---

[13] Originally edited by Philip Mairet; additional editing by Heinz Ansbacher.

solicitude by getting into danger and terrifying the parents. The appearance of such characteristics as jealousy, envy, or egotism has an obvious relation to the outside circumstances, but he may also indulge in—or prolong—illnesses such as asthma and whooping cough. The tension in certain types (depending upon the bodily organization) may produce headache, migraine, stomach trouble, petit mal, or hysterical chorea. Slighter symptoms are evinced in a tired appearance and a general change of behavior for the worse, with which the child impresses his parents. Naturally, the later the rival baby is born, the more intelligible and understandable will the methods appear which the first child uses in his change of behavior. If dethroned very early, the eldest child's efforts are largely "instinctive" in character. The style of his striving will in any case be conditioned by the reaction of others in the environment and his evaluation of it. If, for instance, the dethroned child finds that fighting does not pay, he may lose hope, become depressed, and score a success by worrying and frightening the parents. After learning that such ways are successful for him he will resort to ever more subtle uses of misfortune to gain his end.

The type of activity which in later life will be based on the prototype was shown in the case of a man who became afraid to swallow for fear of choking. Why did he select this symptom instead of another? The patient had an immediate social difficulty in the behavior of an intimate friend, who attacked him violently. Both the patient and his wife had come to the conclusion that he must put up with it no longer, but he did not feel strong enough to face the struggle. Upon inquiry into his childhood, it appeared that he had had such a difficulty in connection with swallowing before. He was the eldest child, and had been surpassed by his younger brother, but he had at that time been able, by means of difficulty in eating, to make his father and mother watch over him. Now faced with a personal defeat in later life, and not knowing what to do about it, he fell back upon this old line of defense, as though it might make someone watch over him and help him.

## EFFECTS OF DETHRONEMENT

The dethronement of the first child by another may make it turn away from the mother towards the father, and a very critical attitude towards the mother will then persist ever after. A person of this type is always afraid of being "pushed back" all through life; and we notice that in all his affairs he likes to make one step forward and then one backward, so that nothing decisive can happen. He always feels justified in fearing that a favorable situation will change. Towards all the three life questions he will take up a hesitative attitude, with certain problem behavior and neurotic tendencies. Problem behavior and symptoms will be felt by him to be a help and a security. He will approach society, for example, with a hostile attitude; he may constantly be changing his occupation; and in his erotic life he may experience failure in functioning, and may show polygamous tendencies—if he falls in love with one person he very quickly falls in love with another. Dubious and unwilling to decide anything, he becomes a great procrastinator. I met a very perfect example of this type once, and his earliest remembrance was this: "At three years of age I caught scarlet fever. By mistake my mother gave me carbolic acid for a gargle, and I nearly died." He had a younger sister who was the favorite of his mother. Later in life this patient developed a curious fantasy of a young girl ruling and bullying an older one. Sometimes he imagined her riding the old woman like a horse.

## FIRST CHILD MAY KEEP POSITION

The eldest child may, however, be so firmly fixed in the parents' favor that he cannot be supplanted. This may be either by virtue of his own good native endowment and development, or because of the second child's inferiority, if the latter is ugly, organically handicapped, or badly brought up. In such a case it is the second child who becomes the problem, and the eldest may have a very satisfactory development, as in the following case:

Of two brothers, differing four years in age, the elder had been much attached to the mother, and when the younger was born the father had been ill for some time. Caring for the father took the entire time and most of the attention of the mother. The elder boy, trained in friendship and obedience to her, tried to help and relieve her, and the younger boy was put into the care of a nurse, who spoiled him. This situation lasted for some years, so that the younger child had no reasonable chance to compete with the elder for the love of the mother; and he soon abandoned the useful side of life, and became wild and disobedient. His behavior became still worse four years later, when a *little* sister was born, to whom the mother was able to devote herself owing to the death of the father. Thus twice excluded from the mother's attention and spoiled by the nurse, this second child turned out to be the worst pupil in his class, while the elder boy was always the best. Feeling hopelessly handicapped in competition with his brother, unloved at home, and reproached at the school (from which he was finally expelled), this second son could find no goal in life but to dominate his mother by worrying her. Being physically stronger than either the brother or sister, he took to tyrannizing over them. He trifled away his time, and at puberty he began to waste money and to incur debts. His honest and well-meaning parent, provided a very strict tutor for him who did not, of course, grasp the situation, and dealt with it superficially by punishments. The boy grew into a man who strove to get rich quickly and easily. He fell an easy prey to unscrupulous advisers, followed them into fruitless enterprises, and not only lost his money but involved his mother in his dishonorable debts.

The facts of the case clearly showed that all the courage this man ever displayed resulted from his unsatisfied desire to conquer. He played a queer game from time to time, especially when things went against him. His nurse was now an old woman, earning her living in the family as a superior servant; she still worshipped the second boy and always interceded for him in his numerous scrapes. The odd sport in which he indulged was to lock her in a room with him and make her play at soldiers with him, commanding her to march, to fall and to jump up again at his orders; and sometimes he quickened her obedience by beating her with a stick. She always obeyed although she screamed and resisted.

This singular sport revealed what he really wanted, the completest domination in the easiest way. Some writers would describe this as sadistic conduct, but I demur at the use of a word which implies a sexual interest, for I could discover nothing of the kind in it. In sexual matters the man was practically normal, except that he changed his mates too frequently and always chose inferiors. Genuine sadism itself is a domineering tendency availing itself of the sexual urge for its expression, owing to the discouragement of the individual in other spheres.

In the end this man brought himself into very bad circumstances, while the elder brother became very successful and highly respected.

## ATTITUDE OF ELDEST TOWARD AUTHORITY

The eldest child, partly because he often finds himself acting as representative of the parental authority, is usually a great believer in power and the laws. The intuitive perception of this fact is shown in the ancient and persistent custom of primogeniture. It is often observable in literature. Thus Theodore Fontane wrote of his perplexity at his father's pleasure in hearing that ten thousand Poles had defeated twenty thousand Russians. His father was a French emigrant who had sided with the Poles, but to the writer it was an inconceivable idea that the stronger could be beaten; he felt that the status quo should be preserved and that might must, and ought to, succeed. This was because Theodore Fontane was a first child. In any case the eldest child is readier than others to recognize power, and likes to support it. This is shown in the lives of scientists, politicians, and artists, as well as in those of simpler people. Even if the person is a revolutionary we find him harboring a conservative tendency, as in the case of Robespierre.

## POSITION OF SECOND CHILD

The second child is in a very different situation, never having had the experience of being the only one. Though he is also petted at first, he is never the sole center of attention. From the first, life is for him more or less of a race;

the first child sets the pace, and the second tries to surpass him. What results from competition between two such children depends on their courage and self-confidence. If the elder becomes discouraged he will be in a serious situation, especially if the younger is really strong and outstrips him.

If the second child loses hope of equality he will try to *shine* more rather than to *be* more. That is, if the elder is too strong for him, the younger will tend to escape to the useless side of life. This is shown in many cases of problem behavior in children where laziness, lying, or stealing begins to pave the way towards neurosis, crime, and self-destruction.

As a rule, however, the second child is in a better position than the first. His pacemaker stimulates him to effort. Also, it is a common thing for the first child to hasten his own dethronement by fighting against it with envy, jealousy and truculence, which lower him in the parental favor. It is when the first child is brilliant that the second child is in the worst situation.

But the elder child is not always the worst sufferer, even when dethroned. I saw this in the case of a girl who had been the center of attention and extremely spoiled until she reached the age of three, when a sister was born. After the birth of her sister she became very jealous and developed into a problem-child. The younger sister grew up with sweet and charming manners, and was much the more beloved of the two. But when this younger sister came to school the situation was not to her taste; she was no longer spoiled and, being unprepared to encounter difficulties, was frightened and tried to withdraw. To escape defeat both in fact and in appearance, she adopted a device very common among the discouraged—she never finished anything she was doing, so that it always escaped final judgment, and she wasted as much time as possible. We find that time is the great enemy of such discouraged people for, under the pressure of the requirements made on them by social living, they feel as if time were persecuting them continually with the question, "How will you use me?" Hence their strange efforts to "kill time" with silly activities. This girl always came late and postponed every action. She did not antagonize anyone, even if reproved, but her charm and sweetness, which were maintained as before, did not prevent her from being a greater worry and burden than her fighting sister.

When the elder sister became engaged to be married the younger sister was desperately unhappy. Though she had won the first stage of the race with her rival by gentleness and obedience, she had given up in the later stages of school and social life. She felt her sister's marriage as a defeat, and that her any hope of regaining ground would be to marry also. However, she had not courage enough to choose a suitable partner, and automatically sought a second-best. First she fell in love with a man suffering seriously from tuberculosis. Can we regard this as a step forward? Does it contradict her preestablished custom of leaving every task unfinished? Not at all. The poor health of her lover and her parents' natural resistance to the match were sure causes of delay and frustration. She preferred an element of impossibility in her choice. Another scarcely eligible partner appeared later in her life, in a man thirty years older than herself. He was senile, but did not die as the previous one had done, and the marriage took place. However, it was not a great success for her, as the attitude of hopelessness in which she had trained herself did not allow her to undertake any useful activity. It also inhibited her sexual life, which she considered disgusting, feeling humiliated and soiled by it. She used her usual methods to evade love and postpone relations at the appropriate times. She did not quite succeed in this, however, and became pregnant, which she regarded as another hopeless state, and from that time onward not only rejected caresses but complained that she felt soiled, and began to wash and clean all day long. She not only washed herself, but cleaned everything that had been touched by her husband, by the maid servant or the visitors, including furniture, linen, and shoes. Soon she allowed no one to touch any of the objects in her room, and lived under the stress of a neurosis—in this case, a washing-compulsion. Thus she was excused from the solution of her problems, and attained a very lofty goal of superiority—she felt more fastidiously clean than anyone else.

Exaggerated striving for a lofty goal of high distinctiveness is well expressed in the neurosis of "washing-compulsion." As far as I have been able to ascertain, this illness is always used as a means of avoiding sexual relations by a person who feels that sex is "dirty." Invariably it gives the fantastic compensation of feeling cleaner than everybody else.

However, due to his feeling life to be a race, the second child usually trains himself more stiffly and, if his courage holds, is well on the way to overcome the eldest on his own ground. If he has a little less courage he will choose to surpass the eldest in another field, and if still less, he will become more critical and antagonistic than usual, not in an objective but in a personal manner. In childhood this attitude appears in relation to trifles: he will want the window shut when the elder opens it, turn on the light when the other wants it extinguished, and be consistently contrary and opposite.

This situation is well described in the Bible story of Esau and Jacob, where Jacob succeeds in usurping the privileges of the eldest. The second child lives in a condition like that of an engine under a constantly excessive head of steam. It was well expressed by a little boy of four, who cried out, weeping, "I am so unhappy because I can *never* be as old as my brother."

The fact that children repeat the psychic behavior of older brothers and sisters and of parents is, by some writers, attributed to an "instinct" of imitation or to "identification" of the self with another; but it is explained better when we see that a child imitates only that kind of behavior which he finds to be a successful way of asserting an equality which is denied to him on other grounds.

Psychic resemblances to the conduct of ancestors or even of savages do not sig-nify that the pattern of psychic reaction is hereditary, but that many individuals use the same means of offense and defense in similar situations. When we find so much resemblance between all first children, all second, and all youngest children, we may well ask what part is left for heredity to play in determining those resemblances. Thus, as psychologists we have also not sufficient evidence to accept the theory that the mental development of the individual ought to repeat the development of the race of mankind successive stages.

In his later life, the second child is rarely able to endure the strict leader-ship of others or to accept the idea of "eternal laws." He will be much more inclined to believe, rightly or wrongly, that there is no power in the world which cannot be overthrown. Beware of his revolutionary subtleties! I have known quite a few cases in which the second child has availed himself of the strangest means to undermine the power of ruling persons or tradi-tions. Not everybody, certainly not these rebels themselves, would easily agree with my view of their behavior. For though it is possible to endanger a ruling power with slander, there are more insidious ways. For example, by means of excessive praise one may idealize and glorify a man or a method until the reality cannot stand up to it. Both methods are employed in Mark Antony's oration in "Julius Caesar." I have shown elsewhere how Dostoievsky made masterly use of the latter means, perhaps unconsciously, to undermine the pillars of old Russia. Those who remember his representation of Father Zosima in "The Brothers Karamazov," and who also recall the fact that he was a second son, will have little difficulty agreeing with my suggestion regarding the influence played by position in the family.

I need hardly say that the style of life of a second child, like that of the first, may also appear in another child—one in a different chronological position in the family—if the *situation* is of a similar pattern.

## SITUATION OF YOUNGEST CHILD

The youngest child is also a distinct type, exhibiting certain characteristics of style which we seldom fail to find. He has always been the baby of the family, and has never known the tragedy of being dispossessed by a younger, which is more or less the fate of all other children. In this respect his situation is a favored one, and his education is often relatively better, as the economic position of the family is likely to be more secure in its later years. The grown-up children not infrequently join with the parents in spoiling the youngest child, who is thus likely to be too much indulged. On the other hand, the youngest may also be too much stimulated by elders—both mistakes are well known to our educationists. In the former case (of over-indulgence) the child will strive throughout life to be supported by others. In the latter case the child will rather resemble a second child, proceeding competitively, striving to overtake all those who set the pace for him, and in many cases failing to do so. Often, therefore, he looks for a field of activity remote from that of the other members of the family—in which case, I believe, he gives a sign of hidden cowardice. If the family is commercial, for instance, the youngest often inclines to art or poetry; if scientific, he wants to be a salesman. I have remarked elsewhere that many of the most successful men of our time were youngest children, and I am convinced this is also the case in any other age. In biblical history we find a remarkable number of youngest children among the leading characters, such as David, Saul, and Joseph. The story of Joseph is a particularly good example, and illustrates many of the views we have advanced. His younger brother Benjamin was seventeen years his junior and, therefore, played little part in Joseph's development. Joseph's psychological position, therefore, was that of a youngest child.

It is interesting to note how well Joseph's brethren understood his dreams. More precisely, I should say that they understood the feeling and emotion of the dreamer, a point to which I shall return later. The purpose of a dream is not to be understood but to create a mood and a tension of feeling.

In the fairy tales of all ages and peoples the youngest child plays the role of a conqueror. I infer that in earlier times, when both circumstances and men's apprehension of them were simpler, it was easier to collect experiences and to understand the coherent current of the life of the latest-born. This traditional grasp of character survives in folk-lore when the actual experiences are forgotten.

A strange case of the type of youngest child who is spoiled, which I have already given elsewhere, is that of a man with a "begging" style of life. I found another such case in that of a physician who was having difficulties with his mouth and was fearful of cancer. For twenty years he had been unable to swallow normally and could take only liquid food. He had recently had a dental plate made for him, which he was continually pushing up and down with his tongue, a habit which caused pain and soreness of the tongue, so that he feared he was developing cancer.

He was the youngest of a family of three, with two older sisters, and had been weakly and much indulged. At the age of forty he could eat only alone or with his sisters. This is a clear indication that he was comfortable only in his favorite situation—of being spoiled by the sisters. Every approach to society had been difficult for him. He had no friends, and only a few associates whom he met weekly in a restaurant. His attitude towards the three questions of life being one of fear and trembling, we can understand that his tension when with other people made him unable to swallow food. He lived in a kind of stage fright, fearful that he was not making a sufficiently good impression.

This man answered the second life question (that of occupation) with tolerable competence, because his parents had been poor and he could not live without earning, but he suffered exceedingly in his profession, and nearly fainted when he had to take his examinations. His ambition, as a general practitioner, was to obtain a position with a fixed salary, and, later on, a pension. This great attraction to a safe official position is a sign of a feeling of insecurity. People with a deep sense of inadequacy commonly aspire to the "safe job." For years he gave himself up to his symptoms. When he became older he lost some of his teeth, and decided to have a plate made, which became the occasion of the development of his latest symptom.

When he came to me, the patient was sixty years of age, and was still living in the care of his two sisters. Both were suffering from their age, and it was clear to me that this man, aging, and spoiled by two unmarried and much older women, was facing a new situation. He was very much afraid his sisters would die. What should he do in that case—he who needed to be continually noticed and watched over? He had never been in love, for he could never find a woman whom he could trust with his fragile happiness! How could he believe that anyone would spoil him as his mother and older sisters had done. It was easy to guess the form of his sexuality—masturbation, and some petting affairs with girls. But recently an older woman had wanted to marry him; and he wished to appear more pleasant and attractive in behavior. The beginning of a struggle seemed imminent, but his new dental plate came to the rescue. In the nick of time he became anxious about contracting cancer of the tongue.

He himself, as a doctor, was very much in doubt about the reality of this cancer. The many surgeons and physicians he consulted all tried to dissuade him from belief in it; but he persisted in his uncertainty, continued to press his tongue against the plate until it hurt; then he consulted another doctor.

Such preoccupations—"overvalued ideas," as Wernicke calls them—are carefully cherished in the arrangement of a neurosis. The patient shies away from the right objective by fixing his glances more and more firmly upon a point somewhere off a good, productive course. He does this in order to swerve out of a direction which is beginning to be indicated by logical necessity. The logical solution of his problem would be antagonistic to his style of life, and as the style of life rules (since it is the only way of approach to life the individual has learned), he has to establish emotions and feelings which will support his life-style and will insure his escape.

In spite of the fact that this man was sixty years old, the only logical solution was to find a trustworthy substitute for his spoiling sisters before their departure. His distrustful mind could not rise to the hope of achieving this possibility; nor could his doubts be dissipated by logic, because he had built up throughout his life a definite resistance to marriage. Because it improved his appearance, the dental plate should have been a help towards marriage but he made it into an insuperable impediment.

In the treatment of this case it was useless to attack the belief in the cancer. When he understood the coherence of his behavior the patient's symptoms were very much alleviated. The next day he told me of a dream: "I was sitting in the house of a third sister at a birthday celebration of her thirteen-year-old son. I was entirely healthy, felt no pain, and could swallow anything." But this dream was related to an episode in his life which took place fifteen years before. Its meaning is very obvious: "If only I were fifteen years younger." Thus is the style maintained.

## DIFFICULTIES OF ONLY CHILD

The only child also has his typical difficulties. Retaining the center of the stage without effort, and generally pampered, he forms a style of life that calls for his being supported by others and at the same time ruling them. Very often he grows up in an intimate environment. The parents may be fearful people and afraid to have more children. Sometimes the mother, neurotic before this advent, does not feel equal to rearing more children, and develops such behavior that everyone must feel, "It is a blessing that this woman has no more children." Birth control may absorb much of the attention of the family, in which case we may infer tension, and that the two parents are united to carry on their life in anxiety. The care then devoted to the only child never ceases by day or night, and often impresses the child with a belief that it is an almost mortal danger not to be watched and guarded. Such children often grow up cautious, and sooner or later they may often become successful and gain the esteem and attention they desire. But if they come into wholly different conditions where life is difficult for them, they may show striking insufficiency.

Only children are often sweet and affectionate, and later in life they may develop charming manners in order to appeal to others, because they have trained themselves this way both in early life and later. They are usually closer to the more indulgent parent, which is generally the mother; and in some cases develop a hostile attitude towards the other parent.

The proper upbringing of an only child is not easy, but it is possible for parents to understand the problem and to solve it correctly. We do not regard the only child's situation as dangerous, but we find that, in the absence of the best educational methods, very bad results frequently occur which would have been avoided if there had been brothers, and sisters.

## CASE OF HOMOSEXUAL DEVELOPMENT

I will give a case of the development of an only child, a boy whose attachment was entirely to the mother. The father was of no importance in the family; he contributed materially but was obviously without interest in the child. The mother was a dressmaker who worked at home, and the little boy spent all his time with her, sitting or playing beside her. He played at sewing, imitating his mother's activity, and ultimately became very very proficient in it, but he never took any part in boys' games. The mother left the house each day at 5 p.m. to deliver her work, and returned punctually at six. During that time the boy was left alone with an older girl cousin, and played with sewing materials. He became interested in timepieces, because he was always looking for his mother's return. He could tell the time when he was only three years old.

The cousin played games with him in which she was the bridegroom and he was the bride, and it is noteworthy that he looked more like a girl than she did. When he came to school he was quite unprepared to associate with boys, but he was able to establish himself as a favored exception, for others liked his mild and courteous disposition. He began to approach his goal of superiority by being attractive, especially so to boys and men. At fourteen years of age he acted the part of a girl in a school play. The audience had not the slightest doubt that he was a girl; a young fellow began to flirt with him and he was much pleased to have excited such admiration.

He had worn girlish dress during his first four years, and until the age of ten he did not know whether he was a boy or a girl. When his sex was explained to him he began to masturbate, and in his fantasy he soon connected sexual desire with what he had felt when boys touched him or kissed him. To be admired and wooed was his goal in life; to this end he accommodated all his characteristics in such a way that he might be admired especially by boys. His older cousin was the only girl he had known, and she was gentle and sweet, but she had played the man's role in their games and otherwise she had ruled him like his mother. A great feeling of inferiority was his legacy from his mother's overindulgent and excessive care. She had married late, at the age of thirty-eight, and she did not wish to have more children by the husband she disliked. Her anxiety, then was doubtless of earlier origin, and her late marriage indicative of a hesitant attitude to life. Very strict in sexual matters, she wanted her child to be educated in ignorance of sex.

At the age of sixteen this patient looked and walked like a flirtatious girl, and he soon fell into the snare of homosexuality. In order to comprehend this development we must remember that he had had, in a psychological sense, the education of a girl, and that the difference between the sexes had been made clear to him much too late in his development. Also he had experienced his triumphs in the feminine role; and had no certainty of gaining as much by playing the man. In the imitation of girlish behavior he could not but see an open road to his goal of superiority.

It is my experience that boys who have this type of upbringing always look like girls. The growth of the organs and probably also of the glands is partially ruled by the environment and the child's attitude toward it; and they are adapted to them. Thus if such an early environmental training towards femininity is succeeded by a personal goal of the same tendency, the wish to be a favored girl will influence not only the mind, but also the carriage and even the body.

This case illustrates very dearly how a pervert trains himself mentally into his abnormal attitude towards sex. There is no necessity to postulate an inborn or hereditary organic deviation.

When the boy in question came to me he was involved in a relationship with another boy who was the neglected second child of a very domineering mother; this boy's striving was to overcome men by his personal charm. It was by his charm that he had succeeded early in ruling his weak father. When he reached the age of sexual expression he was shocked. His notion of women was founded upon experience of his domineering mother, who had neglected him. He felt the need to dominate but he entertained no hope of dominating women for, in accordance with the generalization he had made of his early experiences connected with a strong and ruling mother, he had come to feel that a woman was too powerful to control. His only chance to be the victor, he felt, was in relationship with men; so he turned homosexual. Consider then the hopeless situation of my patient! He wanted to conquer by female means—by having the charm of a girl—but his friend wanted to be a conqueror of men.

I was able to make my patient realize that, whatever he himself thought or felt in this liaison, his friend felt himself to be a conquering man-charmer. My patient, therefore, could not be sure that his was the real conquest, and his homosexuality was accordingly checked. By this means I was able to break off the relationship, for he saw that it was stupid to enter into such a fruitless competition. This also made it easier for him to understand that his abnormality was due to a lack of interest in others, and that his feeling of inadequacy, as the result of being pampered, had led him to measure everything in—terms of personal triumph. He then left me for some months; when he visited me again he had had sexual relations with a girl, but had tried to play a masochistic part towards her. He obviously wished, in order to prove to himself that his original view of the world was correct, to experience with her the same inferiority that he had felt with his mother and cousin. This masochistic attitude was shown in the fact that his goal of superiority required that the girl should do to him what he commanded, and he wished to complete the act at this point, without achieving sexual intercourse, so that the normal was still excluded.

The great difficulty of changing a homosexual lies not only in his lack of general social adjustment, but also in the invariable absence of right training toward the sexual role, which ought to begin in early childhood. The attitude towards the other sex is strained in a mistaken direction almost from the beginning of life. In order to realize this fact one must note the kind of intelligence, of behavior, and of expectations which such a case exhibits. Compare normal persons walking in the street or mixing in society with a homosexual in the same situations! Those who are normal are chiefly interested in the opposite sex, the homosexuals only in their own. The latter evade normal sexuality not only in behavior but even in dreams. The patient I have just described used frequently to dream that he was climbing a mountain, and ascending it by a serpentine road. The dream expresses his discouraged and circuitous approach to life. He moved rather like a snake, bending his head and shoulders at every step.

In conclusion I will recall some of the most disastrous cases I have known among only children. A woman asked me to help her and her husband in the case of their only boy, who tyrannized over them terribly. He was then sixteen, a very good pupil at school, but quarrelsome and insulting in behavior. He was specially combative toward his father, who had been stricter with him than had the mother. He antagonized both parents continually, and if he could not get what he wanted he made open attack, sometimes wrestling with his father, spitting at him, and using bad language. Such a development is possible in the case of a pampered and only child who is trained to give nothing but to expect everything—and gets it, until the time comes when indulgence can go on no longer. In such cases it is difficult to treat the patient in his old environment, because too many old recollections are revived, which disturb the harmony of the family.

Another case was brought to me, a boy of eighteen, who had been accused of murdering his father. He was an only child, and a spoiled one, who had stopped his education and was wasting, in bad company, all the money he could extort from his parents. One day when his father refused to give him money, the boy killed him by hitting him on the head with a hammer. No one but the lawyer who was defending him knew that he had killed another person several months before. It was obvious that he felt perfectly sure of escaping discovery this second time.

In yet another case of criminal development, an only boy was brought up by a very well-educated woman who wanted him to be a genius. At her death another experienced woman continued his nurture in the same way, until she became aware of his tyrannical tendencies. She believed it to be due to sexual repression, and had him analyzed. His tyrannical attitude did not cease, however, and she then wished to be rid of him. But he broke into her house one night intending to rob her, and strangled her.

All the characteristics which I have described as typical of certain positions in the family can, of course, be modified by other circumstances. With all their possibilities of variation, however, the outlines of these patterns of behavior will be found to be substantially-correct. Among other possibilities, one may mention the position of a boy growing up among girls. If he is older than they are he develops very much the same as an elder brother close to a younger sister. Differences in age, in the affection of the parents, and in the preparation for life, are all reflected in the individual pattern of behavior.

Where a female majority and feminine influence dominates the whole environment, a single boy is likely to have a goal of superiority and a style of life which are directed towards femininity. This occurs in various degrees and various ways: in a humble devotion to women and worship of them, in an imitative attitude, tending towards homosexuality, or in a tyrannical attitude towards women. People usually avoid educating boys in a too feminine environment; for it seems to be a matter of general experience that such children develop towards one of two extremes—either exaggerated vanity or audacity. In the story of Achilles there are many points from which we may assume that the latter case was well understood in antiquity.

## IMPORTANCE OF EVALUATION OF WOMEN AND MEN

We find the same contradictory possibilities in the cases of only girls who grow up among boys or in a wholly masculine environment. In such circumstances a girl may, of course, be spoiled with too much attention and affection; but she may also adopt boys' attitudes and wish to avoid looking like a girl. In any case, what happens is largely dependent upon how men and women are *valued* in the environment. In every environment there is always a prevailing attitude of mind in regard to this question; and it is largely in accordance with the relative value given to men and women in that attitude that the child will wish to assume the role of a man or of a woman.

Other views of like which prevail in the family may also influence the pattern of a child's behavior, or bring it into difficulties, as for example the superstition about character being inherited, and the belief in fancy methods of education. Any exaggerated method of education is likely to cause injury to the child, a fact we can often trace in the children of teachers, psychologists, doctors, and people engaged in the administration of laws—policemen, lawyers, officers, and clergymen. Such educational exaggerations often come to light in the life-histories of problem-children, delinquents, and neurotics. The influence of both factors—the superstition regarding heredity and a fanatical mode of training—appear in the following case:

A woman came to me with a daughter of nine, both of them in tears and desperation. The mother told me that the girl had only recently come to live with her, after having spent years under the care of foster parents in the country. There she had completed the third grade of her schooling, and she had entered the fourth grade in the city school, but her work had become still worse, and she was graded still lower and put in the second. The mother was thoroughly upset at this and obsessed with the idea that her daughter's deficiency was inherited from the father.

At first sight it was evident to me that the mother was treating the child with exaggerated educational insistence, which in this case was particularly unfortunate, because the girl had been brought up in a congenial, easy environment and expected still greater kindness from the mother. But in her eagerness that her child should not be a failure the mother was overstrict, and this gave the child the keenest disappointment. She developed a great emotional tension which effectually blocked her progress both at school and at home. Exhortation, reproaches, criticism, and spanking only intensified the emotion, with consequent hopelessness on both sides. To confirm my impression, I spoke with the girl alone about her foster parents. She told me how happy her life with them had been; and then, bursting into tears, told me also how she had at first enjoyed being with her mother.

I had to make the mother understand the mistakes in which she had become involved. The girl could not be expected to put up with such a hard training. Putting myself in her place I could perfectly understand her conduct as an intelligent reaction—that is, as a form of accusation and revenge. In a situation of this type, but where there is less social feeling, it is perfectly possible for a child to turn delinquent, neurotic, or even to attempt suicide. But in this case I was sure it would not be difficult for the girl to improve if the mother could be convinced of the truth, and could impress the child with a sufficiently definite change of attitude. I therefore took the mother in hand, and explained to her that the belief in inheritance was nothing but a nuisance, after which I helped her to realize what her daughter had not unreasonably expected when she came to live with her, and how she must have been disappointed and shaken by such disciplinary treatment, to the point of utter inability to do what was expected of her. I wanted the mother to confess to the child that she had been mistaken and would like to reform her method, so I told her I did not really believe she could bring herself to do it, but that it was what I would do in the circumstances. She answered decidedly, "I will do it." In my presence and with my help, she explained her mistake to the child, and they kissed and embraced and cried together. Two weeks later they both visited me, gay and smiling and very well satisfied. The mother brought me a message from the third-grade teacher: "a miracle must have happened. The girl is the best pupil in the class."

# 8

# On the Essence and Origin of Character
## An Introduction

JAMES ROBERT BITTER

In September 1929, Agostino Gemelli, an Italian psychiatrist/psychologist, presented a paper to the Italian Society for the Progress of Science, an article later published, according to Gemelli's abstractor Steven Skelton (cited in Adler, 1935/1988), in the *Acts of the Italian Society for the Progress of Science*. Gemelli sought to articulate a comprehensive model of personality that encompassed "biological, sociological, psychiatric, and psychological perspectives" (Adler, 1935/1988, p. 424). While apparently offering a bit of praise for psychoanalysis, which in his response clearly irritates Adler, Gemelli's article generally rejects a causal-mechanistic understanding of humanity in favor of the holistic-teleological orientation shared by Individual Psychology. In Gemelli's model, human beings *acquire* and use character traits rather than *have* them—and these traits are "variable, and amenable to change or correction" (p. 424). Even though Gemelli's ideas were developed at the same time— and in much the same way—that Adler was developing Individual Psychology, he was apparently unaware of Adler's work when he first presented his paper. Adler responds some 6 years later in 1935 in an effort to both honor the man and his work and to clearly delineate the philosophical foundations for Individual Psychology.

In his afterword, Adler (1935/1988) emphasizes the following positions:

- There is a unity to the human personality that is best understood in terms of the individual's movement toward or away from others and by the life-goal each person chooses;
- Human character is a systemic construct; individuals develop character in relation to others and within the social contexts of their lives;

- Individual character is neither inherited nor absorbed; it is self-constructed in relation to the tasks of life (Gemelli's "tasks of character-ology") that the individual sets before him or herself;
- The community feeling (*Gemeinschaftsgefuhl*) and its action line social interest (Ansbacher, 1992), are the determining factors in the development of character and in living a good and productive life.

In the more than 70 years since Adler's death, the fields of psychiatry, psychology, counseling, and social work have moved increasingly away from the reductionistic/mechanistic conceptualizations that originally characterized Freud's (1914/1995) model—and that briefly reemerged in the structural-strategic systemic models of the 1970s (see Bitter, 2009). The systemic holism that was a foundation for Adler's understanding of human nature is today reflected in almost all aspects of the helping professions as well as the psychologies that support them.

## THE UNITY OF THE PERSONALITY

> Every individual is, so to speak, a crystallized unity-become-flesh in the whole evolutionary striving for perfection, with all its mistakes and preferences. (Adler, 1935/1988, p. 426)

Adler is writing less than 2 years before the end of his life. From his earliest formulations, he has authored a growth model for psychology, one that sees human beings as whole entities, striving for an improved and better position in life. It is a teleological perspective: Human beings self-select goals toward which they move, and it is each individual's style of movement that becomes one's character. Of all the possible goals that a person might posit, it is a life-goal that anticipates perfection, self-actualization, and/or fulfillment that brings unity to the personality. With the formulation of a life-goal, every thought, feeling, action, trait or part, belief, conviction, and decision can be best understood as part of the individual's movement toward that goal, as an expression of one's style of living.

This conceptualization of a unified movement toward the future permeates many of the models that constitute modern and postmodern approaches to psychotherapy. It was the foundation for Maslow's hierarchy of needs (Hoffman, 1988), and the overall development of what came to be called humanistic psychology. Such unified movement is evident, for example, in the later developments of Person-Centered Therapy (Rogers, 1961/1995, 1980), Existential Therapy (Bugental, 1992, 1999; May, 1953), and Reality Therapy (Glasser, 1999).

Erv and Miriam Polster (1974) expanded Fritz Perl's (Perls, Hefferline, & Goodman, 1951/1994) emphasis on the *here and now* to include the *there and then*, noting that every moment in the present has a foundation in those moments which precede it. Erv Polster (1987) went on to develop the notion of *tight thera-peutic sequences* and the anticipation in the present of *the next*, thus creating a therapeutic intervention in human movement. There is always a unification of personality in this movement toward the future; even in his delineation and therapeutic use of parts, Polster (1995/2005) recognizes that there is the person, the self, that contains and uses these parts with definite purpose.

Adler (1927/1965) initially defined human development as a movement from a felt minus position (inferiority feelings) to a felt plus position. To be sure, such movement is the basis for all of the growth orientations associated with human-istic psychology as well as those postmodern models that focus on *preferred out-comes*, that is, solution-focused/solution-oriented therapy (Walter & Peller, 2000) and narrative therapy (White & Epston, 1990; White, 2005).

Rasmussen (2005, 2010) makes the most use of Adler's concept of movement when he merges Adlerian psychology with Millon's (1990, 1996, 1999) evolu-tionary psychology. Rasmussen and Millon describe human personality, includ-ing pathological processes, as at once *protective* (Adler's, 1996a, 1996b, concept of *retreat*) and anticipatory of desired outcomes: again, movement from a felt-minus to a felt-plus. Adler (1935/1988) clearly anticipates the development of evolutionary psychology: "Characterology can, therefore, only be an investiga-tion into the relationship of the individual to the entire evolutionary process of life" (p. 426).

## SYSTEMIC THEORY

> The character cannot be separated from social reference (*Soziale Bezogenheit*). Character does not exist in a vacuum. Properly understood, every character trait shows the degree of the capacity for cooperation, coexistence, and common inter-est (*Mitarbeit, Mitleben, Mitlieben*). (Adler, 1935/1988, p. 425)

Although Adler does not develop further his systemic understanding of individ-uals and families in this article, his earlier works (Adler, 1927/1965; Ansbacher & Ansbacher, 1956) literally lay the foundation for the development of systemic the-ory some 40 to 50 years later. The initial incorporation of general systems theory into psychotherapy all but dismissed the importance of the individual (see Bitter, 2009). Because Adler started with a focus on the individual, he also anticipated and proposed a solution for the integration of the individual and the system, a unification that would not be sought again until the 1980s. Adler's phenomeno-logical approach to family constellation and birth order, culture and gender, and purposeful, relational sequences places the perceiving individual at the heart of living systems. In this sense, each individual both affects these systems and is affected by them. The individual is both a changer and the changed. We under-stand each person by the way in which she or he manifests personal living within the systemic, cultural contexts of one's life, a perspective most thoroughly and therapeutically explored today within the postmodern approach called Narrative Therapy (White, 2005).

## CHARACTER AND THE TASKS OF LIFE

> What Individual Psychology has to say, perhaps only explanatorily but certainly surprisingly, about Gemelli's "Tasks of Characterology" ("*Aufgaben der Charakterologie*") is that it gives an essence of the character which is neither inborn nor acquired. What we call character is the outward manifestation of the relationship of a person to a task postulated by him (sic). (Adler, 1935/1988, p. 425)

Adler's response does not describe the nature of Gemelli's *tasks of characterology*, but by the time his response was published, Adler had clearly defined his own universal tasks of life. His response suggests that both he and Gemelli regard character as something one chooses ("neither inborn nor acquired") and then enacts, a stance that people take in relation to the demands and challenges that occur in life.

Adler's three tasks were, from the beginning, based on an evolutionary perspective. Early humans, he noted, were too weak to survive individually, lacking sharp claws, speed, enhanced eyesight or hearing, and especially great size and strength. Like similarly incapacitated animals, humans formed into a herd or community for protection, a communal task that could be accomplished only if its members developed the capacity for cooperation and friendship. This is Adler's social task. It was this same evolutionary demand for cooperation that also required a division of labor; shared work and contribution made the survival of many possible: The growth of all was contained in the efforts of each individual. Adler posited the work task as the avenue for personal meaning: The meaning of life is contribution to the whole. Adler's task of intimacy includes the recognition that the human species is made up of two genders, men and women, and for the species to procreate and continue, both sexes have to learn to cooperate and to get along with each other.

Character, Adler believed, was developed in the stance that each person took in relation to these universal tasks of life. Effective living required a social resolution to the life-demands that each person must face. In this sense, mental health and human contact have always been linked. Indeed, psychopathology almost always involves some form of self-absorption and a retreat from human connection (Adler, 1996a, 1996b). Impairment in social and occupational functioning is today at the center of determining most clinical disorders (American Psychiatric Association, 2000).

Both modern and postmodern approaches to assessment and therapy recognize problems as a part of life: Life without problems is a myth. The current debate about whether psychological problems emanate from within (genetic or chemical) or are manifested in one's response to life's challenges has long been resolved in non-psychiatric clinical practice.[14] In therapeutic applications, practitioners approach their clients with the same optimism that was inherent in the positions of Adler and Gemelli—that is, with a belief that personality (or character) traits are "acquired, variable, and amenable to change or correction" (Adler, 1935/1988, p. 424). Whether therapy is based on cognitive-behavioral interventions, humanistic psychology, or postmodern therapies, the basis for change lies in the belief that the problem is not the problem; coping, one's stance, is the problem. How one chooses to cope is both the essence and origin of character.

## COMMUNITY FEELING AND SOCIAL INTEREST

[C]haracter, moreover, corresponds to the degree of its social interest, whose ideal measuring stick is nothing else but the goal of an ideal attitude (Verhalten) toward the welfare of all humanity and toward eternity. (Adler, 1935/1988, p. 425)

Adler's community feeling has long been associated in the literature of Individual Psychology with mental health. It is an umbrella-term that includes a sense of connectedness to all of humankind, past, present, and future. It contains the evolutionary need to belong and manifests itself in cooperation, courage, contribution, caring and empathy, and compassion and engagement. Ansbacher (1992) called social interest the *action line* of community feeling. It is the way in which the community feeling is enacted in real life. In Adler's response to Gemelli (1935/1988), he suggests that the quality of one's character is directly related to the amount of social interest enacted in one's life.

As noted earlier, Adler's response to Gemelli was published just 2 years before the end of Adler's life. His concepts of community feeling and social interest had evolved, and he was envisioning these concepts as central to the idea of perfection and the actualization of human potential: "Whatever one calls right, valuable, normal, or reasonable derives its worth from the idea of the perfection of the human race and from the idea of a claim for eternity" (p. 425). By over 80 years, Adler is anticipating the importance of spirituality within the psychological sphere. What is good for one must be good for all. Mental health, the soundness of character, and, indeed, the quality of daily living are all enhanced through a common striving for the greater good and for the well-being of humanity. In 1975, the eminent Canadian researcher of stress, Hans Selye, would echo Adler's emphasis on community feeling and social interest: The way to handle stress

---

[14] Even within the psychiatric profession, the chemical treatment of mental disorders is being successfully challenged (see Breggin, 1994, 2009; Glasser, 2004).

without turning it into distress, he would suggest, is to live each day in such a way as to earn your neighbor's love.

Still, Adler is suggesting something greater than the golden rule; he is calling on individuals to imagine and seek in their everyday actions the perfection and completion of human potential, to be more fully human and to be connected with all that there is. Spirituality provides individuals with the experience of bringing a connection to the whole of life into the present. It connects us to all that has gone before and all that may be ahead of us. It allows people to be both fully present and in the process of becoming at the same time. Toward the end of his life as well as the end of his response to Gemelli, Adler (1935/1988) infuses human experience with a call to aim for perfection, to take human growth to its farthest limit: "Characterology can, therefore, only be an investigation into the relationship of the individual to the entire evolutionary process of life" (p. 426).

## CONCLUSION

This introduction is longer than Adler's original article. His response to Gemelli is packed with ideas that represent a lifetime's work. I have attempted to unpack these ideas for consideration in the present, in the 21st century. Adler's concepts were not only central to the development of Individual Psychology; they would also eventually serve as the foundation for both modern and postmodern approaches to psychotherapy. In his response to Gemelli, Adler reminds us that there is a unity to the individual and that personality and character are the result of the stances taken in relation to universal tasks in life. He provides guideposts for assessing both effective living and pathological dysfunction. Most importantly, he suggests that the humanity we dream for the world is possible now.

## REFERENCES

Adler, A. (1965). *Understanding human nature* (W. B. Wolfe, Trans.). New York: Fawcett. (Original work published 1927)

Adler, A. (1988). On the essence and origin of character. *Individual Psychology, 44*(4), 424–426. (Original work published 1935)

Adler, A. (1996a). The structure of neurosis. *Individual Psychology, 52*(4), 351–362. (Original work published 1935)

Adler, A. (1996b). What is neurosis? *Individual Psychology, 52*(4), 318–333. (Original work published 1935)

American Psychiatric Association. (2000). *Diagnostic and statistical manual of mental disorders* (4th ed., text rev.) [*DSM-IV-TR*]. Washington, DC: Author.

Ansbacher, H. L. (1992). Alfred Adler's concept of community feeling and of social interest and the relevance of community feeling for old age. *Individual Psychology, 48*(4), 402–412.

Bitter, J. R. (2009). *Theory and practice of family therapy and counseling.* Belmont, CA: Brooks/Cole-Cengage.

Breggin, P. (1994). *Toxic psychiatry: Why therapy, empathy, and love must replace the drugs, electroshock, and biochemical theories of the "new psychiatry."* New York: St. Martin's Press.

Breggin, P. (2009). *Medication madness: The role of psychiatric drugs in cases of violence, suicide, and crime.* New York: St. Martin's Press.

Bugental, J. A. (1992). *The art of the psychotherapist: How to develop the skills that take psychotherapy beyond science.* New York: Norton.

Bugental, J. F. T. (1999). *Psychotherapy isn't what you think: Bringing the psychotherapeutic engagement into the living moment.* Phoenix, AZ: Zeig, Tucker & Theisen.

Freud, S. (1995). *The basic writings of Sigmund Freud* (A. A. Brill, Trans.). New York: Modern Library. (Original work published 1914)

Gemelli, A. (1935). Uber das Wesen und die Enstehung des Character [On the essence and origin of character]. *Internationale Zeitschrift fur Individual-psychologie, 13*, 29–30.

Glasser, W. (1999). *Choice theory: A new psychology of personal freedom.* New York: Harper.

Glasser, W. (2004). *Warning: Psychiatry can be hazardous to your mental health.* New York: Harper.

Hoffman, E. (1988). *The right to be human: A biography of Abraham Maslow.* Los Angeles: Tarcher.

May, R. (1953). *Man's search for himself.* New York: Norton.

Millon, T. (1990). *Toward a new personology: An evolutionary model.* New York: Wiley.

Millon, T. (1996). *Personality and psychopathology: Building a clinical science.* New York: Wiley-Interscience.

Millon, T. (1999). *Personality-guided therapy.* New York: Wiley.

Perls, F., Hefferline, R., & Goodman, P. (1994). *Gestalt therapy: Excitement and growth in the human personality.* Gouldsboro, ME: Gestalt Journal Press. (Original work published 1951)

Polster, E. (1987). *Every person's life is worth a novel.* Highland, NY: Gestalt Journal Press.

Polster, E. (2005). *A population of selves: A therapeutic exploration of personal diversity.* Gouldsboro, ME: Gestalt Journal Press. (Original work published 1995)

Polster, E., & Polster, M. (1974). *Gestalt therapy integrated.* New York: Vintage.

Rasmussen, P. R. (2003). Emotional reorientation: A clinical strategy. *Journal of Individual Psychology, 59*(3), 345–359.

Rasmussen, P. R. (2005). *Personality-guided cognitive-behavioral therapy.* Washington, DC: American Psychological Association.

Rasmussen, P. R. (2010). *The quest to feel good.* New York: Taylor & Francis.

Rogers, C. R. (1980). *A way of being.* New York: Houghton/Mifflin.

Rogers, C. R. (1995). *On becoming a person.* New York: Mariner. (Original work published 1961)

Selye, H. (1975). *Stress without distress: How to use stress as a positive force to achieve a rewarding life style.* New York: Signet.

Walter, J., & Peller, J. (2000). *Recreating brief therapy: Preferences and possibilities.* New York: Norton.

White, M. (2007). *Maps of narrative practice.* New York: Norton.

White, M., & Epston, D. (1990). *Narrative means to therapeutic ends.* New York: Norton.

## On the Essence and Origin of Character[15]

### *Alfred Adler*

"On the Essence and Origin of Character" by Father Agostino Gemelli, O.F.M.—This is a German translation of an article appearing in the *Acts of the Italian Society for the Progress of Science*, reporting on meetings of September 1929.

A historical review is given of the modern approaches to the understanding of human personality, as presented from biological, sociological, psychiatric, and psychological perspectives. It is mostly German authorities who are reviewed. Professor Gemelli rejects those views that are mechanistic and conceived of as cause-and-effect. He defends those views that recognize personality traits as acquired, variable, and amenable to change or correction. He is interested in developing a comprehensive philosophical interpretation of the problems and expressions of personality that is, at the same time, teleological, of practical value in therapy, and in harmony with a recognition of biological evolution. —Steven Skelton, Abstractor

## ADLER'S AFTERWORD TO GEMELLI'S ARTICLE

The work of the worthy and conscientious scientific researcher, Professor Gemelli, deserves a thorough assessment, not least because it appeared some years ago and thus did not take into consideration the clear presentation of Individual Psychology, which has taken place since that time.

It must be granted that the honored author stands at the very top among modern psychologists and psychiatrists. His conception, shared concurrently by Individual Psychology, that the personality of the normal as well as the abnormal person (and, along with that, what is commonly called the character), shows how imbued his theory is with a measure of the feeling of community (*Gemeinschaftsgefuhl*) with the ultimate conception of the human psychic life, with the fact of the unity of the personality. His fundamental viewpoints draw his theory entirely into the neighborhood of Individual Psychology.

His partial praise for psychoanalysis we do not share. What it could offer to the above-mentioned viewpoints does not fit in with its causal-mechanistic view, and in spite of its many borrowings from the areas of Individual Psychology, one often gets the impression that a foreign headpiece is adorning a body of an entirely different sort. After all, we must observe, too, that Freud's inroad was into the antiquated psychology of utility (*Psychologie von Nutzen*) and that he was on the path that Individual Psychology developed. That he, for the sake of an untenable theory, because of an idea of

---

[15] Translation by Michael Cicero.

pansexualism, developed a causal-mechanistic view; that he became a slave to the heredity theory; that he interpreted degenerations of the coddled life-style (*des verzartelten Lebenstils*) as the norm of the psyche and viewed the fact of social interest (*des Sozialen Interesses*) as a cunning weakness (*listige Schwache*); that he imparted the ego-character (*Ichcharakter*) to each of his artificial, psychic categories, without comprehending the shaping unity (*gestaltende Einheit*) of the ego; these things separate him from Individual Psychology, to which, however, he owes many of the viewpoints of his later research.

What Individual Psychology has to say, perhaps only explanatorily but certainly surprisingly, about Gemelli's "Tasks of Characterology" ("*Aufgaben der Charakterlolgie*") is that it gives an essence of the character which is neither inborn nor acquired. What we call character is the outward manifestation of the relationship of a person to a task postulated by him. The character cannot be separated from social reference (*Soziale Bezogenheit*). Character does not exist in a vacuum. Properly understood, every character trait shows the degree of the capacity for cooperation, coexistence, and common interest (*Mitarbeit, Mitleben, Mitlieben*). This degree is imparted to it by the unity of the ego. That the degree of activity reveals itself in the character, moreover, corresponds to the degree of its social interest, whose ideal measuring stick can be nothing else but the goal of an ideal attitude (*Verhalten*) toward the welfare of all humanity and toward eternity. I have always emphasized that controversy is possible on this matter. But whatever one calls right, valuable, normal, or reasonable derives its worth from the idea of the perfection of the human race and from the idea of a claim for eternity.

This conception has its biological foundation in the overall structure of life. Every individual is, so to speak, a crystallized unity-become-flesh in the whole evolutionary striving for perfection, with all its mistakes and preferences. Characterology can, therefore, only be an investigation into the relationship of the individual to the entire evolutionary process of life. Along this path of our investigations, it is a happy occurrence to encounter the investigations of Gemelli.

# 9

# Character and Talent

## Frank Main

Alfred Adler made his second visit to the United States in 1927, and it coincided with the launch of his new book, *Understanding Human Nature* (Adler, 1927). That same year, he also published "Character and Talent" (Adler, 1927) in *Harper's Magazine*. The magazine of poets and presidents enjoyed a celebrated tradition as the literary launching pad for eminent artists, philosophers, writers, and scientists. Indeed, Adler shared the pages of the June 1927 issue with the likes of Will Durant. Durant, like Adler, had also just published an important book, *The Story of Philosophy* (Durant, 1926).

In a later issue also published in 1927, the man who coined the term *behaviorism*, John B. Watson, published an article titled "The Behaviorist Looks at Instincts" (Watson, 1927). It is not surprising, then, that Adler published this article joining the ongoing nature-versus-nurture controversy over the origins of creativity and talent.

"Character and Talent" was republished with *Harper's* permission in the *Journal of Individual Psychology* under the "Classics Column" edited by Harold Mosak (Adler, 1989). In his introduction, Mosak established Alder's primary intent: "It is the latter theme which Adler develops in 'Character and Talent,' that the creativity of the individual is more decisive than either heredity or environment in shaping the organization of the personality—the Life-style'" (Adler, 1989, pp. 513–514). There is no doubt this was Adler's primary mission, and his language is emotionally charged to communicate the urgency he believed the topic required:

> The thesis advanced by the group of psychological thinkers known as the Individual Psychologists—the thesis that talent is not inherited, and that the possibilities and potentialities of any individual for performance are not fixed—has been a *bombshell* [italics mine] in a camp of the old-line academic psychologists. (Adler, 1927, p. 64)

Adler then presents case-based exceptions to the deterministic reduction of intellectual, artistic, and musical talent:

> And here again we are back at the problem of hereditary faculties and talents. And again I must deny that heredity has a great deal to do with accomplishment or performance. It is not true that with heredity the last word is said, that the chromosomes are inexorable determinants of subsequent genius. (Adler, 1927, p. 67)

Adler offers a remarkable observation; he recognizes that the father of modern intelligence testing (Alfred Binet) came to recognize that although there were high correlations between higher scores and higher body weight and better health, these things were not causally related to exceptionality. Adler also appears to make the distinction between Binet's more constructivist understandings and the more deterministic conceptualizations developed by Lewis Terman at Stanford (Siegler, 1992).

Since Adler's article was republished in the *Journal of Individual Psychology* two decades ago, research has evolved on two fronts. Both of these lines of investigation seem to affirm a number of Adler's clinical and anecdotal conceptualizations.

First, Adler believed that predicting exceptional performance based on early assignment of a number to a child's potential intellectual capacity was not predictive or helpful. His objections to this deterministic prescription seem to be corroborated by contemporary research. Recently, Gladwell (2008) offered quantitative and qualitative data suggesting that in most cases exceptional performance can't be accounted for by talent alone when early measures of the talent in question are assessed as approximately equal.

Indeed, Gladwell assembles a compelling case for the more predictive elements of opportunity, practice, intelligence thresholds, and work ethic. Gladwell's investigations examine talents that include math, music, and computer programming skills.

Gladwell also addressed aptitude assessment through ACT and SAT test scores. The University of Michigan's admissions policy faced a legal suit when plaintiffs challenged the university's admissions policies that granted admission to minority students who earned test scores lower than those of their White counterparts. In response, the university determined, via extensive follow-up studies, that minority students did every bit as well (Gladwell, 2008). In this case *opportunity* seemed to be the sole equalizing factor.

Similarly, Geoff Colvin (2008) entered the fray with a more general condemnation of the very notion of "talent." As he probes the concept of talent, he offers the following:

> A few contend that the very existence of talent is not, as they carefully put it, supported by evidence . . . as the English music study mentioned earlier. In these studies, all the subjects are people of whom we'd say, "They're very talented." Yet, over and over, the researchers found few signs of precocious achievement before the individuals started intensive training. (p. 23)

Although Colvin's disqualification of the importance of talent was for the purposes of extolling the significance of "deliberate practice," it was also anchored in much of the same research that calls into question the notion of "natural," genetically determined talent.

Finally, and perhaps of greater significance, Adler sets forth the notion that heredity and environment do not constitute determining mental variables of either the mind or the developing lifestyle of the child. Indeed, Adler makes a powerful case for the child's internal *creative power*, which is central to the tenets of Individual Psychology:

> Our objection to the teachings of the hereditarians and every other tendency to overstress the significance of constitutional disposition, is that the important thing is not what one is born with, but what use one makes of that equipment. (Ansbacher, 1964, p. 86)

It is in this regard that Adler's conceptualizations about development of the lifestyle or thinking processes and mental development are perhaps most startling. Through case histories and his medical diagnostic skills, Adler inferred and named internal workings of the brain which he described as *creative power*. Adler believed this third element, *creative power*, brought to bear interactional experiences with others in concert with *reflections* upon early experiences. Recent research by Dr. Daniel Siegel (2007) seems to suggest that the interactions of heredity, experience, and emotional/relational contexts create unique and lasting pathways of thought. Siegel and others have attempted to deconstruct the components of these mental processes that give birth to a child's unique interpretations of circumstances.

Adler's early hypotheses seem to be generally affirmed, extended, and refined through Siegel's painstaking research. While Adler's early thinking is affirmed in the work of Siegel and others, it is certain to evolve. Undoubtedly empirical identification of specific emotional and cognitive linkages is on the horizon. Eventually, we may understand how early recollections and cognitions specifically formulate the child's worldview and style of living.

## REFERENCES

Adler, A. (1927, June). Character and talent. *Harper's Magazine, 155,* 64–72.

Adler, A. (1989). Character and talent. *Individual Psychology, 45*(4), 514–526.

Adler, A. (1927). *Understanding human nature*. New York: Greenberg.

Ansbacher, H. L., & Ansbacher, R. R. (Eds.). (1964). *Superiority and social interest*. New York: Norton.

Colvin, G. (2008). *Talent is overrated*. New York: Penguin.

Durant, W. (1926). *The story of philosophy*. New York: Simon and Schuster.

Gladwell, M. (2008). *Outliers: The story of success*. New York: Little, Brown and Company.

Siegel, D. J. (2007). *The mindful brain*. New York: Norton.

Siegler, R. S. (1992). The other Alfred Binet. *Developmental Psychology, 28*(2), 179–190.

Watson, J. B. (1927, August). The behaviorist looks at instincts. *Harper's Magazine, 155,* 228–235.

## Character and Talent[16]

*Alfred Adler, MD*

**I**

The thesis advanced by the group of psychological thinkers known as the Individual Psychologists—the thesis that talent is not inherited, and that the possibilities and potentialities of any individual for performance are not fixed—has been a bombshell in the camp of the old-line academic talent, potentiality, endowment, special gifts are merely elements in the structure of an individual. It has been shown, further, that these elements may be variously employed, depending upon their relation to the total activity of the individual.

The Individual Psychologists have decided to understand the totality of the individual before regarding the partial phenomena of his existence. They hold that a partial phenomenon, such as a talent, a gift, an endowment, can be properly evaluated and properly understood only when the total is first known and thoroughly understood. In other words, we can judge the potential performance of an individual in some specific situation only when we can determine his total reactions, his total behavior pattern, his general style of life, his "distance" from the normal goal of life.

An example will show you how valueless any other viewpoint than that of Individual Psychology becomes in the face of an actual problem. Consider the case of a thirteen-year-old boy who gives the general impression of a backward, mentally retarded, neglected child. He has not made the usual progress at school, has been forced to repeat several grades, and is brought to a social agency because of thievery and vagabondage. The reports concerning this boy are uniformly bad. He is irritable, unsocial, has a poor memory, is unable to concentrate, inattentive. These reports are the results of psychological tests as well as the schoolroom experiences of his various teachers, Closer study of his character and history shows that he was the younger of two children for some eight years, during which time he was inordinately spoiled by his mother. Then his younger brother was born, and at the same time financial difficulties occurred in this family, with the result that the mother had to leave the home to help earn a living. The net result was that the boy began to receive far less attention and love than he had previously been accustomed to experiencing.

School, therefore, found him in an entirely new situation. His thievery occurred chiefly outside of his own home; but everything that he gained by stealing he gave away as presents to other children, in order to gain their

---

[16] Translation by Walter Beran Wolfe, MD.

friendship and affection. You can see by this that one cannot make final conclusions when one brands a child as a "thief."

We next learn that this child often ran away from home when his father was particularly brutal to him, but that he always managed to deposit a bundle of stolen kindling on the doorstep for his mother to cook with. This done, he spent the nights in the streets, sleeping in alleyways or old barns.

We can hardly evaluate this "truancy" or "delinquency" according to the timeworn conceptions. It is quite evident that his thievery is more than mere stealing, and his truancy more than running away from school. And we must call attention here to the inadequacy of branding the actions of an individual with some set label and then believing that we have understood him!

This "delinquency" and this "thievery" mean something different. It is as though this boy were saying, "I want to force my parents into a situation in which they will pay more attention to me, love me more, sympathize with me. I can best do this by showing my mother that I care for her needs!"

I should like to ask whether there is anyone who could suggest to a boy like this, for whom normal activity in the schoolroom seems hopelessly distant because of his bad preparation for life, a better method of winning the affection and love of his parents and school friends than he has chosen? I shall later show why this normal activity seems to him so impossible of realization. For the present I simply want to indicate that we cannot call such a child "delinquent," "criminal," or "backward." If we want to characterize this boy, we could say that he is a child who demands and needs an inordinate amount of mother love. That this boy seeks for this affection in an asocial way, which he does not particularly like, is due to the fact that the normal approach to his goal seems to him effectually barred by circumstances. The normal paths to affection would be industry and progress in school, giving pleasure to his parents and teachers by helpfulness, attention to work, etc. But we have already heard that he was a spoiled child. It is the characteristic of all spoiled children that they cannot change the behavior pattern which they have developed as a result of being spoiled. It is their tragedy. A child has formed and shaped his behavior pattern at the end of his third year of life. A change in the nature of his character as a result of external influences seldom occurs thereafter. Particularly in the case of a child with the behavior pattern of the spoiled child. Such a child never learns from experience. His experiences, good and bad, are all assimilated into his pattern. He takes an experience and twists, turns, distorts, reshapes it until it fits into his predetermined scheme of things.

Naturally, he does not want to go to school, because the warmth and affection which he is used to is found in greater abundance at home. As a result, he comes to school on the first day against his will, and resistant to all attempts at instruction. His teachers will say that he is inattentive, lacks concentration, day-dreams, spoils the games of other children, cannot concentrate, has a bad memory. All these things are explained when we know that he has an entirely different goal in life than that of a normal schoolboy. The truth is that our boy finds himself in a new situation for which he was never adequately prepared. And in this situation occurs the tragedy of the petted child. He is always right! Since he does not play the game in school, school becomes a very unpleasant place for him. To make matters worse, he now finds his home also unpleasant. Bad school reports turn his mother against him. She does not show her love and affection to the same degree as before. The child blames the school for his misfortune at home, but he does not change his style of life. Love and affection he must have. He seeks it in other places, and with other means.

Enough for our example. It proves very simply that when someone characterizes an individual with a definite character trait we really know nothing about him. We are in much the same situation as a musician who is asked for his opinion of a symphony after hearing three chords. But let the musician be acquainted with musical history, play him a simple melody, and he will be able to say "That is Bach!" or "That is Wagner!" We cannot judge a personality unless we have its dominant motif unless we understand it as a totality.

## II

The Individual Psychologists have also shown that the development of a personality cannot be foretold from the phenomena of physical inheritance. The inherited instruments with which we fight the battle of life are very varied. *How we use these instruments*, however, is the important thing.

We can never tell what actions will characterize a man if we know only whence he comes. But if we know whither he is going we can prophesy his steps and movements toward his objective. It is for this reason that we have found the concept of goal-attainment, of goal-appropriateness, the essential one for the understanding of human behavior.

In the case of our boy, knowing that his purpose in life is to achieve warmth and affection, we can understand the means that he will choose toward that end. And we know also what our therapeutic approach must be, for we understand the tragedy of this child's life. Suppose, for instance, that we could discover that the father and the grandfather of this child were thieves also. This would in no way be responsible for the activity of this particular boy. To be sure, it is interesting to know just why the boy should choose thievery as a means to gaining love and affection. This point must be cleared up in order to rule out a possible hereditary influence. But we shall clear up this point, too.

In the earliest remembrances of childhood we often find the key to later activities. Among this boy's earliest remembrances is the following: He recollects that he was present at the burning of a delivery truck. The men on the truck threw many rubber balls out on the street, in order to save them from the fire. Children and adults who had gathered about the burning delivery truck seized upon these balls as the acknowledged booty of the onlookers. Nobody seemed to have any scruples about helping himself to this property. This remembrance served the boy as a model, as a training, if you will, for his future career as a thief. He found that there were, so to speak, extenuating circumstances even in thievery. Later, when the normal development of a child seemed barred to him, he chose the way to enrichment and power for which this scene had prepared him.

A word now about his development in school. In kindergarten things went rather well. He had a very tender, loving teacher, who was not unlike his mother. But in the primary grades he met a very strict and stern teacher—and he immediately withdrew into himself, failed miserably in class, and resigned himself to the conduct mentioned above as a protest.

The great majority of our opponents stand on the theory that the really important factors in the development of a character or personality are hereditary and congenital. These opponents are always anxious to show that subsequent developmental "trends" modify the result. In support of this theory they often make very keen observations, as for instance Kretschmer and his school. We do not deny the findings of Kretschmer; in fact, we have anticipated them long ago when we stated that if an individual gets off to a bad start in life, by reason of congenital defects or hereditary anomalies, it requires an extraordinary beneficent environment to prevent him from developing a warped style of life. Lacking this beneficent influence of a fostering environment, the individual assumes a false and unwholesome behavior pattern which fits perfectly with his defectively developed physique, his inadequate endocrines, his sickly habitus. He is just like a man on a slippery incline: if he falls and sprains his ankle it is not to be wondered at. But wondering is not enough. We must attempt to keep him erect, and actually that is what we have succeeded in doing.

## III

What I have said about the development of character holds also for the question of talent. In discussing this question I rule out those individuals whose equipment is so woefully inadequate as hardly to come under consideration. I mean the congenital idiots and imbeciles whose condition is actually due to a failure of organic development, to enormous defects in the actual nervous substance of their brains.

There remain, however, the great majority of children and adults, who have the materials but have not developed them to the full extent. Is it absolutely impossible for such people to render a good performance with relatively poor tools? In the early days of our human race were there not accomplishments which could be compared with ours of to-day, even though our forefathers lacked our developed technic and worked with poor instruments? Are we capable of imitating to-day what the old guild workers accomplished with relatively poor tools? Of course we are!

And here we are back at the problem of hereditary faculties and talents. And again I must deny that heredity has a great deal to do with accomplishment or performance. It is not true that with heredity the last word is said, that the chromosomes are inexorable determinants of subsequent genius. In fact, it is probable that an organism equipped with deficient organs, with inadequate tools, will actually develop a better and more ingenious technic to combat the rigors of its environment. Such an organism will pay a great deal of attention to detail, will devise more unerring "short-cuts," will undergo a more intensive training. This brings us to the surprising, the terrifying conclusion of reality. The great accomplishments, the really worthwhile achievements, have been made by individuals whose equipment was poor.

Normal individuals with normal organs approach the normal adjustments of everyday life with a greater equanimity, since accomplishing these tasks seems easily within reason. They lack the tremendous tension that is characteristic of an individual who sees less clearly than his fellow, or a left-hander who is forced to work with his weaker and more poorly co-ordinated right hand. The normal individual seeks for no tricks, no legerdemain, because he can adjust without tricks and legerdemain. Try to drive a nail with a hammer. The hammer almost does it by itself, because it is an efficient instrument. But try to drive that same nail with a pair of scissors, or with a pocket-knife! You need tricks and legerdemain now, and a refinement of technic, to accomplish the same result that comes easily with a hammer.

We must come to the conclusion that it is one of the greatest advantages to an individual to be born with defective organs. That is the conclusion that we arrive at when we regard the question of heredity in a purely objective fashion, the great majority of psychologists, physicians, and laymen to the contrary notwithstanding, The average layman believes that he carries his future with him into life, like his milk teeth: a given quantum of creative ability, which need only be unpacked, so to speak, to make him a dolt or a genius. This superstition lies at the basis of the premise which so many investigators use when they say, "Let us see how far this individual has developed his native talent."

We are constantly hearing people say, "Yes, there is a definite quantum of talent given every human being!" But this is not true. What occurs is this: There is a definite human constant of talent and potentiality, but this constant remains only so long as no effort is made to develop and train it. The boy whom I discussed in the beginning of this paper certainly belonged to the "untalented." He had been forced to repeat two grades by the time he had reached the fifth grade. After treatment he became the best student in his class. The psychologist of the old school will counter, "Yes, he had a latent talent." That is precisely my point. Everyone has latent talent.

I shall cite several examples from our experience of so-called "untalented" children who developed a marked "talent." This development, however, does not take place by magic, or occur overnight. I am choosing for illustrative purposes some of the easy cases, but you must not believe that it is always so simple to make a brilliant student out of a backward child. Sometimes one succeeds easily; often it requires great effort and greater patience. In the end, however, it is always better to be able to say that one boy has talent because he was properly and encouragingly trained to overcome a defect and that another boy is untalented because this or that error was made in his education.

If we disregard professional activity for a moment and investigate, rather, very small details of child activity, we can best see the developments of talent. Take for instance a little three-year-old girl who tries to sew dresses for her dolls. She takes a few stitches which are certainly far removed from works of art, and her mother comes to her and says, "Do you know, that is a very good beginning. Now if you take a few more stitches like this" (showing the child), "then you will have a beautifully dressed doll!" Such a mother, by encouraging this child in its efforts, giving it new fields to conquer, appealing to the child's ability to do more, is preparing the way for a "talent." Contrast another mother whose three-year-old daughter makes the same clumsy stitches in a doll's dress, and is met with, "For heaven's sake, don't bother with that needle! You'll only prick yourself! Little girls can't sew dolls' dresses!" In the first case the child is encouraged to find new combinations, new colors, new models, and develops its technic because its efforts are met by encouragement and applause. The second child loses all desire for activity in which its clumsiness is held up as a cause for shame and punishment. The first develops a talent. The second will complain all her life, "I have absolutely no talent for needlework!"

An eight-year-old girl came into the office, weeping, with her mother. The latter explained that the child made no progress in school. She had come in from the country with excellent reports having finished the third grade. She was put in the fourth grade in a city school, failed, was demoted to the third grade, failed again, was finally demoted to the second grade, and was doing very poorly there. The disparity between the previous excellent reports and the present bad reports was very marked. From the standpoint of Individual Psychology the change in reports represented not a change in talent, but the substitution of a bad environment for a good one.

Investigation of the child's life disclosed the fact that until recent months she had lived in the country with foster parents. The mother had been divorced from her husband and, while trying to gain an existence by work in the city, had sent her daughter to the country. Now that she had succeeded in establishing herself financially, she had brought the child home to live with her.

From our standpoint this amounts to a psychological experiment, and the experiment in this case had been unsuccessful. The reasons for the child's failure are not hard to find. We can imagine that this child living in the country with foster parents expected that the return to her mother would be something of a triumphal entry into a promised Eden. She expected her mother to be the apotheosis of beauty, kindness, goodness. One question gives us our clue. I ask, "Did you like it out in the country with your foster parents?" The girl answers, "Yes. They were very kind to me, treated me like their own child, and bought me pretty playthings."

Now I ask the mother, "How did you receive the child, and how do you treat it?" The mother answers, "I have had a very sad life with my husband. He was an habitual drunkard, and I was afraid that the child had inherited his bad traits, and so I have tried to educate her very strictly, and prevent, if possible, the curse of drunkenness falling upon her, too!" "How do you do this?" I ask. "How does one educate a child to prevent the curse of drunkenness from showing itself?" The mother replies, "One must be very strict and severe with the child; not allow it to play with bad children, criticize all faults, punish all lies and moral failings."

Now put yourself in the child's position. This is the promised land, this is the mother from whom one expects the goodness of an angel, the beauty of motherly love! And the mother turns out to be a nagging, anxious, criticizing, punishing sort of an avenging witch.

I take the mother aside and tell her that perhaps under other circumstances her actions would be advisable, but that in this case it might be better if she attempted to win over the child to her with love and affection. "If I were in your shoes," I tell the mother, "I should go so far as to admit to the child that I had made a mistake, that I had meant well but I had followed a bad method, and that now I wish to be reconciled, and to try to forget the past and do better in the future. I know that you will not follow my advice entirely, because it requires great courage on the part of a mother to admit an error to her child, but you can at least try love and affection."

This mother, however, did have the courage. "I shall do exactly as you would do," she said. Mother and daughter were reconciled before my eyes in the midst of ceremonial tears and sobs. Fourteen days later, mother and daughter returned. The picture was entirely different. Both were laughing, both were happy. The little girl was leading her class in the third grade, and brought a note from the teacher saying that a miracle must have occurred.

We have the records of a number of similar cases. With the more complicated cases I do not wish to burden my readers, but it is precisely these most complicated cases which come into our hands, as psychiatrists. These are the cases of patients who have suffered a total shipwreck of their personality upon the rocks of somebody's prejudice and have been miseducated in their childhood. Either the individual believes he is totally untalented and unworthy, or, as frequently happens, the individual or his relatives believe that he is enormously talented, but the talent does not appear because the individual is "so nervous!"

There are hundreds of such individuals, who find themselves duty-bound to live a life of sickness and "nervousness" in order that their "talent" (which they inwardly fear does not exist) shall not rise to the surface. You can see what mischief this conception of "talent" can accomplish in a life. The paradox is that the poorly equipped man, the man who starts behind the line, has the greatest advantage. Progress and achievement result only from the conquest of difficulties. He who conquers difficulties wins.

The question of talent, particularly in America, England, and Germany where the need for trained technicians is great has reached such importance that nowadays half-grown children are tested for their "talent" for some adult profession. It is my duty to point to the fact that the most expert and highly trained experimental psychologists all make timid, unconvincing reports concerning tests of ability. All their experiments point to the fact that no well-defined, actual judgments can be rendered concerning the "talent" of an individual for any particular task. All of them agree that reality is quite different from the tests, and that one finally has to take the stand that the average man can perform the average task. The riddle really begins where we find an individual who cannot pass the tests.

## IV

What science has designated as organic defects are a very general phenomenon. No one has ever seen a normal child, and one can find some kind of organic defect in everyone. What is important is the sense of defect which the child feels because he has an inadequate organ, and more particularly, what that child's environment says about his defect. There are families who believe their children are sick if they do not weigh twice as much as normal children. As a result, a perfectly normal child grows up in an atmosphere of a chronic invalid. We have seen many children who have grown up with the idea they had weak hearts. Despite the fact that no cardiac lesion could be discovered, these individuals could not run or exercise, and shrank from every effort. Their anxiety and care for their preservation from excitement went beyond the bounds of all reason, and the tendency to guard and defend themselves as though they were fragile porcelain remained long after their discovery that they were quite healthy and as capable of work as anyone else. They had prepared a soft berth for themselves in life, and were loath to leave it. But as a matter of fact we find many children who suffer from organic defects, particularly of the sense organs. And we know well that such individuals suffer much more in life than normal children. They experience the deficiencies of their bodies, as for instance a weak digestive tract, a bad skin, poor eyes, more intensely; and they feel a certain pressure which, under normal circumstances, would develop into an added attention, a greater training, a better technic for overcoming their difficulties.

All poets probably belong in this class. Goethe and Schiller both had bad eyes, and the German poet Gustav Freytag writes in his diary that at the age of fourteen he could imagine better than he could see, as his ignorant father refused to let him wear glasses. The organic defect often gives direction to the total activity of the individual.

Under unpropitious circumstances an organic defect is compensated in a useless way. In such cases we have problem children, criminal children, neurotic children. It may be stated with certainty that wherever we see a child occupied with useless or criminal or neurotic behavior it is because he has felt himself "untalented" for the normal activity demanded by our world. Here is another angle to the difficult problem of "talent." You see, the catchwords with which other psychologists finish their work remain the challenge of the Individual Psychologists to begin to do something about it. A boy learns that he is not talented for mathematics, and finds himself in a group of similar boys who have been branded in the same way. Or a girl finds herself in a group who "cannot learn Latin." These individuals present us with a very ticklish problem, because if we cannot prove them otherwise, they maintain that they are right, that they are untalented, or talented only to a certain degree.

One of the greatest contributions of Individual Psychology has come in the discovery that there need be no actual organic deformity or inferiority for a child to consider himself hindered at the start. The sense of pressure which I have described as occurring in the actual presence of organic inferiorities may occur also in the presence of purely social difficulties, or as a result of the position of the child in the family constellation. In other words, a child with a normal digestive tract but bad nutrition may assume a behavior pattern similar to that of a child with a malformed stomach.

It is possible to burden a perfectly normal child with a pressure so great that he feels himself unable to cope with it. This point explains the fact which has been the thorn in the side of other psychologists, namely, that one occasionally finds an individual with perfect organs, with good inheritance, and of good family, who is, nevertheless, untalented, incapable, a poor performer, the proverbial black sheep. We have determined that this is entirely due to the relative picture, the context within which this child finds himself, and that the blind fate of his behavior pattern has been fixed in previous relationships.

Similarly, in children who are educated without love or affection we find a characteristic behavior pattern. The unbelievably large number of illegitimate children who are tossed from pillar to post by our society come in this category. But a child does not need to be illegitimate to grow up with the idea that he is hated. The petted child sooner or later comes to the same conclusion. A petted child in a situation in which he does not get his accustomed love and affection shows all the reactions of a hated child. This becomes particularly evident in the case of first-born children who are followed by other children. The parents may not actually change their attitude toward the first-born, but he interprets the presence of the second born as an insult to his prestige. He considers himself a dethroned monarch, and acts accordingly, making every effort to regain his lost power. Suspicion, hate, envy of the rival are the natural consequences. This type is particularly frequent among firstborn children.

It is at this point that I wish to blast another superstition. It is generally believed that children who grow up in the same home pass through the same environmental influences. This is a fallacy. The tension, the relative context is as different for each individual as can be. No other child ever lives through the same situation that a first-born experiences. Every other child always has a pace-maker. The first-born always occupies the family limelight for a time. Put a child in the limelight and accentuate the situation strongly, and you build up an unmistakeable behavior pattern. This will be the style of life in which one strives always for the center of the stage, in which one must always occupy the main position. Quite different is the second-born. He directs all his energies at making power crash from its throne. He is always under steam, always on the go; he is always looking for short-cuts to power. I do not say that every first-born son and every second-born must follow this pattern; but we are more accustomed to finding these reactions in these situations.

## V

If I have now given brief proof of the influence of the environment in determining the social and professional capabilities and talents of an individual, their preparation or lack of preparation for the solution of the problems of life, what remains of that mystic quantum which we have been accustomed solemnly to call talent? Where is this alchemic thing which psychologists want to weigh and evaluate with scientific instruments? Our problem is quite another one: To make talented individuals out of untalented ones.

The opposite school of thought has always suffered shipwreck. Wherever one has tried to foster the so-called talented individuals, one has come to no good end. The schools for talented, psychologically tested "over-average" pupils hide their heads in shame because of their poor results. What of classes for talented and untalented children? I have always found, particularly in Vienna, that the classes for talented children consisted mostly of relatively well-nourished individuals from the better classes, whereas in the untalented classes the poorly fed and poorly dressed children of the proletariat were to be found. Binet, the father of psychological tests, made the same discovery. In the very beginning of his researches he called attention to the remarkable fact that there was a constant relation between talent and body-weight. We should not be surprised at this constant relationship. But it is not a cause and effect relationship at all.

The elements which the Individual Psychologists have found most necessary to the development of a child into a useful social being are a good relation with the rest of humanity and the feeling that he is equal to other children. Training toward the social feeling should be begun in the earliest years, and continued through life. Courage and the consciousness of power and equality should be fostered wherever possible. If this is done, we find an individual always on the useful side of life, showing the personality of a worthwhile, courageous, socially-minded man or woman.

Rob this child of his courage and the feeling of his equal chance, and you thwart his development. The bogey of talent is one of the most effective means of putting bounds to the development of a child. If you tell a child offhand he is untalented, and he then proves untalented, this does not prove that you were right. You "fixed" him! And you must not wonder at your evil results. A similar damage can be done to the so-called "talented" individual. By constantly giving him tests of his prowess, usually useless ones, one runs the risk of serious damage to his self-confidence and self-esteem. At any rate, a pathological ambition is bound to develop and the chances are that this talented individual will soon have to hide behind a smokescreen of "nervousness" to defend himself from useless tests of powers.

The courage which is the basis of talent must be combined with an adequate training. Many seemingly untalented individuals are simply poorly trained. Their slightest actions bear the inhibitions of this inadequate technic. We know that there are individuals who walk badly, who have no talent for speaking, and of course others who seem to have no talent for studying, or reasoning or thinking, or reading books. It is simply a question of finding the right technic.

Let us refer to the biography of Charlemagne and read the amusing words of his biographer: "Although Charlemagne tried with might and main to learn to read and write, he never accomplished these things because he obviously had no talent for them." But since the days of Pestalozzi, it is no longer necessary to have talent to read and write—every child can do it!

Growing insight into technic and training will doubtless open up new fields for the formerly "untalented," and I prophesy that in not many years the delusion of "talent" will vanish into the limbo of witchcraft, the evil eye, and the casting of spells. If we could develop the technic of teaching composition better, we could make a half-way adequate composer out of everyone.

This sounds like heresy to the composers, to the musical genius. But I need only to remind you that while Beethoven's mother was pregnant with him, his father said, "If this will be a boy, he will be a second Mozart!" We can say that he guessed correctly, that the boy had the appropriate talents. But what was the most outstanding feature about Beethoven? A hereditary organic defect. Otosclerosis, a hereditary disease of the ear ossicles which results in severe deafness about the twentieth year. What would one of our modern vocational guidance psychologists have said to the young Beethoven? Would he have prophesied talent as a musician? Certainly not. He would have made a shoe salesman out of him, would have directed him to leave music strictly alone. And had Beethoven followed his advice, become a shoe salesman, the vocational guidance psychologist would have claimed that he was right. No musical genius would have developed in him!

# 10

# The Child's Inner Life and a Sense of Community

TERRY KOTTMAN AND MELISSA HESTON

Alfred Adler's "The Child's Inner Life and a Sense of Community" is particularly intriguing in three different arenas. First, the various concepts used provide evidence of the evolution of Adler's own thinking given that some of the concerns mentioned were deemphasized in his later work, while others became increasingly powerful. Second, echoes of Adler's stance on the negative effects of gender inequities can be seen today in the feminist movement and feminist psychology, as well as in the literature that emphasizes the differences between boys and girls in their developmental needs within our society. Third, this piece is especially relevant today in regard to Adler's concerns about how parents, education, and society in general affect children's developing personalities for better or worse. We will first consider this work as it relates to the evolution of Adler's thinking, discuss briefly how his views on gender inequities and their consequences presage various topics related to contemporary feminist psychology and children's development in a gendered society, and end with an examination of the ways in which this piece is quite contemporary within the realm of child development, parenting, and education.

Throughout his entire career, Adler was particularly interested in how individuals develop their personalities and what moves them to become the people they are in adulthood. Although he always believed that the seeds for the formation of an adult's personality were sown in early childhood, his conceptualization of the forces that created personality and his understanding of what motivated people evolved during his continued study of psychology (Monte & Sollod, 2003). In 1907, at the beginning of his career, Adler believed that the weakest or least-developed part of a person's body could be negatively affected by the demands of life and could constrain the individual's development, leading to a tendency to compensate for organismically based weakness. He then moved toward the concept that the dynamic force of personality development was based in biological drives, primarily the drive toward aggression (Adler, 1908, as cited in Ansbacher & Ansbacher, 1956; Oberst & Stewart, 2003). In this conceptualization of individual motivation, a person would "act against the environment when thwarted in meeting his or her needs and in obtaining satisfaction" (Oberst & Stewart, 2003, p. 21). As time passed, however, Adler deemphasized drive psychology, and in several works published in 1910 through 1913, he postulated that masculine protest, the desire to "be like a real man," was the primary force that moved individuals forward in the development of their personalities (cited in Ansbacher & Ansbacher, 1956, pp. 44–75; cited in Mosak & Maniacci, 1999, p. 5). "Our civilization is mainly a masculine civilization, and the child gets the impression that while all adults enjoy superior powers the man's are superior to the woman's" (Dreikurs, 1989, p. 47). Adler believed, as a result of their interpretation that being male was superior to being female, children strove to cultivate being masculine, whether they were male or female. By moving toward the masculine, young children could strive "to be in control, to be competent, and to become the master of his or her own life. This reaction has as its goal the elimination of feelings of inertness and inferiority" (Oberst & Stewart, 2003, p. 21).

When the paper "The Child's Inner Life and a Sense of Community" was first published in 1917, Adler had not actually abandoned his earlier ideas about organ inferiority, the aggression drive, and masculine protest. He incorporated all of these ideas about how personality is developed and people are motivated into this paper, along with his newly developed ideas about the basic dynamic force of personality development in which he was shifting to an emphasis on the striving for a fictional goal of superiority, with successful adaption to life depending "on the degree of social interest in the goal-striving" (Ansbacher & Ansbacher, 1956, p. 172). In the 1920s, he expanded on this thinking, suggesting there is "an inherent tendency for individuals to grow and master the challenges of life. There is a trend toward growth and accomplishment" (Oberst & Stewart, 2003, p. 21). In the later stages of his life, Adler expanded this concept, suggesting that individuals strive for perfection, attempting to realize idealized images of themselves (Ansbacher & Ansbacher, 1956; Dreikurs, 1989; Oberst & Stewart, 2003). "The Child's Inner Life and a Sense of Community" was written in the middle of Adler's career— although it includes references to the reactive mechanisms of organ inferiority, masculine protest, and feelings of inferiority as the primary motivation for human growth and development, it signals a shift toward a more proactive stance on personality development: striving toward superiority and perfection.

In "The Child's Inner Life and a Sense of Community," describing the development of the child's inner life and development of a sense of community, Adler developed many of the themes that undergird the theory of Individual Psychology: holism, teleology, and social interest (Carlson, Watts, & Maniacci, 2006; Ferguson, 1984; Kottman, 2003). In this paper, he expounded on the "trend toward unitary development" (p. 417) and the "wholeness of the personality" (p. 418)—these phrases signaled his belief in the "indivisible whole of each person" (Ferguson, 1984, p. 2), the holism which is a fundamental component of the theory. The "constant upward striving" (p. 418), "the child's inner life grows in the direction of and toward the goal that promises peace, gratification, acceptance, superiority, in short, 'expansion'" (p. 419) reflected Adler's teleological stance—that life is guided by the striving toward goals; that all behavior (which includes thinking, feeling, and doing) has a purpose. Even as early as 1917, when this article was published, Adler was already recognizing the value of this contribution: "No matter how great a child's insecurity, and no matter how pressing the urge toward compensatory efforts, the child could not move one stop ahead, whatever his capabilities or strengths, so long as there is no 'goal' to force the way" (p. 419). The emphasis on the development of a sense of community was illustrated by statements like "the good qualities and the defects of society exert a bilateral influence on the child's inner development" (p. 422). This, combined with the suggestion that the absence of community feeling leads to neurotic and psychotic illnesses, underscores the Adlerian concept of social interest.

Throughout "The Child's Inner Life and a Sense of Community," Adler delved into another recurrent theme in Adlerian theory: feelings of inferiority and their centrality in the development of personality. Feelings of inferiority were viewed as an inevitable result of the development of the child's "inner life" (p. 417), which begins to become evident around 6 months of age. This astute observation of a significant shift in the infant's understanding of the world has been well validated by research on infant cognition (Hetherington, Parke, Gauvain, & Locke, 2006). From Adler's perspective, this new understanding would include an unconscious sense of inferiority which the infant strives to overcome. Developments in memory allow the child to recognize what is uncertain in the world, while developments in cause-and-effect reasoning encourage greater efforts to master that world. As children move through toddlerhood, both competence and awareness of moments of incompetence grow, as the children increasingly recognize the greater competence (i.e., the superiority) of the adults and older children around them. Adler argued that the readiness with which young children respond to the efforts of adults to teach them was due to children's sense of inferiority and uncertainty.

By addressing the "social devaluation of women and the concomitant stratagems in the behavior of the sexes toward each other" (p. 420), Adler had already started down the path of serving as a pioneer for the social equality of women (Watts, 1999). In this, he presaged the work of contemporary feminism and feminist psychologists (Bond & Mulvey, 2000; Crawford & Unger, 2004; Denmark & Paludi, 2007; Gilligan, 1993). "Alfred Adler, in the first important synthesis of psychoanalysis and feminism, showed how social power relations structured the development of personality hierarchy in individual desire. His notion of 'masculine protest' as a source of neurosis and social conflict is eerily relevant" (Connell, 2003, p. 250).

The "'battle' of the sexes" that Adler just briefly described in the "The Child's Inner Life . . ." continues to play out in powerful ways in contemporary society, and the literature is replete with concerns about the damage being done to both boys and girls within a society that has not yet successfully grappled with its own deeply held biases (e.g., for boys, see Biddulph & Stanish, 2008; Johnson, 2005; Kindlon & Thompson, 2000; Meeker, 2009; Rao & Seaton, 2009; e.g., for girls, see Deak, 2003; Holland & Eisenhart, 1990; Meeker, 2007; Pipher, 2002; Preuschoff, 2006; Simmons, 2010). This battle and its impact upon the character of young men and women has been powerfully illustrated in the recent Tom Wolfe (2005) novel *My Name Is Charlotte Simmons*, in which an extremely bright young woman with dreams of taking academia by storm (a traditionally masculine goal) cannot resist a culture in which women gain significance through their sexual liaisons with young men who routinely and overtly demean them. In the almost 100 years since Adler published "The Child's Inner Life . . . ," it seems that, despite extensive and explicit social attention to gender roles and gender inequities, there have been only superficial kinds of changes.

In this article, Adler gave particular attention to the role of the education provided by parents, and society more generally, in influencing the development of personality, which he viewed as the general stance a given child takes toward the world that guides the child's way of interacting with that world. Today, developmental psychologists use the language of parenting styles to describe some of the same phenomena. In particular, Adler speaks of "children who have been robbed of their courage by a strict, unfair upbringing" (pp. 418–419). Current research has established that an authoritarian parenting style in which discipline is based on a parent's superior physical power, threats, and humiliation results in relatively poor outcomes for children who can come to see themselves as "helpless or worthless" (Hetherington et al., 2006, p. 463). Such children may be "so bent on eliminating every 'mistake' from their experience that they waste their time in continuous uncertainty and end up in a 'hesitant attitude' for life" (p. 421).

Adler also noted in this paper that children learn through imitation, and when children sense "the increased bellicosity, the tyranny, the will to power, [they] will perceive this behavior as justification for [their] own desire for power, especially if [they experience] this pressure in [their] upbringing" (p. 420). Authoritarian parents make ready use of physical discipline in response to children's behavior, including aggression, thus demonstrating that aggression is a justifiable tool for the powerful. This, in turn, increases the likelihood that these children will become more, rather than less, aggressive in the future (Gershoff, 2002). In Adlerian terms, such children develop both low social interest and respond to the world with a high level of activity, becoming the "sadists, tyrants, and delinquents" (Lundin, 1991, p. 321) of the future.

In Adler's view, children who are pampered by their parents also fail to develop courage, and it is possible to see a similar approach to parenting today. So-called helicopter parents closely monitor their children, even as young adults in college, and are quick to intervene on their children's behalf when a problem arises (Nelson,

2010). Such parents essentially *over-parent*, solving problems for their children that children need to solve for themselves as part of a normal developmental process. This phenomenon is believed to be the result of technological advances that potentially allow parents and children to be in immediate contact at any time and the result of smaller family sizes, which leads parents to invest more heavily in the one or two children that they do have. Extensive research on the long-term consequences of this type of parenting will not be available for some years yet; however, Adler would probably view this apparently growing cultural trend with considerable dismay. It seems unlikely that children who experience over-parenting will develop either the level of social interest that Adler believed essential for a healthy society or the personal problem-solving skills needed to overcome the life challenges that will inevitably arise. Over-parented individuals may develop a strong sense of entitlement, expecting much from society and giving little to it.

In "The Child's Inner Life and a Sense of Community," Adler argued that the essential goal of education must center on preparing children to lead socially productive lives. Indeed, Adler recommended that only people who were committed to creating a sense of community should become educators. This notion that the purpose of education was to develop children into effective members of society was a view shared by John Dewey and Karl Marx (Cleverley & Phillips, 1986). The importance of becoming contributing members of society has found expression in today's schools through a number of curricular initiatives, including programs such as *Character Counts!* (Josephson Institute, 2010) and community service requirements (Kaye, 2010). At the same time, contemporary world events, media (including video games), and the emphasis on competitive sports create a "self-contradictory society" (p. 420) in which the challenge of developing children into adults with strong social interests and high levels of social competence may be impossible to meet.

Indeed, a careful reading of "The Child's Inner Life and a Sense of Community" leaves one with a poignant sense that the more things have changed, the more they have stayed the same. Despite the passage of time, the essence of Adler's views on how children develop their personalities remains relevant today.

## REFERENCES

Ansbacher, H., & Ansbacher, R. (Eds.). (1956). *The Individual Psychology of Alfred Adler: A systematic presentation in selections from his writing.* New York: Harper Row.

Biddulph, S., & Stanish, P. (2008). *Raising boys: Why boys are different—and how to help them become happy, well-balanced men.* Berkeley, CA: Celestial Arts.

Bond, M., & Mulvey, A. (2000). A history of women and feminist perspectives in community psychology. *American Journal of Community Psychology, 28*(5), 599–630.

Carlson, J., Watts, R., & Maniacci, M. (2006). *Adlerian therapy: Theory and practice.* Washington, DC: American Psychological Association.

Cleverley, J., & Phillips, D. C. (1986). *Visions of childhood: Influential models from Locke to Spock* (rev. ed.). New York: Teachers College Press.

Connell, R. W. (2003). Masculinities, change, and conflict in global society: Thinking about the future of men's studies. *The Journal o f Men's Studies, 11*(3), 249–266.

Crawford, M., & Unger, R. (2004). *Women and gender: A feminist psychology* (4th ed.). New York: McGraw-Hill.

Deak, J. (2002). *Girls will be girls: Raising confident and courageous daughters.* New York: Hyperion.

Denmark, F., & Paludi, M. (2008). *Psychology of women: A handbook of issues and theories* (2nd ed.). Westport, CT: Praeger.

Dreikurs, R. (1989). *Fundamentals of Adlerian psychology.* Chicago, IL: Adler School of Professional Psychology.

Ferguson, E. (1984). *Adlerian theory: An introduction.* Chicago, IL: Adler School of Professional Psychology.

Gershoff, E. T. (2002). Corporal punishment by parents and associated child behaviors and experiences: A meta-analytic and theoretical review. *Psychological Bulletin, 128,* 339–579.

Gilligan, C. (1993). *In a different voice: Psychological theory and women's development* (6th ed.). Cambridge, MA: Harvard University Press.

Hetherington, E. M., Parke, R. D., Gauvain, M., & Locke, V. O. (2006). *Child psychology: A contemporary viewpoint* (6th ed.). Boston, MA: McGraw-Hill.

Holland, D. C., & Eisenhart, M. A. (1990). *Educated in romance: Women, achievement and college culture.* Chicago, IL: The University of Chicago Press.

Johnson, R. (2005). *That's my son: How moms can influence boys to become men of character.* Grand Rapids, MI: Fleming H. Revell.

Josephson Institute. (2010). Character counts website. Retrieved from http://character-counts.org

Kaye, C. B. (2010). *The complete guide to service learning: Proven, practical ways to engage students in civic responsibility, academic curriculum & social action.* Minneapolis, MN: Free Spirit.

Kindlon, D., & Thompson, M. (2009). *Raising Cain: Protecting the emotional life of boys.* New York: Ballantine.

Kottman, T. (2003). *Partners in play: An Adlerian approach to play therapy.* Alexandria, VA: American Counseling Association.

Lundin, R. W. (1991). *Theories and systems in psychology* (4th ed.). Lexington, MA: D.C. Heath.

Meeker, M. J. (2009). *Boys should be boys: 7 secrets for raising healthy sons.* New York: Ballantine.

Monte, C. F., & Sollod, R. N. (2003). *Beneath the mask: An introduction to theories of personality* (7th ed.). Hoboken, NJ: John Wiley & Sons.

Mosak, H., & Maniacci, M. (1999). *A primer of Adlerian psychology: The analytic-behavioral-cognitive psychology of Alfred Adler.* New York: Routledge.

Nelson, M. K. (2010). *Parenting out of control: Anxious parents in uncertain times.* New York: New York University Press.

Oberst, U., & Stewart, A. (2003). *Adlerian psychotherapy: An advanced approach to Individual Psychology.* New York: Brunner/Routledge.

Preuschoff, G. (2006). *Why girls are different—and how to help them grow up happy and strong.* Berkeley, CA: Celestial Arts.

Pipher, M. (2002). *Reviving Ophelia: Saving the selves of adolescent girls.* New York: Ballantine.

Rao, A., & Seaton, M. (2009). *The way of boys: Raising healthy boys in a challenging and complex world.* New York: HarperCollins.

Simmons, R. (2010). *The curse of the good girl: Raising authentic girls with courage and confidence.* New York: Penguin.

Watts, R. E. (1999). The vision of Adler: An introduction. In R. E. Watts & J. Carlson (Eds.), *Interventions and strategies in counseling and psychotherapy* (p. 1–14). Philadelphia, PA: Accelerated Development.

Wolfe, T. (2005). *I am Charlotte Simmons: A novel.* New York: Farrar, Strauss, & Giroux.

## The Child's Inner Life and a Sense of Community[17]

*Alfred Adler*

What we find in the newborn—organ functions, reflexes, a totality of movements, instincts, even affects—none of these represent the most important, the most valuable part of our existence which we think of as "inner life." Rather, we might consider [the newborn] as the functional genotype, the living matter from which the inner life is formed.

For in the life of a child and in his physical and mental growth, there is a largely hidden trend that leads "upwards," that unceasingly guides and regulates all the physiological realities mentioned above, thus placing them in its service: Instincts and reflexes are adjusted, recognized as "appropriate," modified and utilized; movement of eyes, limbs, and trunk respond to a "plan"; all emotions—pleasure, joy, grief, pain, anger, love, hate, desire—manifest themselves at appropriate occasions, and by the manner and the degree in which they are expressed, they establish close contact with the environment and with the people in their immediate surroundings. There also soon appear traces of character traits, of a consistent posture which, like call and response to the demands of the environment, represent a further connection to the outside world.

This stage of development begins as early as the second half of the first year, and can only be understood in terms of a trend toward unitary development. It is a "readying" of inner forces to overcome external opposition.

It is only at this stage of development that we can speak of the child's inner life. And now, the growth of a mental apparatus begins which, in manifold testing and groping attempts, undertakes the task of establishing and consolidating a stance vis-à-vis the questions of life.

This apparatus, which we are simply calling "inner life," can be roughly compared to a machine capable of action and purpose. It is, of course, infinitely more complex, a thousand times better equipped to attack and to evade; and in the structure of the organs and the capacity of their function, it incorporates the life experience of the individual as well as that of his forebears. Primarily an agent of attack, collecting useful experiences, exercising self-control, acting with foresight, attempting to protect its tasks by a wide safety coefficient, and never losing sight of its goal—that is how we see the inner life of a human being.

The organs and their function have a limited capacity to start with. Therefore, only a small part of the universe can be understood, received, and utilized in any way—and that only in the manner of a human being.

---

[17] Translation by Lisa Fleisher.

The limits of our mastery of the world are further restricted by the constant demands of our body and our mind at any given moment. This condition of dependency and the resulting sense of restriction burdens the human psyche first and foremost with feelings of smallness, of inferiority, of uncertainty. In this soil, out of archetypes of inherited potentialities, spring the mental instruments of memory and foresight, the essential "safeguards" against fear of defeat in life. Connected to these safeguards—which originated in physical and mental distress—and guided and influenced by them, there arise thoughts, plans, and impulses to increase personal significance as much as possible. This force, which from the sphere of insecurity presses toward an exalted position, toward mastery of matter, is what constitutes our surest guarantee of a route of continued progress. For man's feeling of smallness is acceptable to him only if it gives rise to a constant upward striving, if it awakens belief in the self and in the future, and insight into a common human destiny.

Careful observation of the child's inner life shows, similar to recollections of adults, that this striving for security, this thinking ahead, this preplanning of the future, begins at an early age, molding and forging the "wholeness of the personality," the individuality with unceasing force. But the feeling of insecurity affects the child much more powerfully. It makes him anxious, increases his need for support, causes him to seek adult protection and counsel. The fact that we are able to train a child is an eloquent indication that the child feels inferior and is apprehensive about his future. This uncertainty is often tremendously intensified, and then our ability to train threatens to founder, because the child follows a quite different road of "compensation." We must be prepared for such pathologically heightened feelings of inferiority in three types of children: (1) in constitutionally weak and sickly children; (2) in children who have been robbed of their courage by a strict, unfair upbringing and not by sickness; and (3) in pampered children who have never developed courage.

No matter how great a child's insecurity, and no matter how pressing the urge toward compensatory efforts, the child could not move one step ahead, whatever his capabilities or strengths, so long as there is no "goal" to force the way. It is a lasting service of the School of Individual Psychology to have discovered this fact and to have established it through numerous observations— a fact that is equally valuable for theory and for practice. Let us recall the above-mentioned limits and insufficiencies of our organs and the technical "artifices and strategems" they exact by their sheer existence. To the scientist, the structure of an antediluvian organ clearly explains the purpose and the aim of its function and its mode of operation. He will, in fact, understand these only if, in addition to knowing all the details, he also contemplates the purpose of the organ, its "whither."

On the strength of his inferiority feelings, the child's inner life grows in the direction of and toward the goal that promises peace, gratification, acceptance, superiority, in short, "expansion." Every single symptom points in this direction, and not until we recognize this purposeful direction in its individual mode of expression, can we speak of understanding inner movement or of understanding human nature. Just as a child who is learning to walk can set down his feet only if he has a goal in view—even if he never reaches that goal—so every movement of the human psyche strives for and is contrived in the name of that "fictive goal" which in his naive uncertainty the child has erected for himself as a fixed pole in the chaos of the world.

Not so education which usually aims at a tangible goal! The self-chosen childhood goal incorporates all the characteristics of "divinity" itself, giving rise to psychical phenomena that are in constant and inexplicable conflict with reality. That is not surprising. The fictive goal of a child had other functions: It was supposed to calm, to guarantee superiority. That is why this seemingly "ideal" goal causes the child to experience the world, the environment, his immediate family as hostile agents, as obstacles; why it prepares and forces a battle stance which pure love can break through only once in a while. And so, out of the child's individual life and his family life there arise in him malicious, or on a more lofty level, aggressive traits, running counter to the requirements of societal life and its thrust toward mutual goodwill, fellowship, sense of community, and equality.

What results from the collision of these two "guiding principles" is the nucleus of the personality to come. Further pursuit of this concept goes beyond the scope of our present inquiry.

In our view, then, the life of the individual, as well as human life in general, is enacted both as a goal, unattainable but at the same time giving direction to life, and as a partially unconscious shaping of the future, though imagined and planned for; accordingly, every manifestation of the inner life, apart from its actual and possibly causal significance, shifts into a role which is of singular importance for psychological research: that of a preparatory act which incorporates a direction and a purpose.

Now we perceive questions of the child's inner life in a different and much clearer light. The concept and the essence of education arises out of our understanding of the requirements of the societal life ahead. Its chief requirement, therefore, is clear: It must under all circumstances be "preparation" for a social and socially operative community. And it must be that in all of its nuances. No purpose, however bright its utopian glitter, may divert it from this course, if the meaning and essence of education are not to go astray. Education for our present self-contradictory society torn apart by antithesis would, of course, be asking the impossible and could not succeed. This gives rise to our obvious requirement that we accept as educators only those whose social guideline goes at least as far as affirming a sense of community. The social structure and its tensions are reflected in the rearing and in the constitution of children. The educator must know this source of damage, and if the child threatens to succumb, he must fight it, oppose it, teach him to seek new cultural paths. I was able to demonstrate in countless cases how great is the damage to entire generations, even to the life of an entire nation, that offers its rising generations social devaluation of women and the concomitant strategems in the behavior of the sexes toward each other. The result is deplorable enough: The girls feel slighted, they accept the feminine role only under protest, and raise their desire for compensation to largely unattainable demands. This unhealthy situation affects boys no less strongly, as they feel obligated to demonstrate and to demand continuous evidence of their superiority over women. In the process, they stamp [woman] as the enemy and place the outcome in her hands. All that is permanent in the "battle" of the sexes stems from this imbalance in the social level that weighs on the soul of a child from an early age.

Right from the start, the human psyche has a tendency to strive toward the goal of total superiority. When from the behavior of adults, as in our time, the child senses the increased bellicosity, the tyranny, the will to power, he will perceive this behavior as justification for his own desire for power, especially if he even experiences this pressure in his upbringing. He will then seek to establish a permanent combat readiness. With a generally malicious perspective, which results in constant competition and conflict with others, with a permanently overheated contest for prestige, the child develops from the family into the life of his society. And so it is plainly obvious if all his abilities develop *as if for battle*.

For this reason we must also consider the importance of the question of hereditary characteristics as clearly exaggerated. Many of the manifestations that could be considered hereditary turn out to be the result of imitation. We deny the action of a "drive." Children imitate; at other times, they freely invent what, after tentative preliminary experiments, appears to them to be helpful in their struggle to become God-like.

Character traits and ideals develop in a similar way, under constant urging and shaping by the requirements of society. Their higher or lower level is the result of education—intentional or unintentional—which is capable of putting obstacles in the way of a child's tenacity of purpose. Obedience, for instance, is frequently championed over defiance. Similarly, cowardice over courage which, however, does not prevent occasional development of both traits in a person as interchangeable means. At any rate, human beings seem to have a powerful tendency which we have so far not overcome, that traces such traits as timidity, anxiousness, submissiveness back to the nursery and there conjures up analogous behaviors.

But since the child's sights are always trained on the future, this dependence on social criteria follows automatically, as if by fate. A world full of hostility and adversity will suggest to the adult as well as to the child that faults, weaknesses, and crimes, that self-abasement can operate like an act of revenge, of revolt and exaltation like an instrument of power. On the other side of such forceful attempts to break the social boundaries, there is the equally harmful attitude of others who are so bent on eliminating every "mistake" from their experience that they waste their time in continuous uncertainty, and end up in a "hesitant attitude" for life. We find these two groups so often that they have earned the epithet "neurotic" for our era. The faint-hearted ones are in the majority. This is easily explained by a typical peculiarity of our modern education, which makes the child over-cautious, often simply for the convenience of the parents. It is easy to understand how these fearful views, of life adulterate every value judgment, and cause a permanently pathological approach to the world. The revisions of this point of view are the result of experience recorded without bias: as a rule, making mistakes is of lesser importance than the consequences that a child ascribes to them. This is also surely true of the sexual transgressions of childhood. We must not forget that the child has to solve the questions of his sexuality. When he makes mistakes, let us remember his immaturity, and the shortcomings of educators' attempts thus far at providing a solution. We have come to understand a fact that we consider to be of special importance: The sexual behavior of the developing child is in complete harmony with his individual orientation and can be changed only together with that orientation.

We see the same unity of the "child's life plan" in his favorite games, in career fantasies, in the earliest recollections, in his position vis-à-vis parents, teachers, classmates, strangers, and in certain peculiarities, some of which I want to mention here.

For example, our point of view permits us to conclude from a child's deceitfulness, that his inner growth was subject to a feeling of inferiority to such an extent that he felt pushed into "artifices" and ruses in order to be able to hold fast to a higher goal. Selection of this goal and of artifices such as, for instance, laziness, blushing, shyness, tardiness, etc., pedantry, snivelling, violent temper, and all other characteristics always occur according to available forces, individual experiences, and the effect that will be useful in the battle against the environment. A more in-depth treatment can be found in the works that have been cited. The most prominent impression that always emerges is a "distancing" from societal life, a deficient desire or an aversion to "join the game," or even a tendency to spoil the game for others. The counterpart of social deficiencies, the absence of a sense of community, comes through clearly.

It has been our endeavor to show that the good qualities and the defects of society exert a bilateral influence on the child's inner development as they steer the child's budding ideal and longing into their paths, fill them with their content, strengthen or weaken them. In this way, they influence the child's perspective, force him into a life-long position in which the "non-self" is quite imperceptibly placed on the opposing, the antagonistic side of the ledger. We maintain, then, that the biased, rigidly one-sided view of life, which originates in childhood, causes the sense of community to wither, that it usually remains unrecognized and incorrigible as long as an expanded self-awareness does not force a change. In order to bring this train of thought to immediate fruition, let me in closing point to two main types of spoil-sports, One type develops a system of life whereby they are always prejudiced against others. Their low self-esteem is as obvious as that of the second type who, pointing to their weaknesses, always "blame" themselves, but assume thereby that others must place themselves at their service. How much these people are at odds with the actual requirements of life is evidenced by the fact established by our school, that among other things, they constitute the main contingent of people with neurotic and psychotic illnesses.

# 11

## Individual Psychological Education

### Guy J. Manaster

"Individual Psychology Education" was presented as a lecture to physicians in Switzerland in 1918 and published in 1920. To better understand how Adler's influence on contemporary education is forecast from this paper we need some understanding of where Adler was at that time: geographically, historically, and developmentally.

Adler returned to Vienna from service during World War I touched and inspired by his experience. Although most of the basic tenets of his theory had been formed or suggested by that time, it was a work in progress. He concluded from his war experience that all of the problems of individual development and pathology could not be ameliorated on a one-on-one basis. Individual Psychology therapy could be successful in each case, but society's ills were too great to rely on that technique alone.

Thus Adler broadened the application of his theory to groups, families, and the greater society through education throughout the rest of his life. He exposed the pillars of the educational system, the issues of power and status, for their deleterious effect on society, women, families, and mental health. He could not understand children except in the context of their family and community—views foreign to the strict and impersonal classroom of that time. Adler recognized the loneliness of the downtrodden teacher faced with children from all sorts of backgrounds, with all sorts of problems, with no professional help or practice for alleviating the teacher's pain or the students'.

In taking on the challenge of improving the world through applying and developing his psychology in education and community, Adler was taking on entrenched establishments. In addition to the schools, he was confronting other professions to become involved with the challenge of improving child development and education. This paper is a polite example of his facing physicians with that challenge.

This may not seem to be a particularly courageous move. However, at that time Adler was not securely ensconced in the Vienna medical scene, particularly the academic medical community as Freud maneuvered against Adler receiving an appointment at the prestigious University of Vienna. Adler's socialist sympathies, and his wife's communist leanings, kept him in contrast, if not conflict, with the conservative education authorities. Thus, as Adler developed, broadened, and refined his theory and its clinical applications, he had to be a diplomat and politico to instigate his theory into the entire spectrum of social and educational arenas.

This paper well illustrates his expanding his theory into education and social applications to mental health while trying to appeal to the physician's basic humanitarian and idealistic values.

Today, no one would think of confronting a child's problems, a child in difficulty, without considering the child's health and family situation. Adler's exposition of birth order dynamics comes across as a friendly invitation to the physicians to consider family constellation when considering a child, to remember the family and social context. And, of course, the physician is to do this while focusing on the child's health, bearing in mind the child's perception of his or her relative capabilities and feelings of inferiority.

Sex identification and sex role issues are so imbued as societal and cultural issues that they are, today, recognized and addressed with alacrity in most schools. So too defiance, which now would be termed *oppositional*, is a not uncommon condition and diagnosis in schools. When Adler discusses these, and other issues, in this paper he is presenting the seeds of his eventual overall view and forecasting much in contemporary educational practice.

Adler is speaking to physicians in this paper, but he mentions parents' and teachers' involvement. He did not restrict the application of his theory to particular professionals and, over time, he would make the same plea to all mental health and education professionals. He interacted with and considered all professions as worthy participants in the conversation and efforts of education and mental health. Contemporary team approaches in schools, parent education, democratic collaboration, and the seeds of community mental health in schools can all be seen in this paper.

At the end of the paper Adler makes a final appeal for *prophylaxis*, for prevention. His first requirement is to educate all relevant professionals in psychology, albeit his psychology, developmental psychology and educational theory. Although Individual Psychology is not the primary view taught, psychological theory and practice and developmental psychology are fundamental elements in all teacher training and educational practice. The general goals Adler spells out in this article have been instilled in current educational practice. To further improve education and mental health Individual Psychology should be at the center of the effort.

# Individual-Psychological Education[18]

*Alfred Adler*

The tremendous importance of a thorough, complete understanding of educational questions and the necessity for every physician mastering them up to a certain point, is particularly clear when looked at from the standpoint of the nerve-specialist's treatment. We demand justifiably that the doctor in particular, have a knowledge of men, and we know that such a vital question as the relations between physician and patient, always break down if the physician is either lacking in knowledge of men or in methods of education. It was this attitude and interpretation of his role that made Virchow say: "Physicians will eventually become the educators of humanity."

A question that has become acute in our day and which is bound to become even more acute in a short time, is that relating to the relative spheres of physician and educator. It is quite essential to reach some unanimity in regard to the whole range of problems involved and to obtain a bird's-eye view of them. Both sides overlap but co-operative work is entirely absent.

If we but ask what purpose education serves, all the main points involved will certainly fall within the domain of the physician. The education of children so that they may become individuals actuated by ethical principles, the utilization of their virtues for the good of the community, are regarded by every physician as the self-evident presupposition of life. It may justifiably be demanded that all his actions, measures and moves be in conformity with this object. The immediate direction of the education will always be in the hands of the educator, of the teachers and parents, but we may assume that they will acquaint themselves with those questions and difficulties that only the physician can really plumb to their depths, because he must unearth them from out the pathological interrelations of the psychic life. I wish in particular to emphasize the fact that it is impossible to cover in a short time a field of such tremendous extent and that until a unified conception can be reached, it is only possible to touch briefly on certain questions whose more extensive discussion will be the concern of the following future generations. Nevertheless it is important to become acquainted with those view-points that individual-psychology insists are of fundamental significance and whose misunderstanding, it is claimed, will be visited upon the children in the course of their development.

What brings the physician into the closest contact with educational questions is the relationship between psychic health and bodily health, although

---

[18] Translated by P. Radin.

not however, in that general sense so often spoken of, namely a sane mind in a sane body, a rather unwarranted conception. We all have ample opportunity of seeing physically healthy children and, adults whose psychic condition is by no means healthy. It is difficult, if not impossible, for a child with a weak constitution to attain to that harmony expected of physically normal children. Let us take the case of a child born with a poor digestive system. From the very first days he will be cared for most carefully and solicitously. Such children will consequently grow up in a markedly affectionate atmosphere; they will find themselves always protected, their actions directed and circumscribed by a large number of commands and prohibitions. The importance of food will be markedly exaggerated so that they will learn to prize and even over-value the question of nourishment and digestion. It is the children with digestive troubles who form the main contingent on those who put difficulties in the way of their education, a fact with which the older physicians were already acquainted. It has been claimed that such children must become nervous. Whether such a definite compulsion exists is doubtful. It is however true that the "inimical" character of life weighs more heavily upon the souls of children who suffer and invests them with an unfriendly *pessimistic attitude* toward the world. Sensible of their deprivation they demand stronger guarantees for their importance, become egotistic and easily lose their contact with their fellowmen, because the discovery of their ego has rendered the discovery of their environment a somewhat antagonistic element.

The child is beset with a tremendous *temptation* by its relation to the environment, its attitude toward school, to the frequently intensified discomforts entailed by the weakness of the stomach and intestinal tracts *to obtain compensatory advantages* that can be derived from proving himself ill. He will, for example, develop an extraordinary tendency to being spoiled; from earliest childhood accustom himself to having others clear away all difficulties for him; it will be more difficult for him to become self-reliant and he will invariably *refuse to make increased efforts* in all the dangerous situations of life. His courage and his self-confidence will be shaken almost to their foundations. Such an attitude persists to old age and it is not easy to change a child who for ten, fifteen or twenty years had been a weakling, pampered by everyone, into the courageous man full of initiative, enterprise and self-confidence, demanded by our times.

The harm inflicted upon the community is of course, much greater than the above standpoint lets us see, for we must take into consideration not merely children with stomach and intestinal weaknesses but all those born with inferior organs, those whose sense organs are deficient and who, in consequence, find the approaches to life rendered more inaccessible. We frequently find such difficulties mentioned in biographies or by patients. In such cases the physician will have to concern himself not merely with the psychic educational question—but will endeavour with all his powers, to apply some remedy or treatment for correcting defects so that the child may, at an early stage, be prevented from falling back upon his weakness. We will do this all the more energetically if we ourselves realize that we are here not dealing with any permanent deficiences or with smaller or greater difficulties, and that the important point to bear in mind is that an original organic weakness, *when subsequently corrected,* may yet live on in *a permanent feeling of weakness* and make an individual unfit for life. These conditions become of extraordinary complexity because the children themselves, to an unusual degree, strive to make some compensations and corrections. Only a few succeed in making any good compensations and most of them attempt, *in some fashion or other,* to equalize the differences that exist (between them and healthy children), to make up for their deficiencies either by having recourse to cultural methods or by intensifying both their initiative and their mental powers.

In all these cases we shall find noticeable traits of character causing disturbances such as, for example, psychic sensitiveness always leading to a conflict. We must remember that we are here dealing with manifestations of daily life which we cannot pass over lightly for otherwise both body and soul would be injured.

It is difficult to stress adequately enough how great is the distress and tension reigning in the child's soul. It is an easy matter to understand the mental habits of men who have become useless if we suppose that their uselessness is a persistence of something they have brought with them from the nursery. *Disease and the idea of disease* means much more to the child than we generally imagine. Anyone who wishes to survey the child's psyche from this angle, will soon discover that to a child these are important experiences, and that illness in almost all cases appears not as an increase of difficulties' but as their alleviation, that it is even prized as a means for obtaining tenderness, power and certain advantages at home or in the school.

There are a large number of children who always have the idea that they are ill, who always feel weak. In all these cases where a persistence of the symptoms cannot be explained by any medical findings, it proves that *the children are making use of this feeling of illness* in order to gain prominence, to do justice to their desire for domination and importance in their own family. For example, in cases where long after the whooping-cough has passed, children still adhere laboriously to a similar cough. We find that they invariably succeed in frightening their families by these attacks. This would, for instance, be a case where it would be essential for the physician in his pedagogical capacity to intervene.

On the other hand there are also parents and educators who take the opposite view-point, treating their children with severity, even with brutality, or wish, at least, to give the children the impression of being so severe.

Life is so diverse that it compensates for the errors of the educator. Nevertheless, a man whose childhood has been spent in a loveless atmosphere shows, even in old age, indications of this bringing-up. He will always suspect that people desire to be unkind to him and he will shut himself off from others, lose touch with them. Frequently such people appeal to their loveless childhood, as if that exercised some compelling force. Naturally enough a child does not necessarily develop mistrust because parents have been severe, to be as cold to others as they have been to him, or to distrust his own powers for that reason. It is, however, in such soil that neuroses and psychoses are prone to develop. It is always possible to disclose in such, a child's environment, *some disturbing individual* who, either through lack of understanding or evil intention, poisons the child's soul. Hardly any person except the physician is able in such cases to bring about a change in the environment either by alteration of residence or by explanations.

There are, however, certain complications only discovered through a profound understanding of the individual, which, when grasped, clarify the picture to an extraordinary degree.

There exists, for example, a fundamental difference in the psychic development of the first-born as contrasted with that of the second or last-born child. The individuality of an only child it is also simple to characterize. A family where there are either only boys or girls, either one girl among a number of boys or one boy among a number of girls, expresses itself in a definite psychic manner. It is from such facts and positions that children develop their attitude. Frequently it is possible to pick out the oldest or youngest child by his behaviour. I have always found that the first-born possesses a sort of conservative tendency. He takes the element of power always into consideration, comes to an understanding with it and exhibits a certain amount of sociability. Compare with this, for example, *Fontane's* biography where he states that he would give much if anyone could explain to him why he always had a certain tendency to side with the stronger. I inferred from this and rightly, that he must have been a first-born child who regarded his superiority over his brothers and sisters as his inviolable possession.

*The second-born* always has before and behind him some one who can do more, of more importance, who generally possesses greater liberty of action and is superior to him. If a second-born child is capable of any development he will unquestionably live in a condition of continuous endeavour to surpass his elder brother. He will work restlessly as if under full steam. In fact, the restless neurotics are, to a preponderating degree, second-born children, the first-born rather unwillingly tolerating rivals.

In the attitude of the type perhaps most prominent found among *last born,* we find something infantile, a reserve and hesitation, as if not trusting oneself to perform praiseworthy acts that others are either seen to do or are assumed as doing. Such people easily infer that the whole question is one of stabilizing a situation originally existing. He is always surrounded by people who can do more, meets only people who are more important than himself. On the other hand, he is as a rule able to attract to himself all the love and tenderness of the environment without giving anything in return. There is no need of his developing his powers for he is automatically forced into the centre of his environment. It is easy enough to understand all the injury this entails to his whole psychic development, for he thus learns *to expect to have everything done for him by others.* A second type of last-born is the "Joseph type." Restlessly pushing forward, they surpass everyone by their initiative (Kunstadt) frequently transcending the normal and become path-finders. Both in the Bible and in fairy-tales, people's knowledge of mankind has generally given to the youngest with the greatest gifts, the possession of magic boots, etc.

The behavior of an only girl among a number of boys is also important. Here so many tense situations develop that we may assume that an oppor-tunity for abnormal attitudes to develop will arise; I am not speaking here of absolutely final results. It is made clear to the girl at an early age, that her nature is utterly different from that of the boy and that much will remain forbidden to her that is boy's right by nature, which he may claim as his privi-lege. It is not easy in such a case to have either praise or pampering serve as a substitute. For we are concerned here with emotional values that to the child represent something essential and irreplaceable. The girl is continually bothered, receives orders and instructions at every step. In such children, we find a special sensitiveness to criticism, continual attempts to show the strong side, to appear free from all vices; and at the same time a fear lest her unimportance be discovered. These girls frequently furnish the material for future neurotic diseases.

The same holds true in the case of an only boy among a number of girls. It is just here that the contrast seems even greater. The boy is generally provided with special privileges. In consequence the girls work in unison against their only brother. Such boys often suffer as if at the hands of an extensive conspir-acy. Every word he utters is marked by the sisters; he is never taken seriously; his good traits are decried, his defects made prominent, and as a result the boy frequently loses his self-control and self-confidence and generally shows but poor progress in life. Then people speak of his indolence and laziness. However this is only an external manifestation which with its consequences is based upon a pathological abnormality of temperament, on a fear of fac-ing life. The important point to remember is that we are dealing with people who have either lost their belief in themselves or are prone to lose it. Such boys will habitually recoil from action, are afraid of being made fun of, even when there is no reason for such an attitude. They soon give up all real work, devote themselves to killing time, and become demoralized. Difficulties of the same order are frequently encountered where an older brother is brought up together with a younger sister.

Another point to be taken up by the physician is the explanation of *sexual questions* to children. No single answer covering all cases can as yet be given because of the differences in various nurseries, of individuals and of the environment in which children grow up. One point should however be remembered, that it is an injustice that is very easily visited upon children, if they are kept in ignorance of their sex role longer than necessary. Strangely enough this happens all too often. Patients have not infrequently told me that even up to their tenth year they were not quite certain to which sex they belonged. Throughout their development a feeling manifests itself as if they had not been born like other people as boys or girls and would not develop like them. This gives these children a tremendous feeling of uncertainty noticeable in all their actions. The same is true of girls. There are some who up to the eighth, ninth, tenth, twelfth and even fourteenth year grow up with considerable uncertainty as to their sex and who in phantasy always imagined that, in some fashion or other, they might still be transformed into men. This fact is also supported by certain descriptions in the literature on the subject.

In all these cases the normally certain evolution is interfered with. The years of childhood are spent in endeavouring to supplement their sex role artificially, to develop along masculine lines and to avoid making any decisions that might result in defeat. An uncertainty of a fundamental character is either clearly shown or to be inferred from the pretentious and exaggerated actions in which they indulge. Girls adopt a masculine attitude and force themselves preferably to a behaviour that seems to them and their whole environment as characteristic of boys. They prefer' to romp about, not merely in the wild harmless fashion which we gladly concede to children, but in an emphatic manner as if under some constraint, and do it so consistently that it very early impresses even their parents as of a pathological character. Boys too show themselves as if possessed by some wild turmoil, but, taught by the obstacles they encounter, they generally soon desist and develop an hesitating attitude or turn their attention to girls. The awakened eroticism then takes on in both sexes unnatural and frequently perverse traits that run parallel to their general attitude.

Let me now speak of certain manifestations that are commonly regarded as acts of defiance. A large number of signs are assigned to *defiance* that the physician considers indications of illness. As such are to be reckoned the frequently found form of *refusal to take nourishment* and even those types of rebellion connected with defaecation and micturition. All the pathological symptoms which in more pronounced forms we have found in enuresis, or in an inexplicable or unchangeable kind of constipation, are frequently based upon some deeply-rooted defiance in children, who would like to utilize every opportunity for escaping from the compulsion to which they are subjected, because they feel force, in any form, as an encroachment and humiliation. They derive a feeling of satisfaction from their refusal to adapt themselves easily to the demands of their environment as though this were a measure of their importance. We interpret it as a sign of revolt. It is simple enough to test the matter for we will always find other signs of defiance. The same is true for harmless bad habits like nose-picking, slobbering, and nail-biting. Bad habits clearly indicate a development in a direction antagonistic to the demands of the community. Someone with the role of an opponent is never absent. The symptom itself is almost always due to inferior functioning.

It is exceedingly interesting to follow the whole chain that is formed when we take into consideration the various transformations in the nature of a child's *choice of profession,* as, for example, in the case of a small girl passing successively from the role of princess, dancer, teacher and finally, somewhat resignedly, to that of the house-wife. We frequently find that the choice of profession in the case of grown-up children, is dictated by the desire to do the opposite of that suggested by the father. Naturally this opposition does not develop openly. The logical faculty is constrained by the pressure exerted by the nature of the final objective. The advantages of one profession will be especially emphasized and the disadvantages connected with another just as markedly underlined. In this way it is possible to argue both for and against every point. This attitude must likewise be definitely taken into consideration. But from another angle the physician is also concerned, both in regard to the advice he hazards about the *profession* as in regard to what he says about *the actual choice of a profession.* He must primarily be guided by his knowledge of the person's physical fitness; yet realize on the other hand, that the psychical factor is just as important and may, in some cases, be more fundamental.

It is, of course, an exceedingly disagreeable task to pursue every individual who has gone wrong or who is afflicted with a neurotic illness or a psychosis, in order to improve or heal him. That would constitute a tremendous waste of energy and it is about time that we seriously turn our attention more definitely to *prophylaxis.* There are already an ample number of secured points of vantage. We have for instance, constantly been trying to work toward the goal by educating both parents and physicians. Better results are, however, imperatively necessary in view of the tremendous increase of neurotic and psychotic phenomena in connection particularly with demoralization. Perhaps the first requirement would be to disseminate the ideas derived from a knowledge of men and the educational ideas obtained through individual-psychology; then to apply them so that all can aid us with their strength and in every possible manner. The psychic anomalies of development which at first seem but minor bad habits afterwards lead to the forms of neurotic disease and crime.

# 12

## *The Problem of Distance*[19]

### ROBERT MCBRIEN

Reading Adler's *The Problem of Distance* (1925/1983) is similar to browsing through a museum of psychotherapy. The sentence structure, constructs, and technical terms (i.e., *neurosis* and *psychosis*), developed in the early 1900s, are rarely used in professional literature today. We remind ourselves that the knowledge base for someone studying human behavior during the 1920s was limited when compared to our current knowledge base.

As we read Adler's words the question arises, are these constructs about safeguarding tendencies and the problem of distance useful today? By studying literature, old and recent, we can review the key constructs developed by Adler and his followers as they created Individual Psychology. Further, we learn how contemporary Adlerians have updated these basic teachings and are applying them in their work with clients.

Beginning in 1902 and continuing until 1911, Adler was an active member of Freud's Wednesday Psychological Society. This circle of professionals was invited by Freud because they shared an interest in his theories (I think of the group as an earlier form of a think tank), and was instrumental in the creation of psychoanalysis. Over time it was apparent that Adler's thinking was not in harmony with Freud's. These basic differences came to light in February 1911 when Adler presented to the Vienna Psychoanalytic Society three papers that described his theories. The Ansbachers report that the end result of these presentations was Adler's "complete separation from Freud" (Ansbacher & Ansbacher, 1956, p. 56).

According to Dreikurs (1953) their irreconcilable differences developed due to a basic difference between psychoanalysis and Adler's psychology of the individual. Dreikurs wrote, "For Freud human conflicts are intra-personal caused by opposing conflicts with the personality structure, i.e., between the person's Ego, Super Ego and Id, the unconscious. For Adler, all problems and conflicts are interpersonal. This implies a different emphasis on both the origin of conflicts and on the therapeutic procedure" (p. 3).

---

[19] A basic feature of neurosis and psychosis.

In *The Problem of Distance*, Adler (1925/1983) continues to contrast his Individual Psychology with "the so-called sexual psychology" (p. 101). A construct that Freud and Adler disagreed upon, and challenged each other on, was Adler's (1925/1983) *the masculine protest*. Taking my museum trip metaphor a step further would be to find in the museum a room filled with 100-year-old artifacts and discover in a corner an ancient movie machine. Imagine viewing a flickering faded film of Adler and Freud playing tennis. On the ball is written *neurotic* and Adler's racket is labeled *masculine protest*, while Freud's racket is labeled *penis envy*. We can watch this tennis match that represents a continuation of the rivalry that existed between them.

## ADLER'S PSYCHOLOGY OF THE INDIVIDUAL

How important is the masculine protest today? Grounded in the early development of Adler's theories on understanding human behavior, at first this concept focused on the experience that girls had living in a time when their brothers were placed in a position of privilege and being a girl meant having a second-class citizen's status.

Of the daughter who is being pampered Adler (1931/1980) wrote,

> Many girls who have been pampered find it difficult to adjust themselves to the feminine role. There is always the impression in our culture that men are superior to women; and in consequence they dislike the thought of being women. Now they reveal what I have called "the masculine protest." (p. 191)

Later Adler (1931/1980) expands on this construct. He wrote, "It is not only girls who suffer from a 'masculine protest,' but all children who overvalue the importance of being masculine see masculinity as an ideal and are dubious whether they are strong enough to achieve it" ( p. 192). Today we consider earlier discussions about masculine protest as the roots for current theories on the environment's (especially society's) contribution to symptoms, a key principle of Adler's psychology. Recall that Adler (1925/1983) highlights this construct to drive home his "fundamental and at the same time, the determining factor in the psychic life of both healthy and nervous people—'*the feeling of inferiority*'" (p. 100).

For Adler, both healthy and neurotic individuals experience feelings of inferiority. What is the difference between the healthy person and the neurotic person in overcoming the doubts connected to succeeding with the pursuit of life goals? It is private logic.

Private logic, also known as apperception, when rooted in feelings of inferiority prompts the person to set lofty goals. Pursuing lofty goals is also known as striving for superiority. During the formative years of Individual Psychology this striving for superiority to compensate for one's sense of being inferior was considered to be *neurotic* behavior. It may be helpful for our understanding of this term to use Shulman's (1930/1995) definition: *Neurotic* means "a person who has become discouraged by the interaction between life events and his own lifestyle" (p. 5). Today we think of this construct as self-actualization.

In healthy individuals, this sense of overcoming encourages positive actions that result in goal achievements. We describe these successful persons as self-actualizing and as optimistic. Adlerians describe them as having social interest and recognizes their positive contributions to the community. Adlerians would describe the person's lifestyle as moving on the *useful* side of life.

Adler (1925/1983) wrote, "Every psychic expression of the neurotic possesses within itself two presuppositions—the feeling of *inferiority* on the one hand, and the compelling, hypnotizing striving toward *the goal of godlikeness* on the other" (p. 102). Adlerians say the person's life path is moving on the *useless* side of life.

The striving principle and motivations for choosing the useless side of life are constructs that highlight Adlerian views on the impact of the environment on human behavior. For Adlerians, the motivations for someone moving along the useless side of life explain the need for and uses of *safeguarding tendencies*. In addition, our understanding of the usefulness of safeguards provides the foundation for our understanding of how distancing functions as a "safety mechanism of the ego consciousness" (Adler, 1925/1938, p. 100).

## SAFEGUARDING TENDENCIES

Safeguarding tendencies are an Adlerian construct that helps us understand the purpose for employing a self-defeating pattern of actions prompted by feelings of inferiority. These actions are intended to avoid threats of exposing perceived deficiencies. These discomfort-dodging behaviors are repeated despite the person's experiencing problems

We return to the tennis match again. This time Adler switches to a new racket labeled *safeguarding tendencies* and Freud picks up one labeled *defense mechanisms*. These constructs are described in Ansbacher and Ansbacher (1956). We understand the source of the Adler-Freud rivalry when the Ansbachers describe Freud's defense mechanisms as protecting the ego against instinctual demands while Adler's safeguards served to protect the self-esteem from perceived external threats and problems of life. They wrote, "These respective explanations are consistent with Freud's biological and Adler's social orientation" (p.265).

Can contemporary therapists make use of these constructs from the last century? Contemporary uses of safeguards, especially distancing, have been updated by Clark (2000). His contribution answers the question in my title. It is yes.

Adler's safeguarding and distance constructs are definitely *useful* for students of Individual Psychology and Adlerian counselors today. We turn to Clark's update.

Apparently Adler did not provide a definition of his construct, but Clark offers this: Safeguarding refers to "a self-deceptive evasion that deters functioning in experiences which evoke threat and feelings of inferiority" (p. 192). Clark contributes to the usefulness of the safeguarding construct by offering a counseling model to use with discouraged clients who are employing safeguarding strategies inappropriately.

We are reminded that we all use a safeguarding strategy on occasion. Think of an alibi you used or you heard someone use to explain being late for an appointment. According to the theory this use of an alibi would be to protect our self-esteem. However, the discouraged person using safeguards consistently finds that nothing changes and a goal is not reached or a problem is not solved. Recall that safeguards are *not known*. This was Adler's term for the unconscious (Ansbacher & Ansbacher, 1956, p. 1).

A key theme in all safeguards that counselors can investigate is the evasion of responsibility. Because the person's private logic hides the purpose for the self-defeating behaviors, any success with positive changes will probably require effective counseling. Effective counseling strategies would guide discouraged clients to move away from their chronic use of safeguards and move toward overcoming obstacles as they move to the useful side of life.

## THE PROBLEM OF DISTANCE

Adler's essay on the distancing safeguard calls for the reader's awareness of the Northern European culture he lived in, his classic education, and the reality of the phenomenon known as *lost in translation*. What we read in English was translated from his native German language. To better understand Adler's message, I found it necessary to gather background on the meanings implied in unfamiliar terms and references. Thanks to Google I was able to learn the term *denouement* (p. 101), a term used in theater and film today that refers to the final outcome of a complex sequence of events. Adler refers to Kraft-Ebing, a psychiatrist, educator, and author. He published a controversial book on human sexology in the 1880s. Controversy arose when he described homosexuals as normal people with a different sexuality. Adler (1925/1983) recognized that Kraft-Ebing's unpopular views on homosexuality were in alignment with Individual Psychology theory (p. 102). It seems that Adler's reference to Kraft-Ebing was to point out the therapist's need to look for the purpose for any symptom.

When Adler (1925/1983) mentions Penelope (p. 105) he refers to Odysseus's wife, in Greek mythology. She wove a garment by day and then undid her weaving at night, thus never finishing the garment. This reference can serve as a metaphor for any task someone undertakes but never finishes. Thus hesitating and marking time are safeguards and these actions serve some useful purpose for the actor. Adler is using a literary term in discussing the lifeline of the *tragic hero*. He uses *perpetitia* (p. 108) to describe the interplay of ambition or vanity (superiority) and inferiority with the result that the problem of distance prevents the hero from decisive action.

Clark (2000) expands these understandings of distancing tendencies with the insights of Dreikurs, Mosak, and other second-generation Adlerians. Clark states,

> Through the employment of safeguarding tendencies, individuals consequently demonstrate an outward appearance of attempting tasks or appear to endure sufferings in pursuit of obligations, when in actuality they are avoiding situational demands through withdrawal tactics that serve as alibis. (p. 192)

Evidence counselors look for to uncover a distancing complex includes the person's avoidance behaviors when faced with challenges and problems, expressions of doubt and pessimism regarding success with problem solving, and the evasion of responsibility. This description reflects Adler's (1925/1983) fourth mode of distancing, "Construction of obstacles and their mastery as an indication of 'distance'" (p. 106).

I recall the client who was a university senior in his last semester who had only his student teaching assignment left before graduating, obtaining his BS and teaching credentials, and entering the profession he spent 4 years preparing for. His presenting problem was his inability to get to his classroom on time each morning. In trouble with his supervising teacher, his education department faculty, and his family, he sought counseling. After studying Adler's construct on the distancing safeguard, I now have a better understanding of why this young man was late for the three appointments we set, dropped out of counseling, took an incomplete grade for his student teaching credits, and failed to graduate on time.

Clark (2000) presents a progressive three-stage counseling model for helping clients identify and modify inappropriate safeguarding tendencies. Clark's sequence begins with the *initial* stage where encouragement and assessing the lifestyle are key strategies. During the *integration* stage the process focuses on the clarification of conflicts associated with safeguarding tendencies and developing new frames of reference for their approach to life. Stage 3, the *accomplishment* stage, involves action-oriented strategies that help the client gain control over habitual safeguarding and create alternative actions that lead to positive outcomes.

Clark's (2000) systematic counseling process is developmental, strengths-based, and encouraging. Clark's system of structured counseling might have guided me to be more effective counseling my persistently tardy student teacher. Listed are 15 counseling "tools" I could have used with him.

## STAGE ME—THE RELATIONSHIP STAGE

Goals: Enhance client's self-worth, find strengths and abilities, and build hope through developing the power of choice and decision-making.

### COUNSELING STRATEGIES

1. Active listening and empathy
2. Encouragement
3. Self-disclosures
4. Focus on resources, assets, and strengths
5. Assess the lifestyle
6. Sentence completion
7. Early recollections
8. Dreams (Adler comments on dreams, p. 106)

## STAGE II—THE INTEGRATION STAGE

Goals: Focus on conflicts connected to the use of safeguards. Protect against exposure to perceived defects. Explore life convictions. Guide the client to understand the purpose of safeguarding tendencies and related patterns of lifestyle. Teach the client to reframe negative schemas.

### COUNSELING STRATEGIES

9. Confrontation
10. Cognitive restructuring
11. Reframing
12. Interpretation

## STAGE III—THE ACCOMPLISHMENT STAGE

Goals: Guide the client's readiness for change, promote an action orientation, teach strategies for eliminating self-defeating habits.

### COUNSELING STRATEGIES

13. Task setting and obtaining commitment
14. Breaking it down by dividing tasks into manageable steps
15. Catching oneself

Clark (2000) describes his progressive stage model as "a framework for a client's change from safeguarding tendencies to socially constructive directions" (p. 201).

Readers may recognize the Adlerian counseling methods woven through the 15 counseling strategies listed above. Additionally we can take advantage of other contemporary counseling strategies that have taken advantage of Adler's keen insight into human behavior. His recognition of the impact of pessimism on safeguarding and his use of the terms *scheme* and *schema* prompt me to invite readers to learn about the optimistic explanatory style in Peterson and Steen (2005) and Young and Klosko's (1993) schema-focused therapy. These sources may prove useful for counselors seeking to expand their knowledge of cognitive-behavioral therapy strategies.

## A CASE STUDY

To further make a case for how distancing is useful in the 21st century, Stewart (2007) describes how the environment is used in constructing safeguards. He cites Adler's description of people who gain distance from others when winter interferes with face-to-face meetings. With warmer weather there is more contact with others and the people reported their symptoms got worse (p. 346).

Stewart lists five prominent features about weather that make it usable as a safeguard:

1. It can facilitate or deter the opportunities for interacting with others.
2. The conditions serve as elegant safeguards since these events offer excuses for canceling or delaying responsibilities that are not the actor's fault.
3. It serves as a trigger of a physical or psychological symptom. This safeguard provides an acceptable alibi for distancing since the weather can be blamed for the various symptoms.
4. With reference to *personal priorities* (see Pew, 1976) Stewart identifies *to detach* and *to avoid* as the two personality priorities that make weather-focused safeguarding most prominent (p. 347).
5. Our American society today is highly mobile and weather changes impact on travel plans. Weather reports are important for the traveler's actual plans for taking a trip and with regard to safeguarding. Weather is important as an *attribution* for the person as they make excuses and achieve their safeguarding goal.

Stewart (2000) discusses four key implications for counselors for the process of counseling the client using weather as one of their safeguards. The four implications are as follows:

1. Weather-based safeguards serve to protect the self that allows a small amount of functioning despite the person's pursuit of mistaken goals rooted in self-interest rather than social interest.
2. For those whose personality priorities involve detachment or avoidance counselors may find the use of encouragement strategies are needed throughout the stages of counseling. With the goal of guiding the individual to develop social interest and learn the benefits of having positive

relationships with others, support and encouraging tactics will build the individual's confidence in their ability to take perceived risks to make social connections.

3. During the *integration stage* (Clark, 2000) of counseling clients may be assigned the task of recording the weather, their activities, and the emotions experienced each day for a period of time. The log of these events permits counselor and client to identify patterns where weather safeguards may have been employed. Identifying triggers for the safeguard's use permits the client to learn to "catch oneself."

4. Counselors are reminded to sort out uses of weather safeguards to determine if their use is occasional (e.g., students and teachers celebrating a snow day) or more significant due to their widespread, repeated, and pervasive use.

Stewart's case study shows how Mary, his client, used a combination of weather and physical symptoms as a safeguard, thus causing problems with social relationships, in particular a romantic relationship. He described how Adlerian counseling guided Mary to become aware of how her *private logic* impacted on her struggle. Finally Stewart's counseling methods included most of Clark's strategies. For example, he had Mary keep a daily log of the weather and how it influenced her mood and behavior. Completing this task helped her move toward the useful side of life.

## SUMMARY AND A CHALLENGE

The problem of distance involves the evasion of one's responsibility to succeed with the challenges of life. Adler's view of success in life is rooted in social interest and one's contribution to the community. Distancing as a safeguard to self-esteem and a barrier to success with life's challenges was reviewed. To update Adler's 90-year-old theory Clark's three-stage counseling process, designed to use with clients challenged with chronic use of distancing safeguard tendencies, was presented. Finally Stewart's case study involving a client's use of weather as a distancing safeguard offers an example of counseling the client who has the problem of distance.

Now a challenge for readers. Counselors are invited to discover in their clients' life stories how successful they are moving along the useful side the life. How are clients handling the challenges life gives them? Is there evidence of a use of distancing as a safeguarding tendency? Readers using distancing-focused counseling in their work will find it quite helpful for their clients. A personal benefit will be the professional satisfaction gained by adding the effective strategies described here to their counseling toolkit.

# REFERENCES

Adler, A. (1925/1983). The problem of distance. In A. Adler, *The practice and theory of individual psychology* (pp. 100–108). Totowa, NJ: Rowman & Allanheld.

Adler, A. (1930/1995). *The pattern of life* (2nd ed.). Chicago: Adler School of Professional Psychology.

Adler, A. (1931/1980). *What life should mean to you.* New York: Perigee Books.

Ansbacher, H., & Ansbacher, R. (1956). *The individual psychology of Alfred Adler.* New York: Basic Books.

Clark, A. J. (2000). Safeguarding tendencies: Implications for the counseling process. *Individual Psychology, 56,* 192–204.

Dreikurs, R. R. (1953). *Fundamentals of Adlerian psychology.* Chicago: Alfred Adler Institute.

Peterson, C., & Steen, T. (2005). Optimistic explanatory style. In C. R. Snyder & S. J. Lopez (Eds.), *Handbook of positive psychology.* New York: Oxford University Press.

Pew, W. L. (1976). *The number one priority.* Retrieved April 30, 2011, from Adler Graduate School Web site: http://www.alfredadler.edu/pdf/NumberOnePriority.pdf

Shulman, B. H. (1995). Appendix II in A. Adler, *The pattern of life,* 2nd ed. Chicago, IL: Adler School of Professional Psychology.

Stewart, A. E. (2007). The use of weather as a safeguarding strategy. *Individual Psychology, 63,* 345–352.

Young, J. E., & Klosko, J. C. (1994). *Reinventing your life.* New York: Plume.

## The Problem of Distance[20]

*Alfred Adler*

The practical importance of *Individual-psychology* is to be sought in the degree of certainty with which an individual's life-plan and life-lines can be determined from his attitude toward life, *toward society, toward the normal and necessary problems of communal life,* his plans of obtaining prestige and the nature of his group consciousness. Assuming the acceptance of many of my conclusions let me direct your attention to the fundamental and at the same time, the determining factor in the psychic life of both healthy and nervous people—"*the feeling of inferiority.*" Similar in nature must be reckoned the "*urge toward the positing of a goal,* toward the heightening of ego consciousness," a "*compensatory*" function as well as the "life-plan" obtruding itself upon the individual for the attainment of his goal through the employment of various "aggressions" and "deviations," along the line of the "masculine protest" or the "fear of taking a decision." I shall further assume a knowledge of the neurotic and psychotic psychic life, the fixation upon a "guiding fiction" in contrast to its absence in the healthy man, who regards his ideal "guiding principle" as giving only an "approximate orientation" and to be used as a means only. Finally, I assume the acceptance of the fact that, regarded as a whole, neurosis and psychosis are to be interpreted as a "*safety mechanism*" of the ego consciousness.

The manner in which the uninterrupted strivings of mankind "upward," have conditioned, a cultural progress, perfecting at the same time, both a method and technique of life in which all possible eventualities and organic realities become of some utility even if not put to their proper use, must by this time, have assumed sufficient definiteness to place in a proper light the importance of the *denouement* in psychic life as contrasted with causal attempts at explanation. The concrete evidence for the untenability of the so-called sexual-psychology—in which *the sexual attitude of the neurotic* is quietly seized upon by many people as a factor to be thought of as an "*analogy*" of the life-plan, is clearly presented and the untenability of this view is to be regarded as one of the fundamental principles of individual psychology.

In our investigations, we found the tendency to seek the "attainment of pleasure" to be a *variable* and in no way determining factor, adjusting itself completely to the orientation of the life-plans. *Traits of character and affects,* contrary to the almost generally accepted belief, were there shown to be well-tested and, in consequence, tenaciously fixed preparations for the attainment of a *fictive goal of superiority.* The theory of the "inherited" sexual components,

---

[20] Translated by P. Radin.

perversions and criminal tendencies," naturally becomes untenable as soon as this fact is disclosed. We are then justified in defining the general subject of psycho-neurosis to include the study of all those individuals who had possessed from childhood—be it in consequence of organ inferiority, an erroneous system of education or a bad family tradition—*a feeling of weakness*, a pessimistic perspective, and all those familiar and similar contrivances, prejudices, tricks and states of exaltation that develop in connection with the construction of an imaginary and subjective feeling of predominance. Every trait, every facial expression is so definitely connected with the promised goal of peace and triumph that we can justifiably claim that *all neurotic manifestations show a belief in an all-powerful ambition linked with deficient strength if personality, to be a necessary presupposition of their condition. Only when so viewed are they intelligible.*

Exactly similar psychic over-exertions as our school has demonstrated hold true for *phantasies, dreams and hallucinations.* The driving power is always something *in the nature of a preparation, a groping;* in the nature of an "if it were" tendency toward expansion, of a striving for power over others, of search for an outlet, of security against danger. Here we always have to remember that the second purpose lies nearer at hand, that the consequences of an act do not flow from the taking of a decision and that frequently, the social after-effects of the proof of really being ill or its imagined belief, suffice to satisfy the urge toward recognition. To what an extent, however, *all experience* is to the neurotic, merely the material *and means* for obtaining, through the employment of his life-perspective, renewed stimulations along the path of his neurotic leanings, that is proven by his utilization, at one and the same time, of apparently contradictory attitudes[21]—in "double vie," dissociation, polarity, ambivalence. To which we should add, the falsification of the facts of the external world, that may go so far as complete exclusion, the wilful and purposeful shaping of an emotional life and sensations with the externally directed reactions derived from them, and the planned interplay of memory and amnesia, of conscious and unconscious stirrings, of knowledge and of ignorance.

Once having reached this point and made certain that every psychic expression of the neurotic possesses within itself two presuppositions—the feeling of inadequacy, *inferiority* on the one hand, and the compelling, hypnotizing striving toward *the goal of godlikeness*, on the other—then the "multiple meaning" of the symptom which Kraft-Ebing had already pointed out, need no more deceive us. In the development of the psychology of the neurosis this multiple meaning represented no small obstacle. To this is largely

---

[21] We wonder whether it really is so difficult to understand the "semblance" in the so-called introversion and its opposite, to conceive both as means to an end? (Original footnote by Alfred Adler.)

due the fact that phantastic systems and narrow restrictions were permitted to dominate neurology, the first method leading to insoluble contradictions and the second to sterility (in results). The individual-psychological school is committed, on principle, to investigate the "scheme" of a psychic disease consisting in adhering to the route repeatedly taken by the patient. Our work has demonstrated the great importance to be ascribed to the actual material, and even more, to the patient's evaluation of it. A proper understanding of the individual and an individualistic discussion was, for that reason, a necessary preliminary. The perfecting of the life-plan, on the other hand, the rigid insistence upon complete superiority, bring to light its contradiction with the demands of reality—*i.e. with society*; shake the patient free from his helpless behavior and experiences and compel him to oppose the normal decisions inherent in social life with *a revolt in the form of an illness*. A clear-cut psychological-social element thus enters the neurosis. The neurotic's life-plan is always operating with his own individualistic interpretation of society, the family, the relations of the sexes, and discloses in its perspective the uncritical assumption of his own inadequacy in life and of the hostile attitude of his fellowmen. The recurrence of generalized human traits, although without inward adjustment and in an intensified degree, should impress us again with the fact that both neurosis and psychosis are not far removed from the essence of psychic life, that they are indeed but *variants* of it. He who questions this must be prepared then to deny, now and for all time, the possibility of any understanding of psychological phenomena, for the methods of normal psychical life alone are at our disposal for investigation.

Adhering to the conception of a determining neurotic line, rooted in a feeling of inferiority that has as its goal an "upward movement" as posited by our school, we obtain a ceaseless "here and there," a "half and half," as a sort of neurotic hybrid; the attitude found in a *state of exaltation deprived of all force*, in which traits either of fainting or exaltation generally come to the front. As in the case of neurotic doubt, compulsion-neurosis or phobia, the terminal effect is either a "nothing" or almost a "nothing." At best it represents the preparations connected with an apparently difficult situation and a certification of illness, an arrangement to which—in more favorable instances—the actions of the patient seem bound. We shall see why later on.

This peculiar occurrence, demonstrable in all neuroses and psychoses, in melancholia, paranoia, and dementia praecox, has been described by me in detail under the term "*hesitating attitude.*" Favourable circumstances enable me to deepen this conception.

If we follow the patient's life-line in the direction indicated by us and try to understand how in his own individual manner—(that means simply by his manipulation of individually-gained experiences and personal perspective)—he is intensifying his feeling of inferiority *and yet freeing himself from responsibility* by attributing this inferiority to heredity, the fault of his parents or to other factors; and if finally, we recognize both by his demeanor and his maneuvers, his insistence upon impeccability, then it must be all the more astonishing to notice how, *at a given place in his aggressiveness*, his behavior deviates from the direction expected. To enable the reader to get a better idea of this I shall subdivide it into four modes, each one challenging attention by the fact that the patient attempts unerringly to interpose a *"distance"* between himself and the anticipated act or decision at that particular point. As a rule the whole disturbance appears as a sort of stage-fright confronting us in the form of a symptom or neurotic disease. Coincident with this purposeful "distance," frequently *expressing itself in some bodily sign*, the patient is giving shape, in varying degrees of intensity, to his separation from the world and reality. Every neurologist will be able to dovetail this disease-habitus with his own experiences, especially if he take into consideration the manifold gradations.

I. *Retrogressive movement.*—Suicide, attempted suicide; severe attacks of agoraphobia with great "distance"; fainting, psycho-epileptic attacks; compulsion—blushing and severe compulsion neurosis; asthma nervosum; migraine and severe hysterical pains; hysterical paralyses; aboulia; mutism; severe anxiety attacks of all kinds; refusal to take food; amnesia; hallucination; alcoholism, morphinism etc.; vagabond habits and tendency toward crime. Anxiety and falling dreams as well as criminal ones are frequent and indicate what exaggerated precautions are at work—the fear of what might conceivably *happen!* The concept of external compulsion is tremendously extended and every communal as well as humanitarian demand, rejected with exaggerated sensitiveness. In severe cases, which must be included here, every useful activity is interdicted. The sickness-certification naturally has its positive side in the assertion of one's own will-power and triumphs negatively likewise over the normal communal demands. This holds true for the other three categories too.

II. *Cessation.*—The impression obtained is that of *some magic circle* drawn around the sick person preventing him from coming into closer contact with the facts of life, of confronting truth face to face, of permitting either an examination of his worth or a decision. *The direct cause* (for the neurosis) is furnished by professional tasks, examinations, society, love or marriage relations, as soon as they take the form of problems bearing on life. Anxiety, weakness of memory, pain, insomnia with subsequent incapacity for work, compulsion-phenomena, impotence, ejaculatio praecox, masturbation and completely disqualifying perversions, asthma, hysterical psychosis etc.—these are all safety arrangements to prevent any regional over-stepping. The same applies to the less violent attacks of the first category. Dreams of being confined, of impossibility of attainment as well as examination dreams, occur frequently and outline concretely the patient's life-line, how he breaks off at a definite point and then constructs his "distance". Niebuhr in his *History of Rome*, III, 248, says: "National like personal vanity is ashamed of non-success for it is a greater confession of limitation in powers than the most shameful disgrace, which carries in its train, slothful and cowardly cessation of all energy: the former utterly destroys all court-like pretensions while the latter permits them to survive."

III. *Hesitation and mental or actual (oscillations) "to and fro,"* make the "distance" secure and terminate 'with an appeal to the above mentioned diseases, to the doubt that is often combined with them or to a "too late" (fatal delay). We find definite exertions to kill time. This is an inexhaustible field for compulsion-neuroses. Generally the following mechanism is discernible:—a difficulty is called into life, *sanctified* and then an attempt made to master it. Washing-compulsion, pathological pedantry, fear of contact (found likewise as a spatial expression of arrangements of distance), tardiness, retracing one's steps, destruction of work begun (Penelope), always leaving something untouched—all these traits are frequently encountered. Just as often do we find work or decisions postponed because of "irresistible" compulsion toward unimportant activities, pleasures, until action is too late; or a difficulty, generally self-constructed (e.g., stage-fright), makes its appearance just a moment before a decision is to be taken. This behavior is clearly related to the former category but with the difference that in the above instances, the act of decision is prevented. A frequent type of dream consists in any kind of a "to and fro" movement or in tardiness employed as provisional attempts at a life-plan. The superiority and safety strivings of the patient betray themselves in a fiction, frequently mentioned, never unmentioned and never understood. The patient "says it but does not know it!" It begins with an "if" clause:—"if I didn't have (this disease), I would be the first." That as long as he maintains his life-line, he never frees himself from this life-falsehood is intelligible enough. As a rule, the if-clause contains some unfulfillable condition or the patient's arrangement, and any change of it lies entirely in his own hands.

IV. *Construction of obstacles and their mastery as an indication of "distance."*—Here we encounter less severe cases always operative in life and occasionally taking on brilliant aspects. At times they arise spontaneously or (secondarily) out of the more severe cases, by the aid of some medical treatment. At times both physician and patient are under the credulous belief that a "remnant" is nothing but the old "distance." But the patient is then utilizing it differently, with a stronger social meaning. As formerly he constructed "distance" in order to break off, so now he creates it in order to triumph. The "meaning," the goal of this attitude is now easily guessed: The patient is now protected both against his own judgment and, in the main, against others' evaluation of his self-complacency and prestige. If the decision goes against him, then he can fall back upon his difficulties and upon his (self-constructed) sickness-certificate, if he emerges as victor then his thoughts will read "What might he not have accomplished had he been well, he who has accomplished so much though ill, with one hand it might be said !" The arrangements of this category are:—slight conditions of anxiety and compulsions; fatigue (neurasthenia); insomnia; constipation; stomach and intestinal disabilities consuming both strength and time and demanding a pedantic and time-killing regime; headaches; poor memory; irritability; moodiness; pedantic insistence upon a submissive environment and uninterrupted preparations of hostility against the latter; masturbation and pollution with superstitious conclusions etc.— throughout, the patient is testing himself to determine whether he really is efficient, and arrives consciously, or without admitting it to himself unconsciously, at the conclusion of pathological inadequacy. Frequently this conclusion, unexpressed but easily recognizable, inheres in the very neurotic arrangement under the protection of the patient's life-plan. Once the "distance" has been effectively constructed, the patient can permit himself to appeal either to some "other will-power" or battle against his own attitude. His line is then composed of the following factors:—unconscious arrangement of "distance"—a more or less unfruitful attack against it. We must clearly recognize that the battle of the patient against his symptom, and his complaints, his desperation and possible sense of guilt in the stage of the developed neurosis, *are primarily designed to accentuate the importance of the symptom in the eyes of the patient and his environment.*

In conclusion, let me point out in these neurotic methods of life that *all responsibility* in connection with success appears to be *cancelled.* To what far higher degree this factor is concerned in psychoses I shall attempt to present later on. So the life of the neurotic, as is consistent with his atrophied community sense, is spent predominantly within the circle of his immediate family. If the patient frequents wider circles he always exhibits a tendency for and a retrogressive gravitation toward his immediate family.

It is but in agreement with the views of the individual-psychological school that the analogy of neurosis with the behavior of healthy persons, should obtrude itself markedly. The psychic demeanor of either type is to be understood, in the last analysis, as a prepared answer to the questions suggested by society. We consequently regularly find the following constituent, immanent presuppositions and safety devices: a life-plan whose goal is unification, operating with a special purposeful self-evaluation; a goal of superiority and psychic manipulation which—in an integrated connection—has developed out of an infantile, perspective.

Quite as convincing is the similarity of our types with the creations of mythology and poetry. This is not surprising. They are all creations of the human psyche born of the same types of ideas and method of thought. They have naturally influenced each other. In the life-line of these artistic figures the indication of "distance" is again perceptible, most clearly in the figure of the tragic hero where it begins as "peripetia," and is then linked with the "hesitating attitude." This "technique" has palpably been taken from life, and the idea of "tragic guilt" points as an "illuminating intuition" at the same time to activity and passivity; to "arrangement" and the vanquishing of the life-plan. Not merely fate, but predominantly, some prepared experience is portrayed in the person of the hero, whose sense of responsibility is only *apparently extinguished*, in reality persisting, *for he has overheard the ever-insistent question about his adjustment to the demands of society*, so that as hero he may emerge victorious over the rest of the world.[22]

Thus he who seeks new, strange paths for society is threatened with an intensified danger of losing touch with reality. The interplay of vanity and insecurity, common to all these types, brings to the front the peripetia and within its individual "distance" constrains it to decisive action.

---

[22] The "chorus," on the other hand, represents the voice of the community, which, in the later phase of dramatic evolution, is transferred to the hero.

# 13

## Dreams and Dream-Interpretation

DOROTHY E. PEVEN

A dream which is not understood is like a letter which is not opened.

—The Talmud

At night we enter another world, down the wormhole, through the dark matter, and into a parallel universe. A world we create for ourselves full of wonder, creativity, and imagination—sometimes peaceful, sometimes frightening, but always wondrous, a place where the rules of time, space, and logic are suspended: the world of dreams.

Why do we dream? What function does the dream serve?

From the beginning of recorded history there is evidence that all cultures have sought to understand dreams and dreaming. And all believed that the correct interpretation of the dream will lead to understanding the future. The Hebrews, ancient Egyptians, early Greeks, and the Romans all believed that dreams are prophetic: Dreams predict the future. The interpretation of dreaming symbols and the meaning of each dream has fascinated the peoples of the world and in modern times has produced thousands of hours of research and miles of books and articles.

Our current interest in dreams has less to do with prophecy and more to do with the brain and its functions. The discovery of rapid eye movement (REM) during sleep opened a whole new world of research. The neuroscientific version of sleep and dreaming is now investigated with technology instead of shamans. The physiology, chemistry, and structure of the brain are currently subject to examination by machines like the EEG.

The science of dreams began in 1953 when researchers at the University of Chicago noticed that rapid eye movements (REM) and certain brain wave patterns are physical signs that a dream is in progress. Subjects, upon being awakened during REM sleep, could relate the dreams they were experiencing.

Later, researchers learned that people go through four or five REM stages nightly at about 90-minute intervals and that we can also dream when in non-REM (NREM) sleep.

To answer the question of *why* we dream and what *function* it serves, researcher Jonathan Winson looks to the spiny anteater, the only mammal that does not exhibit REM sleep. Winson believes that the large prefrontal cortex of the echidna formulates memories and strategies for the future in the waking state. For humans to learn in the same way would require an oversized prefrontal cortex larger than the skull could accommodate. Instead, we experience REM sleep, which allows us to incorporate new information. Since theta waves are active in the hippocampus during REM, there is some evidence for this theory (Guiley, 1993, p. 7).

The Activation-Synthesis Hypothesis of Hobson proposes that whatever is happening in the dream has to do with what is happening physically in the brain. Neurons receive messages from the brain stem instead of from the usual sources and interpret the signals that get to the brain in unique ways: thus, the dream (Guiley, 1992, p. 4).

Sleep deprivation studies lead to the conclusion that dreaming is a necessary physiological function. People continually awakened from REM sleep become anxious, fatigued, and irritable and have difficulty concentrating and remembering. If deprived of REM sleep for 4 or 5 days they hallucinate. When the subjects sleep normally, REM is greatly increased (as if they were making up for lost time).

For Flanagan, a professor of philosophy at Duke, dreams are the result of our need to create meaning. He demonstrates how brain stem activity during sleep generates a profusion of memories, images, thoughts, and desires, which the cerebral cortex attempts to make into a coherent story. "These narratives shed light on our mental life and our sense of self" (Flanagan, 2000, p. 115).

When Adler wrote the following article research on the brain had not begun. However, the meaning and interpretation of dreams had been given a giant boost from the appearance in 1900 of Freud's *The Interpretation of Dreams*. In that book Freud suggested that dreams are primarily "wish fulfillment," that they employ the same dynamisms used in slips of the tongue and daydreams, and arise from the unconscious.

Carl Jung, a decade later, believed that dreams were a true expression of the individual unconscious, the collective unconscious, and contained universal symbols like archetypes. He believed dreams were to be understood as having meaning and messages and "that the unconscious mind is capable at times of assuming an intelligence and purposiveness which are superior to actual conscious insight" (as quoted in Fromm, 1974, p. 96).

Adler differed from Freud in many important ways but accepted Freud's idea that dreams come from the unconscious and show hidden tendencies and personal conative patterns. Both Adler and Freud believed that dreams reveal the self and are subject to interpretation. But Adler had a much different concept about the nature of humans and how and why humans behave the way they do. Contrary to Freud, Adler believed that human beings are first of all, social animals and human behavior is best understood in a social setting. Within the social setting each human being . . . (is) an organism traveling through time and space to meet a destiny. This destiny is imagined by the individual as an ideal state of being. Since the organism is always moving as if there is an end point [a final goal . . . *telos*]. It is possible to examine behavior from the point of view of the direction of the movement. . . . The movement toward a . . . goal is continuous, it is constant, and it is maintained throughout life. (Peven & Shulman, 2002, p. 9)

Adler's view of dreams and dreaming contains his theory that all of a person's behavior is organized according to an ideal goal. The goal is unconscious and can be interpreted from the varieties of behaviors people exhibit including their dreams, and "that behind the dream exist forces at work striving toward a given goal," and "in dreams all the transitional phases of anticipatory thinking occur as if directed by some previously determined goal and by the utilization of personal experiences" (Adler, 1912, p. 222).

People go through life holding a set of convictions about themselves and the world outside of the subjective self, which lead to judgments about behavior. We form ideas and ideals about the significant issues of life and how to go about living successfully; we create a goal. "One may value honor above all else, another may value prestige or money. And still another will make safety and security important" (Peven & Shulman, 2002, p. 24).

Once the goal is formed, Adler believed that it underlies all behavior including dreams. Later Adlerians, however, do not believe that every dream has a psychological purpose, nor does every dream reveal the dreamer's goal in life.

Shulman focused on other aspects of the dream. For example, he lists the various functions of dreaming: (1) Dreams originate in unsolved problems about which the individual is concerned; (2) people dream to rehearse for future activity (the prophetic function); (3) the dream is meant to evoke feelings and emotions that lure the dreamer from the path of common sense (the dreamer commits self-deception); and (4) dreams purposefully create an emotional state in the dreamer.

Uniquely in the world of psychology Adlerians understand the dream as purposeful, creating an emotion. The purposive nature of the dream is the emotion created. Emotions are energizers of behavior, dynamic forces that produce movement. We learn to use emotions as strategies in the pursuit of our private goals. Thus, we summon anger to intimidate another to display bravery or to win an argument by overpowering another (Peven & Shulman, 2002).

Perlis and Nielsen conducted experiments at the University of Arizona and came to a similar conclusion: "[We] hypothesize that REM sleep and dreaming serve a mood regulatory function . . . [and] There is presently experimental evidence that daytime mood influences REM sleep and dreaming and that the latter, in turn, influence daytime mood" (Perlis & Nielsen, 1993, p. 243).

Adlerians will be delighted to know that Adler and his followers had insights that later research finds reasonable.

Insofar as Adler discussed the future orientation of dreams he did not believe that dreams were prophetic. While dreams can be a preparation for future behavior, they are not to be understood as predicting the future. But insofar as dreams reveal the dreamer's goal, they can be understood as future oriented. To demonstrate this, Adler gives us the dream of a businesswoman as follows: "I enter [my] shop and find the girls playing cards." Then Adler proposes:

> The interpretation is simple. The dreamer put herself into the future situation in which she would be . . . on the lookout for transgressions of rules . . . Her whole psychic life is permeated with the conviction that without her nothing could possibly be in proper order. . . . she degrades everyone . . . [and she demonstrates] her over-strained goal of superiority. (Adler, 1912, p. 218)

Here Adler finds both the future orientation of the dream and the goal of the dreamer's behavior: to degrade others so that she may feel superior. The goal is to put others down so that she may feel morally superior.

The psychology of dreams is often confused with the biology of dreaming. What we do know is that *something* is happening in the brain during sleep that leads to dreaming. Yet we still do not know why dreaming takes place and what function it serves. However, Adlerians believe that dreams must have an adaptive function, that all behavior has a purpose, and that, therefore, the dream must have a purpose.

Adler's view of dreams and dreaming contains his theory that all of a person's behavior is organized according to a plan of salvation (an ideal goal). The goal is unconscious and can be interpreted from the varieties of behaviors people exhibit including their dreams.

The future of scientific research may well lead us to confirm Adler's theory of the dream demonstrating an unconscious goal of the dreamer just as the research has confirmed that dreams produce emotions and can be considered the fuel that drives behavior.

## REFERENCES

Adler, A. (1912). Dreams and dream interpretation. (Lecture delivered in September 1912).
Guiley, R. E. (1993). *The encyclopedia of dreams*. New York: Crossroad Publishing.
Flanagan, O. (2000). *Dreaming souls*. New York: Oxford University Press.
Freud, S. (2000). *The interpretation of dreams*. New York: Modern Library.
Fromm, E. (1951). *The forgotten language*. Canada: Holt, Reinhart and Winston.

Perlis, M. L., & Nielsen, T. A. (1993). Mood regulation, dreaming and nightmares: Evaluation of a desensitization function for REM sleep. *Dreaming, a3*, 243–257.

Peven, D., & Shulman, B. (2002). *"Who is Sylvia?" and other stories: Case studies in psychotherapy.* New York: Taylor & Francis.

Shulman, B. H. (1977). *Contributions to Individual Psychology.* Chicago: Alfred Adler Institute.

## Dreams and Dream-Interpretation[23]

*Alfred Adler*

This is an age-old problem that can be traced back to the cradle of mankind. Fools and wise men have tried their hands at it and kings and beggars have attempted to extend the limits of their world knowledge by dream interpretation. How does the dream arise? What does it do? How are its hieroglyphics to be deciphered?

Egyptians, Chaldeans, Jews, Greeks, Romans and Teutons listened eagerly to the mystic language of the dream and in their myths and poems, we find indicated many traces of their arduous research for its understanding, for its interpretation. We hear them repeatedly insist as though obsessed; the dream can disclose the future! The famous dream-interpretations of the *Bible*, the *Talmud*, Herodotus, Artemidorus, Cicero, and the *Nibelungen-Lied*, impress upon us with undeniable certainty the conviction that the dream is a peering into the future. Even up to the present day the idea of obtaining knowledge of the unknowable is always brought into connection with reflections upon dreams. That our rationalistic age externally repudiated the hope of unveiling the future and laughed at such attempts is intelligible enough and it is this attitude that has made any occupation with the problem of the dream open to ridicule.

In order to circumscribe our field let me insist that I do not hold the view that the dream is a prophetic inspiration, that it can unlock the future or give knowledge of the unknowable. My extensive preoccupation with dreams has taught me one thing, that the dream like any other psychic manifestation comes into being through powers inherent in each individual. At the very threshold of any investigation there appear problems indicating that the possibility of dreams being prophetic was not easy to posit and that dreams are more likely to confuse than clarify the situation. The question to be asked clothed in all its difficulties is:—Is it really impossible for the human mind, within certain definite limits, to look into the future?

Unbiased observations lead to the strangest results. If the question (of the dream peering into the future) is put directly, an individual will generally deny it. But let us not pay any attention to mere external words or thoughts. If I were indeed to question the other portions of his body, (i.e. not his mouth or brain) for example, his movements, carriage, his actions, then we would receive quite a different impression. Although we deny the possibility of looking into the future, our whole manner of life is such that it betrays exactly to

---

[23] Translated by P. Radin.

what an extent we would like to obtain certainty with regard to future events. Our behavior clearly shows that, right or wrong, we do adhere to a possibility of obtaining knowledge of the future. Indeed it can further be shown that we would not be able to do anything if the future complexion of things—either those we desire or fear—did not determine the direction to be taken, furnish us with the incitement to act and disclose to us both the evasions and obstacles. *We continually act as if possessed of fore-knowledge of the future, although we realize that we can know nothing.*

Let us start from the petty things of life. If I buy something I obtain an anticipatory sensation, taste and pleasure. Frequently it is only this steadfast belief in an anticipated situation, with its pleasures and inconveniences, that makes me act or refrain from action. The fact that I am open to error will not deter me. On the other hand I refrain from acting in order, *if doubt develops,*[24] to weigh two possible future situations without coming to any decision. If I go to bed to-night I do not know that on the morrow when I awake there will be daylight, but I prepare myself for it.

But do I really know it? Do I know it in the same sense as I know that I am standing in front of you? No, my knowledge is of an entirely different order. It is not to be found in my *conscious thinking.* Yet its traces are indirectly in my bodily attitude, at my command. The Russian scientist Pavlov was able to show that in the stomach of animals when they *expect* a certain food, the juices necessary for digestion are secreted *as though the stomach had fore-knowledge of what foods it was to receive.* That means, however, that our body must be operating, like our mind, with some knowledge of the future if it wishes to play its role and be adequate; that it makes preparations as though it could foretell the future. This reckoning with the future is as in the last-mentioned instance quite foreign to our conscious thinking. Let us however ponder on this question! Would we ever act if we *consciously* grasped the future? Would not reflection, criticism, the constant weighing of pro and con constitute an insuperable obstacle to what we really desire to do, to act? *Our apparent knowledge of the future must consequently remain in our unconscious.* A condition of diseased psychic make-up exists—it is common and expresses itself in manifold ways—extreme doubt, compulsion-brooding, *folie de doute*—where the inward suffering actually drives the patient *into the only path* for properly safeguarding his importance and his feeling of individuality. The painful examination of one's own future prospects so prominently emphasizes its uncertainty and the anticipatory thinking is so definitely of a conscious kind that a set-back follows. The impossibility of

---

[24] The function of doubt in life and in the neurosis is, as I have shown, always to obtain a cessation of aggressiveness, to evade decisions and to conceal this fact from one's self. (Original footnote by Alfred Adler.)

knowing the future either consciously or with certainty fills the patient with indecision and doubt and thus everyone of his activities is interfered with by considerations of a different character. The contrast is given by that mania which manifests itself where a secret and otherwise unconscious future goal expresses itself impetuously, overwhelming reality with evil intent and enticing the conscious self to irresistible assumptions in order to protect the pathological self-consciousness from making mistakes in its co-operation with society.

That conscious thinking plays but a minor role in dreams hardly needs proof. Similarly the critical faculty and the contradictions brought about by the inactive sense organs are also inoperative. Is it conceivable that the expectations, wishes, and fears connected with the given situation of the dreamer should manifest themselves undisguisedly in the dream?

A patient had been brought to the hospital after he had taken ill with a severe attack of tabes; his mobility and sensibility was in consequence of his disease markedly limited and he had in addition become blind and deaf. As there was no means of communicating with him, his situation was indeed a very remarkable one.

When I saw him he was continually demanding beer and abusing the nurse in all sorts of obscene language. His real strivings, as well as his method of enforcement remained untouched. If, however, we were to imagine one of his sense-organs as functioning it is evident that not only his statements but likewise his thought-connections would have taken a different turn. The non-functioning of touch during sleep is felt in many ways particularly in the displacement of the realm of action and in the *less hampered emergence of a goal*. This necessarily leads as compared with the waking stage, to an intensification and stressing of conation and in content to analogical but more sharply outlined characterizations and suggestions. These latter, however, in consequence of the dreamer's caution may be accompanied by restrictions or obstacles. Even Havelock Ellis (*The World of Dreams*) who offers other explanations mentions this problem. Looked at from other view-points we can understand why in the case of the above patient, as in dreams, only an under-standing of the true situation of affairs could bring about a *rationalization* (Nietzsche) and a "*logical interpretation*."

Nevertheless the direction of the activity and therefore the anticipatory, prescient function of the dream is always clearly discernible; it foreshadows the preparations developed in connection with actual difficulties encountered by the dreamer's life-line, and the safe-guarding purpose is never lost sight of. Let us attempt to trace these lines by an example. A patient with a severe case of agoraphobia, who had taken ill with haemotropia, dreamt the following as she lay in bed incapacitated from pursuing her duties as a business woman: "I enter a shop and find the girls playing cards."

In all my cases of agoraphobia I found this symptom used as an excellent means of forcing upon the environment, relations, husband or wife, employees, certain duties and dictating laws to them like a *kaiser or deity*. This tyranny is accomplished by preventing any person from being absent or withdrawing from business on such excuses as attacks of anxiety, dizziness or nausea. I always in such a case think of the similarity of this attitude to that of the Pope, *the deputy of God*, who regards himself as a prisoner (in the Vatican) and who by this very renunciation of his personal freedom, intensifies the worship of the believers and forces all potentates to come to him ("The journey to Canossa") without their being able to expect a return visit. The dream of my patient occurred at a time when this trial of strength had already become manifest. The interpretation is simple. The dreamer put herself into the future situation in which she would be out of bed and on the look-out for transgressions of rules. Her whole psychic life is permeated with the conviction that without her nothing could possibly be in proper order. This conviction she adheres to in other phases of life, for she *degrades everyone and tries pedantically to improve everything*. In her ever-wakeful distrust she is always endeavouring to discover errors in others. So thoroughly is she filled with experiences emphasizing mistrust that she really developed greater acuteness in detecting mistakes than others. She knew exactly what employees would do if they were permitted to. She also knew what men do when they are alone. "All men are alike!" For that reason her husband always has to remain at home.

Unquestionably considering the nature of her preparations she will, as soon as she recovers from lung-trouble, discover quite a number of omissions in her business, which is situated right near her home. She may even discover that the employees have played cards. The day after her dream she had the servant bring her the cards and on some pretext or other, had the girl-employees called to her bed-side repeatedly in order to give them new directions and to supervise them. In order to obtain light on the future she only has to ferret out in her sleep-consciousness, in consonance with her over-strained *goal of superiority*, some fitting analogies and to take literally and seriously the fiction of the *recurrence of similar*[25] *manifestations in individual experiences*. Indeed in order to prove herself to have been in the right all she need do is, after her recovery, to increase the standard of her demands. Mistakes and omissions would then certainly be found to exist.

As another example of dream interpretation, I would like to use the dream of the poet Simonides as handed down by Cicero, a dream interpretation that

---

[25] The deeper knowledge of this "fiction of similarity," one of the most important assumptions of thought and of the causality principle, I owe to my friend and collaborator A. Hautler. (Original footnote by Alfred Adler.)

I have already used to develop a part of my theory of dreams (cf. the chapter "On the Concept of Resistance"). One night shortly before embarking on a journey to Asia Minor Simonides dreamt "a dead person whom he had piously buried warned him from taking the contemplated journey." After this dream Simonides discontinued his preparations for the journey and stayed at home. According to our experiences in dream-interpretation we may assume that Simonides was afraid of this journey, that he *used this dead person*[26] who was under obligations to him, *to frighten and protect himself* by the thought of the horror of the grave and by presentiments of meeting a frightful end. According to the narrator the boat capsized, an event that probably presented itself to the dreamer's mind on the analogy of other shipwrecks. If the boat had really arrived safely at its destination what would have prevented superstitious natures from assuming that it would have gone down had Simonides not heeded the warning and been on board?

We find consequently in dreams two types of attempts of pre-interpreting, of solving a problem, and of initiating what the dreamer desires to put into a given situation. This he will seek to accomplish along lines best adapted to his personality, his nature and character. The dream may depict a situation which is anticipated in the future as already existing, (the dream of the patient with agoraphobia), in order in the waking state to put this arrangement into effect either openly or surreptitiously. The poet Simonides apparently employed an old experience to prevent him from travelling. If you firmly believed that this is an experience of the dreamer, that it is his own interpretation of the power of the dead man and that it is his own situation that demands an answer as to whether he is to go or not, if you take all these possibilities into consideration then you get the unmistakeable impression that Simonides dreamed this dream in order to give himself a hint that he could clearly and without hesitation remain at home. We may assume that even if he had not had this dream our poet would have remained at home. What then about our patient with agoraphobia? Why did she dream of the carelessness and disorderliness of her employees? We may detect in her behaviour the following assumptions: "When I am not present everything goes to pieces and as soon as I regain my health and take charge of affairs I shall demonstrate to everyone that nothing can get along well without me." We may consequently be certain

---

[26] I intend further on to discuss in detail the employment of such very broad emotion-provoking reminiscences that serve the purpose of inducing affects and their consequences, cautions actions and at the same time, loathing, dizziness, anxiety, fear of the sexual partner, fainting, and other neurotic symptoms. Much of these I have discussed in my book, *The Neurotic Constitution,* and have been able to reduce it either to a likeness (e.g., incest-likeness, crime-likeness, godlikeness, megalomania, smallness-mania) or to what I have described as a "junktim." As far as I know only Prof. Hamburger has arrived at even approximately similar results. (Original footnote by Alfred Adler.)

that upon her first appearance in the shop she will discover all sorts of der-
elictions of duty and of carelessness for she will be looking about, argus-eyed
in order to show her superiority. She will probably be able to prove she was
right and that is why she anticipated the future in her dream.[27] The dream
therefore like character, affect and the neurotic-symptom is arranged by the
dreamer in accordance with a predesigned purpose.

Permit me now to interpolate here a discussion so that I can meet an
objection which very likely has occurred to many of you. How am I to
explain the fact that the dream attempts to influence the future complexion
of things when most of our dreams appear so clearly to contain unintelligible
and often enough, stupid and meaningless matters? The importance of this
objection is so distinctly felt that most of our authorities have looked for the
essence of the dream in these bizarre, unoriented and unintelligible manifestations and have tried to explain them; or stretching the unintelligibility of the dream-life they have denied to them all importance. Schemer and
Freud in particular among the newer men must be given the credit of having
attempted the interpretation of the mystery of the dream. Freud in order to
give a foundation to his dream-theory, according to which the dream represents a kind of revelling in infantile unfulfilled sexual wishes, regarded
this unintelligibility as a purposive distortion, as though the dreamer in
spite of the restrictions imposed upon him by civilization, did nevertheless
desire, in phantasy at least, to gratify his forbidden wishes. To-day this view
has become as untenable as that of the sexual basis of neurotic diseases or
the sexual basis of our civilization. The apparent lack of intelligibility in the
dream is to be accounted for primarily by the circumstance that *the dream is
not a means* for the attainment of a future position but an accessory phenomenon, an indication of power, a sign and a proof that both body and mind
are making an attempt at anticipatory thinking and at anticipatory groping
in order to justify the personality of the dreamer in connection with some
approaching difficulty. In other words we have here a synchronous movement of our thought, one running in the same direction as the character
and the nature of the personality demand and expressing itself in a difficult
language which even when understood, is not at all clear. Yet this language
indicates the direction toward which the path tends. As necessary as is intelligibility for our waking thought and speech, preparing as it does our actions,
so superfluous does it become in the dream, for the dream is to be compared

---

[27] It may be surmised that Simonides, who as a poet yearned for immortality, was according to this
dream possessed of a fear of death, whereas the patient with agoraphobia, pursuing her fictive goal
of domination, had a queen ideal. Cf. also for the first, "Individual-psychologische Ergebnisse uber
Schlaflosigkeit" (Fortschritte d. Medizin; Leipzig, 1913), where, among other things, the relation
of the infantile fear of death to the choice of a medical profession is emphasized. (Original footnote by Alfred Adler.)

with the smoke of a fire which but points out to us in what direction the wind lies.

On the other hand the smoke may serve to tell us that a fire is to be found in a certain place and experience teaches us to infer the presence of wood from the fire and from that the fact that something is burning.

If we break up a dream into its constituent parts and if we can discover from the dreamer what these individual parts mean then a moderate expenditure of industry and a certain degree of penetration will indicate to us that behind the dream exist forces at work striving toward a given goal. This direction is adhered to by man in other aspects of life besides those of the dream and is conditioned by his ego-ideal and by those difficulties and inadequacies felt by him as oppressive. From this view-point then, which can rightly be called an artistic one we obtain a knowledge of man's life-line or, at least, of part of it and we get a glimpse of that unconscious life-plan by means of which he strives to dominate the pressure of life and his own feeling of uncertainty. We also get a glimpse of the detours he makes in the interests of this feeling of insecurity so that he may avoid defeat. We have the right to employ the dream as much as any other psychical manifestation and just as much as the whole life of man, for the purpose of drawing conclusions concerning his position in the world and his relation to other people. *In dreams all the transitional phases of anticipatory thinking occur as if directed by some previously determined goal and by the utilization of personal experiences.*

We thus arrive at a better understanding of the initially unintelligible details found in dream-structure. The dream rarely gives a presentation of facts—and even when it does, this is conditioned by a specific trait of the dreamer—in which recent happenings or pictures of the present occur. For the solution of an undecided question simpler, more abstract and infantile comparisons are at hand, comparisons frequently suggesting more expressive and more poetical images. For example, an impending decision may be replaced by an impending school examination, a strong opponent by an older brother, the idea of victory by a flight to the sky, and a danger by an abyss or a fall. Affects that play a role in dreams always arise from preparations and anticipatory thinking, and from the protective devices for the actually threatening problem.[28] The simplicity of the dream scenes—simple in comparison with the complex situations of life—represent to such an extent the attempts of the dreamer to find some outlet by excluding the confusing multiplicity of powers present in any given situation, that he is willing to pursue a guiding-line that resembles these simple situations. Just as a pupil who does not understand a teacher's question, for example, often looks quite

---

[28] These may gain tendentious strength from the dream picture if this is necessary for the sake of safety. (Original footnote by Alfred Adler.)

bewildered when asked with regard to the propulsion of energy, "What takes place when you are pushed?" If a stranger were to enter the room, as this last question was asked, he would look at the teacher with the same lack of comprehension that we exhibit when told a dream.

Lastly, the unintelligibility of a dream belongs together with the problem first discussed. There we saw that *in order to obtain protection for an act we require a belief in the future that is steeped in the unconscious.* This basic attitude for human thoughts and actions, according to which an unconscious guiding-line leads to a personality ideal within the unconscious, I have discussed in detail in my book *The Neurotic Constitution.* The construction of this personality ideal and the guiding lines leading to it contain the same cognitive and emotional material as does the dream and the emotional processes that lie behind it. The same necessity that forces one kind of psychic material to remain within the unconscious presses at the same time so heavily upon the thoughts, pictures and auditory impressions of the dream that the latter, *in order not to endanger the ego's unity of personality* must likewise remain in the unconscious, or better, must remain unintelligible. (Think, for example, of the dreams of the patient afflicted with agoraphobia). What she tried to achieve by means of her unconscious personality was the domination of the environment. If she could have understood her dream then her despotic strivings and actions would have had to give way to the criticism of her waking thoughts. But as her real desire was to rule, her dream must remain unintelligible to her. From this point of view it is also possible to understand that psychic illness and all forms of nervousness become untenable and are bound to improve if we succeed in bringing into consciousness and blunting the over-strained goals of the neurotic.

Let me now show partially how, with the help of the patient herself, the interpretation of a dream was conducted. The patient came under my treatment on account of irritability and suicide-mania. I wish to stress particularly the fact that the analogical aspect of the dream-thought is always found to be prominent in the supposition[29] with which the dreaming individual begins. The difficult nature of the situation lay in the fact that she was in love with her brother-in-law. The dream follows:—

---

[29] Cf. Vaihinger, *The Philosophy of As If,* whose theory of knowledge is in complete agreement with my beliefs on the psychology of the neuroses. (Original footnote by Alfred Adler.)

## A NAPOLEON DREAM[30]

"I dreamt that I was in the dancing-hall, wore a pretty blue dress, had my hair dressed nicely and danced with Napoleon."

"In this connection" (said the patient) "the following occurs to me:

"I have raised my brother-in-law to the role of Napoleon *for it would otherwise hardly be worth while* taking him away from my sister (i.e. her neurotic nature is not at all fixed on the man but on the desire to be superior to her sister). In order to cover the whole matter over with the mantle of righteousness and further, in order not to give the impression as though I had been instigated by revenge because I had come upon the scene too late, I have of necessity to imagine myself as the Princess Louise so that it appears quite natural for Napoleon to divorce his first wife Josephine in order to take a wife of equal rank.

"With regard to the name Louise, I had been using it for some time. On one occasion a young man asked for my Christian name and my colleague knowing I did not like Leopoldine, said simply that I was called Louise.

"That I was a princess I dreamt frequently (guiding-line) and this is indeed my most intense ambition, which in dreams permits me to construct a bridge over the gulf separating me from the aristocrats. Furthermore this illusion is calculated to make me feel, when awake, all the more painfully, the fact that I was brought up away from home and that I am alone and thrown upon myself. The sad thoughts that come over me, enable me *to behave harshly and cruelly to all people* who have the good fortune to be connected with me.

"As far as Napoleon is concerned, let me point out that since I am definitely not a man, I want to bend the knee only before such as are greater and more powerful than all the others. Incidentally this would not prevent me from stating that Napoleon was a burglar (burglar-dreams). Then again I should only bow before him and not really submit to him, for I would like to hold the man by a string, as is to be inferred from another dream—and then, and then I would dance.

"Dancing must be a substitute for many things to me because music exerts a tremendous influence upon my soul.

"How frequently during a concert was I seized with the intense longing to run over to my brother-in-law and almost suffocate him with kisses.

"In order not to allow this desire for a stranger to rise up before me, I must throw myself passionately into dancing or if I have no partner, remain seated

---

[30] Napoleon, Jesus, Jeanne d'Arc, the Virgin, as well as the Kaiser, father, uncle, mother, brother, etc., are frequent compensation-ideals of the intensified lust for superiority and represent, at the same time, the directive and emotionally steeped preparations of the psychic life of the neurotic. (Original footnote by Alfred Adler.)

with compressed lips and stare gloomily into the distance in order to prevent any one else from approaching me.

"*I did not wish to succumb to love,* and yet in my opinion balls and love belong together.

"I selected the blue color because it is most becoming to me and because I had been actuated by the desire of making a good impression upon Napoleon. I had now the desire to dance, something I formerly was not able to do."

From this point on the interpretation might proceed much further and finally disclose the fact that the unconscious life-plan of this girl had as its purpose the will to rule, a purpose now altered and weakened to the extent that she no longer regards dancing as a personal humiliation.

I have come to the end. We have seen that the dream represents a subsidiary psychic manifestation as far as action is concerned, but that as in a mirror it may betray events and bodily attitudes that are related to subsequent acts. Is it therefore to be wondered at the folk-soul at all times with the infallibility that holds true of all universal feelings, accepted the dream as a pointing toward' the future? A very great man, one who united within himself the focal points of all the sensations of man, Goethe, has expressed the dreamer's "glimpse into the future" and the help and strength flowing from it in a wonderful ballad. The count returning to his castle from the Holy Land finds it empty and desolate. At night he dreams of a dwarf's wedding. The conclusion of the poem is: "And were we now to sing of what happened later on, then all the noise and dot would have to cease. For what he saw so nicely in miniature, he became acquainted with and enjoyed on a larger scale. Trumpets and the jingling, ringing peals of music rang out, and rider, chariot, bridal throngs, all approached "and bowed before him, an innumerable happy lot. Thus it was and thus it will ever be."

The feeling that this poem of the dreamer is directed toward thoughts of marriage and children is quite sufficiently stressed by the poet.

# 14

# *Life-Lie and Responsibility in Neurosis and Psychosis*
## A Contribution to Melancholia

MARY FRANCES SCHNEIDER

You are about to read Adler's classic essay "Life-Lie and Responsibility in Neurosis and Psychosis: A Contribution to Melancholia." You should be able to walk away from this reading with a detective-like curiosity for sniffing out the "life-lie" and an understanding of how safeguarding works to evade life task responsibilities. In this article, Adler buttresses his constructs by offering the reader case study examples of hypochondria and depression, which are still among our most common presenting issues. This article models understanding key constructs through exercising them within the context of therapy—still the best way to get your mind around a psychological construct.

This essay is a classic, which means it presents seminal ideas that have formed the development of Individual Psychology. We are rereading this work to experience the emergence of these key ideas. Just a few words about classics:

My nephew, a junior at the University of Chicago, is living with us this summer because he received a grant to write a curriculum for grade school children. The purpose of this curriculum is to teach philosophy to Grade 4 students in the Chicago school system. Sam's goal is to have students read "key selections from philosophers" and "reflect on what these ideas could mean today." Sam is struggling with the task of pulling student attention away from _____ (insert favorite distraction here: electronic gadgets, basketball hoops, open fire hydrant spray, street dance practice for *America's Got Talent*, etc.) and placing that attention for a sustained period of time on a set of historically important ideas about the meaning of life. Dinner conversation during the first week of his summer school experience had to do with the challenges of reflection. "My students are finding the act of reflection to be a very new experience," he said. "They are not used to thinking about big ideas." Well, it's Sam's third week on the project and armed with 2 years of undergraduate philosophy and 21 years of wisdom, in today's lesson Sam is encouraging enactments of the Socratic dialogues.

My agenda in this introduction to Adler's essay "Life-Lie and Responsibility" is similar to Sam's—I'd like to point out a few golden ideas in this text and then encourage you to mull over these ideas by applying them to your own lived experience and practice. Reflective integration of the depth of these ideas comes with applied practice. I also want to mention that you are reading a classic piece of writing and while it may not be as Greek as what Sam is teaching, the form, style, and syntax of Adler's journal article can challenge the reader. In spite of the thickness of text, the key ideas, just like Sam's curriculum, are historical treasures.

In this essay the reader is introduced to cognitive schemata that are central in Adler's perspective on how the neurotic or psychotic client constructs a holistic, highly individualized system of strategies for avoiding personal responsibility and applying the life-lie in the life task areas. This essay begins by laying out the importance of the "individual life-lines" (p. 235), which are not discussed in depth in this essay but instead the reader is directed to recall this foundational Adlerian idea of lifestyle—the style of life—which is going to be key in both understanding and predicting client movement and choice.

Pull from this essay the stunningly brilliant idea of the life-lie. The life-lie is essential to understanding the client and client's lifestyle. Adler is poetic in his description of the life-lie. "The individual helps along with all the powers at his disposal and thus the calming hypnotizing safeguarding currents of the *life-lie* permeate the whole content of life" (Adler, p. 236). The life-lie is a central integrated theme—an individual perspective—around which safeguarding mechanisms are organized to achieve a private goal, avoid social responsibility, and often place blame on or simply use others. This life-lie always has social implications—avoiding responsibility to others while placing others or the resources of others in the service of the unhealthy individual. It is the major headline culled out of the lifestyle analysis and certainly helps the therapist both understand and predict the client's ongoing choices and line of movement. Mulling this idea of life-lie as it relates to each of your clients would be a most useful exercise.

As an example, let us take the very public and not so subtle case of Bernard Madoff. His life-lie probably involved beliefs around financial powers so omnipotent that he could beat high-risk odds—a sort of "mega-gambler" lie. Certainly, in his mind, his greatness entitled him to use the resources of others—retirement savings, charity resources, institutional funds—toward his own private economic goals. Safeguarding and distancing himself from reality, he bought his own delusion and felt little or no responsibility toward these individuals, families, groups, and institutions. Rather, he most likely felt that he had the right to use these resources to fuel his powerful goals and visions. The "calming hypnotizing safeguarding currents of the life-lie" certainly encompassed the whole of Bernie's life. Not only was he hypnotized regarding these powers, but so were his victims. Whistle-blowers blew in the wind. No amount of reality-based data on the improbability of his high rates of return seemed to break the trance. The trance was both powerful and popular, a trance that even affected the U.S. Securities and Exchange Commission's (SEC) ability to competently investigate Madoff's firm. Madoff did create greatness—he created the greatest Ponzi scheme in history. This was a man devoted to and prominently known for economic wizardry—wizardry which turned out to be a life-lie. Too good to be true was, indeed, too good to be true.

These words—"calming hypnotizing safeguarding currents of the life-lie"—are densely packed brilliance not only for those of us who are engaged in individual therapy but also for those practicing marriage and family therapy. This "calm trance" permeates the client's entire life—those in relationship with the client deal with deeply held beliefs that rub up against the realities of daily social interactions. The trance affects others; it is the source of behaviors that we often term *codependent* in partners, family members, and friends. The client presses on with behaviors supporting a life-lie and significant others react, that is, buy into, are at the mercy of, cope with, accommodate, try to cure, and at times even support the lie. Everyone around the client is affected by the life-lie and makes some type of accommodation to it. And as Adler notes in this essay, any attempts to get the client to "face the truth" only engender the client's wrath.

So let us talk about the idea of the "safeguarding tendency," which is the "inclination to resort to detours, truces, retreats, tricks and stratagems as soon as the question of *socially necessary decisions* comes up" (Adler, p. 236). The neurotic lifestyle, especially the life-lie, encompasses safeguarding mechanisms that relieve the individual of personal responsibility both to the self and to others. While other theories call these *defense mechanisms*, Adler views the mechanisms in the service of the lifestyle—protecting and guarding the belief system from any reality-based experiences that might challenge it. Carlson, Watts, and Maniacci (2006) offer both history and description of safeguarding in their work *Adlerian Therapy*. In the following essay, Adler describes case study examples of the safeguarding mechanisms in operation and how safeguards relate to the relief of responsibility. The life-lie relieves the client of authentic responsibilities, excusing or exempting the client from standard expectations regarding what we now call the life tasks.

Just a few more words on responsibility before you dive into this essay: As Adler has pointed out, the neurotic's goal within the line of movement of the lifestyle creates safeguards around authentic expressions of responsibility. It is so fixed in its safeguarding agenda that it cannot participate in authentic responsibility, which is actually a cooperative act. Meeting the life task responsibilities in marriage, work, or friendship requires creative collaboration with others—a give-and-take in the moments of life with an eye on fulfilling specific tasks. The neurotic's individually fixed agenda makes collaboration around responsibilities impossible.

I hope you enjoy reading this essay and, in the process, spin your own set of associations to the work. I hope you walk away with ideas that resonate in your therapeutic work as well as your life experience. Enjoy this classic.

## REFERENCES

Adler, A. (1924). Life-lie and responsibility. *The Practice and Theory of Individual Psychology.*

Carlson, J., Watts, R. E., & Maniacci, M. (2006). *Adlerian therapy: Theory and practice.* Washington, DC: American Psychological Association.

## Life-Lie and Responsibility in Neurosis and Psychosis:
## A Contribution to Melancholia (1914)[31]

*Alfred Adler*

This essay is essentially based on the belief that all psychogenic diseases, which we reckon as belonging to neuroses and psychoses, are symptoms of a higher kind and consequently constitute the technique, representation and products of individual life-lines. The detailed proof I reserve for another essay. However it is impossible even here not to take into consideration this provisional assumption. In doing so I gladly acknowledge my indebtedness to the views of some well-known scholars. To mention but one psychiatrist, Raimamn has pointed out clearly the connection between individuality and psychosis. The development of psychiatry likewise shows the progressive blurring of boundaries. Ideal types are disappearing both from literature and practice. Let me also mention here the "unity of neurosis" upon which I have laid emphasis. In general it may be said that we are approaching a point of view to which individual psychology has made important contributions. That view-point is that the neurotic methods of life seize with an apparently unalterable regularity, based upon individual experiences, upon the means of a utilizable neuroses or psychoses, in order to triumph.

Psychological results of individual psychology are well adapted to cor-roborate this view-point. For they suggest as one of their final results that the patient is constructing an inner world of his own on the basis of a defective individual perspective in definite contrast with reality. Nevertheless this per-spective which dictates his attitude to society, is from a human point of view easily understood and is in other connections quite general. We frequently call to mind individuals who in life or in poetry have skirted around such an abyss. Up to the present there is not the slightest proof that either heredity, experience or the environment *necessarily lead* to a general or specific neu-rosis. This etiological necessity, which is never free from personal tendencies or personal connivance, exists simply in the rigid assumption of the patient who thus safeguards his neurotic or psychotic inference and with it the integ-rity of his disease. He might be able to think, feel and act in a less etiological manner if he were not impelled onward upon this journey by his goal, by that imagined final scene. However it is a categorical command of his life-plan *that he should fad either through the guilt of others and thus be freed from personal responsibility*, or that some fatal trifle should prevent his triumph.[32] The essentially human nature of this longing is strikingly manifest. The indi-

---

[31] Translated by P. Radin.
[32] Cf. the chapter on "The Problem of Distance." (Original footnote by Alfred Adler.)

vidual helps along with all the powers at his disposal and thus the calming hypnotizing safeguarding currents of the *life-lie* permeate the whole content of life. Every therapeutic treatment and certainly every clumsy and tactless attempt to tell the patient the truth, deprives the patient of the very source of his irresponsibility and must expect to encounter the most violent resistance.

This attitude which we have so often described originates in the "safeguarding tendency" of the patient and exhibits his inclination to resort to detours, truces, retreats, tricks and stratagems as soon as the question of *socially necessary decisions* comes up. The analyst is well acquainted with all the excuses and pretexts used by the sick man in order to evade his tasks or his own expectations. Our contributions have thrown a clear light upon these problems and exposed them to view. There are very few instances in which the attribution of guilt to others appears to be missing. Among these instances, the disease-pictures of *hypochondria* and *melancholia* force themselves most upon our attention.

I should like to raise the question of the *"opponent"* which can be employed as a very useful guide in making the nature of the psychogenic disease picture more transparent. The solution of this question no longer exhibits the psychogenically diseased individual in his artificial isolation but in his socially determined system. It is easy to understand from this fact the belligerent tendency of the neurosis and psychosis. What might otherwise be regarded as the termination namely, the specific disease, now takes its proper place as a means, a method of life, a symptom indicative of the path taken by the patient either to attain his goal of superiority or to feel his right in possessing it.

In many psychoses and also in neurotically-diseased individuals the attack as well as the accusation fall not simply upon one person but upon a number of people, occasionally upon the whole of humanity, hetero-sexuality or the whole world order. This behavior is unusually clearly apparent in the case of *paranoia*. The complete withdrawal from the world which means, of course, *at the same time, condemnation of it*, is expressed in *dementia praecox*. In a more concealed fashion and limited to only a few persons do we see the struggle of the hypochondriac and the melancholic. Here the view-point of individual-psychology allows us a sufficiently wide field of vision for understanding even the artifices used in these cases. Thus, for example, when an ageing hypochondriac succeeds in freeing himself from work in which he fears disappointments, at the same time forcing some relative to take charge of his house and make sacrifices for him. The "distance" to the decision—in this case his literary talent—is sufficiently great not to be overlooked. He emphasizes this "distance" by resorting to an unusually effective agoraphobia. Who is at fault? He was born in the revolutionary year (1848) and insists that this is a hereditary stigma. His digestive disturbances represent in the *enumeration of the means* he adopts (Stern) important aids to his lust for dominating his environment.

This lust for domination is thus incited to increased work. These disturbances *are caused* by air-inhaling and purposive constipation.

A craftsman fifty-two years old has an attack of melancholia one evening when his daughter before going out on a visit, forgets to take leave of him. This man had always insisted upon his family looking up to him as the head of the family and forced definite services and strict obedience upon them by means of his hypochondriacal troubles. His neurotic stomach could stand no restaurant food. His wife was consequently compelled when he went upon his vacation, "necessitated by his condition of health," to prepare his food in a kitchen which she rented in the country. The fact that he was ageing he attributed to the "unfilial" actions of his daughter and he regarded it as an indication of weakness. When his prestige was threatened, his impending melancholia was to bring home to his daughter her guilt and to show his family the full significance of his capacity for work. Now he had discovered a way of acquiring and enforcing that prestige which he seemed to have failed to obtain in the world in spite of his achievements. He was thus on the road to *irresponsibility* if for any reason his personal role should fail him.

A manufacturer twenty years old, was as he grew older, subject every two years to a fit of melancholia which lasted a few weeks. As in the case mentioned above, he also began to take ill when through, an unfortunate event, his prestige *was threatened*. He also neglected his work and frightened his family, who were dependent upon his work, by continual complaints about impending poverty. The situation he thus called into existence resembled in every detail an overwhelming of his environment. All complaints and criticisms stopped in his presence, *he was freed from the responsibility for his reckless adventures* and his importance as the maintainer of the family became clear to everyone. The stronger his melancholia became, the more bitterly he complained, *the higher did he rise in value*. He became well when the resentment against his adventure had disappeared. Subsequently, his melancholia always recurred whenever he found himself in a financially insecure position and on one occasion because of the intervention of the tax officials. His condition always improved as soon as his troubles were over. It was quite easy to see that he was carrying on a policy of *prestige-attainment* within his family, seeking safety in his melancholia whenever discussions on vital matters came up. In this way he could excuse himself and also relieve himself of any responsibility if anything went wrong and if everything ended well, receive *increased recognition*. Our example thus shows clearly the symptom of the "*hesitating attitude*" we have described and also the creation of "*distance*" wherever a decision is to be taken.

Before I enter upon a description of the last-mentioned example of melancholia, let me attempt to define more sharply from the view-point of individual psychology the mechanism of melancholia and to throw some light upon that aspect in which it is in marked contrast with paranoia. If we once admit the social-conditioning and the belligerent attitude of melancholia we shall easily discover what it is in the goal of superiority that hypnotizes the sick man. The path he takes in the beginning is certainly rather strange. For instance, he minimizes himself, *anticipates* situations of intense misery and, identifying himself with them, acquires a feeling of sorrow and the outward expression of being completely broken up.[33] This seems a contradiction of his affirmation of a goal of greatness. As a matter of fact his exhausting physical weakness became in his hands a rather fear-inspiring weapon for securing recognition and escaping responsibility. For anyone to be able to achieve a true melancholia is, to my mind, something in the nature of a work of art except that, of course, the creative consciousness is wanting and *that the patient's attitude represents a condition with which he has been acquainted since early childhood.*

Tracing it back to his earliest childhood we find that this attitude is in reality an artifice, an automatically conditioned method of life, taking the form of a rigid life-line when he is passing through a period of uncertainty. *Actually this consists in the desire to force his own will upon others and in safeguarding his prestige by threats of becoming ill.*[34] He bends all his energies with their accompanying bodily and psychic possibilities, towards the achievement of this purpose. He disturbs his sleep, his nourishment, his stool and urinary functions so that he may lose strength and prove that he is ill. He is quite willing to follow this course to its logical conclusion of suicide. An additional proof of the aggressive nature of melancholia is furnished by the occasional appearance of the murder impulse and by the frequent presence of paranoiac traits. In these cases the attribution of guilt to others becomes prominent as for example in the case of the woman who believed herself to be suffering from cancer because her husband had forced her to visit a relative suffering from that disease. Summarizing we may say that the difference between the melancholic and paranoidal attitude seems to consist in the fact that the melancholic feels himself to be guilty whereas the paranoiac accuses somebody else. To make the matter clearer let me add that these individuals resort to this procedure *only if they find no other method of establishing their superiority.* We might incidentally point out that both these types represent universal human traits and as soon as we look for them they will be seen to have an extensive distribution.

---

[33] Just as, for example, the actor in Hamlet. "He weeps for Hecuba! What's Hecuba to him or he to Hecuba that he should weep for her?" In his complaints the psychotic individual betrays in much the same way as the neurotic, the nature of his "arrangement." (Original footnote by Alfred Adler.)

[34] Often the melancholic type of procedure shows itself to be either incidentally or predominantly the revenge impulse of impotent rage. (Original footnote by Alfred Adler.)

The psychical susceptibility to psychoses is frequently diminished by the fact that the goal of superiority[35] possesses even greater strength. The asserted impossibility of correcting "maniacal" ideas is partially true but flows logically from the compelling nature of the goal. We were able to show above how the psychotically diseased individual protects his personality-feeling at all times by creating "distance" which he attains by the subterfuge of a life-falsehood. In order to cure his neurosis it is necessary for the patient to "*temporarily*" weaken his guiding ideals. A success running counter to his symptoms will only then be really efficacious if the patient is disposed to let himself be healed or if he is able gradually and unnoticed to slacken the rigidity of his goal. As far as we can see the maniacal idea commits no mistakes. It is under the compelling influence of the guiding idea and fulfils its ultimate purpose which is to make itself irresponsible and protect the ego-consciousness by the creation of "distance." *A logical examination hardly touches the mania because in its capacity as a well-tested modus vivendi et dicendi, it fulfils its purpose and because, moreover, the patient runs for protection to his limited appreciation of that communal sense of reality which we all share.*

The melancholic individual we have just been describing betrayed the whole arrangement of his illness in a dream which he had at the very beginning of the treatment. He had become ill *when removed from a place where he occupied the principal position* to one where he would have to prove his worth. Twelve years before, at the age of twenty-six, under similar circumstances he had also had an attack of melancholia. His dream was as follows:—

"I am at a pension where I eat my mid-day meal. A girl in whom I have been interested for some time, serves the meals. I realized suddenly that the world was coming to an end, and at the same time the thought occurred to me that I might now be able to rape the girl, *for I could not be held accountable.* However, after I had committed the rape it became evident that the world was not going to end." The interpretation is simple. The patient wishes to evade all decisions relating to love because he is unwilling to shoulder the responsibility. He has often toyed with the idea of a world-catastrophe (enemy of mankind). The dream, in a sexual disguise, indicates that he would have to believe in a world-catastrophe in order to be able to conquer, for in this manner a sense of irresponsibility could be created. His final act (the rape) shows him on the way to the attainment of his goal through a fictitious arrangement, an "as if," a provisional testing of a method of attack which consists in doing violence to others.[36]

---

[35] I am not here considering the intermediate conditions ranging from marked incapacity for fixing attention to idiocy produced by inactivity of the reasoning powers, of long duration. (Original footnote by Alfred Adler.)

[36] Cf. *Dream and Dream-Interpretation,* in this volume and the author's dream-theory in his *The Neurotic Constitution.* (Original footnote by Alfred Adler.)

We are now in a position to examine the guiding line of the patient. He shows himself to be a man with no trust in himself, and one *who does not expect to succeed by a direct line of attack*. We should therefore expect to find from the facts of his early life and from the study of his present melancholic stage, that he is going to attempt to attain his goal along some circuitous path. We may also assume that he is going to create "distance" between himself and the direct approach to his goal. Perhaps we are even justified in assuming that should he have to decide he will lean toward an "ideal situation" because in such a situation, confidently anticipating a threatening catastrophe, he will himself be free from all responsibility. He will only regain his confidence, it may be assumed, when certain of victory. *This idea obtained from the dynamics of the dream coincides with the view expressed above about melancholia.* Now this attitude, be it remembered, is typical, to a certain extent, for the majority of mankind and is frequently encountered among neurotics. It is part of the essence of the specific power, the singleness of the guiding superiority-belief and the defective connection with the logical demands of life, when irresponsibility and its related ideas are driven into the realm of the psychotic. To account for this we might provisionally assume a special degree of stubbornness and an unsocial craving for domination in our patient, although he denied possessing these traits when asked.

Let me now mention a few of this patient's reminiscences. Once in boyhood when dancing he fell down pulling his dancing-partner down with him and losing his glasses. Before raising himself he reached out for his glasses but carefully held his partner down with his other hand, a fact that led to an unpleasant scene afterwards. In this occurrence we may already detect his unsocial attitude, his tendency to violence. His customary means of enforcing his will are also clearly perceptible from other childhood reminiscences. For example, he remembers lying on the sofa and weeping for an unconscionably long time.[37] He did not know how to account for this last reminiscence. His older brother, who corroborated the patient's stubbornness and will to dominate, informed me quite spontaneously when interrogated, that his younger brother (our patient) had on that occasion forced him by his incessant crying to surrender the whole sofa to him.

I cannot discuss in detail here the manner in which the patient disturbed his sleep, his nutrition, his nutritive and excretory functions, how he lost strength and thus gave proof of being ill. Nor can I dwell on the manner in which by positing unfulfillable conditions and guarantees he attempted to demonstrate both to himself and to others the hopelessness of his condition;

---

[37] I have discussed the purposive molding and survival of childhood reminiscences in *The Neurotic Constitution,* and in a paper delivered before the congress of psychotherapy at Vienna in 1913. (Original footnote by Alfred Adler.)

nor how he felt the steps taken by his family and the interference of the physician as an additional affront. He went so far as to deny to himself all ability and all possibility of making a living, in that way forcing his family and his friends into his service and into his power, using them then in connection with attempts to make his business superiors more amenable to his wish, which was that he should be transferred to a place where he could again play the role of master. His hostility was therefore directed against all the officials under him, and it took the form of interfering with all their demands. His plan was to pass from a condition of irresponsibility to one of violence. Then having finally attained his goal he would allow himself to be convinced that the world was not coming to an end.

In my book, *The Neurotic Constitution*, I found the necessary conditions for the development of mania, to judge from selected cases, to be the following:

1. An intensified feeling of uncertainty and inability to face an imminent decision.
2. The mechanism is a marked deflection from and devaluation of reality. (Among other things this means a denial of the value of rationality as a function of society.)
3. Intensification of the guiding-line leading to the fictive goal of superiority.
4. Anticipation of the guiding ideal.

With regard to its bearings on melancholia I would like to add to this last trait, the fact that the sick man tried to approximate to this well-tested picture of a helpless weak, needy child for he discovered from personal experience that it possesses a great and most compelling force. His attitude, symptoms and his irresponsibility are formed with them in mind.

Psychiatrists insist that the essential character of psychosis is to be found in the absence either of a motive or at least of an adequate motive, for an act. This manner of presenting the problem is almost incomprehensible. The problem of "motive" we individual psychologists are well aware of and it is never absent from our discussions. The vital role assigned to-day to individuality and character in modern psychiatry is a real sign of progress, and leads directly to our own problems.

We must remember that the most important question for the sound or the diseased psyche to answer is not the where-from? but the whither? For it is only after we are acquainted with the impelling goal and with a knowledge of its direction that we can attempt to understand its various movements, movements which we take to be in the nature of individual and special preparations.

According to the Viennese psychiatric school melancholia is defined as follows (Pilz, *Spezielle gerichtliche Psychiatrie;* 1910): "The essential trait of melancholia is a primary (i.e. not induced by external circumstances), depression in the nature of sadness and anxiety accompanied by thought interference." It is a natural conclusion from our view to lay stress upon those motivations caused either by the nature of the goal or by those special guiding lines that we interpret individualistically. This motivation is synonymous with the disguised activity of melancholia. In melancholia we find in complete form the "hesitating" attitude and the "progressive advance backwards," both conditioned by the "fear of taking a decision." Melancholia is thus an attempt, a contrivance for conducting in a round-about way what we have designated as the "remnant" and the "distance" of the individual, to its true goal of superiority. As in all Cases of neurosis and psychosis this is accomplished by the voluntary assumption of the "cost". Thus this illness resembles an attempt at suicide in which it frequently actually terminates. Thought interferences, speech-disturbances, stupor and bodily carriage enable us to visualize concretely the "hesitating attitude" which as intentional disturbances of social functions, point to a decreased community feeling. Fear at all times serves the purposes of security, a weapon of defense and a proof of illness, and paroxysms of rage and the raptus melancholicus break out occasionally in the form of expressions of a fanaticism of weakness, an indication of disguised emotions; maniacal ideas point to sources of purposive phantasies which both furnish and "arrange" the patient's affects in the interests of his illness. The mechanism of anticipation and absorption in the role of a person about to perish is unmistakable. The illness always seems to be most intense in the morning i.e. as soon as the patient enters upon the activities of life.

The experienced observer has unquestionably not overlooked the "*belligerent attitude*" of the melancholic individual. Pilz, for example (l.c.), shows among other things, that the conscience-qualms of the sick man often have as their consequence the bestowal of senseless gifts or of testamentary provisions. We object only to the phrase "senseless." An apparently passive psychosis *is always teeming with feelings of hate and with tendencies toward depreciation.* The sick man, for that reason, after having satisfied his desire to punish his family, is seized with the proper conscience-qualms accompanying his act, so that he may be freed from responsibility.

The previous history of our patient shows very clearly that all persons afflicted with melancholia belong to a certain type who are not intensely interested in anything, who easily become uprooted and who easily lose their belief in themselves and in others. Even when quite well they exhibit an attitude of ambition, of hesitation; they recoil before responsibility or they construct a life-falsehood whose content is their own weakness and whose inference leads to a struggle against others.

# 15

## Physical Manifestations
## of Psychic Disturbances

Len Sperry

It is surprising to some that Adler's initial theoretical work focused on psychosomatics (i.e., organ inferiority) rather than on some psychotherapeutic topic. In fact, his first book was titled *Study of Organ Inferiority and Its Psychical Compensation* (Adler, 1907/1917). This chapter provides a context for reading Adler's seminal paper, "Physical Manifestations of Psychic Disturbances." It begins with a definition and description of organ inferiority and describes Adler's personal and professional interest and involvement with the concept. Then, it contrasts Adler's view of psychosomatics with that of Freud's. It ends with the recognition accorded Adler for his seminal contribution to psychosomatic medicine.

### PSYCHOSOMATIC MEDICINE AND ORGAN INFERIORITY

Adler's contribution to psychosomatic medicine involves the concept of organ inferiority. He described organ inferiority as an inherited defect, weakness, or deficiency of an organ or organ system. Adler noted that an inferiority triggered a compensation, and depending on the attitude taken by affected individuals, the compensation would be satisfactory or unsatisfactory. One of Adler's favorite examples of organ inferiority and compensation was the Greek orator Demosthenes, who became a great speaker in compensation for an early speech defect.

Adler later recognized that while some individuals experienced organ inferiorities, everyone experienced psychological inferiorities. He concluded that individuals are motivated by feelings of inferiority to strive for greater things. Accordingly, his overall view of inferiority evolved. In its final formulation, an individual with an organ inferiority could compensate at the somatic level, a sympathetic or neurological level, or the psychic level (Driekurs, 1948). Of the three, psychic compensation is most likely to influence the formation of the life-style (Carlson, Watts, & Maniacci, 2006).

Adler himself was troubled by organ inferiorities and reportedly exerted considerable effort in compensating for them. Not surprisingly, his early recollections are reflective of this and involve themes of illness and death. He suffered from rickets from birth and, on one occasion while experiencing an exacerbation of symptoms related to rickets, recalls his older brother moving around effortlessly while Adler struggled to walk. In another recollection he nearly dies of pneumonia at age 5. He recollects hearing the doctor tell his parents that he would probably die. Although very fearful of dying, he miraculously overcame the infection and made a full recovery, and "then and there decided his future occupation. He vowed to become a doctor" (Hoffman, 1994, p. 8).

Another indication of the influence of psychosomatics on his life is Adler's early career choice. After completing medical school Adler's medical practice involved working with individuals with physical and psychosomatic problems including tailors, laborers, and circus performers.

## PSYCHOSOMATIC THEORIES: ADLER VS. FREUD

There are various theories of how brain-body interactions result in psychosomatic symptoms, whether they be asthma, pain, migraine headaches, scoliosis, flat feet, or gastrointestinal disturbances. Throughout history many attempted to explain brain-body interactions. Among these was Freud, who believed that physical symptoms were "organic," meaning that they resulted from a disease process and were then "used" by the psyche to serve some neurotic purpose. In contrast, Adler's final formation of organ inferiority went well beyond Freud's formulation. In fact, Adler's formulation of psychosomatics "was the first to recognize that the psyche could induces physical symptoms by initiating physiological pathology" (Sarno, 2007, p. 69). In other words, the mind can actually activate physical condition, and the physical expressions of emotions indicate that the mind is acting and reacting to situations it interprets as favorable or unfavorable.

## PHYSICAL MANIFESTATIONS OF PSYCHIC DISTURBANCES

In his landmark paper, "Physical Manifestations of Psychic Disturbances," first published in 1934 (Adler, 1964), Adler posited that individuals express themselves through their organ systems—for example, the endocrine system, the cardiovascular system, the muscular system, and the nervous system. Adler provided psychosomatic explanations for a wide variety of medical conditions including pseudopregnancy, scoliosis, and flatfeet. In explaining flatfeet, Adler insists: "There can be but one explanation of this, namely, that depression can cause a loss of muscle tone. . . . he shows by his bearing what goes on inside him;

he speaks with his muscular apparatus. We must learn to understand the organ dialect" (Adler, 1934/1964, p. 231).

Utilizing the construct "organ dialect," Adler insisted that every organ is capable of expressing emotions and physical symptoms. He also noted that the organs most likely to be expressive were those that were somehow weaker or deficient. This organ expression in which the lifestyle is expressed through the body rather than with words is called "organ dialect" or "organ jargon." For example, the organ jargon in an individual with arthritis might be: "I can't stand it. I'm freezing up. I'm rigid. I can't change" (Griffith, 2006, p. 87).

## RECOGNITION OF ADLER'S CONTRIBUTION TO PSYCHOSOMATIC MEDICINE

Adler has been recognized for inaugurating the field of modern psychosomatic medicine (Ellenberger, 1970, p. 645). Walter Langdon-Brown, MD, Emeritus Professor of Medicine at Cambridge University, is quoted as saying, "There is hardly an aspect in medicine which has not undergone some change as the result of Adler's teaching. It has even had effect upon the views of many who have never read him, but who are conscious of a change in the medical atmosphere that surrounds them" (Orgler, 1976, pp. 67–68). Not only has Alder been recognized for his seminal theoretical contribution to medicine, but his basic theory of psychosomatics has been experimentally verified as well. "He would have been delighted and astonished to learn of the elaborate peptide network that connects brain and body, validating his psychosomatic concepts" (Sarno, 2007, p. 70).

## CONCLUDING NOTE

Adler's personal and professional interest in psychosomatics has been described along with his conceptualization and formulation of organ inferiority. It is noteworthy that Adler's final conceptualization formulated several decades ago has now been empirically validated. Within this context the reader can better understand Adler's paper, "Physical Manifestations of Psychic Disturbances."

## REFERENCES

Adler, A. (1910/1917). *Study of organ inferiority and its psychical compensation: A contribution to clinical medicine.* (S. Jellife, Trans.). New York: Nervous and Medical Diseases Co. (Original work published in German in 1907)

Adler, A. (1964). Physical manifestations of psychic disturbances. In A. Adler (H. Ansbacher & R. Ansbacher, Eds.), *Superiority and social interest* (pp. 224–232). Evanston, IL: Northwestern University Press.

Carlson, J., Watts, R., & Maniacci, M. (2006). *Adlerian therapy: Theory and practice.* Washington, DC: American Psychological Association.

Driekurs, R. (1948). The socio-psychological dynamics of physical disability. *Journal of Social Issues, 4,* 39–54.

Ellenberger, H. (1970). *The discovery of the unconscious: The history and evolution of dynamic psychiatry.* New York: Basic Books.

Griffith, J. (2006). Adler's organ jargon. In S. Slavik & J. Carlson (Eds.), *Readings in the theory of Individual Psychology* (pp. 83–92). New York: Routledge.

Hoffman, E. (1994). *The drive for self: Alfred Adler and the founding of Individual Psychology.* Reading, MA: Addison-Wesley.

Orgler, H. (1976). Alfred Adler. *International Journal of Social Psychiatry, 22,* 67–68.

Sarno, J. (2006). *The divided mind: The epidemic of mind-body disorders.* New York: HarperCollins.

## Physical Manifestations of Psychic Disturbances

*Alfred Adler*

Some day it will probably be proved that there is no organ inferiority which does not respond to psychic influences and does not speak their language, a language which corresponds to the problem confronting the individual. This is important in regard to symptom selection, particularly in regard to what we still call hysteria, or functional neurosis. It also justifies one of the basic tenets of Individual Psychology: Men a transitory or permanent defect becomes apparent in an organ, this organ must be scrupulously examined, so that it may be determined in what way it is characteristic of the individual himself. Sometimes one organ, sometimes another, is more influenced by outside impressions. In this paper I will deal chiefly with those psychological influences which transmit the excitation to the body through the arousal of feelings and emotions.

Psychic influences are being accepted more and more today. Even from the standpoint of general medicine it is no longer denied that the uniqueness of the individual causes variations in every illness. The doctors of yesterday realized that a child who was always subject to infectious diseases was a hypersensitive child. But only recently has it been discovered that in less sensitive children also, organs such as the endocrine glands can become involved.

It is important to observe whether these general phenomena induce transitory or lasting changes. For instance, people usually respond to shock with heart symptoms, but what is important is the duration of this change in the functioning of the heart. Only occasionally is it lasting, as in certain neurotic cases. But we know very definitely that an inferior heart, or a heart that has been injured through illness, is more susceptible to such influences, and that they can open the door to subsequent lasting and serious illnesses. You must not forget that the organism is a unit, and that through a shock in one place the entire organism is set to vibrate. We know too little to lay down any rules, but it is fairly certain that through such a shock an organ may be damaged.

Not much is known as to how a psychic impression reaches the organs, but without doubt its effect is a general one. The organism has a strong tendency to preserve its equilibrium. There is plenty of evidence that disturbances can be caused by affects. Here the uniqueness of the individual must be considered and must first be explored. Individual Psychology finds this not too difficult. We usually succeed during the first interview.

I may point out how frequently we are dealing with people who expect others to step in for them, who seek help, alleviation. This disposition can almost always be traced back to their training in early life. In a world such as ours it is such individuals who appear to be the most heavily burdened, for to them the world is a place of enmity, a place in which difficulties cannot be overcome, but must be avoided. If we wish to see this in relation to organic disturbances, I hardly know of any organ which cannot be used as an example.

## MENSTRUATION

For instance, most gynecologists agree that many disturbances during menstruation can be attributed to emotional reasons. The patient herself understands little about her feeling of irritation, her frame of mind. She does not comprehend why she should feel so oppressed by such an insignificant event. She is reconciled to the fact that something happens once a month, but she does not realize that her whole disposition exerts the greatest influence upon this relatively minor occurrence.

We must realize that many girls quite instinctively oppose menstruation by adopting a defensive attitude. They are not helped if we merely tell them this. We all know from experience in other walks of life that good suggestions are not necessarily accepted. What we must do is to study the patient so as to find out why she is not prepared to face her difficulties, and then explain this lack of preparedness to her. Wherever there are menstrual troubles we will find a certain disposition, one which occasions a defensive attitude and leads to some kind of occlusion. We must consider that perhaps this instinctive defensive attitude of a girl would not be of such significance if her uniqueness would not have to be taken into account. The peculiar idiosyncrasy of a particular girl can give us an important key as to why the customary defensive attitude was intensified. Perhaps the girl has learned of, or experienced, the difficulties in which a girl can become involved during and after puberty. This is a point which must be given serious consideration; it is the exogenic situation which releases the trigger, which affects the whole disposition.

## PSEUDOPREGNANCY

This also belongs here. Today we still know very little of how pseudo-pregnancy is caused. But I once had a case which was most revealing. The patient had had sexual relations with a man for many years and he had told her he would marry her if she should ever become pregnant. Her abdomen began to swell just as in pregnancy and continued to do so for six or seven months. It was then that I saw the woman and became suspicious; I advised her to consult a gynecologist. An hour later she returned; her abdomen had shrunk to its normal size. The gynecologist had found that she was not pregnant at all. Under heavy manipulations the flatus had been expelled through mouth and anus. It had been a case of meteorism [flatulent distention of the abdomen] the non-conscious creation of the woman herself, possible only in the case of a person desirous of taking on this symptom.

## AIR SWALLOWING

I have found that many men and women are able to develop meteorism. They swallow air. This is a fact which is too often neglected in internal medicine. There may be various other accompanying manifestations, and the gulping down of wind can cause symptoms of anxiety neurosis. This I have frequently observed. It is plain that a person with a tendency to anxiety symptoms can be seized by a state of giddiness arising from inflation of the stomach. Other symptoms, as well, can be caused by this. It should be understood that the swallowing of air takes place when the patient does not feel able to face a certain situation, when the inferiority feeling is intensified and a sense of oppressiveness arises. If we study these individuals, quite apart from their symptoms, we always find that from their earliest childhood they have been well aware of the social significance of anxiety, i.e., of how other people can be impressed by a display of anxiety.

## ENDOCRINE GLANDS

In recent years I have had plenty of opportunity for studying the influences of the feelings and emotions upon the endocrine glands. It has been very clear to me that the endocrine glands can be affected by the emotions, and it seems to me that the sex glands, also, can be put in a passive state by emotional influence. Here again we must not fail to take the individual's opinion into account.

Take for instance the case of a youngster who feels he is unmanly and, accordingly, does not live a life conducive to the development of the sex glands. He eliminates certain activities which the normal glandular development demands. Some boys are kept in an environment in which only girls are found as a rule; they are made to sit quietly at home, interest themselves in dolls and cooking, and are prevented from behaving actively. This can result in their having feminine appearance in later years. I have seen such youngsters become more masculine looking once they have been brought into proper contact with other boys.

The New York anthropologist Boas has pointed out that sports have made the American girl approach closer to the masculine type. There can be no question that, apart from whether the individual takes the sexual role seriously or not, the sex glands and thereby the physical structure are influenced by athletics. We also find that the sex glands of individuals who have an unusually strong leaning toward the other sex develop an increased activity and efficiency if this attitude persists.

When we consider how effective such influences can be we realize the nature of what we call "functional inadequacies." For instance, the retrogression of the woman during the climacteric is by no means an unvarying occurrence, but is also conditioned by the woman's mood—she may regard the climacteric as a danger or an illness. We physicians are particularly obligated to remove damaging beliefs.

## THYROID GLAND

A most important role is played by the thyroid, particularly in the case of Graves' disease (Basedow's disease, exophthalmic goiter). I once had an opportunity to examine a number of such patients in Zondek's clinic in Berlin. Zondek claims that Graves' disease cannot be investigated without the individuality of the patient being taken into consideration. Now this is not always easy. For instance, there was one patient, a mechanic of 26, who had suffered from Graves' disease for two years. The symptoms were distinct; the basic metabolism was increased 30 per cent. I found that the patient had been the only boy in the family and was most hypersensitive. He said to me: "When a person's ill, he's put under observation because human beings are always suspicious." He spoke reproachfully, in a tone which suggested that he was very sensitive and found it difficult to make contact with other people. I could see that he was very impatient and probably prone to outbursts of emotion. He would tell me no dreams, but his earliest recollection showed that he greatly disliked any change of situation. Nothing would have induced him to leave the place in which he was working.

These details told little about the exogenic factor, the situation which had provoked the illness. I asked him if anything had happened which might have contributed to his trouble; whether he had been upset by anything. But he made little response. Finally he mentioned a love affair. Six months before he fell ill, the woman had gone off with another man, but he assured me that this break had been a very trifling matter. "On the whole I was rather glad," he said. "She did not suit me." Knowing that nervous persons want to keep their hold on another person and feel deeply injured if a third person is preferred, one will regard this break as the exogenic factor, especially since it occurred at the same time as the first symptoms of trembling set in.

## OTHER ORGANS

Let us now discuss what little we know about the influence of the psyche on the organs. It is obvious that the psychic force must pass through the sphere of consciousness; there must be a transformation of the absorbed influences, followed by irritation of the vegetative system. Through the latter the irritation is transmitted further in very diverse ways, in accordance with the uniqueness of the individual and the uniqueness of the organs. His organs begin to respond.

The irritation always excites the whole organism; however we are able to observe the excitation only in those parts of the organism which manifest it more clearly. Many glands can be affected, including the liver, which like other organs responds differently in each individual case. There are some persons who, while one might expect the irritation to induce anger, respond with attacks of pain in the liver area. It has been demonstrated that the irritation also causes a change in the bile outflow, and that it can affect the pancreas and the Islands of Langerhans. Certain people respond to the irritation by hyperglycemia and glycosuria, and it is obviously the physician's duty to put such patients in a frame of mind which does not expose them to disturbances of this nature.

When the vascular system is affected by the psyche, the skin is often affected too. It is recognized that skin diseases may be provoked by psychological influences. Of course this does not apply rigorously to all patients with skin troubles.

## THE BRAIN

Psychosis and epilepsy are still more complicated problems, and no sensible psychiatrist can fail to realize that here, too, a part is played by the exogenic situation. (The same applies to melancholia and schizophrenia.) To touch on but a single aspect of the problem, we can state that in psychogenic epilepsy a part of the brain responds to the irritation. It is possible that there are also certain organic changes. E.g., old cases of schizophrenia show changes of the brain substance. This can in part be regarded as a variation of the brain structure which characterizes the uniqueness of the individual from the start. Perhaps edema can affect the brain. Neurotic manifestations can be conditioned through the tissues' being influenced by the retention of water, as demonstrated in cases of sudden withdrawal of morphine (Alexandra Adler).[38] This aspect is significant for the study of other similar processes, and is not in contradiction to the views of Individual Psychology.

## SCOLIOSIS AND FLATFOOT

Structural changes, resulting from psychic irritation, are seen particularly clearly in cases of scoliosis and flatfoot. Such eases as I have seen were predisposed to these troubles; they had not always had them, but began to be troubled at some definite time—usually when the patient lost his poise and self-confidence on being confronted by a particular situation.

We have known now for twenty-five years that pains in the spine are more complicated than appears at first glance. There are pains which become localized on the anterior wall of the chest and begin when the patient is in

---

[38] Adler, Alexandra. "Die Storung des Wasserhaushaltes Wahrend der Morphiumentziehung und dere therapeutische Beeinflussung durch Euphyllin." *Klin. Wschr.,* 1930, 9, 2011–2015. (Original footnote by H. & R. Ansbacher.)

a depressed state. This we find, for instance, among melancholics, but also among nonmelancholics when they feel unfairly treated.

I do not believe that the simple explanation of the nerves being pinched is correct; it is too naive an idea. Also, I have little faith in the idea of radiating pains, say according to the theory of Head's segments. Long before people began talking about "orthostatic albuminuria" I drew attention to the fact of how often curvatures of the spine are connected with manifestations in the kidneys. It is possible that the whole segment is irritated during embryonic development. All curvatures indicate very clearly that a congenital defect exists, which is characterized by the naevus (birthmark) at the top of the curvature or in the segment. I have had astonishing experiences in regard to this and have been able to predict where the naevus lay.

Cases of flatfoot are very similar; the sufferers of such pain are often depressed individuals. There can be but one explanation of this, namely, that depression can cause a loss of muscle tone. You can see this on the entire person; whether he is flatfooted or not, he shows by his bearing what goes on inside him; he speaks with his muscular apparatus. We must learn to understand the organ dialect.

## PREDISPOSITION, ILLNESS, ACCIDENT

If a person is endogenously predisposed for an illness, is he bound to contract it? Say, for instance, that he is predisposed to schizophrenia (we have partial knowledge of the physical make-up of a schizophrenic), does that mean that he is really bound to contract schizophrenia? The answer is: As long as the physical peculiarity of the patient would be brought under conditions in which he maintained his equilibrium, he would not have to fall ill. We can influence him so that psychological influences will not have this decisive effect upon him.

On the other hand, it seems that even if an organ is subject to psychological influences over a long period of time, it can be lastingly harmed only if it is already inferior. Here again we are faced with the question: Where does the inferiority of the organ begin? Perhaps one must think more of injury through the whole system which manifests itself in "the place of least resistance" (*locus minoris resistentiae*).

There are many examples which show injury in the physical sphere. Accidents belong here. E.g., a man was run over by a car on the day on which, through his malicious disposition, he had been trying to force his attentions on a girl in his office. She mobilized friends to consult what should be done with him. Such coincidences being possible—which to us are not mere coincidences—one can imagine that in the difficulties which always surround man, those persons will be more likely to be injured who are psychologically not strengthened. We see the same also in epidemics.

## PHYSIOGNOMY

I wish to mention one other phenomenon—the external formation of the human body, the physiognomy. Although we cannot say how much, there is some value in physiognomy, because it is shaped by movement; it is movement which has become form. We recognize this transition all too little. We judge by external appearances, often most rashly, but without always realizing that moods affect the physical substance, making the features appear pleasant or unpleasant. Anyone who has observed the appearance of a melancholic during his melancholic phase and afterwards will be amazed. Similarly in everyone the mood leaves its aftereffects in the expression.

We are returning to our fundamental view, to the foundation of all proper functions: the proper embeddedness in the evolution of mankind. Only in this way can we understand how we assume that one man is sympathetic, another not; that this takes place automatically; that we understand this better only when we succeed in formulating this process into concepts. This is a thought which fits only in an evolutionary view. From this vantage point we shall understand what is to be regarded as erroneous and as approximately correct.

A widespread error exists regarding the concept of society. To understand it correctly we must realize how strongly it is interlinked to the evolution of mankind as something to strive for. The physiognomy is bound up, far more than we have ever realized before, with the degree of harmony existing between the individual and the society for which to strive.

# 16

## What Is Neurosis?

Timothy S. Hartshorne

What is neurosis? Does anyone care? The term left mainstream psychiatry/psychology with the DSM II. So why read a paper on neurosis? For that matter, why read a paper by Alfred Adler? Not for his brilliant prose. While noting the need for a "clear and straightforward answer" to the question of "What is neurosis?" Adler is anything but clear and straightforward. So, why read this chapter?

In 1971 I was promoted from orderly to psychiatric technician. To earn this promotion I had to take a class offered by the hospital where I worked. In this class we were taught about the ego, id, and superego. There was no mention of Freud by name. There was no need, because this model was fact. Psychoanalysis and psychiatry were tightly linked, and neurosis was understood from the psychoanalytic model. When the DSM III was developed, a decision was made to move away from diagnoses that were linked to theory. Instead disorders would be described by their symptoms only. This was considered a victory for the behaviorists.

The world of empirically supported treatments and manualized therapy is a natural evolution from this move to understand psychiatric conditions on the basis of symptom lists. There is no need to understand where a client's agoraphobia, for example, comes from. You only have to diagnose it and then treat it using the current best practice. This makes a great deal of sense. It is hard to argue that if there is research to suggest that a particular treatment is effective for a particular disorder you should nevertheless ignore that and do something different.

It is not that all interest in etiology has been lost. However, much of the work today focuses on brain-behavior relationships and genetics. For example, a quick search shows 412 journal articles on the genetic basis for obsessive-compulsive disorder. Once again, this is not unimportant, but the genetics of a disorder are of somewhat limited use in treatment and many therapists continue to be convinced that understanding the roots of a disorder is extremely helpful in its treatment. Such an understanding might actually better guide the choice of a particular supported intervention or manualized therapy.

Adler does two things in the chapter. One is to provide an understanding of the dynamics and development of neurosis. The other is to distinguish neurosis from other non-psychotic conditions. I will describe these and then return to the question of why these might be relevant and the chapter worth reading.

To understand neurosis, Adler beings with feelings of inferiority. Of course everyone experiences feelings of inferiority, but in some cases events take place in early childhood convincing children that they cannot cope with the tasks of life. They then become hypersensitive about their experiences and they reduce their attempts to actively deal with life problems. In other words, they retreat from the problems they face.

A second concept that must be understood is that all problems in living require cooperation with others, or what Adler calls in this chapter "social preparation." A person lacking social preparation struggles with friendships and may avoid social contact and react with embarrassment around other people. This person may experience work or business failings as supporting their conviction that they cannot succeed. Most people experience some rejection in their love relationships, but those individuals with no preparation for social living retreat and, as Adler says, "come to a standstill." Problems with friendship, work, and love are normal life experiences, but "neurotic" individuals react with heightened emotion and withdrawal from the life tasks, because they realize they do not have the skills to solve these life problems.

The suffering of the neurotic, Adler claims, is preferred by that individual over the threat to their self-esteems if their basic worthlessness as a person is disclosed. The symptoms that develop, the obvious suffering, protects the person from this great fear. So in plain language, if children do not learn early on how to cooperate and navigate their social world, they come up against the problems of making friends, being productive, and falling in love without the necessary skills. This becomes a particular difficulty for them when they encounter an event that they find they cannot manage. They then retreat into a state of chronic inaction and develop the neurotic symptoms as a mask for their complete sense of personal failure and worthlessness. By their symptoms they are saying, "Look how I suffer. If it were not for my suffering I could manage and solve the problems of life."

Not all non-psychotic problems are actually neurosis, and Adler makes the distinction between those with neuroses and those others who fail to cooperate with the social world and life tasks. He provides various terms to describe these others: criminal, suicidal, drunkard, "bad" child, arch-reactionary, ultra-radical fanatic, and the voluptuary (hedonist). While neurotics reduce or constrict their level of activity by their retreat to the rear, these others instead increase their activity as they attack the front. Their approach to life problems is to fight. Like the neurotic they do not know how to cooperate, but unlike the neurotic they believe that they can cope with the demands of living. Of course they do not succeed.

Adler provides a case study in this chapter which helps to illustrate many of his concepts. Running through this chapter is the central concept of retreat, or as he puts it, the "advance to the rear." Retreat, Adler says, is a "Law-of-Movement" or lifestyle. It comes to characterize the way these individuals step forward only to fall back due to their suffering.

Adler does not focus a great deal in this chapter on treatment, other than to note it must focus on developing insight and community feeling. The major contribution of this chapter is to understand the movement of the person with a neurosis. This is what is so often missing in the world of the DSM and manualized therapy. The DSM lists symptoms in a static system. Manualized therapy focuses on the elimination of those symptoms. Adler shows individuals with a neurosis in their dynamic state. Understanding their movement, and catching them in the act, is the foundation for helping them to change directions.

Therapists looking for an understanding of those mental health issues that at one time fell under the "neurosis" classification, but who are not interested in the traditional psychoanalytic model, will find in this chapter another way of making sense out of the dynamics of the person with one of these disorders. Such an understanding may be fundamental to choosing an intervention strategy.

## REFERENCES

Adler, A. (1912). *Uber den nervosen Charakter: Grundzuge einer vergleichenden Individual-Psychologie und Psychotherapie* [The nervous character: Outline of comparative individual psychology and psychotherapy]. Wiesbaden, Germany: Bergmann.

Adler, A. (1933). *Der Sinn des Lebens* [The meaning of life]. Vienna: Leipzig: Passer.

Adler, A. (1935a). What is neurosis? (E. B. Menser & I. C. Stark, Trans.). *International Journal of Individual Psychology, 1*(1), 9–17. Original work published in 1933 as Was ist wirklich eine Neurose? [What is really a neurosis?], *Internationale Zeitschrift fur Individual Psychologie, 11,* 177–185.

Adler, A. (1935b). Prevention of neurosis. *International Journal of Individual Psychology, 1*(4), 3–12. Original work published in 1935 as Vorbeugung der Neurose [Prevention of neurosis], *Internationale Zeitschrift fur Individual Psychologie, 13,* 133–141.

Adler, A. (1938). What really is a neurosis? In J. Linton & R. Vaughan (Trans.), *Social interest: A challenge to mankind* (pp. 156–181). London: Faber & Faber.

Ansbacher, H. L. (1990). Alfred Adler, pioneer in prevention of mental disorders. *Journal of Primary Prevention, 11*(1), 37–68.

Ansbacher, H. L. (1992a). Alfred Adler, pioneer in prevention of mental disorders. *Individual Psychology, 48*(1), 3–34. (Reprint of 1990 with some changes and corrected references)

Ansbacher, H. L. (1992b). Alfred Adler's concept of community feeling and of social interest and the relevance of community feeling for old age. *Individual Psychology, 48*(4), 402–412.

## What Is Neurosis?[39]

*Alfred Adler*

Anyone who has occupied himself with this problem year in, year out, will understand that the question "What then is the real nature of neurosis?" has to receive a clear and straightforward answer. If we explore the literature on the subject with the objective of finding an explanation, we discover such a confusion of definitions that, in the end, a uniform conception of neurosis can scarcely be reached.

Whenever there is a lack of clarity concerning a question, there are a great many explanations and much contention. So it is in this matter of neurosis. Some of the many explanations are: that neurosis is irritability, sensitive weakness, a disease of the endocrine glands; the result of infection of the nose or teeth, of genital disease; the result of weakness of the nervous system; the result of certain glandular diatheses, of the birth trauma; the result of conflict with the outer world, with religion, with ethics, with the bad unconscious and the compromising conscious; the suppression of sexual, sadistic, and criminal drives; the result of the noise and dangers of the big city; of a sheltered or strict upbringing, of family training in general; of certain conditioned reflexes; etc.

There is much in these views that is pertinent and that can be taken as the explanation of more or less significant partial manifestations of neurosis. Most of the factors given in the foregoing list as explanations for neurosis are found more frequently, however, in the lives of people who are not suffering from neurosis than of those who are. There is very little in them which can lead to clarification of the question: "What really is neurosis?" The great frequency of neurosis, its extraordinarily bad social effects, the fact that only a small portion of nervous people are ever treated, and that they carry their burden of suffering all through life as immense torture: these, together with the great interest in this question of neurosis which has been stirred up in the lay world, justify a dispassionate scientific clarification, before a large forum, of the question: "What is neurosis?" One will see that much medical knowledge is necessary for understanding and treating this illness. It should be kept in mind that prevention of neurosis is both possible and necessary. But such prevention can only be expected through a clearer recognition of the root of the trouble. The measures used for preventing and recognizing the small beginnings of neurosis are derived from medical knowledge. However, the help of the family, the teacher, the educator, and other assistants is indispensable. This justifies a wide dissemination of the knowledge as to the nature and the origin of neurosis.

---

[39] Translated by John Linton and Richard Vaughan; additional translations by Heinz Ansbacher.

Arbitrary definitions such as have existed for a long time (e.g., that it is a conflict between the conscious and unconscious) must be unconditionally rejected. There can be little discussion on this point, for the authors who support this view must ultimately have realized that nothing at all can take place without conflict; so this statement sheds no light on the nature of a neurosis. Nor, too, is any light to be received from those who take up a lofty scientific standpoint and want to mislead us by attributing those organic changes to chemical action. They will find it difficult to make any contribution in this way to solving the problem, since we can make no pronouncements about chemical action. Neither do the other current definitions tell us anything new. What is understood as a nervous state is irritability, suspicion, shyness, etc.—in short, any kind of manifestations that are marked by negative qualities, by character traits that are not suited to life and seem to be loaded with affects. All authors agree that the nervous state is connected with a life of intensified affects.

## HYPERSENSITIVITY AND IMPATIENCE IN NEUROSIS

When, many years ago, I set about describing what we understand by the nervous character, I brought to light the hypersensitivity of the nervous person. This trait is certainly to be found in every nervous subject—although in some exceptional cases it cannot be discovered very easily, since it is concealed; closer examination, however, shows that such persons are nonetheless acutely sensitive.

Individual Psychology, by its more thorough research, has shown the source of this sensitivity. Anyone who feels at home on this poor earthcrust of ours (who is convinced that he has to share not only its delights but its drawbacks, and is resolved to make some contribution to social well-being) will not exhibit any undue sensitivity. Exaggerated sensitivity is an expression of the feeling of inferiority. From this, there follow quite naturally the other traits of the nervous person, such as, for example, impatience. This, too, is not shown by the person who feels himself secure, who has self-confidence, and has reached the point of coming to terms with the problems of life. When these two character traits of hypersensitivity and impatience are kept in view, it will be understood that there are people who live in a state of intensified emotion. And when we add that this feeling of insecurity leads to a violent struggle for a state of repose and security, then it can be seen why the nervous person is spurred on in his striving for superiority and perfection. It can be understood, too, that this trait with its implication of a struggle for preeminence takes the form of ambition—an ambition that is solely concerned with the person himself. This is intelligible in the case of a person who is in [difficult] straits. Occasionally, this striving for preeminence takes other forms, such as greediness, avarice, envy, and jealousy, which, as a matter of course, are universally condemned. Here it is a question of persons who are violently straining every nerve to outwit their difficulties, because they have no confidence in their own powers to find a straightforward solution. Add to this that the intensified feeling of inferiority goes hand in hand with an imperfect development of courage (that instead of this [courage] we find a number of cunning attempts to evade the problems of life, to make existence easier, and to throw the load on the shoulders of other persons). This evasion of responsibility is bound up with a lack of interest in other people. We are far from setting out to criticize or condemn the large number of people who to a greater or lesser extent show this attitude; we know that even the worst mistakes are not made with a conscious sense of responsibility, but that the person in question has become the victim of a wrong attitude toward life. These persons have before them a goal, the pursuit of which brings them into conflict with reason.

## THE DEVELOPMENT OF NEUROSIS AND A REDUCED RANGE OF ACTION

Still, nothing has been said yet of the nature of the nervous state, of the way in which it has been brought about, or of the factors which go into its formation. We have, however, taken one step in advance; and, taking into account the defective courage of the nervous person and his hesitant attitude toward the tasks of life, we are able to show the meager result of his life process in facing the problems of life. It is certain that we can trace this meager amount of activity back to the period of childhood. As Individual Psychologists, we are not surprised at this because the lifestyle is developed in the earliest years of childhood and is only accessible to change if the person in question understands the error in his development and has the power to come once more into contact with other people [and] with a view to the welfare of humanity as a whole.

It may be assumed that a child who shows more than the normal amount of activity of the wrong kind, if he becomes a failure in later life, will never be a nervous subject. His failure will take another form, and he will become a criminal, commit suicide, or become a drunkard. It is possible that he may be a "difficult" child of the worst sort, but he will never develop the traits of a nervous person. We have approached, then, a little nearer to the solution of our problem. We can assert that the range of action in the case of the nervous subject does not extend very far; it is much more restricted than that of a more normal person.

It is important to know the source of the greater amount of activity in the other cases. If we can prove that it is possible either to develop or restrict a child's range of action—if we can understand that in a wrong education there are means of reducing this [action] to a minimum—then we also understand that the question of heredity does not influence us in this direction, but that what we see is the product of the child's creative power. The condition of the body and the impressions of the external world are the building materials which the child uses for the construction of his personality.

## NEUROSIS AS A CHRONIC STATE

The fact to be noted in connection with symptoms of nervousness is that they are all chronic. These symptoms can be classified as physical disturbances of certain bodily organs and as psychic shocks—manifestations of anxiety, obsessive thoughts, signs of depression (these seem to have a special significance), nervous headaches, compulsory blushing and washing, and similar forms of psychic expressiveness. They persist for a long time; and if we do not remove ourselves to the obscure region of fantastic ideas, if we are willing to admit that their development has some meaning, and if we seek their connection with one another, we shall discover that the task which confronts the child has been too difficult for him. In this way, the permanent nature of nervous symptoms seems to be established and explained.

The outbreak of these symptoms is due to the reaction that follows on a certain definite task. We have made extensive investigations in order to discover what constitutes this difficulty in solving problems; and Individual Psychology has offered a permanent contribution to this whole issue by establishing the fact that human beings are always confronted by problems, the solution of which requires a social preparation. The child must obtain this preparation in his earliest years, for any augmentation of it is only possible given this early foundation. When we have undertaken the task of making it clear that such a problem actually results always in a shock, then we can speak about the effects of shock. Such shocks can be of various kinds. In some cases, it may be a social problem, say, a disappointment in friendship. Which of us has never experienced this or has not received a shock from it? But the shock itself does not signal a nervous disease. It is a sign of nervous disease, and actually becomes nervous disease, only when it persists, when it develops into a chronic condition. In that case, the person in question avoids suspiciously all personal intimacy and shows clearly that he is always prevented from coming into closer contact with other persons by shyness or embarrassment or by bodily symptoms like a quickened pulse, perspiration, gastro-intestinal troubles, and urgency of micturition (urination). This is a condition that has an unmistakable significance in the light thrown upon it by Individual Psychology. It tells us that this person has not sufficiently developed a sense of contact with other people; and it follows from this that his disillusionment has brought him to a position of isolation. We are now at closer grips with the problem, and we can give some idea of the nervous state. When, for example, someone loses money in business and feels the shock of this loss, he has not yet become a nervous subject. This happens only when he remains in that state, when he feels the shock and nothing else. This can only be explained if we understand that a person in this state has not acquired a sufficient degree of cooperative ability and that he goes forward only on condition of being successful in everything he attempts.

The same holds true for the problem of love. Certainly the solution of this problem is not a trifling affair. For its solution, some experience and understanding are required, and a certain sense of responsibility. If anyone becomes excited and irritated on account of this problem (e.g., if after having been rejected once, he makes no further advances, if all the emotions that secure his retreat from the problem in question play a part in that retreat, if he has such a conception of life that he keeps to his path of retreat), then, and not until then, is he a nervous subject. Everyone feels a shock when he is under fire, but the effects of the shock will only become chronic if the person who has suffered them is not prepared for the tasks of life. In that case, he will come to a standstill.

## NEUROSIS AS AN AVOIDANCE OF THE APPEARANCE OF WORTHLESSNESS

We have already substantiated this complete halt when we said that there are people who are not properly prepared for the solution of every problem, who from their childhood have never been real co-workers. But there is something more than this to be said. It is suffering that we see in the nervous state, and not something that the victim enjoys. If I were to propose to anyone that he should give himself headaches like those that result from confronting a problem for the solution of which he was unprepared, he would not be able to do so. We must therefore reject at once all explanations which imply that a person produces his own suffering, or that he wants to be ill. Without doubt, the person concerned does suffer, but he always prefers his present sufferings to those greater sufferings he would experience were he to appear defeated in regard to the solution of his problem. He would rather put up with these nervous sufferings than have his worthlessness disclosed. Both nervous and normal people offer the strongest opposition to the exposure of their defeats, but the neurotic carries his opposition much farther. If we try to imagine what is meant by hypersensitivity, impatience, intensified emotion, and personal ambition, then we shall be able to understand that such a person, so long as he thinks himself in danger of having his worthlessness revealed, cannot be brought to take a single step forward.

What, then, is the mental state that results from these effects of a shock? The sufferer has not caused them; he does not want them: they do exist, however, as the consequences of a psychic shock, as the result of his sense of defeat and of the fear of being unmasked in all his worthlessness. He has no real inclination to struggle against the result, nor does he understand how he is to free himself from it. He would like to have it removed. He will persist in saying, "I should like to get well again. I want to get rid of the symptoms."

Accordingly, he even consults a doctor. But what he does not know is that he is still more afraid of something else: of being proved worthless. Somehow, the sinister secret might come to light, the fact that he is of no value. We see now what a nervous state actually is. It is an attempt to avoid a greater evil, an attempt at all costs to keep up the appearance of being of some value, to spare no expense in the attainment of this goal; at the same time, there is also the desire to reach it without any cost at all. Unfortunately, this is impossible. There is nothing else that will help, but to supply the person in question with a better preparation for life, to encourage him, and give him a firmer footing. This cannot be done by driving him on, by punishing him, by being severe with him, or coercing him. We know how many people there are who, when they have a certain amount of activity at their disposal, would rather do away with themselves than solve their problems. That is clear. We cannot, therefore, expect anything from coercion; a systematic preparation must be taken in hand, so that the sufferer shall feel himself secure and in a position to approach the solution of his problem. Otherwise, we have a person who imagines he is standing before a deep abyss and is afraid that he is going to be pushed into it, i.e., that his worthlessness is going to be revealed.

## A CASE ILLUSTRATING THE USES OF NEUROSIS

A thirty-five-year-old attorney complained of nervousness, continuous pain in the back of the head, various pains in the region of the stomach, dullness in the whole head, and general weakness and fatigue. Further, he was continually excited and restless. Often he had a fear of losing consciousness when he had to speak with strangers. In the family circle, at home with his parents, he felt relieved—although even there the atmosphere did not quite satisfy him. He was convinced that his symptoms would keep him from success.

The result of the clinical examination was negative, except for a scoliosis, which, with loss of muscle tone as a result of depression, can be taken as an explanation of the pain in the back of the head and the pains in the back. The tiredness can be ascribed to his restlessness, and certainly the dull feeling in the head can be understood as a partial manifestation of depression and of continuous emotion.

From the general diagnosis which we here employ, the discomfort in the stomach region is more difficult to understand. It could come from nerve irritation as a result of the scoliosis. But it could also be the expression of a predilection, the answer of an inferior organ to a psychic irritation. The frequency of stomach disorder in the patient's childhood and a similar complaint of his father's, likewise without organic findings, speak in favor of the latter explanation. The patient stated that whenever he was excited, he lost his appetite and occasionally vomited.

### Neurosis as a Mistake in Striving for Success

One complaint, perhaps regarded by him as a trifle, makes it possible for us to perceive the lifestyle of the patient a little more closely. His restlessness speaks clearly in favor of the fact that he has not completely given up the battle for "his success." His statement that he does not feel well even at home speaks [perhaps] less clearly for the same conclusion. His fear of meeting strangers (therefore his fear of stepping out into life) cannot leave him, even at home.

The fear of losing consciousness affords us a peep into the workroom of his neurosis. He tells us (though he is not aware that he is saying it) how, when he has to meet strangers, he artificially increases his excitement by pre-conceived ideas of losing consciousness. We can name two reasons why the patient, "as if" by intention, artificially increases his excitement to the point of confusion.

One reason is clear, although not commonly understood: the patient, so to speak, "squints" closely only at his symptoms, and not at their connection with his whole lifestyle. The second reason is that the relentless retreat, the "advance toward the rear," is not allowed to be interrupted. This I described a long time ago as the most important neurotic symptom (Adler, 1912).

### Neurosis as a Retreat From the Tasks of Life

In the case of this patient, the retreat was connected with weak attempts to pull himself together. The excitement into which the patient falls when he is confronted by the three problems of life—society, occupation, and love (for which he evidently is not socially prepared)—affects not only the body, pro-ducing functional changes in it, but also the psyche. This excitement has to be proved (for up to now it has only been guessed) with the aid of general diagnosis, medical-psychological intuition, and Individual Psychological experiences. The functional disturbances of soma and psyche are the conse-quences of the faulty preparation for life of this personality. The patient, who formerly has experienced smaller failures, recoils from the *exogenic factor*. He now feels himself continuously *threatened by defeat*. The more so since, as a pampered child (a fact which we later have to prove), he finds his self-erected goal of personal superiority—a goal which is without sufficient inter-est in others—more and more unattainable. *This state of heightened emotions always springs from the fear of a final defeat*. Fear, in the ordinary sense of the word, however, need not always be clearly evident. Those symptoms which we find in psychosis and neurosis originate, as we know, in accordance with the physical constitution (for the most part inborn), and in accordance with the psychic constitution (always acquired). These physical and psychic fac-tors are always mixed together and influence each other reciprocally.

## Neurosis as a Lack of Preparation in Community Feeling

But is this yet neurosis? Individual Psychology has truly done much to show that, for the solution of the tasks of life; one can be either badly or well prepared; that, in between the extremes of good and bad, there are thousands of varying degrees of preparation. Individual Psychology has also done much to make us understand that the inability to solve the problems of life cause the vibration of the whole soma and psyche to increase incalculably in the presence of disturbing exogenic factors. It has also shown that poor preparation originates in earliest childhood, and that it cannot be corrected through experience, nor through emotion, but only through understanding. It also has discovered community feeling (*Gemeinschaftsgefühl*) as the *integrating* factor of the lifestyle that must be present to a decisive degree for the solution of all the problems of life. The physical and psychic phenomena which accompany and characterize the feeling of failure I have described as the *inferiority complex*. The manifestations of shock, in the case of inferiority complex, are greater in those individuals who are socially less prepared than in those who are better prepared; less in those who are more courageous than in those who are discouraged and who constantly look for help from the outside. Everyone has conflicts which upset him more or less. Everyone feels them, physically and psychologically. Due to the kind of bodies we have, and to the external social circumstances, no one living is spared from the feeling of inferiority toward the outside world.

Hereditary organ inferiorities are all too frequent in human beings for them to avoid the probability of attack by the harsh demands of life. The factors of the outside world which affect the child are not of a nature which makes it easy for him to build up a "right" lifestyle.

Pampering or neglect (imagined or real)—but especially pampering—lure the child all too often to set himself in opposition to the community feeling. To that, add the fact that the child finds its "law-of-movement" for the most part without correct guidance: He strives according to the deceptive law of trial and error, according to his own free will, within his limits as a human being, but always he strives towards a goal of superiority, of which there are innumerable varieties. The creative power of the child takes and uses all its impressions and sensations as impulses toward a final attitude, toward its individual, unique "law-of-movement." The fact, emphasized by Individual Psychology, was later called *Einstellung* (Attitude) or *Gestalt* (Form, Configuration), without, however, doing full justice to the whole of the individual and to the fact of his inseparable "connectedness" with the three great problems of life.

Are these conflicts—of the "bad" child, of the suicidal, of the criminal, of the arch-reactionary, of the ultra-radical fanatic, of the voluptuary whose comfort is disturbed by the misery which he sees in the world—are these conflicts, including their physical and psychic consequences, neurosis? In their persistent mistaken "law-of-motion," these people all run counter to the idea of cooperation as emphasized by Individual Psychology. They come into contradiction with what is "right" (sub specie aeternitatist), that is, according to the relentless demand of an ideal community. Of course, they feel the manifold consequences of this collision. To be sure, there are countless physical and psychic variations of these consequences. But is this neurosis?

Were it not for the relentless demands of the ideal community, everyone could, in the course of life, satisfy his wrong "law-of-motion." Speaking more imaginatively, it might even be said that he could satisfy his "drives," his "instincts," his "conditioned reflexes"—then there would be no conflict. No social (normal) person could make such an absurd demand. Such a demand dares to stir timidly only when one overlooks the "connectedness" of the individual and the community or tries to separate them. Everyone bows more or less willingly to the iron law of the ideal community. Only a child, pampered to the utmost, will expect and demand, *"res mihi subigere conor,"* as Horace says reproachingly—freely translated: "to make use of the contributions of the community for myself, but without contributing in return." Even such a question as "Why should I love my neighbor?" springs from the inseparable connectedness of mankind and arises out of the stern criterion of the community ideal.[40] *Only he who carries within himself, in his "law-of-movement," a sufficient degree of the community ideal, and lives according to it as easy as he breathes, will be in a position to solve, in the sense of the community those conflicts which are inevitably his.*

## NEUROSIS: THE INDIVIDUAL IN FULL RETREAT

Everyone experiences his conflicts, the neurotic as well as other people. However, it is the way in which the neurotic attempts to solve them which differentiates him from others. Among the manifold variations of these attempts, there are constantly to be found partial neuroses and mixed forms of neurosis. Within his "law-of-movement," the neurotic trains, from childhood on, for the retreat from social tasks. These tasks, because he fears defeat, threaten his vanity, threaten his striving toward a personal superiority which is too much separated from community feeling. These tasks threaten his striving to be the center of attention, to be first. His life motto, "All or nothing" (usually moderated very little); the oversensitivity of one constantly threatened by defeat; his impatience the heightened emotion of one living as if in an enemy country; his greed: all these bring out more frequent and

---

[40] Alfred Adler, "Der Sinn des Lebens"-Dr. Passer, Vienna, 1933. (Original footnote by Alfred Adler.)

more severe conflicts than would be necessary. They make the retreat, prescribed by his lifestyle easier for him. The tactics of retreat, trained and tested from childhood, can easily appear to be a "regression" to infantile wishes. But these wishes are not the important things to the neurotic.

To the neurotic, the thing of importance is not so much such infantile wishes as it is his *retreat*. For this retreat he gladly pays with sacrifices of all sorts. But here, too, one might be misled into confusing these sacrifices with "forms of self-punishment." However, it is not the self-punishment that is important; it is rather the feeling of relief that he gets through the retreat, which saves him from a collapse of his vanity and his great pride.

Now, finally, it will be understood what the problem of "securing" (safeguarding) means in Individual Psychology. It can only be understood in its whole connection: not as something "secondary," but as the chief concern. The neurotic "secures" himself by his retreat, and "secures" his retreat by aggravating the physical and mental manifestations of shock. These shock manifestations arise when he finds himself confronted with a problem which threatens him with defeat. He prefers his suffering to the collapse of his great personal pride. The strength of that pride Individual Psychology has demonstrated repeatedly. Often that exalted pride becomes clearly visible only in psychosis. His superiority complex, as I have called it, is so strong that the neurotic himself senses it only from afar with shuddering awe. So strong is it, that he gladly turns his attention away from it, when a test of it in real life seems imminent. It impels him forward, but he dare not risk the test. *Only in retreat is there security for his prestige.* For the sake of the retreat, he has to discard everything, forget everything that could hinder his retreat. He gives room only to retreat ideas, retreat feelings, and retreat actions.

The neurotic turns his whole interest toward the retreat, until it becomes an elaborate "Retreat Complex." Every step forward becomes for him a fall into an abyss, which seems full of all sorts of horrors, because he sees before him no possibility of success. With all his might, with all his feelings, with all his tested devices for retreat, he tries to keep himself securely in the background. There are two things which permit him to cling to those securities which save him from defeat. The first of these is the building up and glorification of his shock experiences, to which he devotes all his interest; at the same time, he turns away from the one important factor, namely, his fear of recognizing how far he is from his high egoistic goal. The second of these is the display of feeling, metaphorically clothed and artificially stirred up as they are in dreams, in order to allow him, contrary to common sense, to persist in his own lifestyle. These securities he has ready at hand so as not to be driven toward the defeat which he fears.

## The Neurotic Use of "Yes-But"

The greatest danger to the neurotic is the disapproval of others. At the outbreak of the neurosis, extenuating circumstances are acknowledged by others—and with approval. Were it not for these extenuating circumstances, the people around him would not give recognition to the trembling prestige of the neurotic. In short, *neurosis is: the utilization of shock experiences for the protection of the threatened prestige.* Still, shorter, we can summarize the neurotic's whole frame of mind in the phrase: "Yes-but." In the "yes" is imbedded the recognition of the community feeling; in the "but" the retreat and its securities.

When our patient left the university, he found employment as an assistant in an attorney's office. He stayed there only a few weeks, leaving, as he said, *"because his field of activity was too insignificant."* After he had changed jobs several times for this or some other reason, he decided to devote himself preferably to theoretical studies. He was invited to give lectures about questions of law, but he declined "because he could not speak before a large audience." At this time (he was then thirty-two years old), his symptoms appeared. A friend who wanted to help him offered to give a joint lecture with him. Our patient consented on the condition that he be allowed to speak first. He stepped upon the platform, trembling, bewildered, and in fear that he would lose consciousness. He saw only black spots before his eyes. Shortly after the lecture, his stomach trouble set in, and he imagined he would die if he had to speak again before so many people. After this, he occupied himself only with the instruction of children.

A doctor whom he consulted told him that in order to get well he would have to become active sexually. We could readily have foreseen the absurdity of such advice. The patient, who already was in retreat, answered this advice with the fear of syphilis, with ethical considerations, with the fear of being betrayed and of being accused of being the father of an illegitimate child. His parents counseled him to marry. They chose a girl and he married her. She later became pregnant and left the house to go back to her parents, because, as she said, she could not endure his constant criticism from "above"—as though he were the "superior" one.

Now we see how arrogant our patient could be when he was offered an easy opportunity, but how he began a retreat at once when matters seemed to him uncertain. He did not bother himself about his wife and child. His only concern was, always, *not to appear inferior,* and this concern was stronger than his striving for the success he longed for so much. He went to pieces when he came to the battlefront of life. He fell into a tide of feeling which closely resembled extreme anxiety, with its physical and mental consequences. He strengthened his retreat by setting up phantom scarecrows, because in this way the retreat was made easier for him.

A motorist can easily imagine such a mechanism. He has his goal, he is on his way; now he steps on the gas in order to reach his goal more quickly and more surely. His goal in this case was the retreat.

### RETREAT AS A "LAW-OF-MOVEMENT" (LIFESTYLE)

Stronger proofs? We want to supply them in two ways: first, by going back to his early childhood in order to establish the fact that he was misled into the lifestyle which we have found to be his; second, by gathering out of what we know of his later life more incidents which resemble each other. I always consider it the strongest proof of the correctness of a finding of this nature, if it turns out that the incidents which contribute further to the characterization of a person agree perfectly with those already found. Should they not agree, then the conception of the person under examination must be altered accordingly.

As the patient states, his mother was a meek, yielding woman, to whom he clung tenaciously, and who pampered him thoroughly. Also, she always expected great achievements from him. The father was less inclined to spoil him, but gave in to him every time the patient cried when he wanted something. Among the children of the family, the patient preferred a younger brother, who worshipped him, fulfilled his every wish, and who ran after him like a little puppy, and whom he easily managed. Our patient was the hope of his family; he always got his own way with the other brothers and sisters. This unusually easy, warm home situation unfitted him for the outside world, and he created for himself the "pampered" style of life.

This became apparent at once when he went to school for the first time. He was the youngest in the class and used this fact as his motive for changing schools twice and for the purpose of expressing his dislike of this outside position. Then, however, he studied with tremendous zeal in order to surpass all other pupils. When he was not successful in surpassing them, he retreated. He frequently stayed away from school on account of headaches and stomach aches and often was tardy. When he was not among the best pupils, he and his parents ascribed it to the circumstance that he was frequently absent. At the same time, our patient strongly emphasized that he knew more and had read more than all the other pupils.

On the slightest provocation, the parents put him in bed and nursed him with great care. He had always been a timid child and often cried out in his sleep in order to occupy his mother with him, even in the night.

It should be understood that he was not clear about the meaning and the connection of all these manifestations. They all were the expression of his lifestyle.[41] Neither did he know that he read in bed at night until early morn-

---

[41] Neither in the conscious, nor the unconscious, but in the "non-understood." (Original footnote by Alfred Adler.)

ing in order to enjoy the privilege of getting up late, and so rid himself of a part of his day's work. He was more shy with girls than with men. And this behavior extended over the whole time of his development into manhood. It can easily be understood that in every situation of life, he lacked courage; that under no consideration would he risk his vanity. The uncertainty as to whether he would be well received by girls was in strong contrast with the certainty with which he could expect devotion from his mother. In his marriage, he wanted to establish the same mastery which he enjoyed at home over his mother and brothers. Such an attempt must meet failure.

## EARLY RECOLLECTIONS, ATTITUDES, AND DREAMS: AVENUES TO UNDERSTANDING NEUROSIS

I have established the fact that the lifestyle of an individual is to be found in the earliest childhood recollections. To be sure, it is often well hidden. Our patient's earliest recollection is as follows: "A little brother had died and the father sat in front of the house and wept." We remember in this connection how the patient fled home before a lecture and *pretended to die.*

One's attitude toward the question of friendship characterizes very well one's ability to be a social human being. Our patient stated that all during his life he had friends for a short time only and that he always wanted to rule them. Friendship, to him, was an opportunity to exploit others. When this circumstance was pointed out to him in a friendly manner, he answered, "I do not believe that anyone exerts himself for the community; everyone does it only for himself."

The following shows how he armed himself for the retreat. He wanted very much to write an article or a book, but when he sat down to write he became so agitated that he could not think. He declared that he could not sleep unless he read beforehand. But if he read, he got such a pain in his head that he couldn't sleep.

At the time the patient was visiting another city, his father died and he returned home. Shortly afterward, he had the opportunity to accept a position in the city where he had been visiting. He refused the position under the pretext that he would die if he should enter that city again. When he was offered a position in his own city, he refused that upon the ground that he would not be able to sleep the first night, and for that reason would fail the next day. He would have to get well first.

To show that his "law-of-movement"—this "Yes-but" of the neurotic— is to be found even in the dream of the patient, we will give an example. With the technique of Individual Psychology, one can find the dynamics of a dream. The dream says nothing new, nothing which we could not recognize otherwise from the behavior of the patient.

From the contrivances of the dream, when rightly understood, and from the choice of dream content, one can recognize how the dreamer, guided by his "law-of-movement" (his lifestyle), endeavors to enforce his own way, contrary to common sense, by artificially arousing appropriate feelings and emotions. Often one finds hints as to how, under stress of a fear of defeat, the patient produced his symptoms. Our patient told the following dream: "I was supposed to be going to visit friends who lived on the other side of a bridge. The railing was freshly painted. I wanted to look in the water and leaned against the railing. This pushed against my stomach which began to hurt. I said to myself: 'You should not look down in the water below. You could fall.' But I risked it nevertheless, went again to the railing, glanced below, and fell back again quickly, as I reflected that it was after all better to be safe."

The visit to friends and the freshly painted railing indicate the trace of some community feeling and the building up of a new style of life. The patient's fear of falling from his heights, his "Yes-but," are emphasized clearly enough. His stomach troubles as a result of his feeling of fear are, as described earlier, always constitutionally present. The dream shows us the patient's rejecting attitude toward the efforts of the doctor up to that time, and the victory of the old lifestyle. This was accomplished by the aid of a vivid picture of danger, when the security of his retreat was jeopardized.

The neurosis is the automatic use of functional symptoms which have their origin in the effect of shock, and whose utilization is not understood by the patient.

Those who are too fearful about their prestige and who even in childhood (usually as pampered children) have been enticed to this way of utilization are more inclined to neurosis than are others. The cure can only come about by way of understanding, through the growing insight of the patient, and through the development of his community feeling.

# 17

# The Structure of Neurosis

Jill D. Duba

Perhaps you are a counselor or a coach. Or perhaps you are a teacher working with a group of many children. When you reflect upon the many people that you are in contact with each day, namely the ones you are striving to help, is there one or two that strikes you as "nervous" or particularly anxious, fearful, and/or unsettled? For many of us, we have encountered such individuals and have worked diligently at helping them overcome their anxieties, worries, and the accompanying physiological responses. According to Adler the cure for such nervous states is twofold. First, the individual must develop social interest or "community feeling." Second, one must come to an understanding of the use and functionality of the symptoms. In "The Structure of Neurosis" Adler presents a concise explanation of how such neurotic symptoms came to be in the first place, as well as how the symptoms service the individual. While his article does not focus on how to help clients increase awareness, insight, and community feeling, "The Structure of Neurosis" does provide an informative baseline for how today's counselors can begin to understand the self-defeating behaviors, mistaken goals, and movement of clients who are struggling with neurosis.

To illustrate how these concepts can be applied to a present-day scenario, I am going to frame the ideas that Adler presents within the context of a client case. As in any counseling context, Adler would argue that it is important to gather as much information about the client prior to coming to any definite conclusions about their presenting problem and lifestyle. For the purposes of brevity, however, we will use this short case example as a backdrop for understanding how Adler's principles might be applied.

Let's consider "Ellen," a 44-year-old female. Her presenting concern includes complaints of persistent headaches, excessive appetite, and weight gain. She also worries every day about "dying too early." Ellen has seen multiple medical doctors who have all confirmed that besides needing to lose at least 50 pounds, she is healthy. She is finding it increasingly difficult to socialize with anyone. She reports that it is easier to come home after work, eat, and retreat to her bedroom to drown out her worries by watching TV. Although she insists that she would never harm herself, she is beginning to question her worth in society—as a family member, coworker, and community member. She tells herself that "no one notices I am gone anyway." Ellen is a high school librarian. She has worked for the same school for the last 18 years. Last year she became increasingly worried when word got out that the school district was cutting various staff positions. Ellen confesses that although she has thought about switching schools and even moving, she is "comfortable" and very afraid of change. After a couple of sessions, Ellen reports that she has been dating a very "obese" man for the last 3 years whom she is neither attracted to or in love with. She explains, though, that "this situation is better than being alone." After exploring her childhood we find that what Ellen remembers most is that she "was overweight." Although she knows that her mother and grandmother meant no harm, they would say to her, "Come here, my chubby girl." She also recalls being ridiculed at school. She tried to be as quiet as possible so that the other students would not notice her. Ellen remembers being happy when another "fat girl" came to her school in the third grade. This was her only friend throughout elementary school. Ellen broke her leg during the summer when she was 5 years old. She recalls feeling excluded from the activities the rest of the children were involved in. She says that after that summer she never could "quite get back to a normal size." After a couple of years, she began to think that she would "always be fat" and as a consequence she would never have "real friends."

## LIFE AS MOVEMENT

Adler suggested that all individuals have a "capacity for motion . . . as long as life exists." This movement is understood in terms of the direction and goal. Adler argues that everyone is striving to "overcome all imperfections and achieve completion." What varies among individuals is the direction or movement toward this goal of *overcoming* feelings of inferiority. So, in the case of Ellen, we can assume that she is striving to overcome feelings of inferiority. For example, instead of experiencing "less than" among family or friends, she drowns herself in the TV, overeats, and tells herself that she may play or have a significant role in social settings. What we need to know more about is the nature of her movement—namely the way in which she strives to overcome feeling inferior.

## INTENSIFIED MINUS SITUATIONS

What is the nature of one's insecurities? As previously mentioned Adler argued that everyone experiences a certain degree of insecurity and thus works through life to try to overcome this (either by becoming courageous or by ignoring it and/or taking manipulative measures). However, Adler also recognizes that some individuals experience severe or "intensified" cases of inferiority. In modern-day terms, this would be an example of psychopathology or any given mental health "disorder." Such "intensified minus situations" originate from three different early life experiences: organ inferiority, pampering, or neglect. In the case of an organ deficiency (i.e., physical shortcoming, physiological limitation or flaw), the child "experiences the weakness of his organic equipment" and "feels impelled to reorganize it accordingly." Essentially, the child takes the position that he/she is "less than" and behaves according. Pampered children, on the other hand, develop "like parasites" who are either always looking for assistance and influence or "extremely disinclined to accept any suggestion." Finally, neglected children will likely grow up feeling neglected and will find situations in his/her adult life that will "make him feel neglected."

For a moment, let's consider the case of Ellen again. When Ellen was a child, how did her weight impact the way she felt about herself? How did this interpretation impact how she made sense of who she could be as a student, daughter, and friend? When she faces current situations that induce feelings of insecurity, what does she do to overcome those feelings? The way in which she developed movement to overcome her feelings of insecurity as a child is the same way (or movement) she overcomes feelings of insecurity as an adult.

## EXCEPTIONS: CREATIVE POWER AND SOCIAL INTEREST

Adler was a hopeful individual and thus saw exceptions to any explanation of behavior. That is, not all children who have organ deficiencies are spoiled or neglected and will grow up to feel especially nervous, anxious, and unhappy. As mentioned in the above section, Adler believed that how children make sense of (attitude and interpretation) a given organ deficit or environment (being spoiled or neglected) will impact how they strive to overcome any and all future imperfections or feelings of inferiority. We already have considered how Ellen's attitude toward her organ deficit (overweight) transformed itself into how she overcomes feelings of insecurity even as an adult (law of movement).

Might there have been another route for Ellen, another way of interpreting her weight as a child? Adler suggested two other ways in which children can create a response that is courageous and will likely contribute to the formation to a law of movement that does not contribute to pathology later in life, namely creative power and social interest. In "The Structure of Neurosis" Adler explains that it is the "creative power of the individual" or how the child makes "use . . . of that equipment" that will impact how the child overcomes his/her inferior position. Consider Ellen. What if as a child she decided that children who judge her on her appearance are not worth being friends with anyway? What if she decided that although she was overweight, she would work to simply enjoy activities despite the discomfort of the extra weight? What if she saw this "deficit" as a challenge that she was determined to cope with? Finally, if Ellen responded to her weight in these ways, how might this have molded how she dealt with other challenges in her life as an adult? That is, her "creative power" to find ways of overcoming her weight as a child would directly impact how she would "strive to overcome" all imperfections throughout her life.

In "The Structure of Neurosis" Adler explained that although all three groups of individuals "face life with a feeling of insecurity," the solution depends on how they are "prepared to make contact with . . . fellow human beings." Further, he suggested that "only the individual who is socially prepared for cooperation can solve the social problems which life imposes." This is because the "insecure individual is always more concerned with himself than others." Although we may not have a report of how Ellen was raised and prepared to connect with and interact with others, we can make some speculations. What we do know is that she is very self-focused. She is more concerned about what her contributions may be than the people that she would be impacting in a positive way. Instead of looking for and believing in the support that other people can provide her, she withdraws from any human contact and remains depressed, worried, and anxious in her bedroom. What if Ellen was prepared and encouraged to interact with others? What if she was taught the value of social interaction and of relationships? Further, how might this have contributed to her law of movement?

## ADLER TODAY

Many of us have encountered Ellen. Unfortunately Ellen has likely been diagnosed with a disorder or two, has been overmedicated with anti-anxiety medications, and has been limited in talk therapy because of reimbursement limitations. Adler's perspective, on the other hand, is a holistic and systemic one. Furthermore, his message about the cure for one's emotional and mental "pathology" is clear. That is, the solution must involve others. The client must have a desire to be a part of and a contributing member of a group. In addition, the individual must be courageous enough to change and reconsider his/her attitude about challenges and the problems of life. Finally, Adler's perspectives are quite fitting for the counselor or helper who is interested in empowering and motivating individuals, for helping persons find valor and bravery that lies within, and for looking at "problems" as an opportunity for change.

## REFERENCES

Adler, A. (1914). Das Problem der "Distanz": Uber einen Grundcharakter der Neurose und Psychose [The problem of "distance": A basic trait of neurosis and psychosis]. *Zeitschrift fur Individual Psychologie, 1*, 8–16.

Adler, A. (1932). Die Systematik der Individualpsychologie [The systematics of individual psychology]. *Internationale Zeitschrift fur Individual Psychologie, 10*, 241–244.

Adler, A. (1935). The structure of neurosis. *International Journal of Individual Psychology, 1*(2), 3–12. (Original work published in 1932; reprinted in Ansbacher & Ansbacher, 1979)

Ansbacher, H. L., & Ansbacher, R. R. (Eds.). (1979). *Superiority and social interest: Alfred Adler—A collection of later writings* (3rd ed.). New York: Norton. (Original work published in 1964)

# The Structure of Neurosis

*Alfred Adler*

The subject I have chosen to discuss here, namely, the structure of neurosis, is one of the most difficult problems in psychology. We frequently observe fear in people without considering it as a manifestation of neurosis. Frequently, also, there may be found a certain inelasticity or rigidity of thinking in people who are not neurotic; in individuals, for instance, who lay great stress on rules and formulae. But we cannot take this as characteristic of neurosis. The same applies to other neurotic symptoms. The symptom of fatigue occurs in the neurasthenic as well as in so-called normal people. The symptoms found in functional neurosis may also be found outside of a neurosis. Every human being under certain psychic tensions will react according to his individual makeup. In one suffering from fear, we may notice various reactions such as heart palpitation, breathing difficulties, etc. Normal human beings may be subject to these symptoms. Contractions of the throat may be brought on in them by a feeling of insecurity. Other individuals will, under stress of fear, react with stomach symptoms, or intestinal disorders, or bladder irregularities. There are a great number of individuals whose fear manifests itself through the sexual organ. There is a special type in whom fear creates sexual excitement. Individuals of this type consider such a reaction normal, and even go so far as to construct theories about it. We want to keep in mind that phenomena beyond the range of human psychological life do not occur in neurosis either.

## THE SOUL AS PART OF LIFE

Here, I must briefly touch on the basic views of Individual Psychology, especially the concept of the soul or mind. It is quite clear that, thereby, we venture into transcendental territory.

Watson and his school, who refuse to do this, ignore the existence and meaning of the soul. There are other schools, also, which take a purely mechanistic viewpoint on these matters, thus eliminating the mind and psychic life. In the true sense, this is impossible since the very word "psychology" means science of the soul. Many call themselves psychologists who, in fact, are physiologists and, according to the structure of their scientific training, eliminate the concept of the soul or think of it in a mechanistic way. The psychologist, however, takes it for granted that a basic conception of psychic life includes the various manifestations of the personality. These manifestations are arranged in definite order and direction.

Speculative insight is necessary to understand the context data which may lead beyond the province of experience. But even here, in the sphere outside immediate or tangible experience, there is no evidence which precludes the assumption of psychic life or disproves the existence of it. Let us assume, therefore, that the soul is a part of life.

## LIFE AS MOVEMENT

Now the most important characteristic of life is motion. That does not mean that living things cannot be in a state of immobility, but that the capacity for motion is present as long as life exists, and that all psychic life can be interpreted in terms of movement. Hence, all phenomena which pertain to the psychic life can be seen in space-time relationships. We observe these movements and see them as if in a congealed state—as forms in repose, so to speak. Once we see psychic expression as movement, we approach an understanding of our problem; for the chief characteristic of a movement is that it must have direction and, therefore, a goal. Moreover, this direction toward which every psychic movement proceeds could not exist if the entire psychic life did not have a goal, which, as must be stressed at this point, is, in the case of every individual, determinable and capable of formulation, even though the individual himself cannot formulate it. In relation to this we may note that we have in our consciousness a great number of impressions which are not clearly defined concepts and which, under certain circumstances, we can formulate. In this connection, it is sometimes erroneously concluded that if we clothe the non-understood in words, we have moved it from the realm of the unconscious to the conscious, which is certainly not the case.

## THE GOAL OF OVERCOMING

I have said that every movement has a goal. "Drives" and "natural tendencies," such as sexual drives, for instance, have no direction. These abstract concepts cannot, therefore, be well utilized in the understanding of psychic occurrences. The direction which we seem to observe in these drives is merely the direction imparted to them by the movement of the individual-as-a-unity toward his goal. The movement toward a goal shows a unified pattern. It is this goal of the psychic life which makes the whole psychic life a unity. The result is that the aspiration toward this goal is immanent in every part of the psychic movement; therefore, the goal becomes a part of the unity. We must conclude, then, that we understand a part of the psychic life only when we conceive it as a part of a unity which proceeds along the same course toward the same goal with other characteristics of the individual. In the practical application of Individual Psychology, this viewpoint is of the greatest importance. Hence it is essential to the understanding of psychic life to explain how the goal originates.

Striving toward a goal, toward an objective, we find everywhere in life. Everything grows "as if" it were striving to overcome all imperfections and achieve completion. This urge toward perfection we call the "goal of overcoming," that is, the striving to overcome.

Language is inadequate to express the full range of interpretations of what "overcoming" means. The interpretation varies with each individual because the goal of each individual is different. If we say that such a striving is for "power" or "force," or a "running away from reality," we have made typical generalizations which do not give a clear insight into a particular, individual case. But we have gained one point. We have illuminated the field under consideration, and must then narrow down the meaning so that we are able to perceive the particular direction of movement of the individual in question. For this we need experience, alertness, and a closely 'critical, objective, unbiased examination of each individual case.

The phenomena to which we allude imply the existence of a minus and plus situation simultaneously in the same individual—that is, an inferiority feeling and at the same time a striving to overcome this inferiority. The inferiority feeling can show itself in a thousand ways, for instance, as a striving for superiority. The question, then, arises as to how the fictitious goal or guiding fiction, which is different in each individual and which he carries within himself from the beginning to the end of life, is established.

## THE CREATIVE POWER OF THE INDIVIDUAL

We concede that every child is born with potentialities different from those of any other child. Our objection to the teachings of the "hereditarians" and every other tendency to overstress the significance of constitutional disposition is that the important thing is not what one is born with, but what use one makes of that equipment. Still, we must ask ourselves: "Who uses it?" As to the influence of the environment, who can say that the same environmental influences are apprehended, worked over, digested, and responded to by any two individuals in the same way? To understand this fact, we find it necessary to assume the existence of still another force: the creative power of the individual.

We have been impelled to attribute to a child creative power, which casts into movement all the influences upon him and all his potentialities—a movement toward the overcoming of an obstacle. This is felt by the child as an impulse that gives his striving a certain direction. There is no doubt that all phenomena in the psychic life of a child tend toward overcoming his inferior position and consequently, the views of those who believe in the "causative" influence of "heredity" on the one hand, or "environment" on the other, are, as complete explanations of his personality, made untenable by the assumption of this creative power of the child. The drive in the child is without direction as long as it has not been incorporated into the movement toward the goal which he creates in response to his environment. This response is not simply a passive reaction but a manifestation of creative activity on the part of an individual. It is futile to attempt to establish psychology on the basis of drives alone, without taking into consideration the creative power of the child which directs the drive, molds it into form, and supplies it with a meaningful goal.

There are, however, certain factors which affect the child and allure him to mold his life in a certain direction. These factors are not primarily causative agents, but rather alluring, stimulating phenomena. The attitude toward these factors varies very widely in different individuals. No mathematical rule is conceivable that could teach us how to make the proper use of anything which we possess. However, unprejudiced research cannot observe the disposition or constitution individuals possess, only the "use" they make of what they possess. These factors, as I have indicated, appear as alluring or stimulating opportunities to the individual. It would be erroneous to assume that they act as causes, for, with deepened understanding, we see that a different use is made of the same stimuli by different individuals, and therefore we are justified in assuming, merely, that it is probable on a statistical basis that they will evoke in an individual certain seemingly typical uses of them. So much we may understand. Any assertion beyond that we may regard as a bit unscientific. In other words, it is the creative factor that comes into play here, and it is this factor which we have to train ourselves to understand better in its working.

## INTENSIFIED MINUS SITUATIONS

### ORGAN INFERIORITY

As a result of our experience we understand that children with inferior organs will feel inadequate for the tasks of life and that the minus situation will be felt by a child with inferior organs more intensely than by the average child. This is very significant because our experience confirms the fact that where a situation is felt to be especially insecure, the results are very striking and they show a greater striving for a plus situation. These observations apply to children who are born with inferior sense organs, with inferior brain structure, (and with) inferior endocrine glands. The organic weakness does not necessarily function as a "minus" situation, but the child experiences the weakness of his organic equipment for average social tasks, and he feels impelled to reorganize it accordingly.

There are innumerable forms of life in which we may observe the striving to overcome the sense of inadequacy rooted in an experience of organ inferiority. Some individuals seek to eliminate problems; some act so as to avoid them. By the avoidance of problems, some feel relieved and so more secure. Others wrestle and struggle with their problems—such, for instance, as that of left-handedness—and accommodate themselves more courageously to outside influences.

The outcome depends on the creative power of the individual, which expands outwardly according to no rule except this: that the determining goal is always "success." What constitutes success for him depends upon the individual's own interpretation of his position.

During the first three or four years of life, the child forms his way of life (*Lebensform*). He has then shaped his concrete goal, determining the way in which he overcomes his problems. From then on one may perceive in his attitude the result of this process of creative goal formation. There are millions of variations of such goals. They differ from each other, metaphorically speaking, in color, shape, rhythm, and intensity.

## Pampering

A second group of individuals will show a life pattern very similar to that of children affected by organ inferiority. I have in mind those individuals who have been pampered in childhood. The more deeply I have delved into the problem of neurosis and searched the cases presented, the more clearly have I come to see that in every individual with a neurosis some degree of pampering can be traced. Dependence on another person for the solution of a problem or the carrying out of a task has a determining influence on an individual.

But we must not think too loosely of pampering. When we speak of a pampered child we do not simply mean a child who is loved and caressed, but rather a child whose parents are always hovering over it, and assume all responsibilities for it, who take away from the child the burden of fulfilling any of the tasks and functions it could fulfill. Under such circumstances the child develops like a parasite and emerges as one of innumerable varieties of individuals, ranging from those who are extremely disinclined to accept any suggestion or influence from others to those who are always seeking assistance. Between these extremes, there are, as I have indicated, thousands of differences in type and kind.

I would like to prevent an easily made mistake, however, by stating here that the pampered style of life should not be understood as simply resulting from the attitude of parents or grandparents, but that it, too, is the creation of the child himself. This creation may be arrived at even in cases where there is no question of pampering by other persons. It is the exacting attitude of the child which induces pampering.

## NEGLECT

A third group consists of neglected children, those who are, for instance, illegitimate, undesired, or ugly. The feeling of being neglected is, of course, relative. External circumstances can contribute to it, and every pampered child will automatically find himself, later in life, in situations which will make him feel neglected.

## INSECURITY FEELINGS AND LACK OF SOCIAL INTEREST

What we want to get at now is the basic, underlying structure which unites all these types. All three groups face life with a feeling of insecurity. This feeling of insecurity and inadequacy is characteristic of all failures. From the way they attempt to solve their problems we may judge how well individuals in the three categories with which we are dealing are prepared to meet these problems, which are always of a social nature. All problems with which we are confronted are of a social nature. For the purpose of clarification we may classify them as problems of social, occupational, or love relationships. Their solution depends, consequently, upon how well an individual is prepared to make contact with his fellow human beings.

All failures—problem children, criminals, suicides, neurotics, psychotics, drunkards, sexual perverts, etc.—are products of inadequate preparation in *Community-Feeling (Gemeinschaftsgefühl)*. They are all noncooperative, solitary beings who run more or less counter to the rest of the world; beings who are more or less asocial, if not antisocial.

This viewpoint tends to make of Individual Psychology a value psychology. What does this signify? The very far-reaching implication is that only the individual who is socially prepared for cooperation can solve the social problems which life imposes. By this we mean that there should exist a certain degree of contact feeling (*Kontaktgefühl*)—of striving for cooperation (*Streben nach Kooperation*)—in the "law-of-movement" of the individual. Where it is lacking we meet with "failures." I have already shown that this inclination for cooperation and social achievement has not been properly developed in children who feel insecure. These insecure ones build a lifestyle which shows a lack of social interest (*soziales Interesse*), because an insecure individual is always more concerned with himself than with others. He cannot get away from himself.

We cannot stress too much that in the neurotic there is a lack of interest in others, a lack of social interest (*sociales Interesse*). We must not be confused by the fact that some neurotics seem to be benevolent and wish to reform the whole world. This wish to reform the whole world can be merely a response to a keenly felt minus situation. Where the minus situation is strong, the striving to overcome will also be strong. We can perceive this also in the organs of the human body, for where the obstacle to be overcome is great the tension is also great. The neurotic places the goal of his overcoming high. It is related, just as in the case of a normal individual, to the feeling of personal value. The feeling of personal worth can only be derived from achievement, from the ability to "overcome." A lack of social feeling (*sociales Gefühl*) prevails, in the law-of-movement of the neurotic and decreases his ability to "overcome." This lack is not as great in the neurotic as it is in the criminal. The criminal is more actively aware of his fellow creatures but opposes them at the same time. The neurotic does not oppose them openly, but his efforts are bent toward testing and utilizing, or exploiting, the community feeling (*Gemeinschaftsgefühl*) of others.

This is characteristic of all neurotics, so that in the structure of a neurosis we find the utilization of the community feeling (*Gemeinschaftsgefühl*) of others and simultaneously the arresting of an individual's cooperative participation by a "but." This "but" is the epitome of all neurotic symptoms. It offers an alibi to the neurotic. The neurotic lives according to the formula "yes-but." All the symptoms which hinder the neurotic from going forward to achievement are found to be covered by this formula. His estimate of his value, therefore, depends upon how much another person contributes to it, and not upon his ability to overcome—not upon his own achievements.

Even in considering functional neurosis we maintain the foregoing viewpoint. In such cases we have to deal with an arrangement of emotions, such as anxiety, insecurity, hyper-sensitivity, rage, impatience, greediness, etc. These emotions all arise from living outside the scope of cooperation. The tension in which the neurotic lives makes it easy to work himself up into a state of heightened emotion.

This tension makes itself felt at the point of "least resistance," and the characteristic effects show up in such places as I have mentioned before, for instance, the stomach, bladder, intestines, heart, etc.

So we come to see that functional neurosis can be understood only when we recognize the individual as a unity.

## UNPREPAREDNESS IN THE FACE OF LIFE PROBLEMS

*When scrutinized, the neurotic will be found to be an individual placed in a test situation who is attempting to solve his problems in the interest of his own personal ambition rather than in the interest of the common welfare.*

This holds true of all neuroses. All neuroses grow out of the psychic tension of an individual who is not socially well prepared, when he is confronted with a task which demands for its solution more community feeling (*Gemeinschaftsgefühl*) than he is capable of.

The true nature of the so-called endogenic factors in neurosis becomes more clearly marked when the individual finds himself placed in a test situation. Here the individual's interpretation of his own qualities plays a great role. We do not share the opinion that a neurotic is incapable of solving those problems before which he breaks down, but we recognize that he has not yet acquired that ability to join (*Anschlussfähigkeit*) necessary for him to make an approximately correct solution of them. He does not possess sufficient "contact ability," that is, capacity for making contact with others. There then develops in him that psychic tension which can be found in everyone who feels insecure. This tension affects the whole body and the whole psychic life and always differs in different individuals.

There are individuals—those who are greatly concerned with rules, formulae, and ideas—whom this tension affects intellectually. We can observe this most clearly in compulsion neurosis and in paranoia. With others, another sphere of psychic life is set in motion—namely, the emotional sphere. This is seen for example in anxiety neuroses and phobias.

I want to lay some stress, also, upon the exogenic factor. Both endogenic and exogenic factors play a part in every neurotic symptom. The true bearing of the exogenic factor on the individual can, however, only be understood when we understand the whole individual in the expression of his lifestyle. The therapist has to put himself in the individual's place in order to see that for this particular individual a certain situation seems too difficult.

Recently, a patient came to me who had been previously treated with success up to a certain point by another Individual Psychologist. Before his previous treatment, he was sexually stimulated only when he saw animals (platonic). It would be interesting to discuss why he chose animals, but I cannot go into that part of his lifestyle here. Anyway, he had, due to a strong inferiority feeling, excluded the normal phase of love relationship. This exclusion I find is characteristic of all sexual perversion. When he came to me he was planning to get married. He said, "I want to marry," the problem now arises of confessing to my future wife what has gone on before. If I do this, I am sure that she will refuse me. This refusal is just what he was aiming at. He wanted another excuse for evading the solution of the love problem. I said to him, "You should not confess to everybody all the disagreeable happenings in your life for which you are not really to blame. It is unfair and not good taste to speak of certain things. It is only the last remnant of your cowardice which makes you think of talking about it to your fiancée. You must expect that other people are apt to misunderstand what/you wish to tell." He perceived this and understood the purpose of his determination to confess to his fiancée. I hope that his increased understanding has enabled him to rid himself of his fear of the love problem.

## NEUROTIC TYPES OF MOVEMENT

If one understands the law-of-movement of neurotics, one will always find that in each patient the mental phase (compulsion neurosis), or the emotional phase (anxiety neurosis), or the motor phase (hysteria), is predominant, although the other psychic processes, too, are always dynamically present. In the treatment of such cases, however, the *whole* psychic process must be clearly and definitely determined. There are no pure cases. There are only mixed cases in which it can be seen that at one time one aspect, at another time another aspect of the whole psychic process comes to the foreground.

People who do not sufficiently understand this predominance of one aspect of life over the other frequently talk about the "unconscious." The unconscious, however, is nothing other than that which we have been unable to formulate in clear concepts. These concepts are not hiding away in some unconscious or subconscious recesses of our minds, but are those parts of our consciousness the significance of which we have not fully understood.

If we focus our attention on the goal, direction, and form of an individual's "movement," which alone gives us true understanding of him, we find among neurotics several different types of "movements."

### Distance

There is first the *distance complex*. This first type of movement characteristic of neuroses shows an attempt to establish distance as a safeguard. There are neurotics, then, in whom the most striking characteristic is that they keep themselves at a significant distance or apartness from the solution of the problem with which they are confronted. This distance may be produced by means of hysteria, fainting, indecision, a tendency to doubt, etc., but all these symptoms mean nothing more than an attempt to stand still in a world that is moving. If an individual cannot decide whether he should do this or do that, one thing is certain—namely, that he does not move. This keeping oneself at a distance can also be seen very clearly in anxiety neuroses. Functional neuroses, too, are capable of hindering a person from solving social problems. Thus an individual may be compelled to urinate just when he is about to go to a party. Also, the compulsion neuroses are well designed to effect this "distance," and consequently bring about a standstill, whenever the neurotic feels himself forced to do something.

### Hesitating Attitude

The second form of movement manifests itself in a *hesitating attitude*: the neurotic advances, but advances hesitatingly. An example of this is stuttering. Any problem may be met with a "stuttering approach." This hesitation may lead to a postponement of a solution of one's problems by means of insomnia. The patient with this symptom is so tired that he can solve his task only very hesitatingly. In neurasthenia, the symptom of fatigue is one of the chief characteristics. In agoraphobia it is obvious that the neurotic hesitates to solve his problem without the assistance of another person.

## Detour

The third form of movement characteristic of all neurotic symptoms is the detour around the solution of a problem and the refuge in a secondary field of operation. This becomes especially clear in a compulsion neurosis. The patient sets up a countercompulsion in opposition to the compulsion of social demands. In doing this he only postpones the solution of his problems. An example of this is the washing compulsion.

## Narrowed Path of Approach

The fourth form of movement is the most complicated and the most striking. I might call it the narrowed path of approach. The person does not give himself up fully to the solution of a problem; he takes up only part of it and eliminates other parts, generally those which are most pertinent. This is the case in perversions. Another phase of this same form of movement is one that sometimes leads to great cultural achievements.

## CONCLUDING SUMMARY

The goal of "overcoming" is approached by each individual differently. Proceeding toward a general diagnosis, we may recognize traits of unconcealed despotism purposing to make the other person a slave to the patient, as is the case of anxiety neurosis. Such individuals have learned in their childhood to force others to come to their rescue by frightening them. Another group of individuals use the "alibi" as the chief form of movement toward the goal of "overcoming." Their ambitious tendency becomes obvious when we see them insisting upon their point of view. For instance, they will say: "If I only could sleep, I could be the first or among the first." But they content themselves with having this alibi. Of course, not everyone will present that alibi in such an easily understandable form; therefore we have to take into account the whole of a patient's attitude toward his problems. In a third group we find individuals who create fictitious values within themselves. Neurotics, for instance, pride themselves on how much they have attained in spite of their neurosis.

I want to stress only one thing more: in psychic processes the single spheres are not as separated as some schools of psychology tend to assume. There is no area where only the emotional or the mental side, either action or volition, can be found to be present. The psychic process comprises the whole of an individual. When we observe a part of it, we should feel forced to search for the rest of it. So, if an individual tells us his first childhood recollections, we may gather from it the mental, emotional, and attitudinal aspects, and only after that may we arrive at an understanding of the unity of his personality. By virtue of our experience we are, with all due precaution, in a position to ascertain the dynamic value of mental, emotional, and attitudinal movements as movements directed toward or determined by a goal that, for the individual, has the meaning of securing for him what *he regards* as *his* position in life. It is in such a way only that we become capable of understanding these goal-directed movements as the individual's efforts to secure for himself what he interprets, or misinterprets, as success, or as his way of overcoming a minus situation so as to attain a plus situation.

We thus come to the understanding: all neurotic symptoms are safeguards of persons who feel too weak to face the problems of life, but have a certain platonic appreciation of social feeling (*Sozialgefühl*). This appreciation often becomes apparent only in that they count on the community feeling (*Gemeinschaftsgefühl*) of others, to claim it for themselves.

As soon as, after long toil and great experience, one has recognized the meaning of this connection, the real expert has the insight that in neurosis one always deals with the pampered type, the type of individual who has not become a cooperative fellow-being because in his earliest childhood he was trained to count on others for the solution of his problems.

# 18

# Trick and Neurosis

DANIEL ECKSTEIN

My first comment on Adler's article relates to the creative title itself. On Halloween, Western children all dressed up in costumes utter the classic phrase "trick or treat" as they open their bags in hopes of obtaining a treat. Adler takes the term *trick* and creatively uses it to illustrate the many ways in which we trick ourselves by devising various ways of coping with life.

Consistent with Adler's commitment to encouragement he makes a special point of noting that "nothing depreciatory" is meant by that term. Indeed, he asserts that most discoveries and advances in science utilize such tricks.

Although contemporary clinical diagnosis avoids the actual term *neurosis*, one way to translate that into contemporary counseling practice could be to consider "how we make trouble for ourselves." Adler gives several case studies, all illustrating how clients have tricked themselves in creative ways.

Tricks, of course, are not all self-destructive. Mark Twain's classic 1876 story of how Tom Sawyer tricked a boyhood friend into painting a fence comes to mind (2010). The boxer Mohammed Ali utilized the "rope a dope" phenomenon, where his trainers loosened the ropes so he could lean into them and absorb the early-round punches of George Foreman in the Heavyweight Championship match held on October 30, 1974, in Kinshasa, Zaire. Many of the best-selling novels and Hollywood movies also involve a trick of some sort. And of course tricks are the trade of magicians.

Adler's focus is on how one uses a trick in a purposive nature. The goal-directed purposeful nature of human behavior is one of Adler's most enduring legacies. In his several case studies he describes how various individuals adopted a strategy to gain them special significance in one way or another. Some of these strategies included being pampered and overprotected, payoffs for nervousness, and advantages gained by what he called a "flight into illness."

In all his case studies the adopted trick was at the expense of the community. In other writings Adler used the concept of "social interest" to refer to the connection as contrasted to utilizing a trick to be disconnected from the group. Contemporary existentialists and socialists use the term *anomie* to refer to the sense of footlessness and disconnectedness that comes from utilizing what Adler calls *tricks* in this article.

Adler also utilizes the concept of "private intelligence," which later was called "private logic," whenever a person uses a "personal, private view of the world to assert his own sense of superiority" over someone else. In this context the term *private* was used in contrast to a more general public view of human behavior. Later the concept of private logic became more synonymous with George Kelly's (1970) concept of "personal constructs." Understanding the inner personal world of another person through empathy, for example, meant to understand Piaget's (1971) concepts of personal schemes, or ways we all organize our own inner world.

While Adler does not mention how counselors can trick clients, often the concept of reframing, for example, is one intervention where another equally true hypothesis is offered. A counselor might trick a client into changing the negative label of "stubborn" into a more positive one of "persistent," for example. Since Adler mentioned the private ways a criminal goes about getting things for himself or herself, another trick, as it were, was in this writer's own experience in juvenile corrections. One of the incarcerated young men was an expert at breaking into homes. He could pick any lock. He was so good that he would not break into any house; rather, he specialized in the ones with large warning signs of "Protected by Brinks," for example.

My trick as his counselor was to get him a job after his sentence was completed working for the very security systems he had helped dismantle. Moving from a more socially useful application of his skills was the trick instead of the previous socially useless strategy.

Adler also spoke about what he called "the providence of guesswork." His protégé Rudolf Dreikurs (1975) later used a similar phrase, "digging gold mines." A contemporary application of a similar concept was in Malcolm Gladwell's book *Blink* (2005). His term was "thin-slicing"; it refers to the idea that we often make decisions based on just small amounts of information.

Another similar concept shared by both Adler and Gladwell is what Adler called the style of life. In the various case studies Adler presents, he notes the consistent personality themes that later became called lifestyle. Gladwell introduces a concept similar to the notion of lifestyle in his description of what are called "fists." He notes that "Morse code is made up of dots and dashes, each of which has its own prescribed length. But no one ever replicates those prescribed lengths perfectly. When operators send a message . . . they vary the spacing or stretch out the dots and dashes or combine dots and dashes and spaces in a particular rhythm. Morse code is like speech. Everyone has a different voice" (p. 27).

In World War II Gladwell notes that such recognition of individual differences in sending Morse code was a valuable way the Allies were able to track Nazi troop movements. A person sending out Morse code messages was assigned to each Nazi troop. But through the concept of individual fists, the Allies learned to distinguish the individual style of each man sending out the messages. Even in the simple act of sending a Morse code message, each person has a personal typing style, as it were. Some would strike a certain letter harder than others, for example. By knowing who was sending the message from what troop the Allies correctly predicted where troops were being assembled in the war.

Adler also uses such metaphors in his descriptions such as "like a motorist who feeds more gas to speed up his car." In a contemporary adaptation of that concept, Kopp and Eckstein took Adler's suggestion of using metaphors and suggested the following six types of metaphors clients can use. They include the following:

1. Self—"I am a teakettle about to explode."
2. Other—"My husband's a locomotive barging into the house."
3. Situation—"I am a barren wasteland."
4. Relationship of self to self—"I keep beating myself up."
5. Relationship of self to other—"Dealing with him is like trying to tame a wild tiger."
6. Relationship of self to a situation—"I am slowly sinking into quicksand." (p. 165)

Another contemporary counseling application is the concept of a therapeutic double bind. While Adler does not use that term himself, he richly describes the dual "push-pull" tensions of one of his case studies of a man who wants to be happy and yet that would mean having to take a test he dreads if he is well enough to do so. "This means that he must not strengthen the impulse to rid himself of his symptoms even though he suffers from them. They are useful to him in aiding him to postpone the test he fears . . . He is on the way to eluding his problem, not solving it" (p. 7). Gregory Bateson (1972) later used the actual term *double bind* and also *paradoxical communication* to describe how schizophrenia often occurs, for example.

Not only does this again point out the payoff for the trick of negative behavior but Adler also points out several times in his article the holistic connection between the mind and the body. *Somatization* is the term used today to describe how people manifest the disease of cancer in their bodies as one consequence of such negative emotions of anger, for example. Adler was one of the original therapists who noted such a mind-body connection.

In summary, it is the author's contention that Adler's "Trick and Neurosis" has the following eight contemporary applications:

1. The purposeful goal-directed nature of tricks
2. A feeling of being connected or of being disconnected with others
3. "Private intelligence," later called "private logic" and similar to George Kelly's concept of personal constructs

4. "The providence of guesswork," which later was called "digging gold mines" by Dreikurs and then "thin-slicing" by Gladwell
5. The *style of life*, which later became *lifestyle* and was described as "fists" by Gladwell
6. The therapeutic use of metaphors
7. Therapeutic double binds, in which to gain more happiness clients have to give up a behavior that has useful payoffs for them
8. The interrelationship of mind, body, and spirit, an essential component of holistic medicine today

## REFERENCES

Bateson, G. (1972). *Steps to ecology of mind: Collected essays in anthropology, psychiatry, evolution, and epistemology.* Chicago: University of Chicago Press.

Dreikurs, R. (1975). *Fundamentals of Adlerian psychology.* Chicago: Adler School of Professional Psychology.

Gladwell, M. (2005). *Blink.* New York: Time Warner.

Kelly, G. (1970). *A brief introduction to personal construct theory.* New York: Academic Press.

Kopp, R, & Eckstein, D (2004). Using early memory metaphors and client generated metaphors in Adlerian therapy. *Journal of Individual Psychology, 60*(2), 163–174.

Piaget, J. (1971). *Biology and knowledge.* Chicago: University of Chicago Press.

Twain, M. (2010). *The adventures of Tom Sawyer* (135th anniversary ed.). San Francisco: University of California Press.

# Trick and Neurosis

*Alfred Adler*

The topic that I shall discuss here really requires a philosophical explanation at the outset, by way of introduction. I shall restrict myself, however, to pointing out that we human beings, with our limited understanding, can never do more than draw lines of connections and relationships between things; that we really know very little of the reality, of the facts that lie behind our impressions. If you compare this brief statement with the title, you will surmise the point that I am trying to get at—the fact that actually the greater part of our lives is characterized by something that we might call "trickiness" or the use of device, if we think of the term "trick," not as something reprehensible, not as something conflicting with the spirit of community and fellowship, but something upon which human nature has come to be absolutely dependent. That is, we must enter the province of guesswork if we hope to make any progress. I could prove this fact by illustrations drawn from art.

To anticipate criticism, I wish to make clear the fact that "trickiness" is something universal and general, and that we must first determine whether the use of a particular "trick" or device is compatible or incompatible with the aims of the communal spirit. You will soon realize that it is my purpose to show that our entire lives are marked by a certain "tricky" quality, which becomes apparent as soon as we consider our relationship to the natural forces that compel us to adapt ourselves successfully to our environment.

The course of evolution demonstrates that, in the life of the senses, there is a something that does not operate by the rules and formulas of logic, but which works through a process of adaptation effected by guesswork. All inventions are based upon a trick. Now anyone who thought he saw in the title of this article a condemnation in the offing, can set his mind at rest— there is nothing depreciatory in the term "trick." I might call attention to Hegel, who says, "The human mind is crafty." This is true not only as it applies to art, to discoveries and inventions, to every instance of progress in science; it is equally true in narrower applications. For example, the ability to catch and hold the evanescent word through the craft of book-printing was not bestowed by nature. We cannot suppose that some powerful agency implanted in the evolution of the human race a natural talent that led a priori to the art of printing. If anyone grants such an assumption, he only expresses a pious wish that cannot be verified with facts. Similarly, we can show that all achievements, of whatever sort, have led to progress, not through the forms of logic, but by a device or trick—through the discovery of a strategem for evading the difficulty in order to solve it.

We could mention many provinces in which tricks are common—in literature for example. There trickery is at its height—in, for instance, the trick of representing a man who never lived, but from whom we can learn, who arouses our emotions, and so on. All these phenomena provide us continually with evidence that tricks play a considerable part in life.

When you think of the development of a child, you will have difficulty in supposing that his development proceeded according to conscious laws of logic, through equation of cause with effect. Even the smallest child possesses the quality of trickiness—the ability to find a stratagem with which to meet his difficulties. So it seems certain that this quality (described variously as instinct, reflex, the unconscious, intuition, etc.) has its basis, is inherent in the development of human life; and that the ability to guess (a power that cannot be further explained) is not supervised and regulated by the reason until later on—the exact time cannot be determined. The power of reason develops only with experience, but the talent for tricks has, to some degree, an organic foundation.

A young child does not think and reflect when subjected to a test in the course of an experiment—when he is pricked, tickled, left by himself, and the like. It is not the understanding that produces the result, but the cunning of the child's personality. Our inquiries must begin at this point if we are to understand the nature of trickiness—the use of device—and its development.

With regard to poetry, for instance, a consideration of metaphor is in place here: if a poet views an object in an exaggerated form and clothes it in metaphorical garb, he succeeds in producing an effect. I might also refer to the interpretation of dreams in Individual Psychology: the dreamer, deceiving himself, employs a trick to fortify his position, which seems to be threatened from without; he strengthens his incentive toward a certain kind of behavior by awakening appropriate feelings and emotions. He will do quite the same thing that he ordinarily would do without the dream, but with the dream a stronger impulse is added—like a motorist who feeds more gas to speed up his car. The same destination, the same direction—only more energy is brought into play.

Tricks are interesting, too, in many other connections. Take the case, for instance, of the professional conjurer. Children never tire of the tricks in their magic games. And magicians in many different fields arouse our interest—in photography, radio, motion pictures, etc. Through a trick the illusion of reality is produced. Then consider the way a locksmith can open a door with a picklock; not everybody can do that. But if you ask a locksmith how he does it, he scratches his head and answers, "Why, I guess you just have to have the knack of it." He cannot explain it; you have to find out the trick for yourself.

Mathematics abound in tricks. The mathematicians do not hesitate to reveal artful dodges like this:

$$x^2 + px = q$$

In that form the equation cannot be solved; no mind could ever puzzle it out. But it can be solved by this trick.

$$x^2 + px + (p/2)^2 = (q + p^2/2)$$

And the same sort of thing occurs in life. Years ago I began to reflect on the nature of jokes. In jokes, too, it is a trick that steers away from common sense and presents the "private intelligence" of a human being. Take, for instance, the anecdote of the man who wanted to attend the synagogue on a high Jewish holiday, but had brought no admission-card. He announced to the temple official at the entrance, "I only want to look for Mr. Miller," and received the indignant answer: "You swindler, you! You want to pray!" Here we see the sharp distinction between the private intelligence and common sense, and here we see the quality of the trick that renounces the spirit of community and goes its own private ways. We must understand reason as being connected with common sense—the sense that can be shared.

Now I have arrived at my subject proper: the part that tricks play in psychic aberrations. In discussing this problem I shall continually speak of the "private intelligence" according to which one may attempt, through a personal, private view of the world, to assert himself and enhance his own sense of superiority by injuring that of someone else. "Private intelligence" is at work whenever a person tries, unfairly, to turn to his own advantage the social contributions of another. But here, too, we shall have to add a qualification: the injury inflicted is not deliberately intentional. I should like to extend this assertion to the criminal, despite the stress laid by the legal codes upon the element of premeditation in crime. Since it is not in keeping with the criminal's style of life to make a distinction between good and evil, we must adhere to the conviction that he simply represents a mode of living that goes its private ways in order to attain its ends by means which to him seem easier than those that have social value.

But we will begin with other types of aberration in which an intent to injure is out of the question. Here we are confronted with a style of life that refuses to be changed as long as the person concerned fails to realize that he is in the snare of a trick. To clarify this point I shall describe a few cases, divested of their factual circumstances. Take, for instance, a difficult child, who wishes to make himself the center of attention without earning this position by his contributions; he is not yet convinced that he can win attention and recognition by contibuting his share, and is deluded into believing that he can meet the requirements of life only by being pampered. If you are looking for the quintessence of this child's behavior, you will find that it consists in his use of a trick—a trick, by which he is attempting to achieve his purpose by evading reason. Every person must decide in favor of one or the other—either the tricks of his individual style, or the spirit of comminity. We are citing extreme cases here, but we must not forget that between the extremes lie thousands of variations; and we must always be prepared to find extremely divergent forms of the same phenomenon.

By way of a brief general diagnosis, we can say that in "bad" children we recognize a type that hopes through naughtiness to become the center of attention. Such a child does not act according to abstract laws of cause and effect, but by direct intuition; he stumbles upon the trick of getting what he wants through naughtiness and continues to use it as long as it works. Another example, a boy may be dominated by a severe, nagging mother; and finally, to avoid similar oppressive situations, he hits upon a trick and says, "I'll cut out women altogether." And so we are led to the opinion that even what we call a "principle" is in reality a trick.

Now let us glance at a case that comes within the province of neurosis. Let us suppose that we have a man who has a splendid record of achievement behind him. Let us suppose that he is an only child, pampered and burdened with hopes and expectations that actually have been fulfilled and attained. He is now a successful business man, well-educated, esteemed by his friends. But he takes a partner into his firm, a man of great force and energy, who begins to outstrip him. Our young man's purpose in life, his highest ideal, is to be the first in everything. He is possessed by a morbid spirit of ambition, which is not generally apparent as long as he is on the up-grade. But now because of his new business relationship he is confronted with an obstacle. At first he falls into a state of mental tension; he stops short, and hesitates to proceed in his usual way for fear the outcome might be against him. This process is not conscious, but intuitional. He senses it in his physical condition and in his daily experiences. His agitation increases. He begins to suffer from insomnia and a continual feeling of tiredness—all this the result of the strain of not finding a way to maintain his high position and of his fear of falling from it. But suddenly the man begins to realize that people are treating him with unusual delicacy and tactfulness; that they are concerned about him and are making allowances for his nervous strain. This gives him a feeling of relief, assures him a certain importance, and helps him bear up more easily under the tension; and, like a clever, cagey lawyer who defers the verdict, he postpones the decision regarding his own potentialities and importance. Although he feels insecure, he is actually secure de facto; for even if he gives up the race, his own attention, and that of his associates, will remain focussed on his nervous condition and not on the essential question of his ability and capacities. He will, by the trick of "nervousness," have maintained his importance and position when he felt himself unable to maintain it otherwise.

The puzzle of psychoneurosis has always been the question: What really has happened here? In attempting to answer it many people have grasped at the idea of an advantage to be gained through illness ("flight into illness"), a theory originated by the ingenious Griesinger—which is accepted today by many psychologists, but which can be shown to be untenable.

The nervous symptom is not produced by a desire for an advantage attainable through illness, but arises from the tension and shock produced when the potentially neurotic patient is confronted with a new problem to which he does not feel equal. This would not constitute a neurosis. A neurosis begins a step farther on, when the individual affected begins to make use of this tension and the resultant symptoms as a trick—not deliberately, it must be understood, but as an element in his general life-process—in order to evade a difficulty and produce the illusion of being able to overcome it. The impulse to obviate the nervous symptom is wanting.

The question whether such a person enjoys a feeling of happiness, a sense of advantage gained through illness, is naive. He would be glad to give up his neurotic symptom—we must give the patient that much credit. But his work is cut out for him: in order to maintain his prestige and self-esteem he must evade the decision regarding his ability, for fear he will be shown to be worthless—and that no human being can endure. This means that he must not strengthen the impulse to rid himself of his symptoms even though he suffers from them. They are useful to him in aiding him to postpone the test he fears. He lacks this impulse to rid himself of his symptoms because he is setting out on a course which is incompatible with common sense and community feeling. He is on the way to eluding his problem, not solving it. The manner in which he does this, the results of the strain that we observe in him—these evidence his personal style of life revealed in his effort to postpone a decision.

There are innumerable styles of life, hence the many divergent forms of neurosis. But a neurosis is produced only when a person stabilizes the tension and excitement that arise from a situation in order to give the appearance of getting through it more successfully. The neurosis is the holding on to the shock-effects, the symptoms.

And now let us consider a case of compulsion neurosis. A married woman, who has always been a little morose and irritable, is living in moderate circumstances. She has a good husband, but a child that causes her considerable difficulty. The family finances are more limited than they once were, and she is depressed because she has to do the housework. Let us remember that, as the oldest child in the family, she was forced by her mother to stay at home and look after the other children. From early childhood on she had literally cursed her fate, using strong language; and now she has a whole diction-ary full of profanity at her disposal. After her husband's financial failure, this woman is forced to live in a very poor district, and her time is taken up, as it had been in her childhood, with housekeeping and the care of her child. Suddenly she becomes obsessed with the idea that she is going to cut off someone's head. She is terrified and goes to a psychiatrist.

Anyone who has followed my narrative can see how this symptom was produced. Ever since she was a child the woman had been accustomed, whenever a difficult situation arose, to follow up the painful excitement with a stream of profanity dictated by a striving for a seeming superiority. She learned this as a child; and now, whenever such a situation arises, she simply overflows with invective. But this, in itself, would not be a neurosis. If it were, we should have to consider every Viennese cabman an obsessional neurotic. The neurosis is produced when the woman affirms, "I'm at the end of my tether; these thoughts are a torment, and someone must help me"—when she cries over herself. Here the neurosis begins. To wish someone death, suffer-ing, defilement is the mildest sort of an attack. The neurosis did not begin until the woman, through her obsession elevated herself to a rank of impor-tance and dignity; when she began to turn it to her advantage, to utilize it for the betterment of her situation; when she allowed herself to give way to these grisly thoughts whenever anything happened that did not please her, and came to expect others to grant her a special indulgence for the exertion of pelting them with abuse.

And we cannot overlook the fact that she actually obtained these indul-gences. She let her housework slide, put her child into a children's home, and insisted on circulating in good society, on dressing better, and so on. She achieved all this; but she could preserve her advantageous position only so long as she continued to raise a very common, vulgar practice—the use of profanity—to a place of importance; so long as she turned her swearing to good advantage. Thus she employed a trick, the obsession; though she really was not conscious that she was using it as a device.

And now another case—this time one in which sexuality is turned into a trick. In all instances of sexual perversion, it must be realized, we have to do with a trick: a stratagem to evade normal sexual life and to snap one's fingers at common sense and community feeling.

A young man, extremely pampered, has been under the constant surveil-lance of his father. The father was kind, but a little too critical; yet the son had great respect for him. The father, however, could not help reproaching the young man for incompetency. The son was not on good terms with his mother. Moreover, he had an older sister who had turned out splendidly, and her success seemed to him a handicap. With his character formed in this pattern—too much respect for his father, too great a fear of women—the boy reached an age when the sexual impulse called for satisfaction. Since his father had robbed him of all self-confidence, he naturally could not rely on himself in love—especially since his mother and his sister had exerted an injurious influence on him from the other side. We can guess what form of sexuality he would adopt. In the urgency of his desire, and with his fear of life, he will be thrown on his own resources, and will have to be content with self-gratification. There are thousands of variations of this mistaken way of attempting to solve the problem of love. Individuals who make such mistaken attempts approach the problem as if love were a task for only one person when it is really a task for two.

The boy arrives at puberty; yet he shows no signs of interest in girls. A great many boys are in this predicament, and their only possible means of sexual satisfaction is auto-eroticism. But onanism is not neurotic; it is a simple act, in the practice of which there is no implication of neurosis. The neurosis does not begin until the individual learns the trick of making a strength out of a weakness and stabilizes the process with a definite end in view. Later on we find the young man in this very situation. In his feeling of insecurity he must elude his sense of inferiority and assert his self-importance. So he practices masturbation in such a way as to attract attention to himself. He spends whole nights in coffee-houses, in the company of women, but indulging only in auto-eroticism, until people finally realize what he is doing. And now his family and associates have to grant him a place of importance, because they feel they must attempt to reform him. He has forced them to it by the trick of turning to his advantage the conduct to which his style of life impelled him.

His stock rises. Now his father has nothing more important to worry about than his son. The boy relieves himself of all the pressure formerly brought to bear upon him. His mother and sister treat him nicely. These are the external influences generally brought into play when a family attempts to overcome a trick of this sort in one of its members. But do you believe that this does any good ? No. The boy rightly fears that, if he changes himself, if he gives up his symptoms, he will no longer be able to enforce this pampering and solicitousness. As long as he sticks to his old ways he can feel certain that the others will tag after him; and there is little danger of anyone's hitting upon the idea of giving him up and letting him ruin himself if he so chooses. He is afraid that he could accomplish nothing, could not amount to anything, through the normal social channels of contribution and co-operation. The only way to change him is to give him new courage to try the useful social channels; he will be able to see through his old delusions and errors once he is made to see through the trick that he has employed.

And now I have arrived at the last point of my discussion. These all are matters that lie close to the root of the human psyche. We need not make lengthy reference to diplomacy and politics in this connection. The best diplomat is the one who turns the best trick. The quality of trickiness, the use of device, plays an unbelievably important role in our lives. In neurosis the trick is always at some odds with common sense and is employed according to the particular life style of the individual. Since the person employing the trick has eyes only for his own weakness and his distressing symptom and fails to see the larger context of his trouble, he cannot by himself be expected to rid himself of his symptom. What must be done is to help him see things in their true relationships and understand that he is using a trick, making an excuse, seeking relief from a situation which he fears and maintaining a prestige and position that he believes he can secure in no other way.

Now we can readily see how analysis through the methods of Individual Psychology achieves its result. It shows the individual his trick and convinces him that he has employed this trick without knowing it. It shows him that he has been utilizing symptoms in an attempt to maintain his high position and to avoid a "defeat." It makes him realize that, in his feeling of insecurity, the earliest impressions of his childhood have led him to the use of the trick. And it shows him that his insecurity is not real; that childhood impressions are not an adequate foundation on which to build a whole life. It throws light upon his life-style and makes him see how, in his desire for relief, he has attempted to play tricks on life.

With that accomplished the task of the Individual Psychologist is well under way, even though he may not at once succeed in convincing the patient, who may then confidently be left to his own thoughts and reflection. And if he asks, "What is going to become of me?" you can answer: "Go on using your trick if you honestly think that it marks the limit of your powers. At the best you will be deceiving yourself; at the worst, deceiving others; but in no case will it be a neurosis any longer. For neurosis is the use of psychical impulses and of symptoms for the purpose of exploiting others by means of a trick—but without understanding that the symptoms are being so used. But now you understand."

No therapist can say, with truth, "The patient understood everything, but he still has his symptoms." If a therapist says this, he has not done enough. He has not seen through the whole trick nor brought the patient to see through it. The point is always to illuminate the field of vision until you yourself see the connections clearly enough to convince the patient and make him see them too.

It is the use of trick whenever a person commits suicide to elude the pressing duties of life; when an individual becomes a sexual pervert to avoid the difficulty of fulfilling the normal social requirement of communal life; whenever a problem child attempts to secure advantages through unsocial behavior; or when a criminal so underestimates the importance of others that he does not hesitate to take the shorter route of acquiring something that belongs to someone else.

We must not forget that tricks play a most prominent and important part in the evolution of mankind. The element of trickiness, the use of device, explains, for instance, what others have called intuition or the faculty of guessing. Returning to our point of departure, we can easily show that the trick of guessing is indispensable to evolution and progress since everything that lives really receives nothing but sensations and impressions, without ever grasping clearly what lies behind impressions; for life is activated by the physical and can never be quite certain of the metaphysical.

# 19

## Nervous Insomnia

PAUL R. RASMUSSEN AND KEVIN P. MOORE

Adler begins this 1914 paper with the following statement: "A description of the symptoms of insomnia will not give any essentially new information" (p. 163). Now, 96 years later, in reference to Adler's report, we come to the same general conclusion; there is, essentially, no new information to report. Adler was clearly ahead of his time and we might argue, certainly in the case of insomnia, we are still waiting for others to catch up. But, such a claim may be presumptive. There is no doubt that research conducted into the nature of insomnia over the last 96 years has led to a more complete and detailed understanding of this pervasive condition. As an introduction to this 1914 report, we will summarize our sense of Adler's contribution, putting our own spin on the ideas, and then compare these ideas to some of the most recent findings from the contemporary literature.

At the core of Adler's argument is the belief that the symptoms of insomnia reveal efforts by the afflicted individual to manage life challenges and crises; or they serve to protect the individual from failures brought about by lack of ability, lack of effort, or lack of opportunity for success—any of which would reveal the individual's basic inferiority fears. Adler makes his argument convincingly . . . at least to those couched in the holistic and teleologically oriented model presented by Adler. To those not grounded or well versed in the model, the ideas may appear superficial (e.g., failing to understand the biological complexity of insomnia), accusatorial (e.g., suggesting an intentional manipulation by the "sufferer"), or fanciful (e.g., referring to an outdated concept of unconscious influences). Arguing Adler's point to the first group is preaching to the choir. Convincing the second group is more difficult. However, to those willing to suspend preconceived notions, Adler's perspective can be quite accessible.

We all do what works. This is a basic tenet of the Adlerian approach to understanding the human experience. As a function of conditioning, nonverbal learning, and adaptive regulatory mechanisms, which are not immediately accessible to conscious awareness, we humans strive to maximize the quality of our experiences. This is the teleological model. The notion of "maximal experience" suggests that we are oriented toward enhancing outcomes—referred to by Adler as a "felt plus"—and oriented to move away from (i.e., resolve) aversive states, which can include physical threats, integrity threats, or simply comfort threats—states referred to by Adler as "felt minus." The validity of this perspective is supported by considering the basic premises of models in evolutionary psychology (see Millon, 1990). Thus, we live our lives moving toward perceived enhancements and away from disturbing experiences. As a function of our experiences, we have developed strategies that "work," which means they give each individual some sense of control over the events in life that he or she finds desirable and those he or she finds threatening. These factors can be sufficiently explained by considering basic learning principles associated with classical, operant, and vicarious models of learning. The "sense" that the individual develops is explained in cognitive theory as "schemes" and in Adlerian psychology as "private logic." While the two concepts might appear interchangeable, subtle difference in the theories render them unique. Schemes are generally referred to as "the organizational processes that provide a guiding frame of reference for how events will be interpreted and processed relative to situational demands" (Rasmussen, 2005, p. 22). Private logic refers to how one has come to interpret situations relative to one's desire to maximize outcomes. Therefore, private logic is more consistent with the understanding of goals than are schemes—at least as they are generally described. Thus, as the result of experiences early in life, the individual has determined what he or she likes and what he or she does not like, and has subsequently developed strategies for bringing about those desired outcomes. Taken together, these qualities, along with the compelling and validating role of emotion, come to define an individual's style of life—lifestyle. The notion of lifestyle is similar to the concept of personality, yet the idea of lifestyle better captures the goal orientation of the individual.

With this basic foundation, we can talk about the case of insomnia. Let us begin this discussion with a simple description of the nature and consequences of insomnia. First, the person, despite efforts to induce sleep, which may include various forms of distraction (counting, music, podcasts, etc.), either cannot fall asleep or cannot maintain sleep, thereby decreasing the hours of restorative sleep attained and impairing maximal functioning. Of course, this presumes that the individual is required by circumstance to awaken at a particular time in the morning. It is probably the case that those who do not need to get up are not as impaired by their sleep onset difficulties as are those who do need to get up in the morning. The second problem, related to the first, is that the individual either cannot stay awake during the day or must endure the consequences of suboptimal performance secondary to one's fatigue.

Considering the sleep onset difficulties, except in the case of primary insomnia, which is less common and more typically the result of various metabolic conditions rather than a psychological problem (Morin, 2010), the problem typically emerges when the issues contemplated while trying to sleep are issues that are not readily resolved and are of such importance to the person to be obsessive.

Therefore anxiety frequently accompanies, and often precedes, cases of insomnia (Ebben & Spielman, 2009). Worry tends to occupy an individual's mind anytime that individual is not forced by some external saliency to attend to something else. Also, the issues are typically those that have some intensity (are important to the person's physical or psychological welfare) and urgency (need quick resolution).

What is important to consider at this juncture is why the issue or issues are of such urgency and intensity and are not readily resolved. This brings into the equation a variety of idiosyncratic factors. The issue may include an outcome that, if sought, while difficult to attain, would provide worth validation for an individual struggling with inferiority feelings or it may reflect a sense of obligation and burden that the individual dreads. While the specific parameters for the individual may differ, we can generalize the nature of the problems. In one case, the problems can be so great that they cannot be ignored and must be resolved. In these cases, most individuals would likely experience some degree of distress and subsequent insomnia. This can be explained by the physiological parameters of obsessional thought and sleeplessness. In fact, excessive worry has been shown to be an accurate predictor for the symptoms of insomnia (Kallestad, Hansen, Langsrud, Hjemdal, & Stiles, 2010). The onset of sleep requires a reduction in residual tension in the body, which requires a quieting of the mind. When the mind remains active, particularly with distressing thoughts, the body is not able to reduce the body tension sufficiently to allow the physical processes of sleep to take over. Insomnia disrupts sleep either by creating a state of physical and mental hyperarousal or by disrupting the non-REM/REM sleep cycle. Physical arousal can be triggered by the activation of the hypothalamic-pituitary-adrenal axis responding to anxiety. This results in the secretion of cortisol as well as epinephrine and norepinephrine, excitatory neurotransmitters that prevent sleep onset by preventing the body from relaxing (Perlis, Gehrman, Pigeon, Findley, & Drummond, 2009). Additionally, patients presenting with insomnia have been shown to spend significantly less time in restful REM sleep than their non-insomniac counterparts (Feige et al., 2008) and this contributes to daytime drowsiness. In some cases, life demands are such that they are not resolved during the day and are brought to the bedroom and occupy the mind at a time when it would be better that the mind not be so occupied.

In other cases, situations that might not be universally or culturally defined as distressing may be disturbing to the individual because they hold some importance to that individual. For instance, the individual may be distressed about a personal, financial, or job crisis. It may be that the problem (or problems) occupying the individual's mind is beyond his or her control; thus resolution is not immediately available. Common here would be those situations that require some specific response, action, or change in another person or group of individuals. Because the situation is one of urgency and intensity for the individual, the mind becomes occupied, anxiety emerges, and insomnia ensues.

In some situations, the circumstance occupying the individual's thoughts might relate to personal dreams or expectations, or the expectations of others, which may include expectations of quality performance at some task by the sleep-deprived individual. The individual may believe that he or she does not possess the skills necessary for success (and is unwilling to admit it and face the consequences) or does not desire (whether admitted or not) to put forth the effort necessary for success, this latter possibility being common among those who as children failed to develop the psychological muscle necessary for success-ful adulthood. Psychological muscle (Walton, 1980) refers to the ability to endure the hardships and sacrifices necessary for most successes.

In any of these situations, the person's mind is going to become occupied when not constrained by external demands. That the person will often have these thoughts during wakeful hours when not immediately occupied by external con-strains underscores the urgency and intensity of the issue for that individual. The mind will orient itself to the most pressing issues in the individual's life when not constrained by the demands of other circumstances. Of course for some, the ability to deny and resist the pressure is more present and may not disrupt sleep onset; for others, the realities of the life challenges are realized in hidden forms. For these individuals, the consideration of dreams that may or may not disrupt sleep may be important as they might reveal current issues that are not a part of the individual's conscious processes.

Understanding the sources of the problem is not too challenging. Determining the benefit of the problem is somewhat more difficult; however, it is far from beyond an available grasp. To be sure, for some facing insomnia, benefits may not occur. For others, benefits may emerge and sustain the difficulties. It is typically during the daytime hours that one is faced with the realities of most life chal-lenges. Unless the individual has determined a resolution, or external realities are changed in some way, the stress during the day is less the result of obsessional, evening ruminations and is more direct. What is the person to do when faced with the crisis? One option is to do what needs to be done for resolution! This would appear simple enough; however, for those reasons previously mentioned (e.g., lack of perceived skills, unwillingness to put forth necessary effort, lack of beneficial options), resolution may not be so "immediately" achievable. To have success and resolve the issue, it may be necessary for others to accommodate the sleepless one's desires (e.g., not expect him or her to fulfill an agreement or expec-tation or to provide critical assistance) and those others may not be inclined to make those accommodations. The sleepless one may have to perform at a level beyond his or her perceived abilities or may have to admit personal inadequacies and then be forced to face the self-esteem- and career-damaging consequences associated with such an admission; or he or she may have to sacrifice engagement in more appealing activities (e.g., recreational activities) to meet the obligation. While asserting more effort or acknowledging inadequacies would be better in the long run, doing so is associated with unpleasant, "immediate" consequences that one would want to avoid if possible. And here we find a secondary benefit of insomnia. Via the insomnia the individual is able to derive relative resolution of life challenges and is able to manage, albeit ineffectively, the consequences of one's lifestyle and associated choices. For these individuals, via the insomnia, they are able to avoid meeting critical life-task obligations (related to work and to social and intimate relationships). Unfortunately, the benefit is not optimal and is associated with many unpleasant consequences—most notably anxiety, anguish, depression, sleeplessness, and task failure (Peterson, Rumble, & Benca, 2008), all of which function to exacerbate the cycle of sleeplessness and daytime drowsiness and various personal and interpersonal failures. For instance, by giving into one's drowsiness and taking naps during the day (which may suggest the emergence of depressive symptoms), the individual successfully escapes immediate task demands and, for a period, avoids the consequences of task failure. In addition, there may be others willing to assist the individual and even resolve the crisis for him or her or take the responsibility for it. This would then serve to reinforce insomnia and increases the likelihood of future episodes of insomnia. To be sure, avoiding stress and failure and getting others to assist can be an effective resolution, yet if the individual experiences insomnia each time he or she is confronted with an unpleasant issue, rescue may become less reliable as others begin developing resentments and refuse to assist. Further, by way of the daytime naps, the individual fulfills his or her sleep deficit and, as Adler suggests, is not sleep deprived.

This benefit of insomnia emerges as the individual is able to elicit sympathy and accommodations from others. The fact is that humans have a natural tendency to help those in an expressed state of need. The help that might be provided could be any of many possible options; the critical point is that another's distress elicits in most others feelings of concern, compassion, or perhaps guilt if one feels personally responsible for the distress of the other. As a result of our inherent capacity for compassion, nurturance, and guilt, the distress experienced and expressed by others elicits our sympathies and often our accommodations, and this sets the foundation for the usefulness of insomnia. If, for instance, an individual is in a relationship, he or she can elicit sympathy and various forms of accommodation from a relationship partner as an outcome of his or her sleep troubles. Further, if the individual him- or herself feels some degree of guilt for his or her relationship shortcomings, that person is able to rationalize his or her failures by ascribing them to insomnia rather than to his or her unwillingness to meet or negotiate relationship goals or expectations. For example, the spouse who fails to fall asleep at night while lying next to his or her partner may be obsessing over the failure of the relationship, while failing to accept his or her partner's disengagement or resentments or his or her need to be personally more committed to the success of the relationship. Via the sleeplessness and subsequent drowsiness he or she is able to advertise his or her state of dissatisfaction with the relationship without having to be assertive and subsequently run the risk of eliciting a conflict or hearing feedback that is hurtful and/or discouraging.

The good news for the insomniac is that the prognosis for treating an insomniac improves when, as Adler suggests, the individual accepts responsibility for his or her role in perpetuating the disorder. Specifically, what is it about the individual's lifestyle and current life circumstance that is creating the opportunity for insomnia? While there may be limits on how the circumstance can change, there are most typically aspects of the person's lifestyle and private logic that can be altered. Typically, this will include a renewed orientation to the circumstance or a renewed stance toward the challenges faced. When the individual is able to derive some sense of control over the situation prompting the sleeplessness, the obsessive thoughts are lessened and the natural process of sleep is able to return. Recent reports of effective strategies fit well an Adlerian perspective. For instance, Kaplan, Talbot, and Harvey (2009) discuss safety behaviors, suggesting that the insomnia dwells on threat and the need for safety. Adler argued that successful treatment cannot be achieved without accepting responsibility for the disorder and consciously changing one's own maladaptive behaviors and confronting the challenges that life provides. In other words, one must decrease the focus on safety behaviors and be willing to meet challenges, which can at times be daunting. This is consistent with findings that indicate the shortcomings of purely physiological treatments for insomnia (Morin, 2010), because in such a situation the onus is on the physician and the patient resumes a state of irresponsibility. The challenge to those struggling with insomnia is to face life, however difficult it may be at times.

As a final point, humans periodically face significant challenges and crises and immediate solutions are not readily available. Adler recognized the social embeddedness of each person, understanding that we need one another. In the face of stress, humans need to reach out to those who can provide emotional support and practical assistance. Often those struggling to sleep are hesitant to seek assistance and this perpetuates the sleep disturbances by preventing effective solutions. With the help of others, one is able to face and manage challenges contributing to insomnia.

## REFERENCES

Ebben, M. R., & Spielman, A. J. (2009). Non-pharmacological treatments for insomnia. *Journal of Behavioral Medicine, 32,* 244–254.

Feige, B., Al-Shajlaw, A., Nissen, C., Voderholzer, U., Hornyak, M., Spiegelhalder, K., Kloepfer, C., Perlis, M., & Riemann, D. (2008). Does REM sleep contribute to subjective wake time in primary insomnia? A comparison of polysomnographic and subjective sleep in 100 patients. *Journal of Sleep Research, 17,* 180–190.

Kaplan, K. A., Talbot, L. S., & Harvey, A. G. (2009). Cognitive mechanisms in chronic insomnia: Processes and prospects. *Sleep Medicine Clinics, 4,* 541–548.

Millon, T. (1990). *Toward a new personology: An evolutionary model.* New York: John Wiley & Sons.

Milner, C. E., & Belicki, K. (2010). Assessment and treatment of insomnia in adults: A guide for clinicians. *Journal of Counseling & Development, 88,* 236–244.

Morin, C. M. (2010). Chronic insomnia: Recent advances and innovations in treatment developments and dissemination. *Canadian Psychology, 51,* 31–39.

Kallestad, H., Hansen, B., Langsrud, K., Hjemdal, O., & Stiles, T. C. (2010). Psychometric properties and the predictive validity of the insomnia daytime worry scale: A pilot study. *Cognitive Behaviour Therapy, 39,* 150–157.

Perlis, M., Gehrman, P., Pigeon, W. R., Findley, J., & Drummon, S. (2009). Neurobiologic mechanisms in chronic insomnia. *Sleep Medicine Clinics, 4,* 549–558.

Peterson, M. J., Rumble, M. E., & Benca, R. M. (2009). Insomnia and psychiatric disorders. *Psychiatric Annals, 38,* 597–605.

Rasmussen, P. R. (2005). *Personality-guided cognitive behavior therapy.* Washington: American Psychological Association.

Walton, F. X. (1980). *Winning teenagers over in home and school: A manual for parents, teachers, counselors, and principals.* Columbia, SC: Adlerian Child Care Books.

## Nervous Insomnia[42]

### Alfred Adler

A description of the symptoms of insomnia will not give any essentially new information. The complaint of the patient will refer either to decreased duration and insufficient depth of the sleeping state or to the time of wakefulness. The main emphasis, and it seems rather trite to mention it, always falls on the insufficient rest and its resultant tiredness and inability to work.

For the sake of accuracy let me state that quite a number of patients complain of the same fact (*i.e.* tiredness, etc.), although enjoying undisturbed or even more than normally lengthened slumber.

The nature of the illness of which insomnia is a symptom can be easily circumscribed. There is no psychic disease and no accompanying group of symptoms in which this suffering is not to be found either of long-standing or intermittent. The most serious forms of psychic diseases, the psychoses, are generally heralded by exceptionally severe types of insomnia.

The attitude of the patient to his symptoms is interesting. He markedly stresses the tormenting nature of his disease and the numerous remedies taken against it which are always of no avail. One man spent half the night ardently trying to conjure up sleep, while another did not retire till past midnight in order to fall asleep from extreme tiredness. Others repeatedly attempt to remove even the gentlest noises or count up to one thousand a number of times, occupy themselves with long trains of thought or experiment and changing from one position to another until daybreak.

In some instances—in milder forms of insomnia—sleeping rules are formulated and adhered to. In one case sleep could be obtained only if the patient drank some alcoholic beverage, took some bromide; if he ate a little or a good deal, early or late at night; after his card-game; if he had company or was alone; had taken neither black coffee nor tea; or on the contrary imbibed one of these drinks. The not infrequent antithetic nature of the conditions propitious for sleeping is a striking fact; all the more so because a fairly large number of explanations are given for their attitudes, some insisting that sexual intercourse is a well-proved expedient, others that on the contrary, abstinence is.

It is easier to snatch an afternoon sleep, but here too there are a series of conditions ("if no one disturbs me," "if I can retire at the proper time," "immediately after eating," etc.). It may, on the other hand, tire a person or cause headache or drowsiness.

---

[42] Translated by P. Radin.

If we look over the descriptions given by the patients, we get the impression not only of being in the presence of sick people—especially if we consciously fix our attention upon the effect of the disturbance—but of individuals with diminished, increased or nullified capacities for work, of there being some obstacle in life for which they lack all sense of responsibility.

For the sake of simplicity let us dismiss older examples where alcoholic intemperance or misuse of narcotics have gained control over the patient and engendered new symptoms and obstacles. The examination of insomnia due to organic causes does likewise not fall within the compass of this work.

It deserves to be mentioned, however, that frequent use of narcotics aids the patient in gaining the same excuse for increased difficulty of his work as does insomnia. He will get up later, suffer from a feeling of drowsiness, lack of concentration, and waste, as a rule, a good part of the day trying to recuperate from his slumber.

The "harmless methods" on the other hand, have a bad reputation. They either are only efficacious at the beginning of the treatment or not at all. They work initially with those patients who, in all walks of life, are characteristically known by their external obedience and good-natured amiability. The stopping of a successful cure always shows the patient's attitude to the new treatment, as if he wished to demonstrate the uselessness of the physician's endeavours. More obstinate and unwilling neurotics occasionally begin the treatment by insomnia and try *to put the blame upon the physician.* Generally during their anamnesis we discover that they have on past occasions, likewise" employed insomnia as a means and as a sign of increased aggravation of their condition, in order thus to be able to demand that they be spared certain work and to be able to force their own will upon other people.

All that we can infer from the patient's descriptions, or all we ourselves can feel intuitively, indicates the pronounced estimation in which sleep is held. No physician will underestimate the importance of sleep but those who obtrusively force into the foreground self-understood facts should be asked the object of their procedure. What, in the long run, is meant by this marked stressing of sleep, and what here manifests itself definitely enough, is this—that the patient demands recognition of his difficult position. For only if this acquiescence is obtained will he be excused from responsibility in his mistakes of life and be permitted to attach double importance to his success.

If, one follows the psychic trial of strength leading to the arrangement of insomnia which develops later into a weapon and protection for the threatened personality-feeling, we soon learn to understand how insomnia has taken its proper place in connection with the endangered situation of the patient. The feeling of the applicability of the means (insomnia) used the patient obtains from experiences either of his own or others, or from the effect of the suffering inflicted upon his environment and upon himself. We should not be surprised then, if the physician or any other method adopted, are frequently designed to serve no other purpose but that of confirmation, *i.e.* as long as the psychic situation of the patient is unknown and remains unchanged.

Here it is where Individual-Psychology can set in. Its therapeutic purpose should be that of bringing the patient to the realization of the true nature of the interconnections of his symptoms and his giving up of his secret desire of not being held responsible for his plans. He will be impelled to assume responsibility, to take definite action or to renunciation, as soon as he acknowledges to himself and the physician that his insomnia is a means to an end, and when he refuses to see any mysterious destiny in it. Its coincidence with other nervous symptoms such as compulsion and doubt, in so far as their technical employment in the neurosis is concerned, is clearly visible.

We are quite clear now as to the type of person who will develop the symptom of insomnia and we can describe him to the patient with astounding accuracy. Such a type exhibits lack of faith in his own powers and an ambitious personal goal. Traits like the overvaluation of success and of the difficulties of life, of a certain unwillingness to face life, will never be found missing any more than the hesitating attitude and the fear of making decisions. Generally the minor means and artifices of the neurotic character are clearly manifested, such as pedantry, depreciating tendency and lust for domination. Occasionally the tendency to self-depreciation appears, as in the hypochondriac and melancholic attitude. In short, insomnia may represent an important connecting link in the chain of every neurotic's method of life.

Speedy success in treatment is not to be obtained with any certainty. If such a success is imperatively required it is possibly best accomplished by informing the patient directly and tactfully, that insomnia is a favourable sign of a curable psychic disease. The next step would be to endeavour, by showing great interest, to discover the nature of the patient's thoughts at night and to pay no further attention to the insomnia. Occasionally insomnia is then displaced by a very deep sleep extending far into the day—which, like insomnia, prevents him from accomplishing his task.

The patient's thoughts during his sleepless hours are, in my opinion, of great significance from two aspects. They are either a method of remaining awake or contain the basis of the personally conceived psychic difficulty for whose sake insomnia has been called into existence. The latter I shall discuss in the following chapter, "Individual-psychological Conclusions on Sleep Disturbances." I always detected the following meaning in the train of thoughts of a sleepless person, *obtaining some object without incurring any responsibility, otherwise either apparently unattainable or attainable only by the employment of one's whole personality and conscious responsibility.* This meaning was frequently to be read "between the lines," at other times to be inferred as the purpose, but occasionally appeared quite clearly from the context. Insomnia thus fits easily into the group of psychic manifestations and arrangements that have as their object the construction of a *"distance"* between the imagined goal and the patient, the initiation of an "actio in distans."

The task of individual-psychology is to describe this "actio," to furnish us with an understanding of the patient's attitude to his world and to demonstrate the connection of insomnia with individual difficulties. The therapeutic and truly valuable part of such a study lies in the fact that it discloses to the patient his fictive, misunderstood and logically contradictory leading idea, and frees him from the obstinate immobility of thought derived from it. At the same time the patient is carefully forced out of his position of irresponsibility and compelled to accept responsibility even for his unconscious fictions. That this gradual clarification is to be attempted only with the kindliest of attitudes' on the part of the physician, our school has frequently enough emphasized.

The means for engendering insomnia are comparatively simple and easily understood as soon as the utility of the symptom has once been demonstrated. The methods coincide absolutely with those a person would employ who purposely desired to be sleepless. To mention only a few: card-playing, paying visits or inviting people to the house; restless movements in bed; occupying one's thoughts with business; thinking of difficulties of all kinds and exaggerating them; planning, counting, indulging in phantasies; insistent desire to sleep; counting the strokes of the hour when awake and permitting them to wake one up; falling asleep and permitting one's self to be awakened by a dream or by a pain or fright; getting out of bed and walking up and down the room; waking up at an early hour. They are always acts that almost anyone would be able to accomplish after some practice if they were at all necessary to free him from responsibility. For example, a patient makes up his mind to get up early the next morning in order to study for an examination. He is terribly afraid that his insomnia may interfere with his plan which thus proves his sincerity. *He wakes up, i.e., wakes up at three in the morning,* remains sleepless, complains bitterly about his mysterious fate and is thus quite freed from any guilt in connection with his examination. Is there anyone who doubts the possibility of waking up *at any predetermined hour?*

More puzzling is the disturbance of slumber through pain. In my examples it was always a question of pain in the leg, abdomen, back of the head and the back. My explanation of the first is that it is caused by spasmophilic susceptibility induced by unconscious but planned *over-reaching.* The last I found in people who were accustomed *to inhaling of air* and who generally had *scoliolithic curvature of the spinal column.* Incidentally, these anomalies in position play a great role in the symptomology of neuroses and can easily be employed by unconscious tendencies for engendering pain, particularly in the group of symptoms connected with neurasthenia and hypochondria. Frequently the patient can be lifted out of his fixated susceptibility to pain, provided one has a certain degree of luck, by persuading him that he has a segmental naevus in his head (a sign of inferiority).[43] Subsequent orthopedic treatment is important and valuable. Frequently the patient's carriage tells us of the existence of such an interconnection.

Of much rarer occurrence but very illuminating are those instances where according to the patient and his family, sleep can be obtained by the patient's allowing his head to hang downwards over the edge of the bed, of making movements with the head or striking it against the wall. Many people will perhaps regard as less certain. the method adopted by patients with purposeful intensified hyper-sensibility who attempt to prevent every conceivable noise or glimmer of light, and being almost inevitably defeated, in view of the impossibility of their task, awake up (that being their object).

I shall now give a few examples to illustrate my views. A patient whose illness and conscious behaviour was to dominate and annoy his wife, began to suffer from insomnia due to the fact that (as he says), the slightest noise awoke him. Even the breathing of his sleeping wife annoyed him. The house-physician thereupon advised him to sleep alone. A painter whose frightful conceit prevented him from ever finishing a painting and placing it before the public, is attacked at night by spasms in the leg, which compel him to jump out of bed and walk up and down his room by the hour. On the following day he is, of course, incapable of work. A female patient suffering from agoraphobia developed in order to dominate her household more effectively,[44] was nevertheless not able to prevent her husband from going to the tavern in the evening. She developed the habit of waking up at night a number of times, frightened and groaning, and annoyed her husband to such an extent that on the following evening, he became sleepier earlier and came home earlier. She thus attained her object. Another patient who was compelled against his will to travel occasionally and who in general wished to prove to himself and others that illness incapacitated him for his profession, interrupted his sleep continually by means of stomach-ache and pains in the back as described above, and slept consequently far into the day, increasing his tiredness and consequently his inability to work in the day-time, by taking sleeping potions. His condition had hardly improved when he discovered two valuable ideas that would in similar fashion, excusably make him incapable of work. He found that riding in the morning was very beneficial for his health and he

---

[43] Cf. my Studie uber Minderwertigkeit von Organen. (Original footnote by Alfred Adler.)
[44] Cf. chapter on "Dreams and Dream Interpretation," in this book. (Original footnote by Alfred Adler.)

had himself consequently awakened at six o'clock. Nevertheless he retired at midnight. In order to harden himself for the bad beds in which he slept when away from home, he bought a field-bed and slept very poorly until two in the morning and then crept into his comfortable bed. In both cases the result was inability to work. Another patient wished by conscious exaggeration to make his rich relatives shoulder the blame for the bad state of his business. Although according to him, the cause of his illness they refused to help him. He had learned the trick of pressing his arm, on which he lay when asleep, so hard that it would wake him up. Now that in addition to everything else he had also become sleepless, the guilt of his relatives was self-evident.

The physiology of sleep has, as its main specific trait, the piling up of enervating materials and the flooding of the blood vessels in the brain. There certainly are forms of insomnia caused by primary disturbances of the sleep-regulating mechanisms (painful vascular and kidney diseases, psychic shocks, etc.). Neurotic insomnia is of an entirely different nature. Like other nervous symptoms it helps the nervous expansion tendencies and *to a certain extent this nervous insomnia forces its way through, irrespective of the physiological condition of insomnia.*

## APPENDIX

### ON POSITIONS ASSUMED IN SLEEP

The individual-psychological methodology thus shows us that the phenomena in sleep are adapted to the individual life-line and as long as these phenomena are, according to the superstitions of mankind, regarded as the effects of powerful causes, they are quite removed from the influence of human caprice and responsibility. We are convinced, however, that the actual and real foundations for dream-building and the desire for sleep, never manifest themselves in an undiluted physiological manner but that they are always understood by the tendency of each individual and utilized and elaborated in the interests of an individual's expansion-tendency. A careful examination based on extensive data will certainly show that the *sleeping-posture* of a person indicates his guiding-line. A few examples follow below. Generally it is possible to tell an individual who has been thoroughly analysed by individual-psychology, what his sleeping-posture is. The following are a few examples. I respectfully invite psychiatrists, neurologists and teachers to increase this list.

1. K. F. sixteen years old, apprentice, suffering from hallucinatory confusion. An examination of his sleep-posture showed that he was accustomed to sleep on his side *with drawn-up arms,* a rather provocative position. I frequently met him in the day with his arms drawn up. His psychic condition showed complete dissatisfaction

with his profession. He had wanted to become either a teacher or a pilot. When asked whether he knew how he had developed the habit of holding his arms drawn up, he stated that that was the way in which his favourite teacher M. had always walked. It was this M. likewise who had made him think of the idea of becoming a teacher, a plan that had to be abandoned owing to the poverty of his parents.

His sleep-posture consequently very clearly indicated hostility to his present occupation and was an imitation of Napoleon arrived at by the circuitous route of the imitation of the teacher who had the same psychical make-up. The obsession of young Kellner, we should remember, was that he was destined to be the field-marshal in the attack on Russia, an idea that in the following year was taken up by other apprentices.

2. S. suffering from progressive paralysis. In sleep he drew himself together covering even his head. From his medical history I extracted the following—"No megalomania, apathetic, helpless, without initiative."

Let me in conclusion on the basis of personal observations of sleep-postures taken by children, again insist upon the great significance their proper understanding might have for teaching.

# 20

# Neurotic Hunger Strike

## ALAN E. STEWART

At slightly less than 700 words, "Neurotic Hunger Strike" is the briefest chapter in *The Practice and Theory of Individual Psychology* (Adler, 1925). This work originally appeared in *Zeitschrift für Individualpsychologie* in 1914 under the title of "Zur Sitophobie" ("Eating Phobia") before becoming a chapter in Adler's (1920) *Praxis und Theorie*. Despite the brevity of this chapter, it effectively conveys the Individual Psychological position about the etiology of what would be referred to today as an eating disorder, specifically anorexia nervosa. With his customary directness and emphasis on practical applications, Adler convincingly discussed the neurotic hunger strike from the perspective of his theory. A synopsis is provided below followed by a discussion of the contemporary relevance of the "Neurotic Hunger Strike."

Adler (1925) began the chapter with a rather bold statement that the neurotic hunger strike occurs almost invariably in women and usually has its first onset at approximately age 17 years. As is characteristic of all neurotic striving that Adler described, the person responds to the one-down, felt-minus, or inferior position in concrete and self-defeating ways en route to making a dramatic attempt to secure a sense of power and safety and, ultimately, belongingness. In the case of the hunger strike, young women choose the transaction of eating as a vehicle for garnering power. From childhood onward the lesson is learned that eating, along with its restriction and regulation, can be used to focus the attention of parents and siblings. The parents attend to the woman who is beginning to refuse or restrict food for fear of her health. The parents attend to the food to try to make it more palatable, and they attend to the atmosphere of the home so that its favorable nature may lead to the resumption of eating. Of course, these responses by the family are doomed to failure because the hunger strike is pursued as a way to gain power.

In this chapter, Adler (1925) discussed restrictive eating behavior (anorexia) as well as overeating and purging (bulimia) because the latter also becomes a focusing mechanism for giving the young woman some degree of power. If the young woman is not sickly, gaunt, and thus unattractive, she may become obese, unhealthy, and thus similarly unappealing. But, the pursuit of power over self and especially others remains. Wrapping and concealing the symptom are socially recognized rationales that are above reproach, such as a weakened or diseased digestive system. Present along with such rationales for restriction of eating are fleeting efforts by the young woman to resolve it, which *have to fail*. As Adler (1925) terms it, the *to and fro* between restrictive eating, binge eating, and attempts to resolve both, at one level protect the self and also represent nascent, fleeting attempts to engage reality. This result underlies a hesitating attitude and a frittering away of time and opportunities. The person attempts to psychologically stand still while the flow of life moves onward. Thus the position of the person pursuing the hunger strike becomes, *I could do_____ or be_____ but for my problem with food.*

Following the appearance of "Neurotic Hunger Strike," in 1925, Adler (1930) provided a somewhat more lengthy presentation of the topic along with a case study in his chapter "The Hunger Strike" in *The Pattern of Life*. Early contributors to the *International Journal of Individual Psychology* wrote about children's relationships with food, eating, their parents, and the need to obtain a sense of power over their social environments (Friedmann, 1937; Grubl, 1936; Kennleyside, 1937). In addition, contemporary scholars in Individual Psychology have addressed very similar themes (e.g., Strauch & Erez, 2009). In each of these contributions one can discern the original, core etiological and therapeutic principles that appeared originally in "Neurotic Hunger Strike." Overall, 30 theoretical and empirical articles have appeared in *Journal of Individual Psychology* and its predecessors since Adler's first contribution to this topic.

Contemporary scholars working outside of Individual Psychology both echo and reinforce Adler's (1925) original ideas about the development of eating disorders (Altman & Shankman, 2009; Wade et al., 2008; Wilksch & Wade, 2010). Specifically, using a variety of modern psychological and biologically based research methods, these researchers have found temperament risk factors in young women that predispose them to the development of an eating disorder. These risk factors include striving for perfectionism, a higher need for order and control, and a heightened sensitivity to praise and reward (Wade et al., 2008). These researchers also provide evidence from twin studies that some of the temperamental risk factors are biologically based while others emerge from psychosocial origins. The consistency of such contemporary perspectives on the etiology of eating disorders with the Individual Psychological perspective that Adler articulated some 83 years earlier illustrates the prescience of Adler's theory and methods. Such observations also provide an impetus for contemporary clinicians and researchers to consult the works of Adler and other clinician-scholars within Individual Psychology for the valuable and timeless insights that they may provide.

# REFERENCES

Adler, A. (1925). *The practice and theory of Individual Psychology*. London: Routledge and Kegan Paul.

Adler, A. (1930). *The pattern of life*. New York: Cosmopolitan Book Corp.

Altman, S. E., & Shankman, S. A. (2009). What is the association between obsessive-compulsive disorder and eating disorders? *Clinical Psychology Review, 29,* 638–646.

Friedmann, A. (1937). Is your child a fussy eater? *International Journal of Individual Psychology, 3,* 46–47.

Grubl, M. A. (1936). A case of nervous vomiting. *International Journal of Individual Psychology, 2,* 105–109.

Kennleyside, M. C. (1937). Masculine protest by feminine methods. *International Journal of Individual Psychology, 3,* 171–178.

Strauch, M., & Erez, M. (2009). The restrictive personality: Anorexia nervosa and Adlerian life tasks. *Journal of Individual Psychology, 65,* 203–211.

Wade, T. D., Tiggemann, M., Bulik, C. M., Fairburn, C. G., Wray, N. R., & Martin, N. G. (2008). Shared temperament risk factors for anorexia nervosa: A twin study. *Psychosomatic Medicine, 70,* 239–244.

Wilksch, S. M., & Wade, T. D. (2010). Risk factors for clinically significant importance of shape and weight in adolescent girls. *Journal of Abnormal Psychology, 119,* 206–215.

## Neurotic Hunger-Strike[45]

*Alfred Adler*

The fear of eating begins as a rule at the age of seventeen and almost always with girls. Its adoption is generally followed by rapid decrease in weight. The goal, to be inferred from the whole attitude of the patient, is the rejection of the woman's role. In other words it is an attempt by means of an exaggerated abstinence—as is so generally the case—to retard the development of the female bodily form. One of these patients painted her whole body, in addition, with tincture of iodine in the belief of inducing decrease of weight in that manner. At the same time she repeatedly impressed upon her younger sister the importance of eating and was always inciting her to eat. One patient finally reduced herself to a weight of twenty kilo and looked more like a ghost than a young girl.

In all these instances we are dealing with girls who as children had already tested the value and significance of the "hunger-strike" as a means of attaining power. In every developed neurosis this pressure upon the patient and upon the physician is always present. By doing this everything is at once centered about her and her will dominates the situation in every respect. We can now understand why patients of this type lay so much value upon the nature of the food and why they must safeguard this evaluation by means of a "fear arrangement." This process of nourishment cannot be stressed too much, for its over-evaluation permits them to logically pursue their goal to rule over others (like a man I like a father I). It is only then that they feel the right to criticize everything for they have now arrived at the point of view which allows them to make efforts to look down upon the cooking skill of their mother, to dictate the choice of foods, to insist upon punctuality in meals, to force people at the same time to direct their attention to them and to solicitously inquire whether they are not going to eat.

One of my patients changed her attitude after some time, and insisting suddenly upon the importance of eating, began to crave and devour huge quantities of food, a behaviour that evoked the same solicitude from her mother. She was engaged and apparently desired to marry as soon as she was "well." However she obstructed the progress of her female role by all sorts of nervous symptoms (depressions, outbursts of rage, insomnia) and particularly by resorting to continual "fattening cures," thus developing into a monstrosity. She continually consumed bromide and declared that without it she felt worse; she complained at the same time of marked bromide acne, which disfigured her just as much as her excessive fatness. (Nervous

---

[45] Translation by P. Radin.

constipation, desire for defaecation, tic, cutting of grimaces or compulsion-neurosis frequently serve the same purpose.) Many patients attain the same goal by eating in public and fasting in private. The enormous importance of hunger-strike in melancholia, paranoia. and dementia praecox, where by means of negativism the will of the environment is rendered impotent, is well known.

The artifice of "*To and Fro*" is analogous to many other neurotic arrangements. By means of it the symptom of "frittering away time" is developed. This is quite intelligible when it is remembered that the patient through "fear of making a decision"—in the above instance, through "fear of his partner"—has decided upon the "hesitating attitude," "retreat" or suicide. The importance of the nourishment is first over-evaluated and then we have the fear of the taking of nourishment so that finally, as might have been expected, there is no other alternative but that of either adopting the hesitating attitude, of a truce, or of retreating before the normal demands of society. In this behaviour we see definitely reflected the old infantile feeling of inferiority in connection with the demands of life. Other "artifices of the weak" are easily enough detected. Impulses toward revenge are always present just as is the exercise of tyranny over the other members of the family.

# 21

## Melancholia and Paranoia

### Gerald J. Mozdzierz

In his paper on "Melancholia and Paranoia," Adler demonstrates an extraordinarily clear understanding of these fascinating clinical aberrations. In making their way through Adler's description of the cognitive "logic" of both melancholia and paranoia, readers will be well advised to be mindful of two competing forces. The first of these forces is that the paper was written almost 100 years ago and yet Adler's understanding of these psychiatric syndromes and abnormal psychological behaviors is as though it could have been written today. While soon to be centennial, they uncannily ooze with contemporary relevance. In Adler's time, psychology and psychiatry were absolutely new frontiers only a few years old perhaps in some ways akin to the strides being made today in understanding the complexities of the human brain by neuroscience research and imaging studies.

The second of the two competing forces is the somewhat awkward use of language and sentence construction. Long sentences and complex phrases are more uncommon in today's literature but quite common in German. These considerations most likely are a reflection of the fact that Adler wrote the paper in German (his native language) for a meeting to be held in Berne, Switzerland, and it was translated into English at a later date.

Rereading this article for the task at hand instilled a resurgence of the admiration I hold for Adler's powers of observation and clinical reasoning. His "nonlinear"[46] understanding of melancholic and paranoiac attitude and disposition astutely reveals the desperate and oftentimes feeling of doom that permeate such individuals' psyches. His understanding is apt preparation for the therapeutic challenges to be faced in working with patients ("clients," if you prefer) demonstrating these conditions.

While some decry the publication of DSM-V and others sing its praises, Adler anticipated some of its current thinking. His use of the term *melancholia* as a distinct clinical syndrome presages its return in DSM-V. Some may quibble over

---

[46] A reference to the dialectical, contrasting, and oppositional nature of human behavior. See Mozdzierz et al. (2009).

what Adler's intention was when he used the term *melancholia*. It is less arguable that his depiction of its clinical manifestations is that of a profound condition, which is exactly that described by *DSM-V*—something quite different than major depression and vastly different from the garden-variety "adjustment disorders and depressions as a result of everyday life discouragements." Consider what Adler is saying in his depiction of the categorical imperative of the melancholic: "act, think and feel in such a way as if the horrible fate that you have conjured up, had already befallen you and was inevitable" (Adler, 1959/1914, p. 250). No clinician worth their salt can deny how accurately that depiction of the melancholic represents the internal workings of their distorted private logic. Such accurate depiction also contains within it a foretelling of the realities of what it is to work therapeutically with someone so disposed and intensely depressed.

It's not just that Adler keenly observes and describes the "unconscious" motivations of these conditions. Interestingly, he analyses these abnormal behaviors using both a dichotomy and principles of scaling. Both of these principles are incredibly useful in developing a foothold of understanding in the quagmire that represents how to get started in therapy with such patients—after, of course, a "connection" (i.e., some sort of human contact) is established. Adler dichotomizes according to whether a patient is more active or more passive in their "movement," a favorite term he uses to depict our progress toward fictional goals in life. Among the "passive" he describes the suicide and the complaining accusatory paranoiac; among the "aggressive" are those whom he "scales." That is, there are those who, along a scale, demonstrate varying degrees of cowardice from avoiding the demands of life, to those who turn to alcohol (and we can assume drugs), to those involved with crime.

No therapist who has ever worked with the severely paranoiac (non-schizophrenic) and heard the racial slurs, the outspoken accusations, and the protestations decrying victimization by allegedly malignant others that emanate from such a person can deny Adler's depiction. Such indictments of fellow human beings simultaneously shout accusation *and* desperation. Herein lays Adler's genius. Using the principles inherent in his theoretical formulations (i.e., the concepts of "private logic," the value of dialectics, and the understanding of goals in behavior and motivation), the paranoiac's pronouncements become understandable for the contemporary clinician. This is a patient in retreat from life, who feels blameless and avoids responsibility. Here is someone desperately proclaiming the guilt of others who simultaneously harbors feelings of an imminent ultimate and total collapse. In this exciting description Adler implicitly demonstrates not only his knowledge of the unconscious thinking of the paranoiac but also a profound empathic understanding (i.e., "putting oneself in another's shoes") of their condition.

When we put aside the hundreds of schools of psychotherapy, the innumerable psychological movements, fads, and trends, and the "technique *du jour*," Adler's description of melancholia and paranoia represents pioneering and staying power that is nothing short of breathtaking. Truly remarkable.

## REFERENCES

Adler, A. (1959/1914). *Individual psychology*. New York: Littlefield, Adams & Company.
Mozdzierz, G. J., Peluso, P., & Lisiecki, J. (2009). *Principles of counseling and psychotherapy.* New York: Routledge.

## Melancholia and Paranoia (1914): Individual Psychological Results Obtained from a Study of Psychoses[47]

*Alfred Adler*

Preliminary remarks:—The following are the forces conditioning neuroses and psychoses discovered and described by me:—infantile feeling of inferiority; safeguarding tendencies; automatically tested methods; characteristic traits, affects, symptoms and attitudes taken toward the demands of communal participation; the employment of all these methods for the purpose of an imaginary increase of the feeling of personality as against that of the environment; the search for a circuitous method and for the creation of "distance" between themselves and the expectations of the community in order to evade both a true evaluation of life and personal responsibility and accountability and finally the neurotic perspective and the purposive, at times insane devaluation of reality. All these facts led me and a number of other investigators to posit some principle of explanation, a principle that has in a very wide sense proved itself both valuable and essential for an understanding of neuroses and psychoses.[48] The above-mentioned mechanisms are described in detail in the author's books The Neurotic Constitution, Studie über d. Minderwertigkeit von Organen, and the present work.

My later conclusions about the mechanism of psychosis can be put in the following way. There are first the three essential meanings of mania already emphasized; the anticipatory and hallucinatory representations of a wish or the fear whose purpose is to secure safety; the purposive devaluation of reality and the resultant heightening of the ego consciousness. To these should be added two more of great significance the struggle against either the immediate or the larger environment and the transference of the scene of activities from the main sphere of action to a subsidiary one.

All these five conditions of mania stand in a logical and psychological relationship to one another.

In the statements that follow, prepared for the Congress of Psychology and Psychiatry, which was to have met in Berne in 1914, and which I now print unchanged, I shall attempt to present the psychological structure of melancholia and paranoia in accordance with the above conclusions.

---

[47] Translation by P. Radin.

[48] Bleuler strangely enough speaks deprecatingly of the fact that "people attempt to explain everything thereby." To me and to others its value consists just in this fact. (Original footnote by Alfred Adler.)

## I. MELANCHOLIA

Attitude and life-plan of individuals disposed to melancholia; outbreak of the disease and the struggle against the environment; transference to subsidiary sphere of action from fear of taking decisions that might bring about humiliation.

1. Melancholia develops among individuals whose method of living has, from early childhood, been dependent upon the acts and the aid of others. Defective activity and manifestations of a non-masculine type are predominant. Such people are generally found to limit themselves to the society either of their family or of a small persistent circle of friends; always try to rely upon others and are not even above forcing others to submit to them and to accommodate themselves to them by making exaggerated references to their own inability. That their tremendous egoism in times of prestige worship like that of our own, occasionally brings them external success does not in any way contravene our statement. The fundamental questions in their own life, their progress, development, even their adherence to their own spheres of action, these they either evade or approach only hesitatingly, especially if difficulties present themselves. The typical manic-depressive on the contrary can be broadly characterized by the fact that he begins every act enthusiastically but loses interest very soon after. This characteristic rhythm which holds for their movements and attitudes when they are well is intensified and reinforced during the period of their illness by calling up maniacal ideas and by their ostentatious and purposeful elaboration.

   Between these two forms lies intermittent melancholia whenever the patient's fluctuating belief in his success is called upon to ward off some demand of life (marriage, profession, society).

2. The whole life-conduct of the "melancholy type" shows its presupposition and starting point to be a fictive but all-permeating standpoint, a melancholic perspective rooted in infantile psychic life, a perspective according to which life resembles a difficult frightful game of chance in a world full of obstacles and in which the majority of men are hostile. We recognize in this attitude of antagonism to the community-feeling an intensified sense of inferiority, one of the contrivances that lie at the basis of the neurotic character as described by me. When protected by their special aggressive tendencies which are transformed into traits of character, affects, preparations and acts (crying !), these people feel themselves able to cope with the facts of life and they try when "sane and healthy"

to achieve a reputation among a small number of friends. By letting their subjective feelings of inferiority take a concrete shape they are in a position to insist from childhood either openly or secretly, upon an increase in their "disablement grant."

3. From the incessant attempts made from early childhood to gain prestige it can be inferred that their self-assessment is quite low and yet all their actions seem to suggest—and these disguised hints disclose the psychical affinity with paranoia—that some neglected opportunity for an extraordinary development had somehow been missed. They indicate familiar unfavourable circumstances (as the source of their failure) or betray in their maniacal melancholic ideas the ineradicable assumption of super-human, even divine powers. It is on such an assumption that are based the complaints in which the sick individual bewails, in what really represents a disguised idea of greatness, the terrible fate which will overwhelm his family when he is gone; or he speaks in a self-accusatory way about his part in the destruction of the world; in the outbreak of the world-war or in the death and ruination of certain people. Often there is found in this enforced complaint about his own unworthiness, a warning reference to real material and moral dangers for his family circle and that of his friends and an equally marked stressing of the personal significance of the patient. Such then is the goal of victims of melancholia and with such an object do they accuse themselves openly of all kinds of inferiority and take upon themselves ostentatiously the blame for all failures and errors. The success of their behaviour is such that, at the very least, they become the centre of attention of their limited circle and are able to induce those individuals who feel obligated to help them to increased activity, to note-worthy sacrifices on their behalf, and always to make advances to them. On the other hand they themselves have become freed from even the slightest feeling of obligation or tie, a condition fitting well into their ego-centric guiding-ideal, for this ideal causes them to feel every connection with others, every adaptation to others or the interference of others with their rights, as an unbearable compulsion and as a serious loss of personal prestige.

Together with these self-accusations and self-reproaches we always find disguised references to heredity, to parents' errors in bringing them up, and to wilful lack of consideration on the part of relatives and superiors. This accusing of others—another phenomenon related to paranoia—can be deduced from the initial melancholic situation. To give examples; if for instance an outbreak of melancholia occurs in a younger daughter when the mother has decided to go on a lengthy journey with the elder daughter, or if a business man is suddenly afflicted with the disease after he has been persuaded against his will to come to certain decisions by the decisive vote of his partner.

References like the above, to melancholia, body anomalies, etc., serve also to establish the fact that, according to the patient, we are here dealing with an unalterable and incurable disease, this of course enormously increasing its importance.

Melancholia thus like every neurosis and psychosis, helps the patient's object of heightening the social value of his own will and personality, at least in his own opinion. Its special compulsory nature, among individuals of infantile mentality, is due to the pressure of a deeply felt dissatisfaction and a feeling of inferiority which objectively considered is unjustifiable. It is an incomprehensibly great payment that these people make for a behaviour in the difficult crises of life which, after all, is inherently consistent. Their sensitive ambition which spurs them on persistently, although with secret trembling, to seek superiority, forces them likewise to retreat or waver before the more important social tasks. By means of systematic self-restriction they thus reach a subsidiary track represented by a circle of friends strictly limited, and by tasks to which they adhere until threatened by what appears to them a change fraught with difficulties. Then the scheme that was constructed in childhood, never revived and which has always remained untested interposes itself and they minimize their own importance in order to gain power through weakness and illness.

4. The most prominent offensive weapon of the melancholic type which he uses for raising his position and which he has employed from childhood on, consists in complaints, tears and depression. He shows his weakness and the necessity for helping him in the most agonizing manner so that he may either force or mislead others to aid him.

5. These patients obtain in their own way, the appearance and conviction of irresponsibility for their lack of success in life, because they repeatedly insist upon the unalterable nature of their weakness and their lack of external help. The psychic affinity with the phobic and hypochondriac type is clearly discernible. However it is characteristic of melancholia that with the object of a more powerful attack and because of a more extensive feeling of inferiority, the realization of inferiority disappears and all criticism of the maniacal ideas is excluded, by means of a marked anticipation of an inevitable tragedy and a determined absorption in the imminent danger.

The categorical imperative of melancholia is "act, think, feel in such a way as if the horrible fate that you have conjured up, had already befallen you and was inevitable." The main presupposition of melancholia-mania is to possess a prophetic insight, to be like a God.

It is only by following up this recognition that, when measured in terms of the common bond of the pessimistic perspective, the interrelation between neurosis and psychosis becomes clear. To take simple examples:—In enuresis nocturna it is "Act as though you were in the lavatory!" Pavor nocturnus: "Act as though you were in great danger." So-called neurasthenic and hysterical sensations, conditions of weakness, paralyses, dizziness, nausea, etc.: "Imagine you have a circlet around the head, something sticking in your throat; that you were on the verge of a fainting-spell; that you could not walk; that everything was in a whirl around you; that you had eaten some bad food," etc.

It is always a question of effect upon the environment. This is true, as I have already insisted for some time, in case of "genuine epilepsy," in which as if in pantomime, death, impotent rage, manifestations of poisoning, warding off danger and defeat, are represented. The nature of the material presented is dependent upon the organism's possibilities often deducible from inherited manifestations of inferiority (cf. Adler, Studie üb. d. Minderwertigkeit v. Organen, 1917), and they begin to play a role as soon as they are able to benefit and to be of benefit to the higher ideals of the neurotic. In every case, however, either the patient's symptom or the attack signify that he has withdrawn either from the present, (by means of anticipation) or from reality (by absorption in his role). The success of this withdrawal is probably most definitely expressed in genuine epilepsy. One of the commonly recurring features of one of the types seems to be the fact that the patient is the last-born (occasionally a person followed at a long interval by another child); an asymmetrical lower displacement of the right side of the face; increase in the protuberance of the parietal bone and traces of left-handedness.

The psychosis discloses, corresponding with the more determined attitude of the patient who is on the point of giving up all honest strivings, a more marked withdrawal from the world and a more extensive depreciation and overwhelming of reality.

6. In the psychosis as in the neurosis, the intensified reference to the unchangeability of the weaknesses and sad destiny awaiting us, prove to be necessary in new and apparently difficult situations, professional decisions and tests of all kinds devised with the object of developing hesitation or abandoning a certain course, as in the rather complicated instance of stage-fright. The investigator must be very

careful not to over-emphasize his own impression of the difficulties of the situation. For what guides the man afflicted with melancholia in his fears, what makes his maniacal ideas "incurable" is not the lack of intelligence or logic, but the lack of desire, the methodical unwillingness to apply this logic. The patient will feel and even act illogically if he can only in this way, and only by means of mania, approach nearer to his goal and heighten his personality consciousness. Anyone who attempts to tamper with his mania appears to him, consequently, as an enemy and he therefore regards all medical measures and attempts at persuasion as directed against his position.

7. It is one of the peculiar traits of the melancholic type that it succeeds in establishing its disease-picture by continuing old well-constructed preparations and that, by freely expressed, intensified reference to its own weakness, it extends the compulsion of continuous and useless helping and the solicitude of the environment. The uselessness of every external pacification after melancholia has manifested itself, is not the result of any lack of logical deduction but flows from the unbendable purpose of the sick man to increase the shock to his environment to the highest degree, to limit the action of all concerned and deprive them of all their prospects. A cure will take place, depending upon the degree of confidence in life still remaining in the patient, as soon as he has enjoyed the satisfaction of having demonstrated his superiority. Promising results have also been obtained by tactful reference to real connections made with no suspicion of posing as superior or a desire always to be in the right. The prophecy when the termination of any melancholic arrangement will take place is certainly not any easier than to foretell when a child will stop crying. Hopeless situations, an unusual degree of lack of interest in life evidenced from early childhood, provocations, and an ostentatious lack of respect on the part of the environment may lead to attempts at suicide as an extreme act of revenge for activity continually directed against one's own person.

The fear of lack of success, anxiety, competition, or expectation of not being able to cope any longer with society or the family, force this type in case of subjectively-felt trouble, to resort to anticipating their ruin. The melancholic view-point growing out of this self-absorption, which by reason of its purposive achievement in waking life and dreams always becomes more and more deeply rooted, in its influences upon the whole organism, is the continual motive for a poorer functioning of the organs. If carefully done the functions of the organs, the carriage, sleep, muscular strength, heart-activity, intestinal manifestations, etc. can be prognostically evaluated. The psychological connections militate against the etiological interpretation of Abderhalden's discoveries in psychosis. From our viewpoint they must represent definitely conditioned manifestations or simply intensified symptoms, appearing in psychosis, of an inherited organ inferiority. We must, among other things, emphasize the fact that organ inferiority may represent the final stage of an important basis of etiologically significant infantile inferiority feelings.

8. Organs, in so far as they can be influenced, come consequently, under the power of the melancholic goal, adjust their functions to the need of the whole situation and thus help to establish the physiognomy of clinical melancholia (heart, body-carriage, appetite, stool, urine activities, trend of thought). In so far as they obey compulsory stimulations they are forced into a melancholic mood. Or it may be that the function remains approximately normal but is felt by the sick person to be diseased and is complained of. At times a disturbance and an irritable condition are induced by the sick man by means of a clear and meaningless behaviour (by sleep disturbances, by enhanced inducing of stool and urine activity).

9. In the last case as well as in connection with the acceptance of nourishment, the patient often shows a series of disturbances automatically induced and which then follow systematically and methodically without sufficient self-criticism. These manifestations as well as the patient's exhaustive demands on the functions of his organisms and his erroneous evaluation of a fictive norm lacking in him, indicate his purpose of visibly procuring a real proof of illness.

10. The acceptance of nourishment is restricted by the calling up of thoughts suggestive of disgust or anxious suspicions (poison) and besides, like all other functions, is under the pressure of purposive melancholic self-absorption ("as if nothing were of use, as if everything must end badly"). Sleep is disturbed by compulsory brooding, by thinking of not sleeping and also by resorting to distinctly purposeless means. Stool and urinary functions can become diseased either by contrary influences or by making continual claims upon them, in some cases by producing a condition of irritation in the respective organs. Heart-activity, breathing, the attitude of the diseased personality, the tear-glands occasionally, come under the pressure of the melancholic fiction tending to a ceaseless self-absorption in a situation of despair.

11. A closer view, one that is made possible only by means of an individual psychological synthetic approach, shows the melancholic attitude to be the picture of a condition which may appear, at the

same time, an offensive weapon among people who find themselves in the position described above, people in whom we otherwise might expect angry perhaps raging and revengeful outbursts. The early acquired deficiency of the social activity conditions that peculiar attitude of attack which, resembling suicide, proceeds from an injury inflicted upon one's self to a threatening of the environment or to acts of revenge.

Occasionally in raptus melancholicus or suicide, which always represents an act of revenge, the affect to be expected is clearly manifest.

12. The presupposition of all activity, the concealed reference to the importance of one's own person, expressed in the demand for the subordination, in the claim upon the services of others, is never absent. Since the insistence upon the guilt of others is likewise always present, the melancholic attitude thus establishes the fictive superiority and irresponsibility of the sick man. By reinforcing the last-mentioned traits (insistence upon the guilt of others), paranoiac nuances are enabled to force their way into melancholia.

13. Since his fellow-man merely serves him as a means for heightening his own personality-consciousness (the pose of friendship and attentive interest is at his disposal as well as disease), the melancholic individual recognizes no limits to the extension of his tyranny over others, robs them of all hope, and will proceed either to suicide itself or the thought of suicide if compelled to surrender his main object of being freed from the demands of others, or actually commit suicide when he comes upon invincible obstacles.

14. In other words an outbreak of melancholia represents the ideal situation for individuals of this type whenever their position is threatened. The question why, nevertheless, he does not enjoy this condition, is unnecessary. The fact is, that melancholia does not permit any other mood to arise and since the patient's object is success, there is no place for any feeling of joy that might interfere with his compulsion-attitude of depression.

15. Melancholia vanishes as soon as the patient has attained, in some manner or other, the imaginary feeling of having regained his superiority and a protection against possible misfortunes by a proof of illness.

16. The attitude of persons who are likely to succumb to melancholia is one of distrust and criticism of society from childhood on. In this attitude likewise we can recognize as one of the primary assumptions a feeling of inferiority with its compensation, and a cautious search for superiority in spite of all statements to the contrary.

## II. PARANOIA

1. Paranoia attacks people whose attitude toward society is characterized by the fact that after a fairly mild upward tendency of their activity or life-line they come to a halt at some distance from the goal that either they or their environment had expected, and that then generally by means of extensive intellectual or, at the same time, active operations in an imaginary struggle directed against self-created difficulties, they obtain an unconscious excuse for either covering up or justifying, or indefinitely postponing, their possible or anticipated defeat in life.

2. This attitude both in toto and in individual questions is prepared early in childhood, tested, blunted and protected against the most serious objections of reality. That is why the paranoiac system possesses, to a greater degree than other psychoses, definite methodical traits and can be influenced only at the beginning and under propitious circumstances. In paranoia neither the communal feeling nor its function, the "universally valid" logic of reality, is ever entirely destroyed.

3. One of the presuppositions of this attitude is shown to consist in a profound feeling of dissatisfaction with life, felt to be unalterable and which compels the patient to try to conceal his lack of success both to himself and others in order not to wound his pride or self-consciousness.

4. To this activity always present and perceptible—as a rule of a belligerent type and, owing to the nature of its devices, directed toward a goal of superiority—is due the fact that the break-down generally takes place in later years. The maniacal idea thus likewise obtains traits of an externally more mature type.

5. This activity whose goal is that of an ideal of superiority, must in its development, automatically lead to an attitude of criticism and hostility toward the patient's fellowmen, an attitude that in the last analysis, is directed against others, against influences and situations behind which humanity as such is suspected of being concealed. In this way others are made responsible for that part of the patient's over-emphasized plans that did not succeed. In paranoia the anticipation of the goal of superiority (megalomania) also serves to put on a firm basis the feeling of superiority and permit the patient to evade responsibility for failure in society by creating secondary regions of activity.

6. In the paranoiac's attitude we find reflected the hostile attitude toward his fellowmen which goes back to earliest childhood. This flows automatically from his active striving for universal superiority which finds expression in the form of the idea that he must be given

consideration, in the persecution-mania and megalomania. In all three of these situations the patient pictures himself as the centre of his surroundings.

7. In the pure form of paranoia, to be taken into consideration only as a boundary case, there is consequently always an upward tendency, which is brought to a halt by the creation of the mechanism of the mania. This is true also of dementia praecox where the fear of life and its demands seem to be greater and which consequently manifests itself earlier. On the boundary line can be noticed cases of zyclothymia, hysterical aboulia, depressive manifestations of a neurasthenic type and conflict-neuroses (cf. The Neurotic Constitution) which show a more marked repression of a temporary kind, following an initial aggression. Dynamically the behaviour of psychogenic epilepsy, chronic alcoholism, morphinism and cocainism, shows great affinity with the above. The differences seem to exist in the more tenacious and intermittent repression of the latter after more extensive activity or a lower degree of connection.

8. Both in the forward as in the backward movement of the psychotic wave, a hostile belligerent trait often ending in suicide, is clearly recognizable. Indeed psychosis may be regarded as the intellectual suicide of an individual who feels himself unequal to the demands of society or of attainment of his own goal. In his backward movement there is discoverable a secret actio in distans, a hostility toward reality, while the forward movement indicates its inward weakness at the time of its exaltation.

9. The self-evaluation of the paranoiac is intensified to the point of similarity to the deity. It is built up on a compensatory feeling of inferiority and shows its weakness in its speedy renunciation of being able to fulfil the demands of society, the surrender of plans, the transference of the field of action to the domain of the non-real, in the marked tendency toward constructing paranoidal excuses of a preoccupational nature and in the insistence on accusing others. The patient clearly lacks faith in himself and his mistrust and unbelief in men, and in the knowledge and ability of men, force him toward the construction of cosmogonic and religious ideas of government as well as to the inherent contrast of these phantasies to the general views. These are all necessary to enable him to get his balance and his additional ballast.

10. The ideas of the paranoiac are very hard to correct because the patient needs them just in this particular form if he is to establish his point of view, the attainment of irresponsibility as an excuse for his lack of success, and if he is to force his activity in society

to become arrested. These ideas permit him, at the same time, to adhere to his fiction of superiority without necessitating a test for he can always ascribe the blame to the hostility of others.

11. If melancholic passivity is an actio in distans for coercing others to subordinate themselves, the purpose of the paranoiac's active phantasy can, on the other hand, be said to consist in obtaining a time-consuming pre-occupation and an excuse that will relieve him from responsibility for his lack of success.

12. In contrast, melancholia is, at least externally, based more on the guilt of others than on that of external circumstances.

13. Every discernible outbreak of paranoia occurs when the patient finds himself in a dangerous situation where he feels his demands for a social position definitely lost. This happens as a rule when on the eve of some undertaking, during its course, or when anticipating either a demotion or the coming on of old age.

14. The final condition results from the intermediate creation of a preparatory mania-mechanism by whose action the patient's feeling of responsibility is destroyed. His feeling of importance is, however, increased by means of his self-identification with his persecution mania, his respect-demanding mania and megalomania. This mechanism represents a compensatory activity that has grown out of his expectation of depreciation and develops in the direction of the "masculine protest" just as we have shown in the case of the psychology of neuroses (cf. The Neurotic Constitution).

15. The construction of maniacal ideas can be traced back to childhood where, in an infantile fashion, they are connected with day-dreams and phantasies relating to situations of humiliation.

16. The paranoiac attitude gives both the soul and body its adequate position in the mania system. Stereo-typed expressions, attitudes and movements are associated with the guiding idea and incidentally are also found abundantly on the confines of the disease and in dementia praecox.

17. Melancholic traits are frequently intertwined with those of paranoia. In particular do we find that complaints about poor sleep, deficient nourishment tend when subsequently amplified, in the direction of ideas of persecution, poison and megalomania. This last path is at times, taken only to emphasize the special nature of the patient's disease.

18. Hallucinations are connected with marked self-absorption in the role to be played and represent both encouraging or warning admonitions. They occur whenever the patient's will-direction is to be regarded as final and yet he is not to be held responsible. These

admonitions are to be taken as analogies like the dream, need not be intelligible to the patient but should be characteristic of the policy he wishes to adopt on certain definite problems. Both hallucinations and dreams thus prove to be contrivances for objectifying those subjective impulses to whose apparent objectivity the patient unconditionally surrenders himself (cf. dream theory of the author in the chapter on "Dreams and Dream Interpretation" in this book, and in his Neurotic Constitution 1.c.). The coercion toward irresponsibility prevents the will from being under one's own direction and substitutes in its place apparently strange faces and admonitions.

19. We must add to the above the fixing of the mania-system by means of a purposive, i.e. a favourable selection of reminiscences, and an evaluation of experiences as viewed from their final object. From our view-point the tendency of this establishing of a system and its vital necessity owing to the nature of the goal-positing, emerges quite positively. (This goal consists in an order for retreat; an arrangement of non-responsibility; that of the guilt of others and the concealment of the personal and evident collapse.)

20. Our attitude thus shows that paranoia makes its appearance at the point where normal human beings lose their courage, where more susceptible natures commit suicide or querulously complain about others, and where the more aggressive types by cowardly avoiding the demands of life, turn to crime or alcoholism. Only people well prepared for adaptation to society maintain their equilibrium. Occasionally we encounter mixtures of the above tendencies.

21. The single-handed struggle of the paranoiacally disposed individual to conquer, results in every person being treated as an enemy or as a figure in a chess game. A feeling of real good-will toward his fellowmen is absent as much in the paranoiac as in all those affected by neurotic and psychotic diseases. Such a person is never a dependable participant in the life of society and enters into normal human relationships (love, friendship, occupation, society, etc.), with an incorrect attitude. This anomalous attitude arises from a low self-evaluation and an over-evaluation of life's difficulties. This it is that misleads him into the creation of an arrangement like neurosis and psychosis. His hostile attitude toward society is, in no sense, inherited or ineradicable but merely a tempting outlet in an extremity.

22. Paranoia rarely disappears because it manifests itself just at that part of the life-line where the patient suspects his inevitable collapse will occur. However, quite senseless subjective exaggerations are amenable to correction in the beginning, and on such occasions the disease may be cured.

23. The attitude of a person predisposed to paranoia, already exhibits in childhood an active aspect which brings the person quite easily to a halt before difficulties. We often discover in the life of a patient frequent interruptions of an apparently puzzling nature, of the direct line of development. All enterprises that retard progress (including therein frequent changes of occupation and vagabondage), are in reality coercions of the guiding idea which demand that time be wasted in order to gain time.

Love of domination, insufferability, lack of fellow-feeling, absence of love relations or the selection of a few docile persons are regularly recurring manifestations in the person's life. He is recognizable by his querulous and unjustly critical nature.

## APPENDIX

### EXCERPTS FROM THE DREAMS OF A PATIENT WITH MELANCHOLIA

An official forty years old is transferred to another bureau. Thirteen years before that he had developed signs of melancholia on a similar occasion. As on the earlier occasion he found himself incapable of performing the necessary duties. Incidentally there appeared certain thoughts in which he hinted at the responsibility of others for his condition. According to him he was neglected and difficulties were put in his way. We have, in short, as is almost always the case in melancholia, the path leading to paranoia vaguely suggested. He asked me for poison in order to escape his torments. No matter what the event was he always succeeded in seeing its worst side. Insomnia, digestive troubles, uninterrupted depression and extreme fears of the future increasing from day to day, allowed us to diagnose the case with certainty.

Above I have shown why melancholia is to be regarded as a "remnant problem" where the sick person, to prove his illness falls back upon the device of accusing and depreciating himself in order to escape taking a definite decision. Our patient, for example, will, in his own way, either try to circumvent a success unfavourable to his plans or weaken it by proving himself to be ill or finally, by having his success interpreted as a part payment for an imagined deficiency transcending everything the world has hitherto known. There is always present the compulsory demand that he be assisted by others whose kindness is to be taken advantage of and they themselves incited to making greater efforts in his behalf by the patient's insistence upon his illness. Interpreting this situation in its infantile meaning we come to the picture of the weeping child. The following are the earliest childhood reminiscences of this patient:—He pictures himself as a little boy lying on the sofa and weeping. When eight years old, an aunt strikes him; he runs into the kitchen yelling, "You have deprived me of my honour!" With this special contrivance, i.e. to shatter the nerves of bystanders by weeping and complaining (to over-power?) he now faces every new situation. Let us not overlook the fact that this contrivance is only intelligible if we assume that we are in the presence of a very ambitious man, one however, who does not believe in himself to the extent of imagining he would be able to attain his goal of superiority by direct methods. It is quite apparent how—and this belongs together with the above—under the pressure of his secret idea of god-likeness he would like to be freed from the responsibility of his achievements in real life so as not to put his god to a test. This explains his "hesitating attitude" and his uncon-scious arrangement of the "remnant" and his "distance" from the goal of superiority which he is afraid of losing whenever a new situation arises.

In the first week of the treatment, the patient dreamt his dream of the world catastrophe narrated in Chapter 19. If you remember we also found there the mechanism of melancholia. He posits the possibility of a complete lack of responsibility interpreted in his own sense and discloses himself as a strong person, in phantasy playing with the fate of the world like a god. When everything is about to end he may do anything.[49] Is not the same sen-timent present in his "You have robbed me of my honour"? When he under-rates himself may we not have the continuation read, "Now I am going to approach with my strongest move"? Is not suicide in the air here and is not depression being employed for the purpose of extortion?

All must submit to his will! That is the object of his melancholia. The following is a second dream: "A girl I saw on the street comes to my room and gives herself up to me voluntarily." What is behind this dream? Simple enough. How far removed am I removed from open aggressiveness! There must be a magical power that compels everyone to submit to me! Like a sleight-of-hand performer he helps things along by a threat of world destruc-tion and by the influence of his depression.

A third dream exhibits the arrangement of his depression. "I find the work easy in another post which I had refused. Everything is pleasant and in the best of order." In other words "Where I am not present there I shall find happiness."[50] This is an assumption suggested by his attitude so that he may make the present situation appear painful. To disprove it is impossible, for if he chooses to imagine himself somewhere else we are dealing with an unful-fillable condition. Unquestionably could we transport him to that place he would discover some other subterfuge.

---

[49] Freeing himself at the same time from the community feeling. (Original footnote by Alfred Adler.)
[50] This is the last line of Schubert's famous song "Der Wanderer" (Original footnote by P. Radin).

# 22

## *Suicide*

### Sharyl M. Trail

The topic of suicide is as relevant today in the United States of America as it was in 1937, when Adler wrote an article devoted to the understanding of suicide in the lives of individuals, family and friend survivors, and society as a whole. It is clear throughout Adler's writing that he was committed to understanding the purposefulness of people's decisions and behaviors. This interest in etiology and the purposefulness of behavior is noted throughout Adler's chapter on suicide. Understanding the causes or origins of suicidal thoughts, feelings, and actions is the key to true primary prevention. Currently there are many government and nongovernment agencies that are devoted to the prevention of suicide. Suicide prevention programs work to identify target groups in the population who are at higher risk for suicide as well as overall risk factors that increase an individual's risk of suicide. Adler's paper on suicide identifies three major factors, outside of mental illness, which increase a person's risk for suicide. It is quite remarkable to review Adler's paper on suicide and find that many of his assertions about the etiology of suicide have been confirmed through modern-day research on the subject.

According to the National Institute on Mental Health (NIMH), in 2007 suicide was the tenth leading cause of death in the United States, and for every completed suicide an average of 11 additional people attempted suicide (NIMH, n.d.). Most alarming, suicide is the third leading cause of death for young people ages 15–24, with the overall suicide rate increasing over 300% in the United States since the 1950s (Miller & Eckert, 2009). Along with youth, other groups including Native Americans/Alaskan Natives and non-Hispanic White men over the age of 85 are at higher risk for completing suicide (NIMH, n.d.). Research also shows that individuals with specific mental health and substance abuse disorders, specific personality traits, and family history are at increased risk for suicidal behavior and suicide completion (Substance Abuse and Mental Health Services Administration [SAMHSA], 2006; Sarchiapone et al., 2009).

Adler begins his paper by making the connection between suicide and "mentally disordered individuals, especially depressed persons," thus coming to the conclusion that the "approximately normal person is inclined to regard suicide as an entirely pathological phenomenon." Current research is in full support of Adler's assertion of the connection between mental illness, especially depression, and increased risk for suicide. Depression is the most prevalent mental health disorder in the United States, with 9.5% or 20.9 million American adults experiencing depression in any given year (NIMH, n.d.). Major depression is the most common diagnosis associated with suicide. Individuals who have multiple episodes of depression are at greater risk for suicide as well as individuals who are depressed in conjunction with dependence on drugs and alcohol (American Association of Suicidology [AAS], 2010). NIMH (n.d.) reported 90% of people who die by suicide also had depression, other mental disorders, or substance abuse disorder at the time of their death. Often both mental health and substance abuse disorders are co-occurring in individuals who complete suicide. The statistics stated above compel mental health professionals as well as public health officials to prioritize the identification and treatment of mental health and substance use disorders to reduce the rates of suicide in this country.

After the discussion of mental disorders, Adler begins his paper by identifying "situational factors" related to suicide. Adler asserts that even the "normal person" can at times be faced with situations that make them feel suicide is the only way to solve the problem. The most relevant situations include money problems and unhappiness or disappointment in romantic relationships. Adler states that although many people experience distressing and unalterable situations, the actual number of suicides committed for this reason is "not so great."

Adler was correct in his statement that environmental or situational risk factors do not in isolation increase an individual's risk for suicide. According to the stress diathesis model, suicide is thought to be a multi-determined act with both distal and proximal risk factors (Roy, Sarchiapone, & Carli, 2007). Adler's understanding of situational factors could be compared to our current understanding of proximal, or trigger, factors, many of which Adler identified in his original paper on suicide. The Suicide Prevention Resource Center (SPRC, 2001) has identified the following environmental or proximal risk factors related to increase in suicide risk: job or financial loss; relational or social loss; easy access to lethal means; and local clusters of suicide that have a contagious influence. Acute stressors do provide a heightened period of risk, but only if someone is already vulnerable to suicide due to distal risk factors such as childhood trauma, family history, or personal history of mental illness/substance abuse and/or is lacking in protective factors (Roy, Sarchiapone, & Carli, 2007; SPRC, 2001).

Adler provided two additional situations he believed increased suicide, one being when women and girls are menstruating and two when individuals become over age 50. In my research for this introduction, I was unable to find a connection between time of menstruation and increase in suicide, but there is a large body of evidence pointing to the significant increase in suicide risk among the elderly. In the United States in 2004 14.3 of every 100,000 people age 65 and older died by suicide, higher than the rate of about 11 per 100,000 in the general population. When looking at all elderly, those at highest risk to complete suicide are non-Hispanic White men over the age of 85, yet the rate of suicide declines for women after age 60. Non-Hispanic White men have a rate of almost 50 suicide deaths per 100,000 (NIMH, 2007; AAS, 2009). Adler stated in his paper that Individual Psychology is capable of explaining these facts, but he did not go on to provide a conceptualization of the problem. Risk factors identified in current research include the recent death of a loved one; physical illness, uncontrollable pain, or the fear of a prolonged illness; perceived poor health; social isolation and loneliness; and major changes in social roles (e.g., retirement) (AAS, 2009). Although Adler did not expound on his conceptualization of the problem, it is quite interesting how current research identifies a negative change in the three life tasks as a possible explanation for the increased suicide rate among elderly White men. Therefore mental health professionals and community supports for the elderly could look to increasing elderly men's social engagement as a possible prevention of depression and suicide.

Adler goes on in his paper to identify "interpersonal factors" connected to increased suicide risk. Adler conceptualizes the problem of suicide through the concepts of lifestyle, feelings of inferiority, and lack of social interest. He begins by explaining that when an exogenous cause (environmental trigger/risk factor) is experienced by individuals, they may be inadequately prepared to manage the crisis due to impairments in lifestyle, including inadequate social interest. To this end, studies have shown a well-established connection between family history of suicide and increased risk for suicidal behavior. It is estimated that up to 40% of the variance of suicidal behavior may be genetic (Sarchiapone, Vladimir, Janiri, Marchetti, Cesaro, & Roy, 2009). Again, heredity is not a single cause or factor in suicidal behavior but should be considered as a distal risk factor.

Along with heredity, environmental factors have also been identified as increasing risk of suicide later in life. Childhood trauma, problematic parenting and family environments, and history of childhood abuse have all been proven distal risk factors for the later development of suicidal behavior (Miller & Eckert, 2009; Roy, Sarchiapone, & Carli, 2007; SPRC, 2001). These experiences early in life inform the lifestyle and provide messages to the individuals that they have an inferior position in the family and in society. Therefore, individuals with feelings of inferiority can potentially develop a lack of social interest due to a fear that other people and society as a whole are a threat to their safety and well-being. Impairments in the lifestyle can then lead to a decrease in resilience when faced with a situational/proximal risk factor.

Adler concluded that individuals who attempt and complete suicide are participating in an active movement away from themselves and others, believing individuals who complete suicide disregard the pain this will cause others. A recent research study has looked at personality style and impulsivity in relation to suicidal behavior (Fazaa & Page, 2009). Fazaa and Page (2009) identified two subgroups of people, self-critical and dependent, which were at heightened risk for suicide. Their findings showed that dependent individuals were more likely to attempt suicide as a means of communication and their attempts were frequently related to interpersonal stressors. They were more impulsive in their attempts and used less lethal means. In contrast, self-critical individuals viewed suicide as a means of escape, with attempts frequently related to intrapsychic stressors. Self-critical individuals were more active in making a suicide plan and used more lethal means. In both subgroups, individuals were ill equipped to manage either situational stressors of intrapersonal feelings of emotional pain and inferiority.

It could be hypothesized that both groups are lacking in social interest and managing their stress or emotional pain takes priority over concern about the impact their suicide or suicidal behavior will have on others. If indeed suicidal individuals are lacking in social interest, experience inferiority feelings, and have inadequate coping abilities based on mistaken lifestyle beliefs, it is imperative to focus our efforts on parent education and the prevention of child abuse and neglect as a way to prevent suicide in this country.

Adler's final section of his paper addresses the "predisposing factors" for suicide. In this section, Adler states, "We are prepared for failures and try to prevent them, always in the conviction that the origin of a misconception of life and its organization can be traced back into early childhood. Therefore we must try and find the type of child, which can be regarded as the potential suicidal type." He concluded that suicidal people combine a lesser degree of social interest with a large degree of activity. Adler identified suicidal adults as problem children, spoiled, oversensitive, and tantrum with willful self-injury. Adler only identified the pampered child who thinks "*too* much of himself, too little of others" as one who develops suicidal behavior. Throughout Adler's paper he has made statements of fact, which still today are supported by research; unfortunately throughout my literature review I found no evidence that the spoiled or pampered child is at heightened risk for suicide. In actuality, it seems the exact opposite seems to be true.

Research indicates that 90% of youth experienced at least one mental disorder at the time of their death. These included most commonly mood disorders, followed by substance-related disorders and disruptive behavior disorders (Miller & Eckert, 2009). Although it is true pampered children can develop these disorders, research indicates neglectful and harmful/abusive parenting is a greater risk factor for developing these disorders in childhood. Risk factors for youth suicide include feelings of hopelessness; peer victimization (bullying); sexual and/or physical abuse; multiple comorbid psychiatric disorders; parental mental illness/substance abuse; family instability and significant family conflict; and exposure to violence (Miller & Eckert, 2009; AAS, 2007; Mullany et al., 2009).

Although research does not support Adler's identification of the pampered individual as one most at risk for suicide, he did have keen insight that events in early childhood have a deep impact on the potential for an individual to develop suicidal behaviors in the future. Adler was ahead of his time, taking into consideration the multifaceted development of the lifestyle and how early childhood experiences shape adult thoughts, feelings, and behaviors. Adler stands correct that stressful life events alone cannot cause a person to become suicidal. The etiology of suicidal thoughts and behavior is multifaceted and complex. We now understand that a combination of chronic risk factors, acute risk factors, protective/resiliency factors, and situational stressors all combine to either increase or decrease an individual's risk of completing suicide. Understanding the lifestyle and how a person developed inferiority beliefs can be a useful intervention when working with suicidal clients. Adler also stands correct in understanding that the primary prevention of any mental illness is developing a child's sense of belonging in the world. The belief of being an equal and important contributing member of society allows people to feel capable of handling a crisis and therefore decreases the risk of seeing suicide as the solution to life's problems.

## REFERENCES

American Association of Suicidology. (2010, June). *Some facts about suicide and depression* [Fact Sheet]. Washington, DC: Author. Retrieved October 5, 2010, from http://www. suicidology.org/web/guest/stats-and-tools/fact-sheets

American Association of Suicidology. (2009, June). *Elderly suicide fact sheet* [Fact Sheet]. Washington, DC: Author. Retrieved October 5, 2010, from http://www.suicidology. org/web/guest/stats-and-tools/fact-sheets.

American Association of Suicidology. (2007). *Youth suicide fact sheet* [Fact Sheet]. Washington, DC: Author. Retrieved October 5, 2010, from http://www.suicidology. org/web/guest/stats-and-tools/fact-sheets

Fazaa, N., & Page, S. (2009). Personality style and impulsivity as determinants of suicidal Subgroups. *Archives of Suicide Research, 13,* 31–45.

Miller, D. N., & Eckert, T. L. (2009). Youth suicidal behavior: An introduction and overview. *School Psychology Review, 38*(2), 153–167.

Mullany, B., Barloe, A., Goklish, N., Larzelere-Hinton, F., Cwik, M., Craig, M., & Walkup, J. T. (2009). Toward understanding suicide among youths: Results from the White Mountain Apache tribally mandated suicide surveillance system, 2001–2006. *American Journal of Public Health, 99*(10) 1840–1848.

National Institute of Mental Health. (n.d.). *Suicide in the US: Statistics and prevention* (NIH Publication No. 06-4594). Washington, DC: U.S. Government Printing Office. Retrieved October 5, 2010, from http://www.nimh.nih.gov/health/publications/ about-nimh-publications.shtml

National Institute of Mental Health. (2007). *Older adults: Depression and suicide facts* (NIH Publication No. 4593). Washington, DC: U.S. Government Printing Office. Retrieved October 5, 2010, from http://www.nimh.nih.gov/health/publications/about-nimh-publications.shtml

Roy, A., Sarchiapone, M., & Carli, V. (2007). Low resilience in suicide attempters. *Archives of Suicide Research, 11,* 265–269.

Sarchiapone, M., Vladimir, C., Janiri, L., Marchetti, M., Cesaro, C., & Roy, A. (2009). Family history of suicide and personality. *Archives of Suicide Research, 13,* 178–184.

Substance Abuse and Mental Health Services Administration. (2006). *Suicidal thoughts, suicide attempts, major depressive episode, and substance use among adults* (Office of Applied Studies Report, Issue 34). Washington, DC: U.S. Government Printing Office.

Suicide Prevention Resource Center. (2001). *Risk and protective factors for suicide* [Fact Sheet]. Newton, MA: Author. Retrieved October 5, 2010, from http://www.sprc.org/library/srisk.pdf

## Suicide

### Alfred Adler (1937)

The frequent fact of suicide is surrounded by mystery for the average observer. When he is not personally touched by the suicide of someone near to him, he usually resorts to a superficial explanation which occasionally makes the suicide comprehensible, but usually leaves it incomprehensible. The members of the suicide's intimate and wider circles also usually find the occurrence strange and inexplicable. This does not seem very significant, since, in general, an understanding of human nature and thinking directed toward prophylaxis cannot be taken for granted. Attempts at explanation often being with the frequency of suicide among mentally disordered individuals, especially depressed persons, to all of whom suicide appears as a way out of their distress even if by their words they seem to reject it. Thus the approximately normal person is inclined to regard suicide as an entirely pathological phenomenon.

### SITUATIONAL FACTORS

Even so, there are certain situations from which the normal person regards suicide as the only way out. These are situations which are too distressing and unalterable, such as torment without any prospect for relief, inhumanly cruel attacks, fear of discovery of disgraceful or criminal actions, suffering of incurable and extremely painful diseases, etc. Surprisingly enough, the number of suicides actually committed for such reasons is not great.

Among the so-called causes for suicide, disregarding the cases of the psychologically ill, loss of money and unpayable debts take the first place. This gives us much to think about. Disappointed and unhappy love follow in frequency. Further frequent causes are permanent unemployment, for which the individual may or may not be responsible, and justified or unjustified reproaches.

Another cause is suicide epidemics which, puzzling as this may be, do occasionally happen. Harakiri, although on the decline, still exists among the Japanese. Among women and girls, suicide or attempted suicide takes place relatively frequently at the time of menstruation. Lastly, suicides increase strikingly after the age of fifty. All these facts ought to be explicable through Individual Psychology.

It is not surprising that qualified and unqualified circles often endeavor to work for the reduction of suicides. So far as we can see, such attempts have not succeeded in reducing the suicide rate. This is because individuals who turn to associations for the prevention of suicide would only be those who still regard the future with a certain amount of hope. In our time, the number of suicides is unchanged, possibly even increasing.

## THE INTERPERSONAL FACTOR

The frequency of suicide is a serious accusation against the none-too-great social interest of mankind. In view of this, a comprehensive exploration of this puzzling phenomenon is urgently needed.

Among inner, endogenous causes, Individual Psychology considers only the style of life which is established out of heredity and environmental influences by the individual's own creative power with his incomplete, humanly limited insight. In addition, one must determine the external, exogenous cause which reveals the inadequate preparation of the individual in question for the urgent situation before him. When the self-consistent life style thus clashes with the external situation, the extent to which the individual stands the test of living with others in society becomes apparent.

Observations of Individual Psychology have shown that every step of an individual is directed toward the successful solution of a presently imminent task in accordance with the total conception of his self-consistency. What the individual considers success is always a matter of his subjective opinion. Our experience has also shown that all tasks which the individual may have to meet require, without exception, adequate social interest for their correct solution. Each individual is so joined to society that he can make no movement, think no thought, and express no feeling without testifying to the degree of his connectedness with society, to his social interest. From this it follows that suicide is a solution only for one who in the face of an urgent problem has arrived at the end of his limited social interest.

This coming to the end of their limited social interest shows itself in all failures, be they active or passive, in their greater development of the inferiority complex. That the suicide departs from the line of social interest is quite obvious. All forms of working together, of living together, and of fellowship are lacking. Further, it must certainly be admitted that this departure occurs in an active way. The activity has a particular curve, however, in that it runs apart from social life and against it, and that it harms the individual himself, not without giving pain and sorrow to others.

The suicide generally gives little or no (conscious) thought to the shock which he causes others. But this difficulty in the way of a further understanding can be resolved. Could it not be that he would have to eliminate others from his thoughts before he could commit suicide? In some cases his social interest might well be great enough for that. Moreover one finds quite frequently, by contrast, that in his last letter or words the suicide hints at asking forgiveness for the sorrow he has afflicted. The movement and the direction of the suicide cannot avoid the fact of sorrow to another. And perhaps there are many on the brink of suicide who, through greater social interest, are deterred from afflicting this sorrow to another.

The "other" is probably never lacking. Usually it is the one who suffers most by the suicide.

## PREDISPOSING FACTORS

Individual Psychology continuously seeks to understand the unity and self-consistency of the individual. We are prepared for failures and try to prevent them, always in the conviction that the origin of a misconception of life and its organization can be traced back into early childhood. Therefore we must try to find the type of child which can be regarded as the potential suicide type. Studies of the past life always bring to light those traits which we have found in similar forms in all those failures who combine lesser social interest with a relatively large degree of activity. Suicidal persons have always been problem children, spoiled at least by one side of the family, very complacent, and oversensitive. Very often they showed hurt feelings to an unusual degree. In case of a loss or defeat, they were always poor losers. While they seldom made a direct attack against others, they always showed a life style which attempted to influence others through increased complaining, sadness, and suffering. A tendency to collapse under psychological pain when confronted with difficult life situations often stood out, in addition to increased ambition, vanity, and consciousness of their value for others. Fantasies of sickness or death, in which the pain of others reaches its highest degree, went parallel with this firm belief in their high values for others, a belief which they usually acquired from the pampering situation of their childhood. I have found similar traits in the early history of cases of depression, whose type borders on that of the suicide, and also of alcoholics and drug addicts.

Among the early childhood expressions of the suicide one also finds the deepest grieving over often negligible matters, strong wishes to become sick or to die when a humiliation is experienced, tantrums with willful self-injury, and an attitude toward others as if it were their duty to fulfill his every wish. Occasionally inclinations toward self-accusation come to the fore which elicit the sympathy of others, deeds of exaggerated foolhardiness which are performed to frighten others, and at times stubborn hunger strikes which intimidate the parents. Sometimes one finds ruses in the nature of a direct or indirect fantasies, wishes, and dreams which aim at a direct attack while suicide follows later.

Examples of suicide in the family have an attraction for those of similar tendency, as do the example of friends and well-known persons and special places associated with suicide.

## SUMMARY

Reduced to the simplest form, the life style of the potential suicide is characterized by the fact he hurts others by dreaming himself into injuries or by administering them to himself. One will seldom go wrong in determining against whom the attack is aimed when one has found who is actually affected most by it. We find in the suicide the type who thinks too much of himself, too little of others, and who is unable sufficiently to play, function, live, and die with others. Rather, with an exaggerated consciousness of his own worth, he expects with great tension results which are always favorable for him.

The idea of suicide, like all other mistaken solutions, of course always breaks out in the face of an urgent confronting exogenous problem for which the individual in question has an insufficient social interest. His greater or lesser activity then determines the direction and development of the symptoms. The symptoms can be done away with through an understanding of the context.

The psychiatrist will do well to keep his diagnosis of a potential suicide to himself, but to take all precautions. He must not tell it to others, but must see to it that something is done for the patient to enable him to find a better, more independent, socially oriented attitude toward life.

# 23

# *Demoralized Children*

## JoAnna White

In April 1920, Dr. Alfred Adler presented a lecture titled "Demoralized Children." It was only a few years after Dr. Adler had completed his military service in World War I. This experience, having had a tremendous impact on his life and his concern for the common good, led him to study societal issues of great concern. One of these concerns was the increase in the number of demoralized youth. These youth were later in the literature referred to as juvenile delinquents. Current literature does not so much employ the term *juvenile delinquent* but rather refers to the concerns related to the topic with terms such as *juvenile justice, juvenile crime*, and *gangs/juvenile vigilantism*. This last term refers to the fact that children who cannot rely on adults to protect them will turn to their peer group to feel safe. These group (gang) members resort to vandalism and other types of violence (Garbarino & Bedard, 2001).

In his lecture, Dr. Adler shared with the group that the published statistics of the day indicated that the number of demoralized youth was significant enough to cause alarm. He went on to say that the majority of cases would go unreported and "run their course in silence" until it was too late to turn things around for the struggling youth. Those youth, who were untreated, would eventually resort to criminal behavior. One need look no further than government and agency statistics of today regarding discouraged juveniles, crime, school crime and safety, and juvenile arrests to know that Dr. Adler was accurately predicting the future. We, the wealthiest nation in the world, have not yet put into place programs to assist parents and educators, policies, laws, and financial support that could prevent our children from becoming "demoralized youth."

In 2008, juveniles accounted for 16% of all violent crime arrests and 26% of all property crime arrests. In that same year, 11% of all murder victims were younger than 18 (United States Department of Justice, Juvenile Justice Bulletin, December 2009). In the 2007–2008 school year, 85% of public schools reported one or more incidents of crime in the schools while 75% of public schools reported one or more incidents of violent crime (Indicators of School Crime and Safety, 2009).

In 2008 5.7 million children lived in extreme poverty with 1 in every 12 children in a household with an income below 50% of the federal poverty line (Southern Education Foundation, 2010).

Marian Wright Edelman, founder of the Children's Defense Fund, asks how it is possible that more than half a million of our youth drop out of school each year. She believes that adults have let children down by not providing safe and nurturing environments for them so that later problems are prevented (Children's Defense Fund, 2010). She states that adults, rather than preventing problems, find it easier to punish children after they get in trouble. This approach requires much less work on the part of the adult so it may be more attractive. However, the ramifications of avoiding early guidance with children are overwhelmingly negative.

The recent statistics and the comments of Dr. Wright Edelman clearly illustrate the main points that Dr. Adler was attempting to make in his lecture 90 years ago: Early experiences and children's interpretations of those experiences are critical in their development, children with feelings of insignificance will find ways (usually negative) to protect themselves and strive for significance, parents and schools play a critical role, children living in poverty are at risk, and persons making decisions about children should be trained to understand their social/ emotional development. These issues are as immediate and in need of attention today as they were in 1920.

Dr. Adler's emphasis in his lecture on the importance of positive childhood experiences for healthy development reminds us of what we know to be true. However, our society tends to ignore this fact when it comes to funding for children's physical and mental health needs, parent education and support, and violence prevention. Adler stated that "in the early stages most of the demoralization takes place within the family circle," yet families continue to struggle because of lack of information, lack of support, and poverty.

With close to 6 million children living in extreme poverty in the United States, we can also learn from Dr. Adler's concerns for the differences in the social classes and the tremendous impact that living in poverty can have on a family and the children. Adler cautions that children living in poverty often view the world with hostility and as a place where difficulties cannot be overcome. These children grow up with a fear of life that develops into extreme pessimism. Thus the demoralized child will find solace in a peer group that also views the world from a negative vantage point. Gang membership today, as it did in 1920, meets a need for youth who have not had experiences in cooperation and have not been encouraged. They feel powerless and are striving for power in ways that fit their life experiences.

Schools can be a toxic place for demoralized youth. Most professionals in schools are not trained to understand these children and teens, and often educators have a strong need for power, which only reinforces a demoralized youth's view of the world as a dangerous place. Adler believed that "the greatest drawback of the school is the prevailing ignorance about the psychic development of the child." An emphasis on academics and obedience at the sacrifice of understanding the whole child is typical in most schools, especially with the constraints placed on teachers regarding performance-based assessments of their students. Students with a positive view of the world and a strong sense of self-efficacy can survive this type of system. Demoralized youth cannot.

There are pockets of educational excellence in which children without means are treated with respect and encouraged. These children are able to learn and contribute to the group. Most go on to college. These unique schools have many of the components of "curative pedagogy" that are essential to a school based on the principles of Individual Psychology. We can learn from these educational successes so that children are saved from a life of poverty, discouragement, and possibly incarceration.

In conclusion, Adler warned that "the feeling of cooperation must suffer where the craving for power exists." All children crave significance/prestige. If they are not afforded experiences that move them toward positive behaviors, they will "choose a side path." Demoralized youth do not easily adjust to society and are not able to engage in meaningful relationships. They are on guard and suspicious. They are unable to trust, which is the most basic element of healthy development. For the sake of these youth and society at large, it is critical that those who make decisions that affect our children view the crisis of demoralized youth from a preventive and holistic approach. Adler's emphasis on the importance of understanding that all children want to feel significant and all children make early lifestyle decisions within the context of their families cannot be ignored if we hope to save children from a life of despair.

## REFERENCES

Children's Defense Fund. (2010). Marian Wright Edelman's child watch column: *Children drop out and into lives of poverty and imprisonment.* Retrieved June 23, 2010, from http://www.childrensdefense.org/child-research-data-publications/data/marian-wright-edelman-child-watch-column/drop-out-into-poverty.html

Garbarino, J., & Bedard, C. (2001). *Parents under siege.* New York: The Free Press.

National Center for Education Statistics. (2009). *Indicators of school crime and safety: 2009.* Retrieved June 23, 2010, from http://nces.ed.gov/programs/crimeindicators/crimeindicators2009/key.asp

Southern Educational Foundation. (2010). *The worst of times.* Retrieved June 24, 2010, from http://www.southerneducation.org/pdf/SEF%20Child%20Poverty%20Sp%20Summary-Final.pdf

United States Department of Justice, Juvenile Justice Bulletin. (2009, December). *Juvenile arrests 2008.* Retrieved June 21, 2010, from http://www.ncjrs.gov/pdffiles1/ojjdp/228479.pdf

## Demoralized Children[50]

### *Alfred Adler*

Of the "blessings" that came in the wake of the Great War perhaps no one thing is of such importance as the tremendous increase in the demoralization of youth. Everyone has noticed it and many have taken cognizance of it with horror. The published statistics were significant enough and their significance must become greater to all who stopped to think that only a small part of the damage inflicted comes to our knowledge and that a large number of other cases are destined to run their course in silence for months and years, until finally we are confronted with individuals no longer to be reckoned as among the demoralized but among the criminals. The numbers are large and the number that never finds its way into statistics, still greater. In the early stages most of the demoralization takes place within the family circle. An improvement is expected from day to day and certain measures are applied. As there are quite a number of transgressions that occur among the demoralized youth that are not directly punishable by law or juvenile courts, and although they inflict extensive damage upon the family, they are covered up without leading to any change in the nature of the culprit. It is, of course, not at all necessary to give up all hope about the mistakes and transgressions of youth, but considering the remarkably deficient knowledge and understanding with which these matters are approached, optimism is not justified. Nevertheless we should point out that in the developmental stages of man, particularly during youth, not everything takes its course along ideal lines, that deviations occur, and if we were to transport ourselves back to our own youth and our youthful companions, we would be able to rake up a number of transgressions committed even by children, who subsequently became either tolerably efficient people or even distinguished men. How extensively youthful transgressions spread, a cursory summary may perhaps show you. I have occasionally attempted to make investigations in schools in such a tactful manner that no one could possibly be hurt. On a sheet of paper on which no names appeared, answers were to be written to the following questions: Has anyone ever lied or stolen? The general results showed that all the children confessed to petty thefts. One of the interesting episodes was the participation of a female teacher in the answers and her recollection of having committed a theft in childhood. But now let us call attention to the complicated nature of such a question! One child may have a kind and intelligent father who knows how to come to an understanding with him and in many cases may succeed. Another child may have done the same thing but perhaps

---

[50] Translated by P. Radin.

more clumsily, conspicuously or brazenly and he will then immediately feel the whole brunt of the family discipline descend upon him and the conviction impressed upon his mind that he is a criminal. We should therefore not be surprised that the difference in the nature of the punishment is correlated with a difference in the subterfuges adopted. It is the worst of all pedagogical principles to tell a child that he will never amount to anything, that he possesses a criminal nature; conceptions that belong to the domain of superstition, although there are scientists who also speak of hereditary criminals. We have thus reached that point at which current educational systems cease to have any method which they can apply for the control of the initial or later stages of demoralization. That ought not to surprise us for we are here concerned with facts in the child's psychic life, whose understanding is as yet confined to an extra-ordinary small circle of people.

Generally when we speak of demoralization we think of the school years. The expert observer will, however, be able to point out a number of cases where the demoralization began before the school days. It is not always possible to attribute them to the bringing-up. Parents must be told that no matter how careful they are that part of the education of which they know or notice nothing and which emanates from other circles, influences the child more than their consciously superior education.

These extraneous influences that find their way into the nursery represent all the events and conditions of life and of the environment. The child is impressed by the difficulties with which he sees his father beset in order to make a living, and he realizes the hostility of life even if he does not speak of it. He will develop a conception with the inadequate means at his disposal, with childish interpretations and experiences. This view of the world then becomes for the child a measure of evaluation; he makes it the basis for his judgments in every position in which he finds himself and will draw the correspondingly necessary inferences. These are in large measure wrong because we are here dealing with an inexperienced child whose reasoning powers are undeveloped and who consequently is liable to make false deductions. But just visualize the tremendous impression made upon a child whose parents live in a poor dwelling under depressing social circumstances, and contrast it with that of a child who does not feel life's hostility so definitely. These two types are so distinct that it is possible to infer from every child's expression and manner of speaking to which group he belongs. How differently will this last-mentioned child's attitude toward life be, with his self-confidence and courage, and how markedly will this be reflected in his whole carriage. The second type makes friends' with the world easily because he knows nothing of life's difficulties or can overcome them more easily. I have asked children among the proletariat of what they were most in fear and practically all answered *of being struck*—in other words, of occurrences taking place in their own family. Children who grow up in fear of a strong father, stepfather or mother, retain this feeling of fear till puberty, and we must remember that on the average the proletarian does not give us the same world-satisfied impression as the average bourgeois who is more courageous. A good deal of this pitiable bearing can be traced back to the fact that he has grown up in an atmosphere of fear of life and punishment. This is the most venomous kind of poison for developing *pessimism* in children, for they retain this perspective throughout life, have no self-confidence and are indecisive. To gain a courageous attitude afterwards requires both time and energy. The children of well-to-do parents generally answered the question of what they feared most, by saying school-work. This shows that neither individuals nor their own environment frighten them and they feel themselves to be in the midst of life where tasks and work exist of which they are afraid. This of course makes us assume the existence of untenable conditions in the schools, which instead of training them to face life gladly and courageously merely filled them with fear.

Let us now go back to the question of demoralization before the school-days. We ought not to be surprised to find, in view of the excitable state of the moods called up by all the disturbing relations that create fear of life, and in view of the envisaging of one's neighbour as hostile, that children will make a persistent effort to gain prestige and not to appear as the insignificant personages to which people often try to reduce them. It is one of the most important principles in any educational system to take the child *seriously*, to regard him as *an equal* and not to humiliate and make fun of him; for the child feels and must necessarily feel all those expressions of his immediate surroundings as oppressive, just as the weaker person possesses a sensibility different from that of an individual who finds himself in an assured position of a mental and bodily superiority. We are not even in a position to state exactly how a child is affected by the fact that it cannot do the things that he wonderingly see his parents and brothers perform daily. This should be remembered. Everyone who has developed a capacity for reading the child's soul, must have realized that every child possesses *an extraordinary craving for power and importance*, for increased self-consciousness; that he wishes to exert influence and appear important. The *young would-be hero* represents but a special case of the power that all wish to have.

Differences between them can be easily explained. In one case the child may be living in harmony with his parents, in another he may fall into a hostile attitude and develop antagonism to the demands of society in order not to utterly succumb to the feeling that he is nothing, plays no role, is quite disregarded. If such a stage of development is actually reached, where children realize their insignificance and their loss of importance, *they set immediately to work to protect themselves*—all children do it—and then indications of demoralization may appear very early. I once met a five-year-old abomination who had killed three children. This somewhat mentally-retarded girl always resorted to the following method in her "crimes." She would look for girls smaller than herself—she lived in the country—take them along to play with her and then push them into the stream. It was only when the third child had been killed that the perpetrator was discovered. She was placed in a lunatic asylum. She did not show the slightest realization of the depravity of her actions. She cried, but passed easily over to other subjects, and it was only with the greatest difficulty that any information could be obtained about the nature of the whole situation and her motives. For four years she had been the youngest child among a number of boys and had been excessively petted. Then a younger sister had appeared upon the scene and the parents lavished all their attention upon the newcomer while she, the elder, was pushed into the background. This could not however endure and she developed a hatred of her younger sister that she was, under the circumstances, unable to gratify because the baby was very carefully guarded, and because she possibly realized that she could be easily detected. She thereupon generalized and transferred her hatred to younger girls, all of whom she regarded as potential enemies. In all of them she saw her own young sister on whose account she was no longer being petted. In this mood she now progressed to the point of even killing them. Attempts made to bring such children back to normal paths, within a short time, go awry, because these children are at times *mentally defective*, oftener than one believes. One must be prepared for a treatment of long duration, and by using infinite tact and a special kind of training, render the child capable of again taking part in the life of society. But these cases, which are exceedingly common, are of lesser interest to us because of their connexion with mental deficiency and we must, in a way, accept them as instances of biological sports, for they probably would never fit entirely into human society. But the great mass of our demoralized youth is free from any taint of mental inferiority. On the contrary we often find extraordinarily gifted children who for a time progress quite well and develop capabilities up to a certain point, but *once they have broken down they are utterly unable to prevent a catastrophe overtaking them along one of the main lines of life.* In every case we find the same regularly recurring traits:—*a marked development of ambition although not outwardly expressed; sensitiveness to being pushed aside or ignored; cowardice consisting not simply in running away but in sneaking away from life and its demands.* From these few traits we can draw a picture of the whole. Only an ambitious child is capable of being frightened away from a task that threatens to extend beyond its powers and of striking out along another path as though covering up its weakness. This is the ordinary course of demoralization found in schools. *This demoralization is connected with some failure* that either has taken place or is about to take place, and shows itself at first in absence from school. But as truancy must, of course, be concealed, we naturally find that at first notes of excuse are forged and then signatures. But what is the child to do with its free time? An occupation must be found. *As a rule a union takes place of all children* who have gone along the same road, all who have been overtaken by the same fate. These children are, as a rule, all tremendously ambitious and desirous of playing a role, but do not trust themselves to attaining if along the main lines of human endeavour, and in consequence seek activities that will give them satisfaction. Some individual is always found to be best fitted for leadership and competition then ceases. Each one has some idea of what should be done. Imitating forms employed by their elders, they will develop a code of ethics applicable to a demoralized group. They try hard and with great ingenuity to think of deeds to perform that will enhance their importance in the eyes of their comrades. These are always carried out by deception, or hyper-deception, for they do not trust themselves to act openly—in consequence of their cowardice. Once on this road there is no turning back. Occasionally mentally defective boys join the group. They are made fun of, have tricks played on them and their pride, then incite them to exceptional efforts and actions. *Or it may be that being accustomed to a definite kind of treatment they are specially trained to obedience and their task becomes one of receiving orders and carrying them out.* It frequently happens that some one plans a specific transgression and the younger, inexperienced, inferior ones undertake it. I shall pass over other temptations although something might be said about them too, such as vicious books, the cinema, but they do not become directing forces until later. The cinema could never survive if it were not for the cleverness and the special skill displayed in selecting subject matter, whether criminal or detective, that stimulates the audience. In this over-evaluation of guile and subterfuge, the cowardice to face life is manifested.

The formation of bands is so common that it is the first thing that comes to mind when thinking of demoralized youths. But the demoralization of an individual distinct from a group is quite frequent. Such a person's life is similar to that we have described above, though apparently the directly impelling motives are different. Let us keep before us the fact that in the cases of group demoralization described above, the fate of the individuals *is foreshadowed as soon as they have suffered some set-back or expect one.* The same is true of a single individual. The simple, almost unwitting, persons come under this rule to the same extent as the more complicated. It is always some offence to one's amour propre, the fear of making a fool of one's self, the feeling of some decline in power or the will to power, that becomes the occasion for a *deviation to some side-line of development.* It looks almost as if these children *were seeking for some subsidiary field of action.* Frequently demoralization shows itself in a special form of laziness, which must then be looked upon neither as hereditary nor as the acquisition of a bad habit, but rather as a method of preventing any of them being put to tests. A lazy child can always fall back upon laziness as an excuse. If he fails in an examination it is the fault of his laziness, and such a child prefers to attribute his failure to laziness than to inability. Thus, like an experienced criminal, he is forced *to prove an alibi*; he must in each case demonstrate that his lack of success is due to laziness. And he succeeds. His laziness covers his failures, and from one point of view, that of sparing his conceit, his psychic situation has improved.

We know the demerits of our schools. The crowded classes, the insufficient training of many of the teachers, occasionally their lack of interest, for they suffer intensely from cramped economic conditions and more is hardly to be expected of them. Primarily, however, the greatest drawback of the school is *the prevailing ignorance about the psychic development of the child*: and that is the reason why hitherto the relations of the teacher and pupil have been so much more hopeless than those existing anywhere else in life. If the pupil makes a mistake he is either punished or given a poor mark. That is about the same as if a doctor called to treat someone who has broken a bone, saying: "You have a bone-fracture! Good-bye!" That assuredly is not the purpose of education! In the main the children take care of themselves under these horrible conditions and progress, but what of the gaps in their development? Children will proceed until they finally come to a point where their deficiencies assume such a form that a halt must be called. It is sad enough to realize how difficult it is even for the best child to progress, how under the weight of the accumulated difficulties he is afflicted with there emerges the painful feeling of being unable to perform the tasks others achieve, and finally to be a witness of his wounded and offended self-esteem! Many pass beyond this stage too, but many prefer to develop for themselves some subsidiary field of action.

Individual demoralization thus develops in the same manner as group demoralization. Here, likewise, the feeling of inferiority, of inadequacy and of humiliation tower above everything else. Let me quote the case of a boy, an only child, whose parents devoted great pains in educating him. At the age of five he already regarded the locking of chests, when the parents were absent, as a great insult and succeeded somehow in procuring a skeleton key and ransacking the chests. He was impelled to this conduct by his striving for independence, his will to power asserting itself in antagonism to his parents and the laws of society. Even to-day, at the age of eighteen, he indulges in household thefts unknown to his parents, although they believe they are aware of all of them. When his father tells him, "Of what use are these acts to you? As often as you steal I discover the fact," then the boy has the proud realization of knowing that his father does not know one in twenty and continues his thefts in the conviction that all that is necessary is to be clever enough to escape detection. Here we have an example of the frequent strug-gle between a child and its parents that induces the former to resort to acts contrary to the moral code of society. When fully grown-up this young man will undoubtedly provide himself with these psychic aids and supports that will enable him to transgress without feeling any pricks of conscience. His father is a business man, and even though the son is not permitted to visit his father's factories, he knows that the latter is engaged in the manufacture of chains, etc. When conversing with people he calls his father's attacks upon him unjust, because the latter is simply doing what he does, simply on a larger scale. So here again we have an example of the educative influence of the environment of which the parents are totally ignorant.

Let me now give one case from proletarian circles. An illegitimate six-year old boy is taken to the home of his mother who is married. His real father has disappeared and his step-father, a cranky old man, although not really interested in children, is very demonstrative to his own daughter, fondles her, brings her sweets while the boy is forced to look on. One day, a fairly large sum of money belonging to the mother disappears without a trace. Shortly after that, after further sums had disappeared, she discovered the culprit to be her son, and that he had spent the money in purchasing sweets, occasion-ally sharing it with his comrades with the object of showing off. So here we have another example of the secondary field of action, serving as usual the old main object of triumphing and gaining prestige at any cost. These thefts happened a number of times, whippings followed, and his step-father did not spare him. I saw the boy myself, covered with stripes, his whole body full of scratches and cicatrices. In spite of the punishments, however, the thefts, as might have been expected, did not cease. The mother, it is true, was rather clumsy, for she had made the thefts rather easy for the child. But how many mothers show any intelligence in such cases? The analysis showed that the boy had been taken care of by an old peasant woman who, when visiting the adjacent villages, had always taken him with her and had given him some sweets from time to time. The child was then transferred to a new environ-ment where he found himself at a great disadvantage compared to his for-mer home. His little sister he sees petted and fondled, given sweets denied him. It is she, not he who attracts attention. He was very good at school. His transgression is found exactly there where he would be expected *to look for an enemy* and appeared almost as inevitable. And so it is in many cases. Demoralization has the effect of an act of revenge and brings to the child a psychic relief.

Let me again emphasize the fact that the transgressions of demoralized people are not of an active, courageous kind, except when they operate in large numbers and this would again point to cowardice. Their most frequent dereliction is theft, which is essentially the crime of cowardice.

If we wish to understand clearly both all the interrelations and the position of the children to society we should bear two things in mind. First that their ambition and vanity are signs of their craving for power and superiority so that in consequence they try to obtain prestige along some side-path as soon as the main-line of development is closed to them. Secondly, their relation to their fellows is somehow deficient; they are not good companions, they do not easily adjust themselves to society, have something of the dog-in-the-manger attitude and exhibit little contact with the outer world. At times, nothing but a meaningless pretence or a mere habit is all that remains of their love for their own people; often even this is missing and they may then even attack their own family. They play the role of people whose feeling for society is defective, who have not discovered the point of contact with their fellowmen and look upon them as hostile. Traits of suspicion are very common among them; they are always on guard lest someone take advantage of them and I have often heard these children exclaim that it is necessary to be unscrupulous, *i.e.*, that superiority must be attained. Suspicion creeps into all their relations and adds to the difficulties of living with them. Cowardly subterfuges develop automatically through this lack of trust in themselves.

The question now to decide is whether this craving for power, this deficient social consciousness is due to different causes? We can definitely answer in the negative for they do but represent two sides of the same psychic attitude. *The feeling of co-operation must suffer where the craving for power exists*, for a person possessed by the latter thinks only of himself, of his power, of his prestige, acts in utter disregard of others. If an individual succeeds in developing a feeling of cooperation the best guarantee against demoralization is given.

I am quite at sea as to what can be done in an age of intensified demoralization like ours. The correct and proper thing is clearly to act immediately. Even in times of complete peace our civilization was not able to gain effective control over demoralization and crime; she could merely punish, revenge herself, frighten people, never solve the problem. She kept the demoralized at elbow distance. Visualize, if you can, the frightful fate of these people, whose loneliness must in itself drive them to crime; people who are criminals only *because they have lost contact*. From that they develop into habitual criminals. It is a piece of utter stupidity, for instance, to herd together during examination, demoralized individuals with their own kind or with criminals.

We must reckon with about 40 percent of the crimes remaining undiscovered. Among the demoralized the percentage is even higher. A short time ago, a youthful murderer was convicted and his lawyer knew that this was the second murder for which he had been tried. When criminals meet they discuss the number of times they have not been caught and this naturally increases the difficulty of combating crime and constantly renews the criminal's courage.

Evils are also noticeable in the type of attitude taken by society. Both courts and police work to no purpose because they always centre their attention upon questions other than the really radical and determining ones. To improve the situation the first requirement is to have a different and a more humane personnel. Institutions ought to be erected for taking care of these demoralized children, for bringing them back to life; not shutting them off from society, but, on the contrary, making them more adapted for it. That can only happen if we have a full understanding of their peculiarities. Nothing can be accomplished if any kind of person whatsoever (*e.g.*, a retired officer or a subaltern) can be appointed director of an institution of this kind merely because he enjoys political protection. Only such people are to be considered for these posts who have a strongly developed community-sense and a full understanding of the people entrusted to their care. The essential point of my argument is this, that in a civilization where one man is the enemy of the other—for this is what our whole industrial system means—demoralization is ineradicable, for demoralization and crime are *by-products of the struggle for existence* as known to our industrialized civilization. The shadows of this struggle fall very early across the soul of the child, destroy its poise, facilitate its craving for greatness and render it craven and incapable of co-operation.

To limit and do away with this demoralization a chair of curative pedagogy should be established. It is indeed hard to understand why such a chair does not already exist. Today a true understanding of the problem is exceedingly rare. All persons in any way connected with this problem should be compelled to take an active part. The institution itself should be in the nature of a central exchange bureau which would give information on all matters relating to the prevention and combating of demoralization.

In addition, county institutions of an advisory nature should exist for the lighter cases. For the more severe forms the relatives of the patients must suggest a method of treating them, for the patients themselves would never be able to find one.

In conclusion teachers should be made acquainted with individual-psychology and curative pedagogy, so that from the very beginning they might be in a position to recognize the signs of demoralization and to intervene helpfully themselves and nip the danger tactfully and lovingly in the bud. A model school for the practical education of the personnel should also be founded.

# 24

# Significance of Early Recollections

## Arthur J. Clark

In the "Significance of Early Recollections," Alfred Adler (1937) presents a culmination of his evolving ideas relating to the projective technique and his theory of Individual Psychology. The paper was originally published in a book chapter (Adler, 1929) and, with the addition of a concluding paragraph and minimal revisions, was reprinted in the *International Journal of Individual Psychology*. In Adler's view, early recollections provide perhaps the most important means for understanding the style of life or basic personality functioning of an individual. Through brief case illustrations, Adler demonstrates how essential concepts of Individual Psychology are integral to the therapeutic utilization of early recollections in treatment settings. These recollections serve an organizing function in the cases for the purposefulness of behavior, the style of life, striving for superiority, holism, and birth order. Each of these uniquely Adlerian theoretical formulations extends the potential richness of his observations and is basic to his discussion of early recollections.

In the introduction to the article, Adler immediately makes reference to the principle of the purposefulness of behavior as it relates to personality dynamics. Through case material, he proceeds to illustrate how a goal-directed process enables individuals to seek adaptive or maladaptive pursuits in life. Adler also suggests that persons often lack awareness of the goal-striving quality of their functioning. In one case, a young adulthood client recalls an early memory: "I was running round the whole day in a kiddy car." From this brief remembrance, Adler empathically infers that the individual's tacit goal-directedness is toward motor activity and movement in general. Among other problems, the man had been having difficulties in adjusting to sedentary occupations. In a somewhat humorous conclusion to the case, he finds a satisfying career as a traveling salesman.

Although Adler emphasizes how early recollections clarify goals and significant strivings, he also points out that when persons recall their memories they usually view them only as experiences from their first years of life. Because the potential meanings of early remembrances are tacit or largely unknown to individuals, they are less subject to the heightened response distortions commonly associated with other self-report measures. Adler also acknowledges that persons largely have a conscious awareness of their first memories, and, as a consequence, it is possible to readily elicit the recollections in a treatment situation or in everyday life. It is apparent in this context that Adler is referring to a contrasting application in psychoanalytic treatment which emphasizes uncovering latent childhood memories through intensive analysis.

In a further discussion, Adler asserts that the full value and meaning of early recollections cannot be estimated until they are viewed in the context of an individual's style of life or lifestyle, and his or her goal of superiority. The lifestyle functions as a sustaining reminder and an enduring guide by epitomizing a person's feelings about life. In the paper's most lengthy case illustration, a young woman came to Adler in conflict over both her desire and her fear of having a child. She expresses that bearing a child would be a potential danger to her health. In Adler's formulation, he thought that the client had been pampered as a child and was fearful of having a baby who would be a rival to her for attention. Indeed, the individual's early recollection involves a dangerous situation in which she is the center of attention of her mother. As in this instance, Adler feels the lifestyle illuminates a person's current perspectives and ingrained long-term beliefs. Related to the lifestyle, an individual's striving for superiority is an inherent tendency to seek a significant goal through a basic motivational process. Consistent with the client's lifestyle and her early recollection, seeking attention is a major quest or goal in the life of the young woman.

Social interest or an identification and kinship with humanity is another prominent construct in Adler's theoretical orientation. Characteristically, a person who demonstrates excessive self-centeredness and isolation from the activities of others has not developed a healthy level of social interest. In another case illustration, Adler discusses the situation of a 30-year-old student who is socially withdrawn and anxious. In a brief early recollection, the client recalls lying on a cot and looking at the wallpaper and curtains. Adler relates that although the man had developed a strong visual capacity, he was not prepared on a human level for an active pursuit of cooperation and intimacy. Further, the client's avoidant pattern of living does not engender a sense of belonging and emotional well-being that is inherent in social interest.

Although Adler does not directly make reference to the prominent Individual Psychology concept of holism in the early recollections paper, he frequently alludes to the holistic quality of an individual's thoughts, feelings, and actions in the case examples. In one instance, a philosophy student complains about a problem of blushing that makes it uncomfortable and stressful for him to participate in social activities. Adler states that the physical manifestation of erythrophobia has a holistic effect on inhibiting his actions and eliciting feelings of tension. In his early recollection, the client was slapped by his parents for wandering away from the family home with his little brother, but his younger brother was not punished. Since childhood, the man felt that his parents favored his younger brother, and he was unable to satisfactorily compete with him. In encountering the tasks of life involving intimate relationships, work, and friendships, the client felt inferior and trapped. In turn, his blushing appears to provide a safeguard or pretext that enables him to avoid those situations where he feared that others would be preferred to him.

Given the importance that Adler attributes to birth order and the broader dimension of the family constellation in influencing a person's development, it is not surprising that he relates both conceptions to early recollections. Citing another case, Adler discusses the situation of a child who felt displaced and dethroned within his family by the birth of a younger sibling. The client, who experiences difficulties with trust and feelings of being let down by others, recalls an early recollection that takes place during a rainstorm in which his mother picks him up and then places him down to hold his younger brother. In such renderings, early recollections provide a brief glimpse into the perceptions of an individual's first years during this formative developmental period.

Beyond the present article, among Adler's extensive commentaries on early recollections, he dedicated three chapters in separate books to the subject (Adler, 1929/1969, 1931/1958, 1964/1933). Since Adler's initial work, early recollections have been a primary focus of hundreds of publications in the professional literature (Clark, 2002). Much of this scholarship relates to practical applications of the projective technique in a treatment context. In this regard, Munroe (1955) states, "Adler's notion of comparing people on the basis of their spontaneous 'conscious' reaction to the fairly simple but dynamic question is the very core of contemporary projective techniques" (p. 429). Other wide-ranging research relates the function of early recollections or the first memories of life to human development, personality, psychopathology, career development, and various other psychological domains. An enduring interest continues in early recollections today, and Adler's original formulations provide a viable theoretical and practical framework for extending knowledge about the topic. In a biography of Adler, Orgler (1939/1965) writes, "the realisation that first memories allow a deep insight into the human soul is one of Adler's greatest discoveries" (p. 29).

## REFERENCES

Adler, A. (1969). *The science of living* (H. L. Ansbacher, Ed.). Garden City, NY: Anchor Books. (Original work published 1929)

Adler, A. (1958). *What life should mean to you* (A. Porter, Ed.). New York: G. Putnam. (Original work published 1931)

Adler, A. (1937). Significance of early recollections. *International Journal of Individual Psychology, 3,* 283–287.

Adler, A. (1929). *Problems of neurosis: A book of case histories* (P. Mairet, Ed.). New York: Harper & Row. (Original work published 1929)

Adler, A. (1964). *Social interest: A challenge to mankind* (J. Linton & R. Vaughan, Trans.). New York: Capricorn Books. (Original work published 1933)

Clark, A. J. (2002). *Early recollections: Theory and practice in counseling and psychotherapy.* New York: Brunner-Routledge.

Munroe, R. L. (1955). *Schools of psychoanalytic thought: An exposition, critique, and attempt at integration.* New York: Holt, Rinehart & Winston.

Orgler, H. (1965). *Alfred Adler: The man and his work.* New York: Capricorn Books. (Original work published 1939)

## Significance of Early Recollections[51]

*Alfred Adler*

The discovery of the significance of early recollections is one of the most important findings of Individual Psychology. It has demonstrated the *purposiveness* in the choice of what is longest remembered, though the memory itself is quite conscious or the recollection is easily brought out upon inquiry. Rightly understood, these conscious memories give us glimpses of depths just as profound as do those which are more or less suddenly recalled during treatment.

We do not, of course, believe that all early recollections are correct records of actual facts. Many are even fancied, and most perhaps are changed or distorted at a time later than that in which the events are supposed to have occurred; but this does not diminish their significance. What is altered or imagined is also expressive of the patient's goal, and although there is a difference between the work of fantasy and that of memory, we can safely make use of both by relating them to our knowledge of other factors. Their worth and meaning, however, cannot be rightly estimated until we relate them to the total style of life of the individual in question, and recognize their unity with his main line of striving towards a goal of superiority.

In recollections dating from the first four or five years we find chiefly fragments of the prototype of the individual's life-style, or useful hints as to why his life-plan was elaborated into its own particular form. Here also we may gather the surest indications of self-training to overcome the deficiencies felt in the early environment or organic difficulties. In many cases, signs of the person's degree of activity, of his courage and social feeling are also evident in the early recollections. Owing to the great number of spoiled children who come under treatment, we find that the mother is rarely absent from the earliest remembrance; indeed, if the life-style is one of a pampered child, the guess that the patient will recall something about his mother is usually correct. If the mother does not appear in the early recollections that, too, may have a certain significance; it may, for one thing, indicate a feeling of having been neglected by her. However, he will never have understood the meaning of his early remembrances. In answer to my question he may, for instance, simply say, "I was sitting in a room playing with a toy, and my mother was sitting close to me." He regards a recollection as if it were a thing by itself and as if it had no significance; he never thinks of its coherence in the whole structure of his psychic life. Unfortunately many psychologists do the same.

---

[51] Originally edited by Philip Mairet; additional editing by Heinz Ansbacher.

To estimate its meaning we have to relate the early pattern of perception to all we can discover of the individual's present attitude, until we find how the one clearly mirrors the other. In the example just given we begin to see this correlation when we learn that the patient suffers from anxiety when alone. The interest in being connected with the mother may appear even in the form of fictitious remembrances, as in the case of the patient who said to me, "You will not believe me, but I can remember being born, and my mother holding me in her arms."

Very often the earliest memory of a spoiled child refers to its dispossession by the birth of a younger brother or sister. These recollections which record the feeling of being dispossessed vary from slight and innocent reminiscences, such as, "I recollect when my younger sister was born," to instances highly significant of the particular attitude of the patient. A woman once told me, "I remember having to watch my younger sister, who was lying on a table. She was restless and threw off the coverlets. I wanted to adjust them and I pulled them away from her, whereupon she fell and was hurt." This woman was forty-five when she came to me; at school, in marriage, and throughout life she had felt herself disregarded, just as in her first childhood when she had felt herself dethroned. A similar attitude, even more expressive of suspicion and mistrust, was expressed by a man who said, "I was going to market with my mother and little brother. Suddenly it began to rain, and my mother took me up in her arms, and then remembering that I was the elder, she put me down and took up my younger brother." Successful as he was in his life, this man distrusted everybody, especially women.

A student thirty years of age came to me in trouble because he could not face his examinations. He was in such a state of strain that he could neither sleep nor concentrate. The symptoms indicate his lack of preparation and of courage, and his age shows the distance at which he stood from the solution of the problem of occupation. He had no friends and had never fallen in love, because of his lack of social adjustment; and his sexuality was expressed in masturbation and nocturnal emissions. His earliest memory was of lying in a cot, looking round at the wallpaper and curtains. This recollection reflects the isolation of his later life, and also his interest in visual activity. He was astigmatic, and was striving to compensate for this organic deficiency. We must remember, however, that any function which is strongly developed but which is not also related to a fair degree of social interest may disturb the harmony of life. For instance, to watch is really a worthwhile activity, but when the patient barricades himself against all other activities arid wants only to gratify his eyes all day, it is possible for watching to become a compulsion-neurosis. Some people are interested primarily in seeing. But there are only a few positions in which interest in seeing is the chief one to be employed. Even those positions cannot be found by a person who is socially maladjusted. This patient, as we have seen, had not been a real fellow man to anyone, so that he had found no use for his peculiar interest.

The earliest remembrances not infrequently disclose an interest in movement, such as: traveling, running, motoring, or jumping. So far as we can see this is often characteristic of individuals who encounter difficulties when they find it necessary to begin work in sedentary occupations. I found this in the case of a man of twenty-five, the oldest son of a very religious family, who was brought to me because of misbehavior. He was disobedient, idle, and a liar, and he had contracted debts and stolen. His sister, three years younger than himself, was a familiar type—striving, capable, and well-educated, an easy winner in the race with him. His misconduct began with his adolescence, and I am aware that many psychologists would ascribe it to some sort of emotional "flare-up" caused by the growth of the sexual glands—a theory which might seem all the more plausible in this case because of the existence of premature and mischievous sexual relations, as is found in many other similar cases. But we ask: Why should the perfectly natural period of puberty be the cause of a crisis and of a moral disaster in this case but not in another—not in the sister's case, for example? We answer: Because the sister was in a more favorable position. The brother's situation was one which we know, from experience of very many cases, to be one of special danger. Furthermore, when we go more deeply into the history of this case, we find that he wanted always to be first, in every situation, and that adolescence did not create any change in this young man's style of life. Before that time the boy had gradually been losing hope of being "first" in a life of social usefulness, and the more hopeless he grew there, the more he had wandered into the easier ways of useless compensation.

This young man's earliest remembrance gives a clear hint of his great interest in motor activity and in movement in general. It was: "I was running round the whole day in a kiddy car." After treatment, when he was improved, he was taken back into his father's office, but he did not find the sedentary life there to his liking. He finally adapted himself to life as a traveling salesman.

Many first remembrances are concerned with situations of danger, and they are usually told by persons with whom the use of fears is an important factor in the style of life. A married woman once came to ask me why she was terrified whenever she passed a pharmacy. Some years previously she had spent a long time in a sanatorium undergoing treatment for tuberculosis, and a few months before I saw her a specialist had pronounced her cured, entirely healthy, and fit to have children. Shortly after this plenary absolution by the doctor she began to suffer from her obsession. The connection is obvious. The pharmacy was a warning reminder of her illness, an employment of the past in order to make the future seem ominous. She was connecting the possibility of having a child with danger to her health. Though she and her husband had agreed that they wanted a child, her behavior clearly showed her secret opposition. Her secret objection was stronger than any reasonable and common sense logic which said that for her there really was now no danger in bearing children. The doctor, as a medical expert, could minimize the danger to her health, but he could not remove the symptom of fear. In this as in many similar cases we know in advance that the real reasons for the symptoms are deeply rooted, and are only to be found if we can discover the most important strivings in the style of life.

Seldom is it true that resistance to having children is based upon *objective* fears of childbirth or illness. In this case it was easy to discover that the woman had been a pampered child who, herself, wanted to be in the center of the stage. Such women do not wish to bring a little rival on to the scene, and they argue against it with every variety of reason and unreason. This woman had trained herself perfectly to be on the lookout for danger, and to perceive opportunities for taking the center of attention. Asked for her earliest recollection she said, "I was playing before our little house on the outskirts of the town, and my mother was terrified when she saw me jumping on the boards that covered the well."

A student of philosophy came to consult me about his erythrophobia. From earliest childhood he had been teased because he blushed so easily, and for the past two months this had so much increased that he was afraid to go to a restaurant, to attend his lectures, or even to go out of his room. I found that he was about to take an examination. He was a faint-hearted man, timid and bashful, and whether he was visiting in society, working, or in company with a girl, in all situations alike he suffered from feelings of tension. His blushing had recently worried him more, and he began to use it as a pretext for retreat from life. From childhood this man had had a strong antipathy towards his mother, who, he felt, was partial to his younger brother. He had lived in the greatest competition with his brother; and he now no longer believed that he, himself, could achieve any success if he went on. Here is his earliest remembrance: "When I was five years old I went out with my three-year-old brother. My parents were much excited when they found we had left the house, because there was a lake near by, and they were afraid that we had fallen into it. When we returned I was slapped." I understood this to mean that he did not like his home, where he felt that he was slighted, and this opinion was corroborated when he added, "I was slapped, but not my brother." But the discovery that he had been in a dangerous situation had no less impressed him, and this was reflected in his present behavior, which was dominated by his guiding idea—not to go out, not to venture too far. Such persons often feel as though life were a trap.

It is easy to imagine this patient's painful experience when in company of a girl. We can understand how he put his blushing between himself and women, thus did not allow himself to come into a relationship with any of them. In this way he avoided coming into a situation where he ran the risk of losing out to another man. He always feared other men would be preferred to him, as he felt his mother had preferred his brother.

When rightly understood in relation to the rest of an individual's life, his early recollections are found always to have a bearing on the central interests of that person's life. Early recollections give us hints and clues which are most valuable to follow when attempting the task of finding the direction of a person's striving. They are most helpful in revealing what one regards as values to be aimed for and what one senses as dangers to be avoided. They help us to see the kind of world which a particular person feels he is living in, and the ways he early found of meeting that world. They illuminate the origins of the style of life. The basic attitudes which have guided an individual throughout his life and which prevail, likewise, in his present situation, are reflected in those fragments which he has selected to epitomize his feeling about life, and to cherish in his memory as reminders. He has preserved these as his early recollections.

# Index